MySQL and Java Developer's Guide

Mark Matthews
Jim Cole
Joseph D. Gradecki

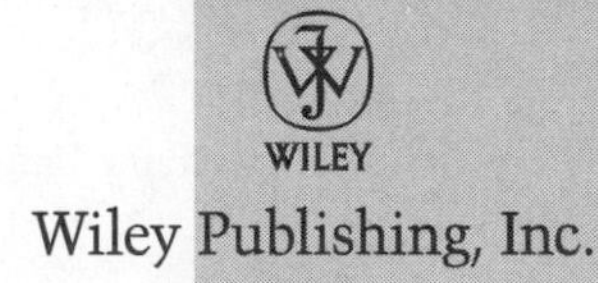

Wiley Publishing, Inc.

Publisher: Robert Ipsen
Editor: Robert M. Elliott
Managing Editor: Vincent Kunkemueller
Book Producer: Ryan Publishing Group, Inc.
Copyeditor: Elizabeth Welch
Proofreader: Nancy Sixsmith
Compositor: Gina Rexrode

This book is printed on acid-free paper. ∞

Published by Wiley Publishing, Inc., Indianapolis, Indiana

Published simultaneously in Canada.

Library of Congress Cataloging-in-Publication Data:

Matthews, Mark.
MySQL™ and Java™ developer's guide / Mark Matthews.
p. cm.
ISBN 0-471-26923-9 (PAPER/WEBSITE)
1. SQL (Computer program language) 2. Java (Computer program language) I. Title.
A76.3.S67M38 2003
005.75'65—dc21

2002155887

Printed in the United States of America

10 9 8 7 6 5 4 3 2 1

CONTENTS

Dedication

To my wife Diane, for all her support in my "geeky" endeavors, and to our new daughter Lauren.

I would also like to dedicate this work to Monty, David, and the rest of the fine group of developers at MySQL AB. Without their contribution to the software community and dedication to free software and open source ideals, this book would not have been possible.

--Mark Matthews

I would like to dedicate this book to my parents. Their ever-present love and encouragement have made so many things possible.

—Jim Cole

This book is dedicated to the trinity: God, Jesus Christ, and the Holy Spirit.

—Joseph D. Gradecki

Acknowledgments

I need to acknowledge the patience and support of my beautiful and loving wife and our boys. Thank you for the opportunity to be your husband and father. Tim, thank you for the opportunities. Jim, welcome to this new adventure and I look forward to many more in the future. Thank you to Liz Welch for the excellent review.

ABOUT THE AUTHORS

Mark Matthews is the creator of Connector/J and its predecessor MM.MySQL, the Java JDBC driver for MySQL. Last year, he joined MySQL AB to further develop Java support in MySQL. Mark specializes in Java, MySQL, XML, and DHTML solutions and has architected major Web applications projects, including a GIS-based retail analytics package. Mark has also taught classes in both Java and UML.

Jim Cole is a senior software engineer specializing in Internet and knowledge management systems. He is an active developer working in Java, C++, Perl, and PHP. He also serves as a system administrator for several Web-based projects, where his duties include custom software development, database management, and security maintenance.

Joseph D. Gradecki is a software engineer at Comprehensive Software Solutions, where he works on their SABIL product, an enterprise-level securities processing system. He has built numerous dynamic, enterprise applications using Java, AspectJ, servlets, JSPs, Resin, MySQL, BroadVision, XML, and more. He has also built P2P distributed computing systems in a variety of languages including Java/JXTA, C/C++, and Linda. He holds Bachelors and Masters degrees in Computer Science and is currently obtaining his PhD.

Introduction

Have you ever been assigned a project and realized that you had no idea how you were going to accomplish it? Many developers have experienced this feeling when asked to interface their code with a database. With a few exceptions, most developers were busy learning Lisp, linked lists, and big-O notation during their formal education instead of learning the fundamentals of relationship database management systems. When the time comes to interface their code with a database, they turn to a book like the one you are holding.

Your challenge might be to write a Web-based system using servlets and Enterprise JavaBeans (EJBs) to transfer shipping records from the home office in Bend, Oregon, to a satellite shipper in New Jersey. Or perhaps your father just opened his new medical office and you volunteered to create a scheduling system over the weekend.

Whatever the situation, interfacing an application to a database is one of the most fundamental tasks a developer is required to perform. This book is designed for developers who either have a pressing task ahead of them or who are curious about how to read database information into their application.

By combining MySQL, the number-one open source database available, with Java, the most portable language ever developed, you can create an undisputable champion. So, sit back in your desk chair with a hot chocolate and get ready to supercharge your coding.

What's in This Book

The primary goal of *MySQL and Java Developer's Guide* is to provide a comprehensive approach to writing code from a Java application to a MySQL database using the industry standard: JDBC. As you will see later in this Introduction, the chapter titles indicate what area of database connectivity and manipulation they cover. The chapters are ordered to reflect the JDBC specification, but we aren't here to simply describe the specification.

We wrote all of the material in the book to highlight how MySQL's Connector/J JDBC driver achieves the interfacing of MySQL with Java while maintaining the spirit of the specification. With this in mind, we provide example code using all major forms of Java development, including

- Applications
- Applets
- Servlets
- JSPs
- EJBs

As you work in Java and JDBC, you will see the true power of the specification. You can write database access code in a Java application and move the code to a servlet with little if any changes. In the case of EJBs and container-managed persistence, we devoted a full chapter to dealing with database access without the cumbersome details of SQL.

We designed the layout of the book to move you through the entire process of writing Java code needed to access a back-end database. Developing the database is one of the first things that you must accomplish in this process. While we don't delve deeply into the theory of database development, you learn how to create databases in MySQL, administer those databases, and handle such details as granting access permissions. From there, we take you into an examination of the MySQL Connector/J driver and how it accomplishes its goal of portable database access. The remainder of the book steps you through Java code that highlights how to accomplish database tasks such as the following:

- Querying and updating
- Handling ResultSets
- Using transactions
- Handling typing issues between JDBC and MySQL
- Working with metadata
- Addressing efficiency issues

Once you're familiar with these concepts, we present a complete application that pulls it all together. Our application illustrates how you can create to a simple authorization service. Using a combination of JSP, servlets, and EJBs, the service allows new users to create accounts, recall the account, and verify a username/password combination. The system is designed to be interactive using JSP pages, which are handled on the server using servlets. The JSPs can be bypassed using the servlets directly. All of the critical information is kept on the database for persistence and management needs.

After reading this book, you should know how to interface Java to MySQL and be able to use the many examples for reference.

NOTE

All the code and examples in this book can be found on the the support Web site at www.wiley.com/compbooks/matthews.

Who Should Read This Book

This book is written for Java developers who need to interface their code to a back-end database. The book's specifics deal with MySQL and Connector/J, but this doesn't limit the information because JDBC is designed to be portable against many databases. If you aren't using MySQL, you still find valuable information.

You don't need to know much about databases—we have included several chapters that provide all of the basics necessary to create databases and make sure they are operational. Keep in mind that we didn't intend these chapters to replace a good reference on MySQL, though.

We do expect that you are an experienced Java developer who is comfortable with the language. This book explains a combination of Java delivery methods, including applications, applets, beans, and EJBs; you may want to begin with what you know best and expand from there.

The Technology Used

In this book, we use the latest Java Developments Kits (JDK) available from Sun at the time of writing. The JDKs we used include J2SE 1.4.0 and J2EE 1.3.1. The Java examples are used in a mixed environment, including Windows 2000/XP, Linux Mandrake, and Linux Slackware. For the most part, we developed the examples using simple text editors and compiled them using the Java command-line compiler. However, all the examples should work just fine in an IDE such as JBuilder.

Two different versions of MySQL are used throughout this book: 4.0.4 and 3.23.52. JDBC connectivity is handled using MySQL's Connector/J driver, and we cover both versions 2.0.14 and development 3.0.1.

Book Organization

The first four chapters of this book provide an overview of databases, JDBC, and installation of the tools you will be using. The remainder of the book is an in-depth guide to building database applications with MySQL, Connector/J, JDBC, and Java.

Chapter 1: An Overview of MySQL

MySQL is one of the most popular open source database systems available today, and it is used as the back-end data storage device for many personal and corporate Web sites. Java is the most portable language in use today and continues to be improved with each new release. In this chapter, we provide a brief overview of each product and begin the discussion of how to interface the two and thus allow Java applications to have access to a vast array of information.

Chapter 2: JDBC and Connector/J

As shown in Chapter 1, JDBC facilitates the interface between Java and MySQL. The JDBC specification defines the interfaces and classes necessary for any Java application, applet, servlet, and so forth to make calls to an underlying database. Because the JDBC specification isn't specific to any one database system, manufacturers create JDBC drivers for their specific database. In this chapter, we discuss the history of JDBC, how it started, and its progress into a version 3.0 specification. We examine in depth the MySQL JDBC driver called Connector/J, and look at its history as the MM.MySQL JDBC driver as well as its future.

Chapter 3: Working with MySQL SQL

Before we delve into the concepts surrounding the interface between Java and MySQL, this chapter provides a basic overview of databases and SQL. Topics include basic concepts behind databases, simple database design, database normalization, and data manipulation.

Chapter 4: Installing MySQL, Java, and Connector/J

All of the coding examples in this book are built using MySQL as the primary database, Java as our coding language, and Connector/J, MySQL's JDBC driver. Although the installation of these components isn't overly difficult, this chapter provides comprehensive instructions for obtaining all of the necessary components and performing a step-by-step installation. We also provide simple examples for testing the installation.

Chapter 5: Using JDBC with Java Applications and Applets

This chapter is the first in a series on the use of Java to access a MySQL database using JDBC. Some of the basic functionality discussed includes loading the JDBC driver, connecting to a local or remote database, building JDBC statements in preparation for queries, executing queries against the MySQL database, working with ResultSets, and accessing MySQL-specific functionality through JDBC.

Chapter 6: Achieving Advanced Connector/J Functionality with Servlets

At this point, you've learned the basics, and it's time to expand into the more advanced topics. This chapter is designed to expand your understanding of SQL, MySQL, and JDBC. The topics include updatable ResultSets, PreparedStatements, date/time types, BLOBs and CLOBs, and joins.

Chapter 7: MySQL Type Mapping

One of the fundamental issues associated with databases and programming language is determining the correct mapping from one to the other. While programming languages have a large variety of types, including simple ones like integer, they also allow more complex ones, like classes. Databases, on the other hand, are limited in their choices for the types of data that can be stored. In the middle of this situation is the JDBC driver. This chapter discusses the types available on the MySQL database, how JDBC interprets those types, and the resulting Java type produced by the mapping.

Chapter 8: Transactions and Table Locking with Connector/J

In a simple world, information is stored in a single table of a database. When you have to update information or insert a new row, you can use a single query. However, most modern databases store information across several different tables to increase the normalization of the tables. In this situation, when you have to update information or insert new rows, you must write two queries instead of one. This chapter looks at inserting multiple pieces of information into multiple tables, what problems can arise, and how transactions can be used to solve these problems.

Chapter 9: Using Metadata

After a query is performed against a MySQL database, the information is returned in a ResultSet object. This object includes all of the rows and columns specific to the query performed. In many cases, additional information is needed about the data, including the name of the columns in the result, the precision of the data in a float column, the maximum length of a column, and maybe even information about the server from which the data was returned. In this chapter, we discuss pulling metadata about both the database and a ResultSet that contains information from a query.

Chapter 10: Connection Pooling with Connector/J

In many cases, a JDBC driver requires between 4 and 10 different communications with a database application before a connection can be established and returned to the requesting application. If an application is constantly creating connections, doing its business, and then closing the connection, the application suffers in its potential performance. To overcome the connection performance problem, you can use a connection pool. This chapter provides a comprehensive introduction to connection pools, presents valuable statistics for creating database connections, and demonstrates how to use the connection pooling mechanisms within JDBC.

Chapter 11: EJBs with MySQL

Enterprise JavaBeans (EJBs) provide the framework for building applications that can handle the rigors of enterprise-level applications. In addition, EJBs can be distributed across a network or a farm of servers. In this chapter, we cover the basic EJB programming model, using DataSources and JNDI, and building session beans to access MySQL. We also discuss container-managed persistence and bean-managed entity beans.

Chapter 12: Building a General Interface for MySQL

All of the chapters to this point have featured relatively simple examples using Java applications, applets, servlets, and JSP to illustrate the finer points of accessing a MySQL database using Java and Connector/J. This chapter pulls it all together using a Certificate Authority application. Using JSP, servlets, and EJB, the application shows how to create new accounts, request certificates, and enable the verification of certificates. All of the information, including the binary certificate, is stored in a MySQL database with multiple tables.

Chapter 13: Database Administration

Once you have a good knowledge of the MySQL database system as well as the fundamentals described in the previous chapters for accessing the data from Java, you must learn some database administration basics. In this chapter, we examine many of the functions within MySQL that benefit administrators, such as granting/revoking permissions, providing security within the server, and recovering from disasters.

Chapter 14: Performance and Tuning

Once the application is written and the information is safely sitting in a database, the users get the final say on whether or not the application meets their performance requirements. If the application isn't running at an appropriate level, you have a couple of options. First, you can profile the Java code to determine where the application is spending the most time and then rework the code associated with the problem areas. Second, you can tune the MySQL server and create indexes for the database tables. In this chapter, we provide the necessary information on performing these two options.

Appendix A: MySQL Development and Test Environments

We developed and tested all of the code in this book on several different test architectures in order to provide a representative reference. This appendix briefly describes those environments and lists the installed software. In addition, we offer some notes for reproducing the configuration.

Appendix B: Databases and Tables

In this appendix, we list all databases and tables used in the examples throughout this book.

Appendix C: The JDBC API and Connector/J

This appendix is a comprehensive review of the entire JDBC API, with annotations for Connector/J. Code snippets are provided to show at a quick glance how to use the various interfaces, classes, and methods.

Appendix D: MySQL Functions and Operators

The list of MySQL functions and operators in this appendix will help you determine when the database should handle computations versus the application. Each function and operator is described, and an example of its use is given.

Appendix E: Connector/J Late-Breaking Additions

The most current, up-to-date additions to Connector/J as it moves from gamma to production version.

CHAPTER 1

An Overview of MySQL

In this chapter, we explain why you might choose to use a database system with your software. We also provide an overview of the MySQL database server and the Connector/J JDBC driver.

For many years, large corporations have enjoyed the ability to deploy relational database management systems (RDBMSs) across their enterprise. Companies have used these systems to collect vast amounts of data that serve as the "fuel" for numerous applications that create useful business information.

Until recently, RDBMS technology has been out of reach for small businesses and individuals. Widely used RDBMS systems such as Oracle and DB2 require complex, expensive hardware. License fees for these systems are in the tens to hundreds of thousands of dollars for each installation. Businesses must also hire and retain staff with specialized skill sets to maintain and develop these systems. Smaller enterprises have relied on systems like Microsoft Access and FoxPro to maintain their corporate data.

Early on, during the explosive growth of the Internet, open source database systems like mSQL, Postgres (now PostgreSQL), and MySQL became available for use. Over a relatively short amount of time, the developers of these systems have provided a large subset of the functionality provided by the expensive commercial database systems. These open source database systems also run on less-expensive commodity hardware, and have proven in many cases to be easier to develop for and maintain than their commercial counterparts.

Finally, smaller businesses and individuals have access to the same powerful level of software tools that large corporations have had access to for over a decade.

Why Use an RDBMS?

Almost every piece of software that has been developed needs to *persist* or store data. Once data has been persisted, it is natural to assume that this data needs to be retrieved, changed, searched, and analyzed.

You have many options for data persistence in your software, from rolling your own code, to creating libraries that access flat files, to using full-blown RDBMS systems. Factors to consider when choosing a persistence strategy include whether you need multiuser access, how you will manage storage requirements, whether you need transactional integrity, and whether the users of your software need ad hoc query capability. RDBMSs offer all of this functionality.

Multiuser Access

Many programs use flat files to store data. Flat files are simple to create and change. The files can be used by many tools, especially if they are in comma- or tab-delimited formats. A large selection of built-in and third-party libraries is available for dealing with flat files in Java. The java.util.Properties class included with the Java Development Kit is one example.

Flat file systems can quickly become untenable when multiple users require simultaneous access to the data. To prevent corrupting the data in your file, you must lock the file during changes, and perhaps even during reads. While a file is locked, it cannot be accessed by other users. When the file becomes larger and the number of users increases, this leads to a large bottleneck because the file remains locked most of the time—your users are forced to wait until they can have exclusive access to the data.

RDBMSs avoid this situation by employing a number of locking strategies at varying granularities. Rather than using a single lock, the database system can lock an individual table, an individual page (a unit of storage in the database, usually covering more than one row), or an individual row. This increases throughput when multiple users are attempting to access your data, which is a common requirement in Web-based or enterprise-wide applications.

Storage Transparency

If you use flat files in your software, you are also responsible for managing their storage on disk. You have to figure out where and how to store the data, and every time the location or layout of the files changes, you are required to change your software. Once the datasets your software is storing become numerous or large, the storage management process becomes cumbersome.

Using a database system gives you "storage transparency." Your software does not care where and how the data is stored. The data can even be stored on some other computer and accessed via networking protocols.

Transactions

When you have more than one user accessing and changing your data, you want to make these changes *transactional*. Transactions group operations on your data into units of work that meet the *ACID* test. The ACID test concept is best illustrated with a commonly used example from the banking industry.

Jack and Jill share a joint checking account with a balance of $1000. They are both performing various operations, such as deposits, withdrawals, and transfers, on the account. Let's see how the four aspects of the ACID test come into play:

- **Atomicity:** All changes made during a transaction are made successfully, or in the case of failure, none are made. If any operation fails during the transaction, then the entire transaction is rolled back, leaving your data in the state it was before the transaction was started. For example, suppose Jack is making a transfer of $500 from his checking account to a savings account. Sometime between the withdrawal of the $500 from the checking account and the deposit of $500 to the savings account, the software running the banking system crashes. Jack's $500 has disappeared! With atomicity, either the entire transfer would have happened, or none of it would have happened, leaving Jack a much happier customer than he is now.
- **Consistency:** All operations transform the database from one consistent state to another consistent state. Consistency is defined by how the database schema is designed and whether integrity constraints such as foreign keys are used. The database management system is responsible for ensuring that transactions do not violate the database schema or integrity constraints. For example, the bank's database developers have declared in the database schema that the balance of an account cannot be empty, or "null." If any transaction attempts to set the balance to an empty value, the transaction will be aborted and any changes rolled back.
- **Isolation:** A transaction's changes are not made visible to other transactions until they are committed under the atomicity rule described earlier. This is best demonstrated by what happens when month-end reports are generated. Let's say that Jack is performing the transfer transaction outlined in the atomicity example, and at the same time you are generating his

monthly statement. Without isolation, the monthly statement might show the withdrawal from the checking account but not the deposit into the savings account. This discrepancy would make it impossible for Jack or the bank to balance their books.

- **Durability:** Once completed, a transaction's changes are never lost through system or hardware crashes. If Jill has paid for $50 worth of groceries with her debit card at the grocery store and the transaction succeeds, even if the database software crashes immediately after the transaction competes, it won't forget that her checking account balance is $50 lower.

Until recently, MySQL did not comply with all components of the ACID test. However, with the new BDB and InnoDB table types (supported in MySQL 3.23 and MySQL 4.0), MySQL can now pass the ACID test.

Not all software requires the robustness (or the associated overhead) of transaction semantics. MySQL is one of the only databases that enable you to decide what level of robustness you need on a table-by-table basis. This becomes important when you are trying to maximize performance, especially when much of the data is read-only (such as in a product catalog).

Searching, Modifying, and Analyzing Data

Any time you store a significant amount of data with your software, your users want to search, modify, and analyze the data you have stored. If you are using flat files, you most likely have to develop this functionality yourself.

As your data stored in flat files takes up more and more space, it takes longer and longer to search. A common solution to this problem is to create an index for your data. Indexes are basically shortcuts to finding a particular piece of data, usually using some sort of key. If you need to develop indexing functionality yourself, you have to learn about data structures, such as hashes and B-trees, and how to store these indexes alongside your data. In addition, you must learn how to implement the index in your software. If you use an RDBMS, you can tell the database system what data you think people will search on, and it does all of the fancy indexing for you.

Users of your software also want to retrieve, modify, and analyze the data you have stored. They expect that your system knows how to compute such values as sums, averages, minimums, and maximums to be used for updating related data or analyzing existing data. They expect that your software will be able to sort the data or group the data by similar attributes. All of this functionality requires you to implement numerous functions and algorithms. If you use an RDMBS, all of these features are built in.

Ad Hoc Queries

It is likely that your software will need to retrieve stored data using arbitrary parameters, otherwise known as *ad hoc* queries. This becomes difficult with flat files because they are not self-describing, and every file layout is different. You also need to consider how you are going to read the data for these queries from your persistent storage mechanism.

Many RDBMSs use SQL (Structured Query Language) for manipulating data. SQL is a declarative language in that you declare *what* data you want, not the procedure for *how* to get it. SQL is also an accepted and widely used standard, so a large set of tools are available (JDBC and Enterprise Java Beans, among them) to help you work with it.

After outlining all of the benefits of an RDBMS, I hope you are ready to consider using one for your software projects. The next question to ask is "Why choose MySQL?"

Why Choose MySQL?

As was the case with many other open source projects, MySQL was first created by someone who needed a better tool to get a specific job done. Monty Widenius and David Axmark started out with another open source project (MSQL), but found that it lacked some features that they needed. They decided to develop their own database system that met their specific requirements. They started building MySQL by using some low-level database storage code they had already developed for other projects and layered a multithreaded server, SQL parser, and client-server protocol on top. They also structured the API for MySQL to appear very similar to MSQL in order to make it easier for developers to port their MSQL-based software to MySQL.

MySQL was eventually released in source-code form, under a proprietary license. Eventually, this license was changed to the GNU General Public License (GPL), which in most cases allows the software to be used without license cost. However, in certain situations you must purchase a commercial license. The exact terms of the license are available in the documentation that ships with MySQL or on the Web at www.mysql.com. Commercial support is also available for those who need it from MySQL-AB, the company that was created by Monty and David to support the continued development of the MySQL software.

The requirements that Monty and David originally had for MySQL were that it be as fast as possible, while still being stable, simple to use, and able to meet the needs of the majority of database developers. Even today, feature requests for future MySQL development are weighed carefully against these original requirements, and are implemented only when and if the original requirements can be met as much as possible.

Over the years, MySQL has evolved into an RDBMS that has the following core features:

- **Portability:** MySQL runs on almost every flavor of Unix, as well as Windows and MacOS X. You can obtain binaries or source code for the MySQL server as well as the tools that access it. More ports of the software become available every day. It is almost a given that MySQL will run on whatever operating system you have available.
- **Speed:** Using techniques such as efficient indexing mechanisms, in-memory temporary tables, and highly optimized join algorithms, MySQL executes most queries much faster than most other database systems.
- **Scalability:** Because of its modularity and its flexibility in configuration, MySQL can run in systems varying in size from embedded systems to large multiprocessor Unix servers hosting databases with tens of millions of records. This scalability also allows you to run a copy of MySQL on a developer-class machine, and later use the same database system on a larger machine in production. Because it is multithreaded, MySQL efficiently utilizes resources for multiple users, compared to other database servers that start full-fledged processes for each user. It is not uncommon to hear of MySQL installations supporting thousands of concurrent users.
- **Flexibility:** MySQL lets you choose the table types you need to meet your software's requirements, ranging from in-memory heap tables, fast on-disk MyISAM tables, merge tables that group together other sets of tables to form larger "virtual" tables, and transaction-safe tables such as InnoDB. MySQL is also very tunable and includes many parameters that can be changed to increase performance for a given solution. However, MySQL comes with sensible defaults for these parameters, and many users never have to tune MySQL to reach a performance they are happy with.
- **Ease of use:** MySQL is easy to install and administer. While other database systems require special knowledge and training, not to mention special operating system configurations, MySQL can be installed in less than 10 minutes if you've done it before. Even if you are a newcomer, you should be able to install MySQL in under an hour. Once it's installed, MySQL requires little maintenance and administration other than adding or changing user permissions and creating or removing databases.
- **Fine-grained security model:** You can restrict users' rights from an entire database down to the column level based on login name, password, and the hostname that users are connecting from. This allows you to create secure systems by partitioning responsibilities and capabilities of different users and applications to prevent unauthorized modification or retrieval of data.

- **Access from other languages/systems:** There are libraries and APIs for connecting to MySQL from Java (the focus of this book), C/C++, Perl, PHP, ODBC (Microsoft Windows applications), TCL, Eiffel, and Lisp. Because of this, a whole set of tools has appeared surrounding the use of MySQL from these languages and systems.

As you can see, MySQL is a flexible and capable RDBMS that has a rich feature set, performs well on the majority of queries, and has a large support base for access from many different languages. This book focuses on using MySQL with JDBC, which is what we talk about next.

MySQL and JDBC

Many developers choose to implement software using Sun's Java technology because of the support Java has for standard Internet concepts such as Web sites, e-mail, and networking. This is the very reason I started to investigate using Java with MySQL in 1994.

Sun created a standardized interface to databases from Java called Java Database Connectivity (JDBC). Early in 1994, I was interested in connecting a Java application I was about to develop with the then-new MySQL database system using JDBC.

At the time, a rudimentary JDBC driver developed by GWE Technologies existed for MySQL. However, it was missing many features that I required for my project. Because many of the features that I needed would have been difficult to implement in the original MySQL driver, I decided to see if I could implement one myself, more as a tutorial than anything else.

After a few weeks of work, I had something that met most of my needs. Through correspondence with other Java developers on the MySQL mailing list, I found that others had a need for a JDBC driver to use with MySQL, and that they required many of the features I had just implemented. Not knowing what would happen, I wrote about the driver I had developed and allowed people to use it. From that small project, the JDBC driver known as MM.MySQL was born.

Over the years, through many hundreds of e-mails from users around the world, chronicling bugs and interoperability issues with development tools and application servers, MM.MySQL was fixed and tuned and eventually stabilized to become a successful open source project with a life all of its own. Downloaded by developers from around the world on average close to a thousand times a day, it is one of the most popular JDBC drivers, commercial or open source.

Monty and David of MySQL AB eventually became aware of the size of the Java developer community wanting to use MySQL, and extended an offer for me to join their team. In June 2002, I did just that, and MM.MySQL became the official JDBC driver for MySQL. It was subsequently renamed Connector/J.

What's Next

Now you understand the need for using a database in many of the applications written today. In this chapter, we explained why MySQL is a logical choice. Using the Connector/J JDBC driver, all sorts of Java applications can access a database and its data. In the next chapter, we provide a comprehensive overview of the JDBC specification and how it has been implemented in the Connector/J driver.

CHAPTER 2

JDBC and Connector/J

In the previous chapter, we discussed how a database can aid in the development of both Web sites and applications. One of the most popular databases is MySQL. Of course, a language is also needed, and our choice for this book is Java. By itself, Java doesn't have any way of directly accessing a database. To allow us to achieve the necessary interface between Java and a database, the developers at Sun created a specification called JDBC. In this chapter, we take a comprehensive look at the following:

- The history of JDBC
- JDBC driver types
- Standards and how they affect JDBC
- The JDBC class
- MySQL's Connector/J driver

What Is JDBC?

In this section, we provide a brief overview of what JDBC is and how it came about. Although many believe that JDBC is an acronym for Java Database Connectivity, the JDBC documentation itself states that JDBC isn't an acronym but actually a trademarked name (you can find more information about JDBC at Sun's Web site: http://java.sun.com/products/jdbc/).

With that said, JDBC is simply an application programming interface (API) for manipulating a database. The manipulation includes everything from connecting to the database, to executing SQL statements, to returning results. JDBC is middleware, or an intermediary between the Java language and a database. Fundamentally, JDBC is a specification that provides a complete set of interfaces that allows for portable access to an underlying database. The issue of portability is one of the key aspects of JDBC. Can you imagine using a language like Java—which provides the absolute best mechanism for writing an application once and executing it on a large number of platforms—and then having to change the code when your organization switches from Microsoft SQL Server to MySQL? That wouldn't be a very portable language in the area of database manipulation.

Fortunately, JDBC provides the standard API, and individual database vendors produce the drivers necessary to perform the actual interface between your Java application and the database. This means that Oracle, MySQL, Microsoft, and many other database vendors have taken the time to write all of the code behind the scenes. Since all of the vendors are writing to a common API, you can be relatively certain that the idea of write once, execute often and anywhere is still intact. Because most of the vendor JDBC drivers are also written in Java (more on this in the next section), the drivers can be used on different platforms as well. Not only can you change the platform on which your application runs or where the database itself resides, but you can also change the platform where the database executes. In the case of MySQL, the database system executes on most flavors of Unix and Linux, Windows, and the Macintosh platforms.

As you know, Java can be used to write different types of executables, such as

- Applications
- Applets
- Servlets
- Java ServerPages (JSPs)
- Enterprise JavaBeans (EJBs)

All of these different executables are able to use a JDBC driver to access a database and take advantage of the stored data. Throughout this book, we use a combination of these applications to illustrate using the MySQL JDBC driver to extract data from a database. For the most part, we use the term *Java application* to refer to any of the executable types we've listed, with the possible exception of EJBs.

What about ODBC?

One of the reasons developers thought JDBC stood for Java Database Connectivity relates to the acronym ODBC (used by Microsoft). ODBC, or Open

Database Connectivity, is an API developed by Microsoft to allow access to databases. The API and subsequent interface code allow access to a wide range of databases on many platforms using a variety of languages. This all sounds wonderful for a middleware product. Surely we could use ODBC as an interface between Java and MySQL. Why don't we?

The answer isn't as simple as not wanting to use a Microsoft product in our development. It is possible to use ODBC from Java using a product called the JDBC-ODBC Bridge, supplied by Sun. This bridge takes Java commands based on the JDBC API and sends them to an installed ODBC driver, which subsequently accesses the database. Any results work through the software in reverse. The bridge was supplied with Java 1.2 and 2.0 as a stopgap for developers who needed quick access to a database from their Java code. At the time, the JDBC specification wasn't mature; there weren't many vendor drivers available that used JDBC, but many were available for ODBC. Now that all major database vendors have pure Java solutions, use of the bridge isn't encouraged.

There are drawbacks to using ODBC in the process of accessing a database through Java. The primary drawback is that the code that implements ODBC is based on the C language and uses a large number of generic pointers. A number of problems occur with interfacing Java to C code, not to mention performance issues. It is much better to have a Java solution to database interfacing in order to provide a seamless solution.

Modeling Database Applications with JDBC

Before we start to look at the specifics of JDBC, let's take a moment and consider how it is used to interface a Java application with MySQL. Figure 2.1 shows a simple two-tier deployment model.

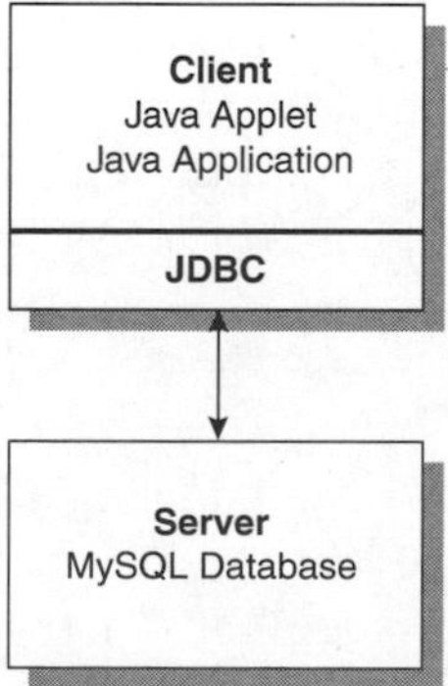

Figure 2.1 A two-tier deployment model.

In the two-tier deployment model, commonly called *client/server*, the client application communicates directly to the database through a JDBC driver. The JDBC API supports both two-tier and three-tier models for database access. The model supports the database being on the same machine as the client application or on a remote machine, with all communication being handled by JDBC. While the two-tier model is effective and has been in use for many years, there are problems with it, including a lack of security for updates occurring on the database, performance issues, and a lack of scalability.

Modern systems use a three-tier deployment model, as shown in Figure 2.2.

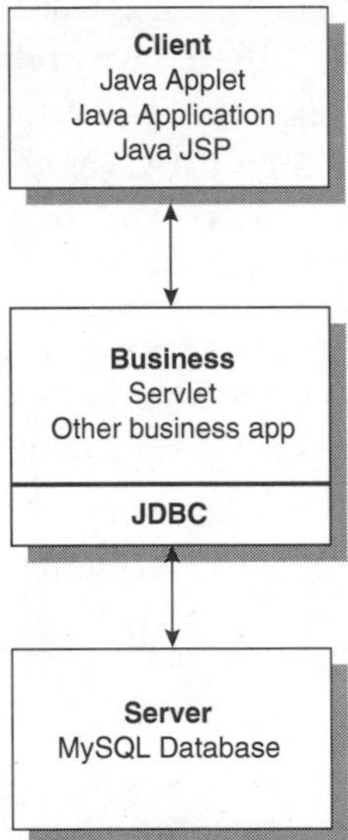

Figure 2.2 A three-tier deployment model.

As shown in the three-tier model, the client doesn't have direct access to the database. Instead, the client sends all its requests to a middle, or business, tier. This tier is responsible for implementing all business rules relating to the application and the data that is received from both the client and the database. Using a third tier has many advantages, the least of which is the ability of the business tier to handle security issues with the client application. The business tier is able to determine what a client is allowed to request and to filter data as needed when it is returned from the database.

Within the Java arena, three-tier models are commonly created using a JSP page communicated to the client via a Web browser. The JSP triggers a servlet on the business, or middle, tier, where rules and logic are applied to the client's request. The middle tier servlet contacts the database, or third, tier either directly or through EJBs.

JDBC Versions

Throughout the history of JDBC, Sun has introduced several different versions, beginning with version 1.0 in January of 1997. This initial specification defined the interfaces necessary to create an instance of the driver in a Java application, building SQL statements to execute against the underlying database, return results through a ResultSet object, and obtain various pieces of metadata about the database as well as the ResultSet.

Next, the 2.0/2.1 specification was released; this broke the original 1.0 specification into two parts. The Core API for 2.0 didn't add much to the original 1.0 specification but instead concentrated on performance and SQL 99 data types. The added functionality included programmatic SQL statements, scrollable ResultSets, streams, and other small updates. The second part of the 2.0/2.1 specification is called the JDBC 2.0 Optional Package. This package includes interfaces for data source interfaces, connection pooling, distributed transactions, and RowSets.

Recently, version 3.0 of the JDBC specification was released. Supported in the 1.4.x version of Java, the new specification includes many enhancements to ResultSets, data types, connection pools, and basic SQL statements. New functionality includes savepoint support (for checkpointing within transactions) and support for ParameterMetaData. You can find a complete discussion of the 3.0 specification at http://java.sun.com/products/jdbc/download.html#corespec30.

In the section "JDBC Support within 3.0.1" later in this chapter, we provide a complete overview of MySQL Connector/J's support of the functionality found in the specification. Appendix C, "JDBC API and Connector/J" also contains a detailed review of the complete specification and Connector/J support.

JDBC Driver Types

This section discusses the basic programming model of the JDBC driver itself. There are four different ways a JDBC driver can be created by vendors to support their database:

- Type 1: JDBC-ODBC Bridge
- Type 2: Native-API partly Java
- Type 3: JDBC-Net pure Java
- Type 4: Native-protocol pure Java

In a Type 1 driver, a JDBC bridge is used to access ODBC drivers installed on each client machine. (This is the JDBC-ODBC Bridge we discussed earlier.) From the standpoint of Java, this is merely a stopgap solution until a Java-based JDBC driver can be obtained.

In a Type 2 driver, JDBC API calls are converted and supplied to a vendor-specific driver. Used in the same manner as the JDBC-ODBC Bridge, the vendor-specific driver must be installed on each client machine. These drivers suffer the same problems found in a bridge situation.

In a Type 3 driver, a pure Java-based driver translates API calls into a DBMS-independent network protocol, which is further translated by a server to a vendor-specific protocol.

In a Type 4 driver, a pure Java-based driver translates API calls directly into the protocol needed by a vendor's database. This is the highest performance driver available for the database and is usually provided by the vendor itself. MySQL's Connector/J driver is a Type 4 driver.

SQL Standards

The standardization of access to a database has been a hot topic in recent years. The standard is called Structured Query Language, or SQL. Although the idea of a standard is appealing, not all database vendors follow the standard, and some cannot because of the feature set of the database itself. SQL92 used to be the defining specification for SQL, but recently a new standard called SQL99 has been adopted. The JDBC version 3.0 specification is designed to support SQL99.

When working with different database systems through JDBC, you can be relatively sure that basic functionality like SELECT, INSERT, UPDATE, and DELETE will work without much change. Beyond the basics, though, getting SQL working from one database to another requires some effort on your part.

By far the most important issue facing standardization is data typing. As you have probably already experienced in your development history, data types between C, C++, Java, PHP, and others can be quite different, especially in the area of data and time. Combine these differences with the various data types that can be stored in a database and you have the makings of a problem. In Chapter 7, "MySQL Type Mapping," we cover the JDBC data types and how they are represented in MySQL and subsequently with a Java application.

Another issue facing standardization is the use of quotes within SQL statements. JDBC attempts to handle this by using escaping and by requiring vendors to implement the escaping as appropriate for their databases.

A developer can also work with standardization by using metadata supplied from the database. Many times, a database will return information in the form of metadata, indicating whether it supports specific features.

Examining the JDBC Interface

Now that we know what JDBC is, where it came from, and its place in a typical system, let's turn our attention to the interfaces used to create the driver. Figure 2.3 shows how all of the core interfaces in the specification are designed to work together.

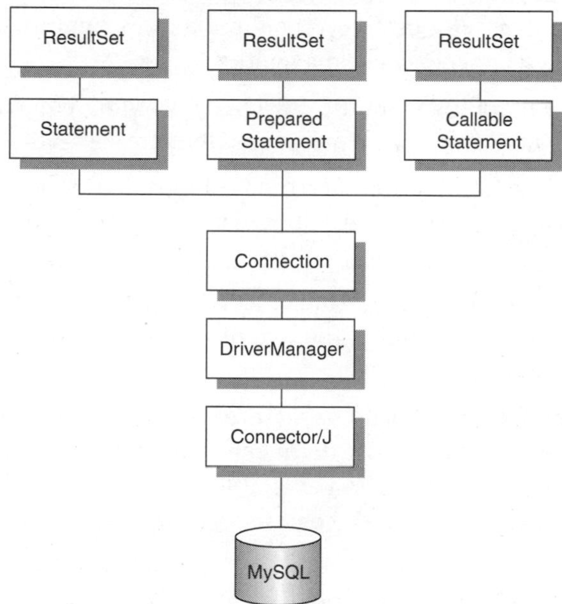

Figure 2.3 The Core JDBC API structure.

As we mentioned earlier, the specification is broken up into two different packages: the Core API and the Optional API. The Core API is implemented in the java.sql package. In this section, we look at the interfaces available in the specification (although we don't indicate here whether Connector/J supports the functionality—that can be found in Appendix C).

The java.sql Package

You can find this information both in Appendix C and in the section "Understanding Connector/J" later in this chapter. The interfaces specifically defined in version 3.0 of the specification are shown in italics. The full Javadoc can be found at http://java.sun.com/j2se/1.4/docs/api/java/sql/package-summary.html.

java.sql.Array: The Array interface is a mapping between the Java language and the SQL ARRAY type. The interface includes methods for bringing an ARRAY value to a client as a Java array or in a ResultSet.

java.sql.BatchUpdateException: The BatchUpdateException is thrown when a batch update operation has failed. The exception includes all of the successful update commands that executed before the failure.

java.sql.Blob: The Blob Java interface is a mapping to the SQL BLOB value.

java.sql.CallableStatement: The CallableStatement interface is used to execute stored procedures if supported on the database. Parameters are allowed with the interface as well as escape syntax.

java.sql.Clob: Clob is a mapping from the Java programming language to the SQL CLOB type. A CLOB is a Character Large Object.

java.sql.Connection: The Connection interface provides a method for creating a connection to a specific database. All SQL is executed in the context of a Connection object.

java.sql.DataTruncation: The DataTruncaction exception is thrown when data will be truncated. On a write, the exception is an error, but on a read, the exception is a warning.

java.sql.DatabaseMetaData: The DatabaseMetaData interface is designed to provide information about the remote database that a connection has been made to previously. The information available to the DatabaseMetaData object will be different based on the database vendor and the information it wants to provide.

java.sql.Date: The Date class is a wrapper for JDBC to use as a map to the SQL DATE value. The value of Date is the number of milliseconds since January 1, 1970, 00:00:00:000 GMT.

A thin wrapper around a millisecond value that allows JDBC to identify this as an SQL DATE value. A milliseconds value represents the number of milliseconds that have passed since January 1, 1970, 00:00:00.000 GMT.

java.sql.Driver: The Driver interface is implemented by all vendor drivers so that they can be loaded by a static class called DriverManager. The Driver object will automatically create an instance of itself and register with DriverManager.

java.sql.DriverManager: The DriverManager class is used to manage all Driver objects.

java.sql.DriverPropertyInfo: The DriverPropertyInfo class provides information for advanced developers who need to set specific properties for loading a Driver object.

java.sql.ParameterMetaData: The ParameterMetaData interface provides information about the parameters in a PreparedStatement object.

java.sql.PreparedStatement: The PreparedStatement interface provides an object for executing precompiled SQL statements against the connected database.

java.sql.Ref: The Ref interface is a mapping between Java and an SQL REF value. A REF value is a reference to an SQL structured type value.

java.sql.ResultSet: A ResultSet interface is designed to represent a ResultSet produced from a query of the database. An internal cursor points to the current row of data, and it can be pointed before and after the data. Methods are used to move the cursor to different rows in the ResultSet. By default, the ResultSet isn't updatable, but can be made both scrollable and updatable.

java.sql.ResultSetMetaData: The ResultSetMetaData interface is used to return specific information about the data within a ResultSet object. The information could include the number of columns, column names, float column precision, and total column size, among other data.

java.sql.Savepoint: The Savepoint interface is used along with transactions to provide rollback points. This allows for the completion of large transactions even when an error occurs.

java.sql.SQLData: The SQLData interface is used to map the SQL user-defined type to the Java language.

java.sql.SQLException: The SQLException exception will be thrown when an error occurs during an attempt to access a database or when the database itself returns an error.

java.sql.SQLInput: The SQLInput interface is used by the developer of a JDBC driver to stream values from the database results. The interface isn't designed to be instantiated by the application developer.

java.sql.SQLOutput: The SQLOutput interface is used by the developer of a JDBC driver to stream data to the database. The interface isn't designed to be instantiated by the application developer.

java.sql.SQLPermission: The SQLPermission interface is designed to allow the driver to determine its permission when an applet calls the DriverManager.setLogWriter or setLogStream methods.

java.sql.SQLWarning: The SQLWarning interface is used to return any database access warnings from the database. Warnings are available in the Connection, Statement, and ResultSet objects.

java.sql.Statement: The Statement interface is probably one of the most important interfaces in the JDBC specification. All SQL statements are executed through a Statement object. Each Statement object returns single ResultSet objects.

java.sql.Struct: The Struct interface is a mapping from a SQL structured type to the Java language.

java.sql.Time: The Time class is a wrapper around java.util.Date to support the mapping from SQL TIME to Java.

java.sql.Timestamp: The Timestamp class is a wrapper around java.util.Date to support the mapping from SQL TIMESTAMP to Java.

java.sql.Types: The Types class is an internal class used to identify generic SQL types or JDBC types.

The classes and interfaces within the Core API are linked together, as shown in Figure 2.4. There is a natural progression from a Connection object to a ResultSet. The path from one to the other occurs using a Statement, PreparedStatement, or CallableStatement; and the Statement class is a parent to both of the others. All of the Statement classes will eventually execute SQL to produce a ResultSet.

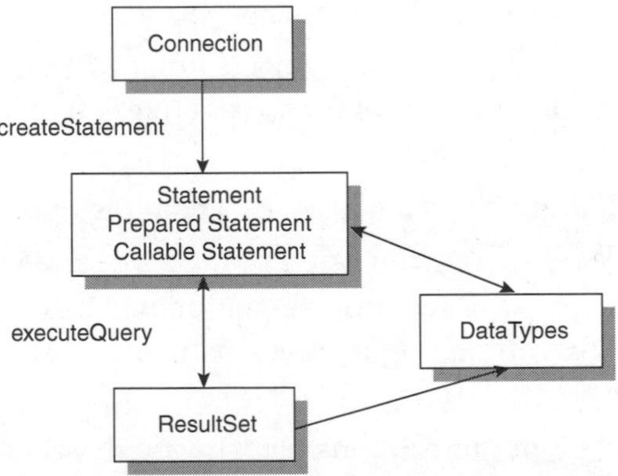

Figure 2.4 JDBC Core API class/interface links.

The javax.sql Package

The Optional API within the JDBC specification is implemented within the javax.sql package. The classes and interfaces are as follows:

javax.sql.ConnectionEvent: The ConnectionEvent class is used to signal a closed pooled connection and an error.

javax.sql.ConnectionEventListener: The ConnectionEventListener interface is used by applications that want to be notified when a PooledConnection object generates an event.

javax.sql.ConnectionPoolDataSource: The ConnectionPoolDataSource is a factor for PooledConnection objects. The object implementing the interface can be registered using Java Naming and Directory Interface (JNDI).

javax.sql.DataSource: The DataSource is a factory for connections. The object implementing the interface can be registered using JNDI.

javax.sql.PooledConnection: The PooledConnection interface provides a connection to the database, but is part of a larger pool. The application developer doesn't use the interface directly.

javax.sql.RowSet: The RowSet is a JavaBeans component that is created and configured at design time and executed at runtime. The RowSet can be configured to connect to a JDBC source and to read data.

javax.sql.RowSetEvent: The RowSetEvent is created when a single row in a RowSet is changed, the internal cursor moves to a different location, or the entire RowSet has changed.

javax.sql.RowSetInternal: The RowSetInternal interface is implemented to allow the RowSetReader and RowSetWriter objects access to the internals of a RowSet.

javax.sql.RowSetListener: The RowSetListener interface is implemented by a component that wants to be notified when an event occurs in a RowSet object. The component calls the addRowSetListener() method of the RowSet in which it is interested.

javax.sql.RowSetMetaData: The RowSetMetaData interface provides information about a RowSet. The information centers around the columns returned from a result.

javax.sql.RowSetReader: The RowSetReader interface is used by a RowSet to obtain results from the database.

javax.sql.RowSetWriter: The RowSetWriter interface is used to write changed data back to the database.

javax.sql.XAConnection: The XAConnection interface allows a connection to handle distributed transactions.

javax.sql.XADataSource: The XADataSource interface is an internal factory for DataSource connections using JNDI.

The classes and interfaces within the Optional API are linked together, as shown in Figures 2.5, 2.6, 2.7, and 2.8, which are referenced within the version 3.0 specification.

Figure 2.5 shows the relationship between the DataSource and Connection classes. The DataSource doesn't act on its own, but instead must obtain a connection to the database through the Connection class.

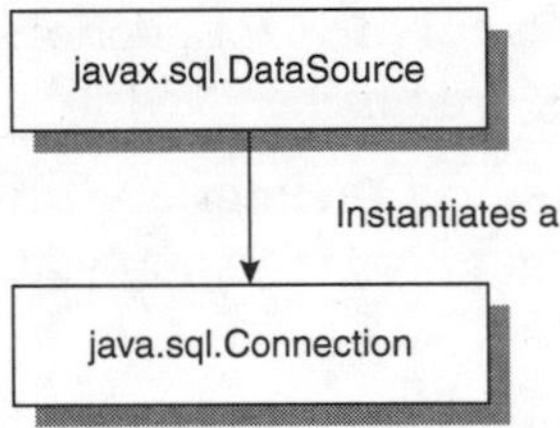

Figure 2.5 DataSource/Connection classes.

Figure 2.6 shows how a PooledConnection class will also use the Connection class to obtain a link to the database. Note the ConnectionEventListener associated with PooledConnection. Any events created by PooledConnection will be sent to those objects that register with the ConnectionEventListener.

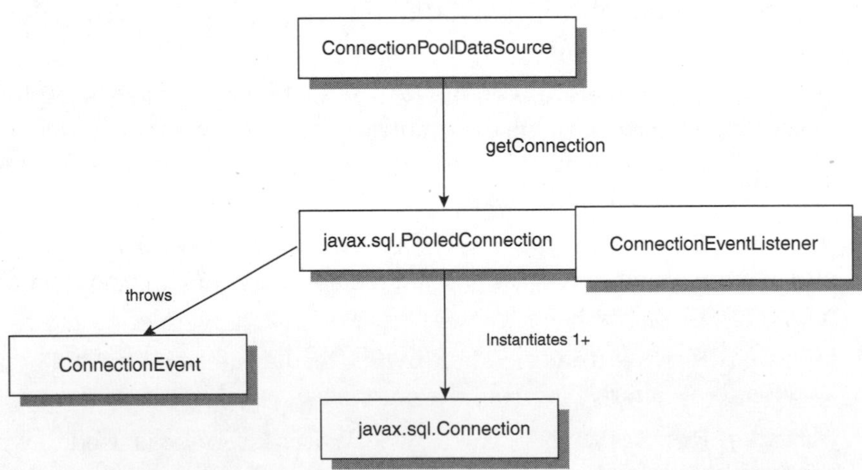

Figure 2.6 PooledConnection/Connection classes.

Figure 2.7 shows how the RowSet classes are constructed from the base Result and ResultSetMetaData classes.

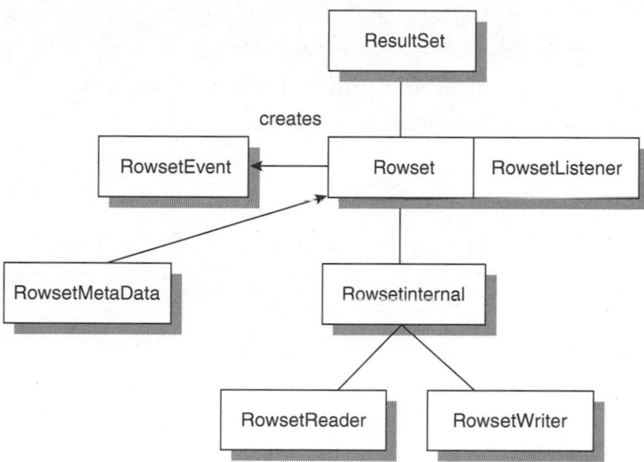

Figure 2.7 RowSet classes.

Understanding Connector/J

Up to this point, our discussion has centered on the general JDBC specification and its related interfaces and classes. In this section, we turn our attention to MySQL's JDBC driver, Connector/J. At the time of this writing, there are two versions of the driver: 2.0.14 and 3.0.1. The drivers can be found at www.mysql.com/downloads/api-jdbc-stable.html and www.mysql.com/downloads/api-jdbc-dev.html, respectively.

The Connector/J driver started as MM.MySQL (written by Mark Matthews) and has been the primary JDBC driver for MySQL. During 2002, Mark joined the MySQL team and subsequently updated the driver and renamed it to Connector/J. The 2.0.14 version is basically the last MM.MySQL version made available on the mmmysql.sourceforge.net Web site. The 3.0.1 version contains numerous changes to the original code. These features will be discussed shortly.

Connector/J is designed specifically for MySQL and attempts to adhere to the JDBC API as much as possible. However, in order for a driver to adhere to the full JDBC specification, the underlying database must support all of the features supported in the latest 3.0 version. For MySQL and Connector/J, strict adherence is impossible because MySQL currently doesn't support stored procedures, savepoints, references, and various other small pieces of functionality. These differences with the specification are noted in Appendix C. For the remainder of this book, we use the latest 3.0 version of Connector/J.

JDBC Support within 3.0.1

As we mentioned earlier, the Connector/J JDBC driver is able to support only those features of the specification that the underlying MySQL database supports. Instead of explaining what *is* supported from the specification, we document here what currently is *not* supported. From a class standpoint, the following classes have some functionality not supported:

- Blob
- Clob
- Connection
- PreparedStatement
- ResultSet
- UpdatableResultSet
- CallableStatement

Next we list each of the major interfaces with the individual methods *not* supported in the current version. As the MySQL database begins to support the underlying functionality needed for each of the classes and methods, the list will get shorter. For example, stored procedures are planned for a future release of the database and thus the CallableResultSet interface could then be implemented.

Blob

Blob.setBinaryStream()

Blob.setBytes()

Blob.truncate()

Clob

setAsciiStream()

setCharacterStream()

setString()

truncate()

Connection

Connection.setSavePoint()

Connection.setTypeMap()

Connection.getTypeMap()

Connection.prepareCall()

Connection.releaseSavepoint()

Connection.rollback()

PreparedStatement

PreparedStatement.setArray()

PreparedStatement.setBlob()

PreparedStatement.getMetaData()

PreparedStatement.setRef()

PreparedStatement.getParameterMetaData()

ResultSet

ResultSet.getArray()

ResultSet.getObject()

RcsultSet.getRef(int)

ResultSet.getRef(String)

ResultSet.rowDeleted()

ResultSet.rowInserted()

ResultSet.rowUpdated()

ResultSet.updateArray(,)

ResultSet.updateClob()

ResultSet.updateRef()

UpdatableResultSet

rowDeleted()

rowInserted()

rowUpdated()

updateBlob()

CallableStatement

All methods

The Connector/J driver does support the use of very large package sizes when used against MySQL 4.0 or later. This means that applications will have quicker and easier access to large data within Blob and Clob columns.

Obtaining JDBC Drivers

While our book concentrates on MySQL's JDBC Connector/J driver, numerous drivers are available for all types of databases. One of the most comprehensive collections can be found on Sun's site at http://industry.java.sun.com/products/jdbc/drivers.

Figure 2.8 shows that there are currently 165 drivers available and growing.

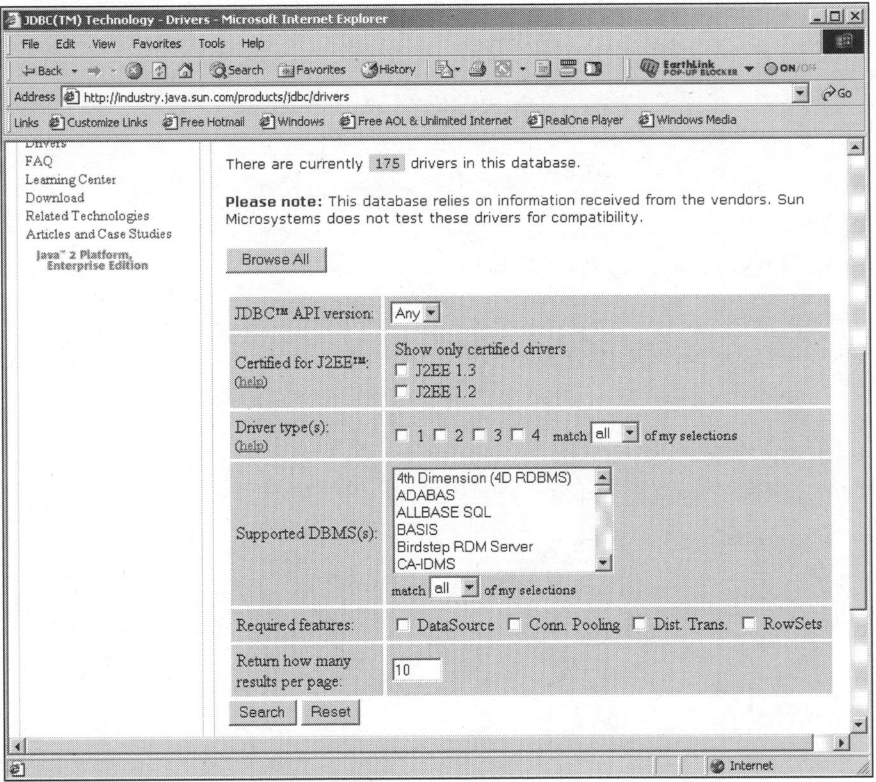

Figure 2.8 The Sun JDBC driver search screen.

What's Next

In this chapter, we provided a comprehensive overview of the JDBC specification and interfaces associated with the spec. We also explored the MySQL Connector/J driver and its support of the specification. In the next chapter, we look at installing all the tools we need for the remainder of the book.

CHAPTER 3

Working with MySQL SQL

If you've used the MySQL database system or any other relational database system, this section of the chapter will be a review for you. Our goal is to present the very basics of database systems, tables, design, queries, and other topics of importance to developers who want to start using a database with their application code. It should be noted that we have space to cover only the basics and not all of the details associated with a database system. We present more advanced topics throughout the book as we discuss JDBC and MySQL. For those who already know this information, skip to the section called "Introduction to MySQL SQL," where we cover some of the MySQL specifics.

What Is a Database?

As we discussed in the opening paragraphs, the most efficient way to store large amounts of data is a database system. The term *database* is generally used as a common identifier of the entire system that constitutes this particular type of storage system. However, a database is actually part of the database management system. A *database management system (DBMS)* is the term given to the entire application that supports a database and includes all server and client components.

In a typical setup, a large machine with plenty of disk space is allocated as a database server. The DBMS is installed on the machine, and a server application executed to handle requests to store and retrieve information. In addition, a database administrator uses the DBMS to administer the server and keep the database stored on the server in order.

The database administrator, who can also be the developer, creates databases by using the DBMS to hold specific data. For instance, an application might include general data such as accounts, addresses, and other forms of basic information. In addition to the account information, the application scans documents into the database from a scanner. This binary data has a much greater space need than the account information, so it is given a separate database. By separating the data into different databases, the DBMS generally allows them to be assigned different disk drive locations. The image data might be stored on a large array of disks, while the account information is stored on smaller disks but configured as a redundant array of independent disks (RAID). Figure 3.1 shows how this might look.

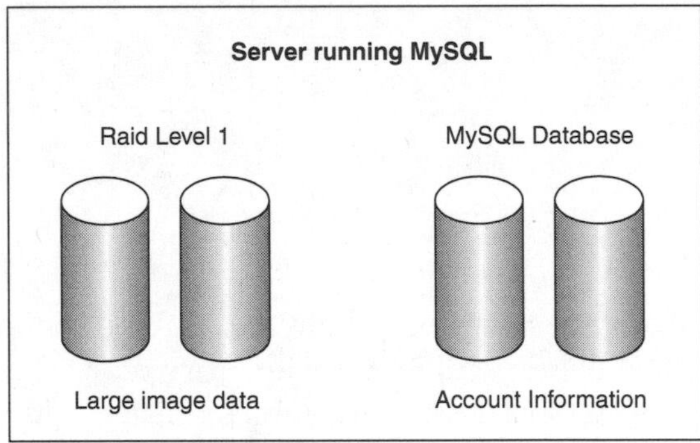

Figure 3.1 A multiple-database system.

Once the databases for the application have been laid out, tables are introduced to each of the databases. While all of the data could be thrown together into the database, it is usually better to group the data into logical bunches. In an account database, you might have a table for account numbers and some identifying information. Another table in the account database could contain address information. Figure 3.2 shows an example.

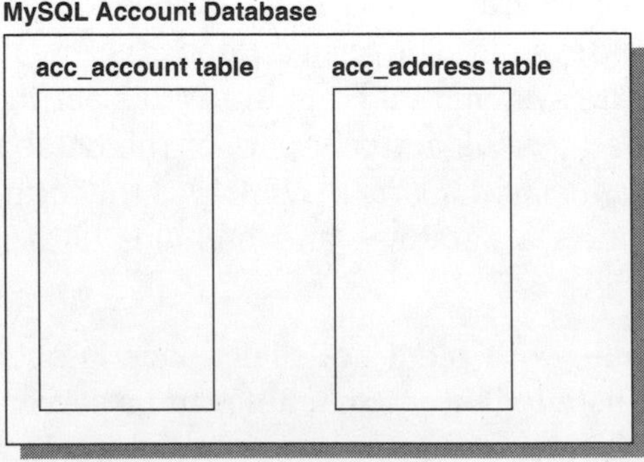

Figure 3.2 Tables within the database.

Each of the tables is further broken down into columns where individual pieces of information are stored. The address table has columns for information such as city, state, and zip. As data is put into the table, it is organized as a series of rows, with each row containing specific information in the various columns, as shown in Figure 3.3.

MySQL Account Database

acc_account table

ID	fname	lname
0	Joe	Smith
1	Jane	Doe
2	James	Shaw

acc_address table

ID	acc_ID	State
0	0	CO
1	1	AZ
2	2	IL

Figure 3.3 Database rows/columns.

So in a nutshell, that is the definition of a database. In the remainder of this section, we examine these concepts in more detail.

Database Models

All databases model data in different ways. A database model is just a description of a container and how data is stored and retrieved from that container. Over the years, a few different models have been developed. Consider the following data that needs to be stored in a database:

Name	Username	City
John Smith	smith	Denver
John Smith	jsmith	Denver
James Doe	doej	Chicago
James Smith	jsmith	Atlanta

The Hierarchy Model

The hierarchy model attempts to organize the data in a parent-child relationship where there is always some root data. Our sample data is modeled as shown in Figure 3.4.

The data is contained within the hierarchy, but getting to it could be a problem since the data is found at different levels.

The Network Model

In the network model, the parent-child relationship is expanded so that children can have multiple parents and a logical layer is applied to the data. Figure 3.5 shows how our sample data is modeled.

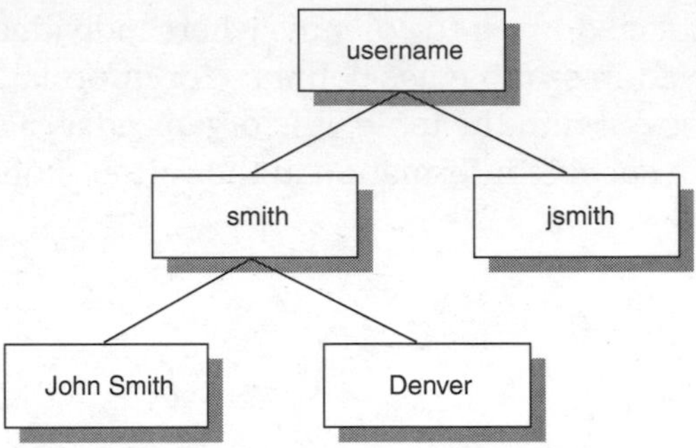

Figure 3.4 The hierarchy model.

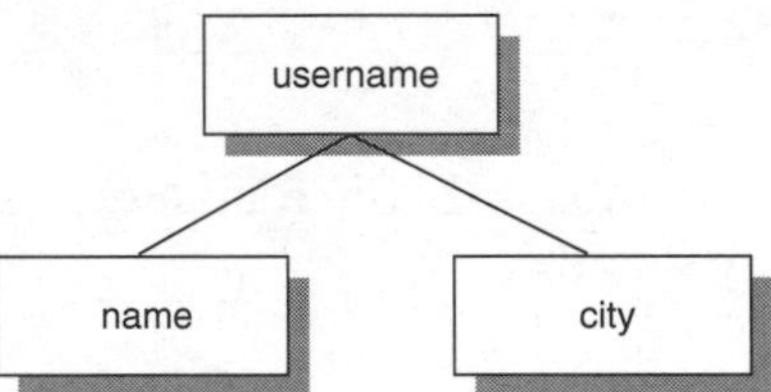

Figure 3.5 The network model.

The Relational Model

In the late 1960s, the relational model was developed. A relational database uses tables with rows and columns. The power of the relational model becomes clear when multiple tables are linked using a relationship. Figure 3.6 shows how our sample data might be put in separate tables and linked using the username.

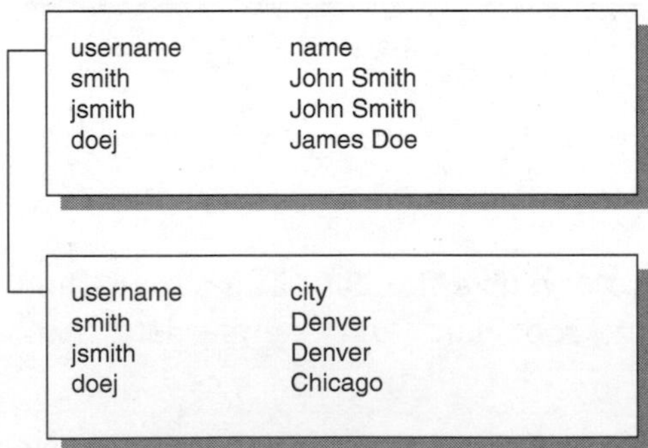

Figure 3.6 The relational model.

The Object Model

In the past few years, the object model has emerged. In this model, a database is created to hold the objects found in a common programming language like

Java. Instead of the data being broken up, the entire object is stored. Figure 3.7 shows how our sample data might look in an object model-based database.

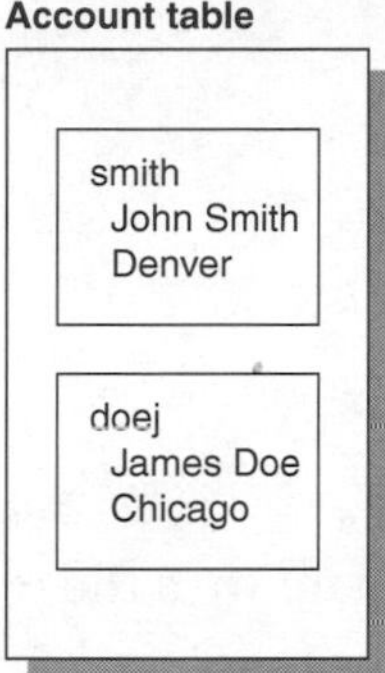

Figure 3.7 The object model.

For the remainder of this book, we assume the use of a relational database management system. MySQL just happens to be such a system.

Data Types

As we mentioned earlier, a database has tables consisting of columns. The columns aren't just names like city, state, and zip, but are created based on a data type such as string, integer, or float. Some of the more common data or column types available are

- **int**—Represents an integer
- **char**—Represents a string of a specific length
- **varchar**—Represents a string of varied length
- **blob**—Represents a large binary piece of data

When you use a type to define a column, the database expects that kind of data when you place information into the table.

Designing a Database

Now let's spend some time on the subject of database design. We know that MySQL and many other databases are relational in nature and that we need to build databases, tables, and columns. However, if we neglect to give some initial thought to the layout or design of these components, the performance and integrity of the database server and the data itself will be suspect. Before diving into this subject, note that very large college textbooks have been written on the subject of database design. This section is just a small glance at the subject.

To illustrate simple design considerations, let's attempt to build the tables within a database to hold data for a simple telephone directory. The data we want to store includes the following:

Name
City
State
Telephone number

First Normal Form

If we were to place our data into a table, we might come up with the following:

Name	City	State	Telephone
John Doe	Chicago	IL	217-333-3333

Of course, we immediately realize that John Doe has more than just one telephone number, so we expand the table to handle more numbers:

Name	City	State	Telephone1	Telephone2	Telephone3
John Doe	Chicago	IL	217-333-3333	800-333-3333	
Jani Smith	Atlanta	GA	403-222-2223		

In our new table, we've added another entry. However, Jani Smith has only one telephone number, so we leave the columns Telephone2 and Telephone3 empty. Unfortunately, our friend Bill Simpson is one of those characters with a home telephone, a business telephone, a cell phone, a pager, and a phone just for messages. Since our table handles only three telephone numbers, we need to add two more columns just for Bill. Most people we add into the table won't have more than three telephone numbers, so the vast majority of Telephone4 and Telephone5 columns will be empty. Of course, just when we limit the table to five telephone numbers, Bill will get a summer cabin with a telephone in it as well. We cannot continue to add columns just to accommodate Bill's communication needs, especially when all of the added telephone columns will generally be empty.

To solve this problem of multiple columns in the database, we apply rules associated with the First Normal Form. The *First Normal Form* is the first in a series of optimizations that should be applied to a database to produce a highly efficient system. The rules in First Normal Form are:

- Columns with similar content must be eliminated.
- A table must be created for each group of associated data.
- Each data record must be identifiable by means of a *primary key*.

It isn't necessary to apply all of these rules to achieve First Normal Form, but they should be attempted nevertheless. For our database, the first and third rules can be applied. Rule two isn't valid for our data because all of the pieces of data are associated with each other. Rule number 1 is the one that will make the most difference in the database. Here's our data after we've applied rules 1 and 3:

ID	Name	City	State	Telephone
101	John Doe	Chicago	IL	217-333-3333
102	John Doe	Chicago	IL	800-333-3333
103	Jani Smith	Atlanta	GA	403-222-2223

We won't include Bill in the example to keep it small. Notice how John Doe's information is being duplicated so we can handle additional telephone numbers. If John Doe gets another telephone number, we just add a new record to the table with duplicate name, city, and state values. The third rule doesn't really help with our telephone number problem, but in order for our table to be in First Normal Form, it needs to be applied.

Second Normal Form

Of course, all of this data duplication simply cannot be a good thing because it is clearly wasting space in the database. We can get some help with the duplicated data using Second Normal Form and its associated rules:

- If the contents of columns repeat, the table needs to be divided into multiple tables.
- Multiple tables from rule 1 need to be linked by foreign keys or their derivative.

Since we have repeating data in the sample table, we apply rules 1 and 2 to create a second table just for the city, state, and telephone information. For example, the following table might be called the name table:

ID	Name
101	John Doe
102	Jani Smith

The telephone table would look like this:

ID	telephone_id	city	state	telephone
201	101	Chicago	IL	217-333-3333
202	101	Chicago	IL	800-333-3333
203	102	Atlanta	GA	403-222-2223

We now have two tables for all of our sample data. The first table, called name, holds just the name of our contact as well as an ID for each name in the table. There won't be any duplicate names in this table. The second table, called telephone, holds all of the contact information for each name in the name table.

Of particular important in the telephone table is the use of the telephone_id column. This column is considered a foreign key and links the name table to the telephone table. The ID column in the name table is copied to each of the telephone table rows as appropriate. If we need to find each of the telephone numbers for John Doe, we look up the ID in the row associated with John Doe. This ID is used as a reference value in the name_id columns of each row in the telephone table. Those rows that have the same ID value are returned. The telephone number value can be pulled from each row and displayed.

Third Normal Form

The last "normal form" we consider is called Third Formal Form and it is the goal for most database designers. There is a single rule in this form:

- Columns that are not directly related to the primary key must be eliminated (that is, transplanted into a table of their own).

In the table called telephone we created earlier, we have to examine the use of the telephone_id column and the data within the table itself. The Third Normal Form rule tells us that the city and state columns shouldn't be part of the telephone table because that data doesn't relate to the primary key of the table. This calls for a new table to hold the city and state information. For example, we might create a table called address to hold this information:

ID	address_id	city	state
301	101	Chicago	IL
302	102	Atlanta	GA

We've provided a brief introduction to database design and the use of Normal Forms to achieve a good design. There is, of course, much more to consider when designing databases, and we recommend you consult a good database theory book for additional information.

Introducing MySQL SQL

The majority of this chapter concentrates on the specifics of the MySQL database and its representation of SQL. In this section, we examine the basics you need to build databases and tables, populate the databases with data, and retrieve the data.

Overview of MySQL

MySQL is a DBMS designed as open source software. It is a relationship DBMS because it supports the idea of building multiple tables and linking those tables using columns within the tables. The application is considered open source because you can download the binaries of the system or the source code.

The MySQL system is entry-level SQL92 compliant, and the developers are constantly striving to expand their support of SQL92—as well as SQL99—while maintaining speed and efficiency. Some of the featured highlights include the following:

Speed and efficiency—MySQL is written in C/C++ using the latest compilers on the various support platforms. The code is multithreaded and takes advantage of kernel threads for extreme efficiency on systems with multiple CPUs. All of the code is highly optimized and makes us of B-trees, in-memory hash tables, and class libraries.

Column types—These include signed/unsigned integers 1, 2, 3, 4, and 8 bytes long; FLOAT; DOUBLE; CHAR; VARCHAR; TEXT; BLOB; DATE; TIME; DATETIME; TIMESTAMP; YEAR; SET; and ENUM types. We demonstrate many of these column types throughout the book in code examples.

A full-featured command set—All of the standard SQL commands, such as SELECT, INSET, DELETE, as well as JOINs, are supported. Support includes the SHOW command for obtaining information about the system. Aliases on table and columns are supported per SQL92.

Functions—A wide range of functions are available, including AVG(), SUM(), MAX(), and many others.

Security—A full privilege and password system gives the database unparalleled security.

Scalability—You can build databases with tens of thousands of tables. Row counts can be in the millions and even billions. Indexes are supported up to 32 per table.

Character sets—MySQL supports many different characters sets and can output errors messages in appropriate languages.

Tools—A full complement of client tools is available for administrative and other uses.

With that small introduction, let's dive into the fundamentals of using MySQL to build storage systems for our Java applications.

Creating Databases

As you learned earlier, a database is just a container for components called tables. A DBMS can have as many databases as needed for a given application. For the most part, you create a database when your application needs a place to store data. In most cases, you need a single database with numerous tables to hold the data. The MySQL server already has its own database, called mysql. We want to create a new one instead of using the mysql database because we plan to use ours for a different purpose.

In order to manipulate a MySQL system, you can use a client tool called mysql. This client tool can be found in the /bin directory of an installation. You execute the tool by entering *mysql* at a command prompt or terminal window. The client tool contacts the local MySQL installation and returns a prompt as shown here:

```
Welcome to the MySQL monitor.  Commands end with ; or \g.
Your MySQL connection id is 139 to server version: 4.0.1-alpha

Type 'help;' or '\h' for help. Type '\c' to clear the buffer.

mysql>
```

Using the mysql client tool, you can determine what databases are currently defined in the local MySQL system. This is accomplished with the following command:

```
mysql> show databases;
+----------+
| Database |
+----------+
| mysql    |
| files    |
| products |
| test     |
| users    |
+----------+
5 rows in set (0.00 sec)
```

In the test database we used, there are currently five databases being managed by MySQL. Two of the tables, mysql and test, are created by the MySQL system when it is first installed. The other three have been added by users of the system. In our example, we want to create a new database called accounts that will hold numerous tables all related to accounts needed by some application. In the most basic form, the database is created with the following command:

```
mysql> create database accounts;
Query OK, 1 row affected (0.00 sec)
```

The accounts database is now available on the MySQL system. Note that on a Windows platform, the database name isn't case-sensitive, but it is on Unix. After a database is created, it will need to be used specifically. To use a database, you execute the USE command:

```
mysql> use accounts;
Database changed
```

The USE command moves the focus of all commands entered into the client tool to the specified database. We now have a database, and it is the focus of our client tool. The next step is to add tables where we can store data.

Creating Tables

The *table* is where all of the data is stored in a particular database. Because we are working with a relational database system, the data is stored in rows and columns. Our goal in creating a table is to determine what will be stored in each table column. Once this information has been established, we can decide on the column types and potential sizes.

You can create a MySQL table based on a number of table types:

BDB—A table that supports transactions; includes crash recovery.

HEAP—A memory-based table that uses a hashed index.

ISAM—An original but deprecated MySQL table.

InnoDB—A table that supports transactions, row-level locking, foreign key constraints, and multiversioning.

MERGE—A group of MyISAM tables used as one. Allows tables to be stored in different locations.

MYISAM—A default nontransactional table type for MySQL.

Each table type has a specific characteristic that determines whether it is appropriate for your application. Note that MySQL allows you to alter the table type after you've created a table—even if you've populated it with data. A large number of options are available, among them the maximum number of rows, the physical location of the table, and the use of a password for the table. However, the most important options are the column type definitions.

First, you need to lay out the data to be stored in the table. In our example, we want to create a table that will hold the username and password for an account in our application. Associated with each username and account is an account ID. The account ID will be used to access specific data within other tables by creating a relationship with the ID. Each of these pieces of data will have a specific data type. The data types available in MySQL are as follows:

TINYINT—An 8-bit integer represented as one byte.

SMALLINT—A 16-bit integer represented as 2 bytes.

MEDIUMINT—A 24-bit integer represented as 3 bytes.

INT, INTEGER—A 32-bit integer represented as 4 bytes.

BIGINT—A 64-bit integer represented as 8 bytes.

FLOAT—A floating-point number; 8-digit precision represented as 4 bytes.

DOUBLE—A floating-point number; 16-digit precision represented as 8 bytes.

DECIMAL(*p*, *s*)—A fixed-point number, saved as a character string; an arbitrary number of digits represented as 1 byte per digit + 2 bytes overhead.

DATE—The date in the form *2001-12-31*, in the range 1000-01-01 to 9999-12-31, represented as 3 bytes.

TIME—The time in the form *23:59:59*, represented as 3 bytes.

DATETIME—A combination of DATE and TIME in the form *2002-10-05 23:59:59*, represented as 8 bytes.

YEAR—The year (1900–2155), represented as 1 byte.

TIMESTAMP—The date and time in the form *20011231325959* for times between 1970 and 2038, represented as 4 bytes.

CHAR(*n*)—A character string with a specified length; a maximum of 255 characters represented as *n* bytes.

VARCHAR(*n*)—A character string with variable length; a maximum of *n* characters (*n* < 256), represented as 1 byte per character or (actual length) + 1.

TINYTEXT—A character string with variable length; a maximum of 255 characters, represented as *n* + 1 bytes.

TEXT—A character string with variable length; a maximum of 216 - 1 characters represented as *n* + 2 bytes.

MEDIUMTEXT—A character string with variable length; a maximum of 224 - 1 characters, represented as *n* + 3 bytes.

LONGTEXT—A character string with variable length, maximum of 232 - 1 characters, represented as *n* + 4 bytes.

TINYBLOB—Binary data with variable length; a maximum of 255 bytes.

BLOB—Binary data with variable length; a maximum of 216 - 1 bytes.

MEDIUMBLOB—Binary data with variable length; a maximum of 224 - 1 bytes.

LONGBLOB—Binary data with variable length; a maximum of 232 - 1 bytes.

ENUM—Selects one from at most 65,535 character strings, represented as 1 or 2 bytes.

SET—Combines at most 255 character strings, represented as 1–8.

TINYINT 8-bit integer represented as 1 byte
SMALLINT 16-bit integer represented as 2 bytes
MEDIUMINT 24-bit integer represented as 3 bytes
INT, INTEGER 32-bit integer represented as 4 bytes
BIGINT 64-bit integer represented as 8 bytes

FLOAT floating-point number, 8-place precision represented as 4 bytes
DOUBLE floating-point number, 16-place precision represented as 8 bytes
DECIMAL(p, s) fixed-point number, saved as a character string; arbitrary number of digits represented as one byte per digit + 2 bytes overhead

DATE date in the form '2001-12-31', range 1000-01-01 to 9999-12-31 represented as 3 bytes
TIME time in the form '23:59:59' represented as 3 bytes
DATETIME combination of *DATE* and *TIME* in the form '2002-10-05 23:59:59' represented as 8 bytes
YEAR year 1900-2155 represented as 1 byte
TIMESTAMP date and time in the form 20011231325959 for times between 1970 and 2038 represented as 4 bytes

CHAR(n) character string with specified length, maximum 255 characters represented as *n* bytes
VARCHAR(n) character string with variable length, maximum *n* characters (*n* < 256) represented as one byte per character (actual length) + 1

TINYTEXT character string with variable length, maximum 255 characters represented as *n* + 1bytes
TEXT character string with variable length, maximum 216 - 1 characters represented as *n* + 2bytes
MEDIUMTEXT character string with variable length, maximum 224 - 1 characters represented as *n* + 3bytes
LONGTEXT character string with variable length, maximum 232 - 1 characters represented as *n* + 4bytes
TINYBLOB binary data, variable length, max 255 bytes

BLOB binary data, variable length, max 216 - 1 bytes
MEDIUMBLOB binary data, variable length,max 224 - 1 bytes
LONGBLOB binary data, variable length,max 232 - 1 bytes

ENUM select one from at most 65,535 character strings represented as 1 or 2 bytes
SET combine atmost 255 character strings represented as 1-8 bytes

We have to pick one of these data types for each of the pieces of data. Clearly, the username and password will be some number of characters. The question is whether we should use the CHAR or VARCHAR data type to represent the characters. The CHAR data type should be used if the character string will be a specific length and never change. In the case of a username and password, this is not the case. The user will be allowed to pick his or her username and password. This means we should use the VARCHAR data type for our character strings.

Next, we need to determine the total number of characters that will be allowed in each of the strings. A value of 64 is more than likely enough.

Finally, our attention turns to the account ID. Should the account ID be saved as an integer whole number or as a character string? If there is ever a chance the account ID will include alpha characters, then the ID should be a character string. With an integer, there are a few different types that can be used based on the potential size of the ID. For our example, let's use an INT data type for the field.

Another characteristic that we want to place on the account ID is a primary key. A primary key basically states that the value in this column will be unique and thus can be used to uniquely identify any specific row in the table.

Once we have identified all of the fields and assigned each a type, we can create the table. To create a nontransactional table, use this command:

```
mysql> create table acc (
acc_id int primary key,
username varchar(64),
password varchar(64),
ts timestamp);
Query OK, 0 rows affected (0.00 sec)
```

To create a table that will handle transactions, use this command:

```
mysql> create table acc (
acc_id int primary key,
username varchar(64),
password varchar(64),
ts timestamp) type=bdb;
Query OK, 0 rows affected (0.01 sec)
```

We can see all of the tables in our database with the following command:

```
mysql> show tables;
+--------------------+
| Tables_in_accounts |
+--------------------+
| acc                |
+--------------------+
1 row in set (0.00 sec)
```

The SHOW TABLES command lists all of the available tables within a given database. To verify that the table was created successfully and to view the various columns, execute the following command:

```
mysql> describe acc;
+----------+---------------+------+-----+---------+-------+
| Field    | Type          | NULL | Key | Default | Extra |
+----------+---------------+------+-----+---------+-------+
| acc_id   | int(11)       |      | PRI | 0       |       |
| username | varchar(64)   | YES  |     | NULL    |       |
| password | varchar(64)   | YES  |     | NULL    |       |
| ts       | timestamp(14) | YES  |     | NULL    |       |
+----------+---------------+------+-----+---------+-------+
4 rows in set (0.00 sec)
```

You can view the columns and their definitions within a table by issuing the DESCRIBE <*table*> command. If you discover a problem with any definition, you can use the ALTER TABLE command. For our example, we are able to verify that the information was created successfully.

Inserts

With our database and table defined, we need to populate it with sample data. Here's the data that we would like to get into the table:

acc_id	username	password
1034033	jsmith	smithy
1034055	jdoe	doey
1034067	jthompson	james2
1034089	sstanford	stanford
1034123	blewis	lewis
1034154	ysheets	sheets

We can place the data in the database table by using the INSERT command. The format of the MySQL INSERT command is:

```
INSERT INTO <table> VALUES(<columnValue>,<columnValue>, €)
```

We have to issue three INSERT commands to get all of the information into the database. Here's the output from one INSERT:

```
mysql> INSERT INTO acc VALUES(1034033, 'jsmith', 'smithy', now());
Query OK, 1 row affected (0.00 sec)
```

Two more INSERT commands and all of our sample data is in the table. MySQL also includes a command called LOAD DATA, which populates a database table from a properly formatted text file.

Let's examine the INSERT command a little more closely. First consider the order of the data. The order must match the columns defined in the table as shown by the DESCRIBE command. The second important factor is the use of single quotes to indicate a value is a string and should be treated as such by MySQL. If you didn't want to insert a password into a row, you could use a NULL value. For example:

```
mysql> INSERT INTO acc VALUES(1034034, 'jime', NULL, now());
Query OK, 1 row affected (0.00 sec)
```

In this example, the NULL value is placed directly into the database in place of a string value.

Selects

Once you've inserted your data into a database, you can extract that data to make business decisions. You pull data from the database by using the SELECT command, which has the following format:

```
SELECT <columns>
FROM <databaseTable>
WHERE <conditions for data>
```

The SELECT command has three different components at its core. The first is the <columns> element, which tells the database the columns where values should be returned. The element can be * (representing all columns) or a list of columns separated by commas. The second component is the <databaseTable> element, which represents the exact table from which the data should come. The third component is the <conditions for data> element, which represents under what conditions the data should be pulled from the database.

First, we pull data using the simplest SELECT:

```
mysql> select * from acc;
+---------+-----------+----------+----------------+
| acc_id  | username  | password | ts             |
+---------+-----------+----------+----------------+
| 1034033 | jsmith    | smithy   | 20021014112438 |
| 1034055 | jdoe      | doey     | 20021014112501 |
| 1034067 | jthompson | james2   | 20021014113403 |
| 1034089 | sstanford | stanford | 20021014113407 |
| 1034123 | blewis    | lewis    | 20021014112252 |
| 1034154 | ysheets   | sheets   | 20021014113416 |
| 1034034 | jime      | NULL     | 20021014112415 |
| 1034546 | jjmyers   | NULL     | 20021014113422 |
+---------+-----------+----------+----------------+
8 rows in set (0.00 sec)
```

This SELECT command tells the database to pull all columns, using the * character, from the acc table. The database responds with a "table" using a heading with the column names found in the database used when we first defined the table. Next, all of the data from the table is placed in the output "table" and displayed accordingly.

Now we can limit the columns of data with our SELECT:

```
mysql> SELECT acc_id, username FROM acc;
+---------+-----------+
| acc_id  | username  |
+---------+-----------+
| 1034033 | jsmith    |
| 1034055 | jdoe      |
| 1034067 | jthompson |
| 1034089 | sstanford |
| 1034123 | blewis    |
| 1034154 | ysheets   |
| 1034034 | jime      |
| 1034546 | jjmyers   |
+---------+-----------+
8 rows in set (0.00 sec)
```

In this example, we have specifically listed the columns we wish to pull data from and at the same time requested all of the data. The system will output the data in the familiar table format. The same query will be used, but a condition is placed on the data we wish to pull.

```
mysql> SELECT acc_id, username FROM acc WHERE username = 'jime';
+---------+----------+
| acc_id  | username |
+---------+----------+
| 1034034 | jime     |
+---------+----------+
1 row in set (0.00 sec)
```

The same query is used here, but a WHERE clause limits the data to be pulled based on the actual value found in the username field. The condition with the SELECT query can hold logical operators to further refine the selection criteria. For example:

```
mysql> SELECT * FROM acc WHERE password IS NULL
AND username = 'jime';
+---------+----------+----------+----------------+
| acc_id  | username | password | ts             |
+---------+----------+----------+----------------+
| 1034034 | jime     | NULL     | 20021014112415 |
+---------+----------+----------+----------------+
1 row in set (0.00 sec)
```

In this query, the system selects all of the rows in the acc table where a value is NULL, and the username value is *jime*.

SELECT Statement Extensions

Up to this point, we have been showing simple SELECT commands both with and without conditions. The SELECT command has a whole list of extensions that can be used to further filter and manipulate the data received from the database. MySQL's SELECT includes the following extensions:

```
SELECT [STRAIGHT_JOIN]
       [SQL_SMALL_RESULT] [SQL_BIG_RESULT] [SQL_BUFFER_RESULT]
       [SQL_CACHE | SQL_NO_CACHE] [SQL_CALC_FOUND_ROWS]
[HIGH_PRIORITY]
       [DISTINCT | DISTINCTROW | ALL]
    select_expression,...
    [INTO {OUTFILE | DUMPFILE} 'file_name' export_options]
    [FROM table_references
      [WHERE where_definition]
      [GROUP BY {unsigned_integer | col_name | formula} [ASC |
DESC], ...
      [HAVING where_definition]
      [ORDER BY {unsigned_integer | col_name | formula} [ASC |
DESC] ,...]
      [LIMIT [offset,] rows]
      [PROCEDURE procedure_name]
      [FOR UPDATE | LOCK IN SHARE MODE]]
```

Let's look at a few of the additions to the SELECT command.

Order By

When we pulled data from the database table in the query examples earlier, MySQL returned the data in the same order it was placed in the table. For the most part, this works just fine because we just want to get the data out of the database. At other times, it might be important that the data be ordered in some specific fashion. For example, suppose you want to sort the data in ascending order (the default) based on the username:

```
mysql> SELECT * FROM acc ORDER BY username;
+---------+-----------+----------+----------------+
| acc_id  | username  | password | ts             |
+---------+-----------+----------+----------------+
| 1034123 | blewis    | lewis    | 20021014112252 |
| 1034055 | jdoe      | doey     | 20021014112501 |
| 1034034 | jime      | NULL     | 20021014112415 |
| 1034546 | jjmyers   | NULL     | 20021014113422 |
| 1034033 | jsmith    | smithy   | 20021014112438 |
| 1034067 | jthompson | james2   | 20021014113403 |
| 1034089 | sstanford | stanford | 20021014113407 |
| 1034154 | ysheets   | sheets   | 20021014113416 |
+---------+-----------+----------+----------------+
8 rows in set (0.00 sec)
```

As you can see in the output from the query, the data is displayed in alphabetical order based on the username. You can also sort based on a numeric column:

```
mysql> SELECT * FROM acc ORDER BY acc_id;
+---------+-----------+---------+---------------+
| acc_id  | username  | password | ts            |
+---------+-----------+---------+---------------+
| 1034033 | jsmith    | smithy   | 20021014112438 |
| 1034034 | jime      | NULL     | 20021014112415 |
| 1034055 | jdoe      | doey     | 20021014112501 |
| 1034067 | jthompson | james2   | 20021014113403 |
| 1034089 | sstanford | stanford | 20021014113407 |
| 1034123 | blewis    | lewis    | 20021014112252 |
| 1034154 | ysheets   | sheets   | 20021014113416 |
| 1034546 | jjmyers   | NULL     | 20021014113422 |
+---------+-----------+---------+---------------+
8 rows in set (0.00 sec)
```

Now the records are ordered based on the acc_id, which is an integer. The ORDER BY clause can also be used with the WHERE clause. For example:

```
mysql> SELECT * FROM acc WHERE ts < now() ORDER BY ts;
+---------+-----------+---------+---------------+
| acc_id  | username  | password | ts            |
+---------+-----------+---------+---------------+
| 1034123 | blewis    | lewis    | 20021014112252 |
| 1034034 | jime      | NULL     | 20021014112415 |
| 1034033 | jsmith    | smithy   | 20021014112438 |
| 1034055 | jdoe      | doey     | 20021014112501 |
| 1034067 | jthompson | james2   | 20021014113403 |
| 1034089 | sstanford | stanford | 20021014113407 |
| 1034154 | ysheets   | sheets   | 20021014113416 |
| 1034546 | jjmyers   | NULL     | 20021014113422 |
+---------+-----------+---------+---------------+
8 rows in set (0.00 sec)
```

As you might have noticed, the default ordering used by ORDER BY is ascending order. You can change this by adding the string *desc* to the end of the clause. For example:

```
mysql> SELECT username, ts FROM acc WHERE ts < now() ORDER BY
ts desc;
+-----------+---------------+
| username  | ts            |
+-----------+---------------+
| jjmyers   | 20021014113422 |
| ysheets   | 20021014113416 |
| sstanford | 20021014113407 |
| jthompson | 20021014113403 |
| jdoe      | 20021014112501 |
| jsmith    | 20021014112438 |
| jime      | 20021014112415 |
```

```
| blewis    | 20021014112252 |
+-----------+----------------+
8 rows in set (0.00 sec)
```

This query returns the username and timestamp for all rows in the table in descending order, thus displaying the accounts most recently entered.

Changing Column Names

If you look back at the previous query, you can see that the output table heading displays the string values for the columns in the table as entered when the table was first created. When we obtain the results of a query both in the client tool and programmatically, the same column names are used. We have the option of changing the displayed values. For example:

```
mysql> SELECT acc_id 'Account ID', username 'Username',
ts 'Timestamp'
FROM acc
WHERE ts < now()
  ORDER BY ts desc;
+------------+-----------+----------------+
| Account ID | Username  | Timestamp      |
+------------+-----------+----------------+
|    1034546 | jjmyers   | 20021014113422 |
|    1034154 | ysheets   | 20021014113416 |
|    1034089 | sstanford | 20021014113407 |
|    1034067 | jthompson | 20021014113403 |
|    1034055 | jdoe      | 20021014112501 |
|    1034033 | jsmith    | 20021014112438 |
|    1034034 | jime      | 20021014112415 |
|    1034123 | blewis    | 20021014112252 |
+------------+-----------+----------------+
8 rows in set (0.00 sec)
```

In this sample query, the three columns pulled from the table aren't displayed with their table names of acc_id, username, and ts, but new names are listed in the query. Although the column name change doesn't have anything to do with the data itself, it does provide a better presentation to the user.

Like

Another common problem with queries against a database is trying to find the exact row you are interested in using. For example, suppose you know that there is an account in the database table acc with a username ending with smith, but you don't know exactly what the full string is. If you attempt to query just using smith, you might find rows with usernames of smith but nothing else.

Fortunately, SQL has a SELECT clause called LIKE that lets you basically search the database for a substring within a column. The LIKE clause requires you to insert a wildcard character, %, into the string you are trying to locate. For example:

```
mysql> SELECT acc_id 'Account ID', username
FROM acc
WHERE username
  LIKE '%smith
';
+------------+----------+
| Account ID | username |
+------------+----------+
|    1034033 | jsmith   |
+------------+----------+
1 row in set (0.00 sec)
```

In this query, we've asked for the account ID and username of all users with a username that begins with any string and ends with *smith*. The wildcard can be used in multiple places throughout the string. Let's say you need to find all usernames containing *stan*. Use the following query:

```
mysql> SELECT acc_id 'Account ID', username
FROM acc
WHERE username
  LIKE '%stan%';
+------------+-----------+
| Account ID | username  |
+------------+-----------+
|    1034089 | sstanford |
+------------+-----------+
1 row in set (0.00 sec)
```

To achieve your intended outcome, place the % wildcard at both the beginning and end of the *stan* string. Note that the more wildcard-matching the database system needs to do, the longer the system will take to return the result.

Group By

One of the things you should notice from the ORDER BY clause is it cannot be used to sort by multiple columns. MySQL includes another clause, called GROUP BY, that can be used to group together common values within multiple columns. For example, suppose you want to group on both the account number and username. The query is as follows:

```
SELECT * FROM acc GROUP BY acc_id, username;
```

MySQL has extended GROUP BY to allow the use of the ASC and DESC descriptors for sorting in a particular order. For example:

```
SELECT * FROM acc GROUP BY acc_id DESC, username ASC;
```

Most dialects of GROUP BY require that the fields used in the clause be part of the SELECT itself. MySQL allows columns to be in the SELECT that aren't part of the GROUP BY.

Limit

In all the queries so far, all of the rows in the result are returned. There are times when you might want only a single row or a small set when there are many possible result rows. In such cases, you can limit the row count by using the LIMIT clause. For example:

```
mysql> SELECT * FROM acc LIMIT 3;
+---------+-----------+----------+----------------+
| acc_id  | username  | password | ts             |
+---------+-----------+----------+----------------+
| 1034033 | jsmith    | smithy   | 20021014165845 |
| 1034034 | jime      | NULL     | 20021014165845 |
| 1034067 | jthompson | james2   | 20021014165845 |
+---------+-----------+----------+----------------+
3 rows in set (0.00 sec)
```

In this query example, the first three rows of the result are returned. We can execute the query again and pull another three rows, but instead of starting at the first row in the result, we use an offset value to get the next three rows. For example:

```
mysql> SELECT * FROM acc LIMIT 3,3;
+---------+-----------+----------+----------------+
| acc_id  | username  | password | ts             |
+---------+-----------+----------+----------------+
| 1034089 | sstanford | stanford | 20021014165845 |
| 1034123 | blewis    | lewis    | 20021014165845 |
| 1034154 | ysheets   | sheets   | 20021014165845 |
+---------+-----------+----------+----------------+
3 rows in set (0.00 sec)
```

In this query, the code offsets to the fourth row and displays three of the results. If there aren't enough rows remaining in the result set, the system returns as many as it can.

Dump to File

Not all applications are able to use the output from a SQL query, but they are able to handle input in the form of a text file. The SELECT command in MySQL includes a clause called INTO [OUTFILE | DUMPFILE] that allows the result of a query to be placed in a file. As listed, there are two options for the INTO clause: OUTFILE and DUMPFILE. The OUTFILE option is used to dump all rows returned in a query. For example:

```
mysql> SELECT * FROM acc INTO OUTFILE 'test.outfile';
Query OK, 8 rows affected (0.00 sec)
```

This query results in a text file with all of the rows, as shown here:

```
1034033  jsmith      smithy    20021014165845
1034034  jime        \N        20021014165845
1034067  jthompson   james2    20021014165845
1034089  sstanford   stanford  20021014165845
1034123  blewis      lewis     20021014165845
1034154  ysheets     sheets    20021014165845
1034546  jjmyers     \N        20021014165845
1034055  jdoe        doey      20021014165908
```

Notice that the NULL values are converted to \N and line terminations are provided. If you need the data sorted, you can add the appropriate clauses to the query. MySQL also includes the clause INTO DUMPFILE, which basically dumps a single row into a file without any sort of special processing. The DUMPFILE is typically used to output a BLOB to a file. Our sample database doesn't include a BLOB, but the query might look like the following:

```
SELECT pic_blob FROM images INTO DUMPFILE 'world.jpg'
WHERE pic_name = 'World';
```

Counting

If you consider the various SELECT queries we've created in this section, you will note that they all output some number of result rows. What if we want a query that counts the total number of rows in a result? The total count can be returned using the count(*) option. For example:

```
mysql> SELECT count(*) FROM acc;
+----------+
| count(*) |
+----------+
|        8 |
+----------+
1 row in set (0.00 sec)
```

Here we execute a SELECT to return the total number of rows in the acc table. Notice that the count value is returned as a column in the result. The column heading value can be changed, as we explained earlier in this section.

Updates

The first major SQL statement we covered was INSERT, which you use to place data into your database. This was followed by the SELECT statement, which you use to pull the data from your database. What do you do if you want to change the data within a row? You have two options. The first is to just make the change. You can do this with the UPDATE command:

```
UPDATE [LOW_PRIORITY] [IGNORE] tbl_name
SET col_name1=expr1 [, col_name2=expr2, ...]
[WHERE where_definition]
[LIMIT #]
```

If you have a user who changes his or her password, you can use the UPDATE command to make the change in the database. Consider the following SELECT, UPDATE, SELECT combination:

```
mysql> SELECT * FROM acc WHERE username='jime';
+---------+----------+----------+----------------+
| acc_id  | username | password | ts             |
+---------+----------+----------+----------------+
| 1034034 | jime     | NULL     | 20021014165845 |
+---------+----------+----------+----------------+
1 row in set (0.00 sec)

mysql> UPDATE acc SET password='ime' WHERE username='jime';
Query OK, 1 rows affected (0.00 sec)
Rows matched: 1  Changed: 1  Warnings: 0

mysql> SELECT * FROM acc WHERE username='jime';
+---------+----------+----------+----------------+
| acc_id  | username | password | ts             |
+---------+----------+----------+----------------+
| 1034034 | jime     | ime      | 20021014204947 |
+---------+----------+----------+----------------+
1 row in set (0.00 sec)
```

In this combination of SQL commands, we display the row where the username is *jime*. The password is shown to be NULL. We use the UPDATE command to change the password to *ime*. Notice that the UPDATE command instructs a specific table to be updated; then the column that needs to be changed is indicated by SET. If we have to change numerous columns, we can use multiple SETs and separate them by commas. Finally, we can use a condition to limit the rows changed. The last SELECT command shows that the row was updated correctly.

The second way to update a database is to never change a row in the database but instead to inactivate one row and insert a new one. In order to do this type of update, you must include two timestamp fields in each row. The first is called an *active timestamp*, and the second is just the *timestamp*. The most active row in the database for a particular key has a timestamp of 0. The active timestamp will be the time when the row was inserted. Once the row is inserted, the active timestamp of the current row is copied to the timestamp (ts field) of the inactive row.

To support this type of update, we've changed the table acc a bit. The new table definition looks like this:

```
mysql> describe acc;
+----------+---------------+------+-----+---------+-------+
| Field    | Type          | NULL | Key | Default | Extra |
+----------+---------------+------+-----+---------+-------+
| acc_id   | int(11)       |      | PRI | 0       |       |
| username | varchar(64)   |      | PRI |         |       |
| password | varchar(64)   | YES  |     | NULL    |       |
| ts       | timestamp(14) | YES  | PRI | NULL    |       |
| act_ts   | timestamp(14) | YES  |     | NULL    |       |
+----------+---------------+------+-----+---------+-------+
5 rows in set (0.00 sec)
```

As you can see, we've added an act_ts column defined as a timestamp; defined the username, acc_id, and ts not to be NULL; and defined the primary key as a combination of acc_id, username, and ts. To show the process of doing the update, consider the row with an acc_id of 1034055. When the initial row was placed in the database, the ts column was set to 0, and the act_ts was set to the actual time the row was inserted. Here's the output of a SELECT showing the row:

```
mysql> SELECT * FROM acc WHERE acc_id = '1034055';
+------ +--------+----------+---------------+----------  --+
| acc_id |username| password | ts             | act_ts        |
+-----  -+--------+----------+---------------+--  ----------+
|1034055 | jdoe   | ime      | 00000000000000 |20021014212444|
+--------+--------+----------+---------------+--------------+
1 row in set (0.00 sec)
```

Next, we need to insert a new row into the database. In order for the database to remain consistent, we need to relate the old row to the new row using a timestamp. The timestamp needs to be the same, so the first step is to obtain the current time and place it in a temporary variable. We accomplish this by using a SET command and local system variable. For example:

```
mysql> set @time=now();
Query OK, 0 rows affected (0.03 sec)
```

The @time variable now holds a timestamp, and it can be used to insert the new row and change the old row. First, the old row is updated and the ts column is set to the current time:

```
mysql> UPDATE acc SET ts=@time WHERE acc_id = 1034055;
Query OK, 1 row affected (0.00 sec)
Rows matched: 1  Changed: 1  Warnings: 0
```

Here's the query to show the new ts value in the old row:

```
mysql> SELECT * FROM acc WHERE acc_id = '1034055';
+--------+--------+---------+----------------+---------------+
|acc_id  |username| password | ts             | act_ts        |
+--------+--------+---------+----------------+---------------+
|1034055 | jdoe   | ime      | 20021014212553 | 20021014212444|
+--------+--------+---------+----------------+---------------+
1 row in set (0.01 sec)
```

Now we can insert the new row:

```
mysql> INSERT INTO acc VALUES(1034055, 'jdoe', 'newpass', 0, @time);
Query OK, 1 row affected (0.00 sec)
Rows matched: 1  Changed: 1  Warnings: 0
```

A final SELECT will show both of the rows and how they relate through the act_ts column of the new row and the ts of the old row:

```
mysql> SELECT * FROM acc WHERE acc_id = '1034055';
+-------+--------+---------+---------------+----------------+
|acc_id |username| password | ts             | act_ts         |
+-------+--------+---------+---------------+----------------+
|1034055| jdoe   | newpass  | 00000000000000 | 20021014212553 |
|1034055| jdoe   | ime      | 20021014212553 | 20021014212444 |
+-------+--------+---------+---------------+----------------+
2 rows in set (0.01 sec)
```

We can always know the active row by including ts=0 in our queries.

Deletes

When data is no longer needed in a database, you can use the DELETE command to remove a row. However, if you want to maintain the history of the rows in the database, you should instead make the row inactive.

First, let's show the removal of a row. The query looks like this:

```
DELETE FROM acc WHERE acc_id = '1034154';
```

The query will select the appropriate row based on the WHERE clause. Another use of the DELETE command is:

```
DELETE FROM acc;
```

This query doesn't include a WHERE clause and thus will remove all rows from the specified database table. To maintain the history of the rows in the database, you shouldn't use the DELETE command because the row will be permanently removed. In that case, the best way to "delete" the row is to make the row inactive by setting the ts of the row to a timestamp other than 0. In most cases, you want to update the current row to a current timestamp value so that the row has a record of when it was made inactive.

Using SHOW

MySQL includes a command called SHOW, which allows a developer or administrator to see details about databases, tables, and the database system itself. In this section, we look at the various SHOW commands and explain what information they provide. Note that in some of the commands an optional LIKE can be used to filter the information provided by the command. The % wildcard is used just like as you do in the SELECT command use of LIKE. We cover the most popular SHOW commands here and save some of them for Chapter 13, "Database Administration."

SHOW DATABASES

The SHOW DATABASES command shows all of the databases available on the current database server. You use the LIKE command to limit the output. For example:

```
mysql> show databases;
+----------+
| Database |
+----------+
| accounts |
| ca       |
| mysql    |
| test     |
+----------+
4 rows in set (0.03 sec)
```

SHOW TABLES

The SHOW TABLES command displays all of the tables within a particular database. The full format of the command is:

```
SHOW [OPEN] TABLES [FROM databaseName] [LIKE wildcardString]
```

Notice that there are a number of optional components to the command. The [OPEN] option will show only those databases that are currently being accessed by a client. If SHOW TABLES is executed, it requires that a database currently be active by executing the USE <database> command. You can use the FROM databaseName option to query the tables available in any database on the system. For example:

```
mysql> SHOW TABLES FROM mysql;
+-----------------+
| Tables_in_mysql |
+-----------------+
| columns_priv    |
| db              |
| func            |
| host            |
| tables_priv     |
| user            |
+-----------------+
6 rows in set (0.03 sec)
```

SHOW COLUMNS

Once you create a table, you can obtain information about its columns, how they are defined, and primary key information by using SHOW COLUMNS. The full format of the command is

```
SHOW [FULL] COLUMNS
FROM <table> [FROM <database>] [LIKE <wildcard>]
```

If you use the basic format, SHOW COLUMNS FROM <*table*>, you see the following:

```
mysql> show columns from acc;
+----------+---------------+------+-----+---------+-------+
| Field    | Type          | NULL | Key | Default | Extra |
+----------+---------------+------+-----+---------+-------+
| acc_id   | int(11)       |      | PRI | 0       |       |
| username | varchar(64)   | YES  |     | NULL    |       |
| password | varchar(64)   | YES  |     | NULL    |       |
| ts       | timestamp(14) | YES  |     | NULL    |       |
+----------+---------------+------+-----+---------+-------+
4 rows in set (0.00 sec)
```

MySQL provides a shortcut to the basic format by using the DESCRIBE <*tablename*> command. The command assumes you have USEd a database. By using the [FULL] option, you display the privileges the current logged-on user has with the table columns as well.

SHOW STATUS

You can obtain a great deal more information about a table by using the SHOW STATUS command. The format of the command is

```
SHOW TABLE STATUS [FROM <database>] [LIKE <wildcard>]
```

For example:

```
mysql> show table status;
```

This command works on all tables from the current database or from a specified database. If you want to limit the tables the command accesses, use the LIKE option.

SHOW PROCESSLIST

The last command we cover in our introduction section is SHOW PROCESSLIST. This command is useful for determining access to the database server—both current access and access in the recent past. The format of the command is

```
SHOW [FULL] PROCESSLIST
```

Using the basic command produces the following:

```
mysql> show processlist;
+--+----+---------+--------+-------+----+-----+---------------+
|Id|User|Host     |db      |Command|Time|State|Info           |
+--+----+---------+--------+-------+----+-----+---------------+
|1 |joeg|localhost|NULL    |Sleep  |8900|     |NULL           |
|4 |ODBC|localhost|accounts|Query  |0   | NULL|showprocesslist|
+--+----+---------+--------+-------+----+-----+---------------+
2 rows in set (0.00 sec)
```

As you can see, the command tells you a user's name, the host the user is connecting from, what database the user is using, and even the command the user is executing.

More on Tables

Let's examine the natural progression of database creation and manipulation. First, you design the database and tables; next you add them to the server, populate the tables with data, and finally retrieve and manipulate the data. Now, what happens when you have to change a table?

In this section, we look at the various commands available in MySQL for changing the definition of a table. Specifically, we consider renaming a table, altering the columns and their definitions, placing tables, and deleting tables. As you'll see, for the first three tasks you use the ALTER TABLE command.

Renaming

You rename a table by using the ALTER TABLE command. For example:

```
mysql> ALTER TABLE acc RENAME account;
Query OK, 0 rows affected (0.03 sec)
mysql> show tables;
+--------------------+
| Tables_in_accounts |
+--------------------+
| account            |
+--------------------+
1 row in set (0.00 sec)
```

Here you use the command to rename the acc table to the accounts table. You can use the SHOW TABLES command to verify that the table name was accurately changed.

Altering Column Definitions

One of the primary uses for the ALTER TABLE command is changing the schema of a table. The change could be adding a new column, changing the column name, increasing the field size of a particular column, or dropping/adding primary keys. First, let's add a new column to our acc table:

```
mysql> ALTER TABLE account ADD access int;
Query OK, 8 rows affected (0.11 sec)
Records: 8 Duplicates: 0 Warnings: 0
```

This query adds a new column called access to the account table and uses a column type of int. The ADD clause of ALTER TABLE has a few options. The full definition is

```
ALTER TABLE <tablename>
ADD [COLUMN] <column specifics> [FIRST|AFTER <columnName>]
```

By using FIRST or AFTER, you ensure that the new column is specifically placed within the table definition. The default placement is at the end of the current table definition. What if you wanted to change a column's data type? For example:

```
mysql> ALTER TABLE account CHANGE access access varchar(15);
Query OK, 8 rows affected (0.11 sec)
Records: 8  Duplicates: 0  Warnings: 0
```

This query changes the access column to a varchar(15). Notice how the column name had to be used twice. The CHANGE clause doesn't know if you are changing the name of the column, the type, or both, so it requires that you specify the column name. MySQL includes a clause called MODIFY that assumes the name isn't going to change:

```
mysql> ALTER TABLE account MODIFY access varchar(15);
Query OK, 8 rows affected (0.11 sec)
Records: 8  Duplicates: 0  Warnings: 0
```

If you want to remove a primary key currently defined on a table, use the following query:

```
mysql> ALTER TABLE account DROP PRIMARY KEY;
Query OK, 8 rows affected (0.11 sec)
Records: 8  Duplicates: 0  Warnings: 0
```

A new primary key can be added with the following query:

```
mysql> ALTER TABLE account ADD primary key(acc_id);
Query OK, 8 rows affected (0.11 sec)
Records: 8  Duplicates: 0  Warnings: 0
```

Placing Tables on Specific Drives

When you are building a large database system, you probably want to disperse the actual tables across disk drives. This is possible using the DATA DIRECTORY clause of the ALTER TABLE command. For example:

```
ALTER TABLE account DATA DIRECTORY="/usr/local/databases/account"
```

Note that the DATA DIRECTORY option in the ALTER TABLE as well as in the CREATE TABLE command is available only on MyISAM tables underMySQL 4.0.

Deleting Tables

If you are absolutely sure that you want to get rid of a table permanently, use the command DROP TABLE <*tableName*>. Here is a simple example of using DROP TABLE:

```
mysql> create table test (id int);
Query OK, 0 rows affected (0.05 sec)

mysql> insert into test values(1);
Query OK, 1 row affected (0.02 sec)

mysql> drop table test;
Query OK, 0 rows affected (0.03 sec)
```

Notice that the table will be dropped without any reservation by the database server. It is vital that you type in the table name accurately because once a table has been dropped, it is no longer available.

Transactions

One of the most powerful aspects of MySQL is its ability to use transactions. A *transaction* is an atomic action that must either succeed or fail. This means that in a transaction consisting of three different queries—a SELECT, an INSERT, and an UPDATE—if any of these operations fail, the other commands must be rolled back to their original state.

The current MySQL system includes two different table types that allow for transactions: InnoDB and BDB. In order for a database table to use transactions, the table must be created using a TYPE clause or the table must be altered with an ALTER TABLE command also using the TYPE clause.

Once you create a table to handle transactions, you must inform the MySQL system that you want to use transactions. You can accomplish this by using the autocommit database server variable. By default, this variable is set to a value of 1, meaning that the database server will automatically commit the query once it executes. To start a transaction, the autocommit variable must be set to 0. For example:

```
mysql> set autocommit = 0;
Query OK, 0 rows affected (0.00 sec)
```

Now you have the ability to execute SQL statements that will be either committed to the database or rolled back. Start with either the BEGIN or BEGIN WORK statement:

```
mysql> begin;
Query OK, 0 rows affected (0.00 sec)
```

Now execute your SQL. Once you have finished, use the command COMMIT or ROLLBACK, depending on your circumstances.

Functions/Operators

In several places throughout this chapter, we have used a MySQL function in a query. A *function* is code written by MySQL that aids in the query being used. For example, suppose you want to determine the largest account ID in the acc table. To do this, use the max() function:

```
mysql> SELECT max(acc_id) FROM account;
+-------------+
| max(acc_id) |
+-------------+
|     1034546 |
+-------------+
1 row in set (0.00 sec)
```

In this query, the maximum value in the acc_id column is returned from the database. MySQL includes a large number of functions—too many to list in this chapter. Refer to the MySQL documentation for a listing of all available functions and examples.

Joins

One of the harder concepts to grasp in the world of databases is the join. Let's begin our discussion by throwing another table into our current database. Right now we have a database called acc that has the following fields:

acc_id	int
username	varchar
password	varchar
ts	timestamp
act_ts	timestamp

This table doesn't hold much information about the actual owner of the account ID. We need to add another table called acc_add that will hold address information for the account owner. Here's the table definition:

```
mysql> create table acc_add (
add_id int not NULL,
acc_id int,
name varchar(64),
address1 varchar(64),
```

```
address2 varchar(64),
address3 varchar(64),
city varchar(64),
state varchar(64),
zip varchar(10),
ts timestamp not NULL,
act_ts timestamp,
primary key(add_id, ts));
Query OK, 0 rows affected (0.00 sec)
```

Let's now add some data to the table for the account ID 1034055. Notice that the acc_add table requires the acc_id of the account whose address is being added to the table. This column value links the acc table with the acc_add table. The full data added to the table can be found on the code download available at www.wiley.com/compbooks/matthews. In this example, we've added two rows:

```
mysql> insert into acc_add
values(30004, 1034055, 'John Doe', '4565 Some St',
'Suite 4', NULL,'Chicago', 'IL', '21734', 0, now());
Query OK, 1 row affected (0.00 sec)
mysql> insert into acc_add values(
30003, 1034055, 'John Doe', '123 Any St', NULL,
NULL,'Atlanta', 'GA', '38394', 0, now());
Query OK, 1 row affected (0.00 sec)
```

Now we want to get data from both tables at the same time. For example:

```
mysql> SELECT acc.acc_id, name
FROM acc, acc_add
WHERE acc.acc_id = acc_add.acc_id and acc.ts = 0;
+---------+----------+
| acc_id  | name     |
+---------+----------+
| 1034055 | John Doe |
| 1034055 | John Doe |
+---------+----------+
2 rows in set (0.00 sec)
```

In this query, we asked for the values of acc_id (from the acc table) and name (from the acc_add table), but only when the acc_id in both of the tables match and the ts field in the acc table is 0. The result is two rows. Let's look a little more closely at what is occurring in this SQL. First, we are asking for data from two tables at the same time, as seen in the FROM acc, acc_add clause. From those two tables, we want two pieces of data: the acc_id and name. Notice how the acc_id has a table name preceding it. This had to be done in order to tell the database server which table we want the acc_id to be pulled from because it can be found in both of them.

Now we want to see data from the tables only when the acc_id is identical between the two tables. At this time, the only data in the acc_add table has an acc_id of 1034055. The database server will analyze the WHERE clause and look for all of the acc_id values in the table acc that also appear in the acc_add table. If you look back in our examples, you can see that there are two 1034055 values in the acc table. One of them is an active row, and one is an inactive row. Both of these rows will be matched against the two rows in acc_add for a result set having four rows. However, we also included a Logical AND in our WHERE clause to return only those rows where acc_id is equal in both tables and the ts field in acc is 0. This logical AND limits the total row output to two rows.

What we have accomplished in this example is a basic join. We have joined two tables by requesting that information be pulled from multiple tables and a condition placed on the values from the tables. Technically this is called an *equi-join*.

Using a Join

When developers talk about a join, they typically use the term *join* without any identifiers. Developers are really referring to a *cross-join*, a *full join*, or an *inner join*. The idea is that all of the rows in one table are crossed with all of the rows in another table. Currently, our acc table has nine rows, and the acc_add table has two rows. If we were to execute a query like the one that follows, we would get a result with 18 rows and all of the columns from both tables. Since this would create a massive table, we won't reproduce it here.

MySQL allows the use of the inner join identified to let the reader of a SQL statement know there is a join occurring. Consider the SQL we used earlier with the acc and acc_add tables. To properly write this SQL using a join, we would have

```
mysql> SELECT acc.acc_id, name
FROM acc
  inner join acc_add
    on acc.acc_id = acc_add.acc_id where acc.ts = 0;
+---------+----------+
| acc_id  | name     |
+---------+----------+
| 1034055 | John Doe |
| 1034055 | John Doe |
+---------+----------+
2 rows in set (0.00 sec)
```

This SQL has several aspects. The first is the use of the inner join clause. The SQL says we want to pull data FROM one table and join that table with another one called acc_add. The INNER JOIN causes a full join to occur with both tables. After the join, there is an ON clause. The ON clause is used exclusively with the join. This clause tells the system what criteria to use when relating the two tables. Finally, our query uses a WHERE clause to further limit the results from the query. In most cases, all of the conditions to use when relating the tables should appear in the ON clause, and final criteria should appear in the WHERE clause.

Outer Left/Right Join

Another common join is called the left join. In a left join, the first table listed in the query returns all of its rows even if a match doesn't occur within the ON clause. The right join does just the opposite and returns all rows in the table listed with the join.

NULL

One of the most interesting features of SQL is the notion that NULL is not 0 as in most programming languages. The value NULL stands on its own in SQL and for this reason, a special equality statement is needed to check whether a field contains a NULL value. The statement is IS NULL and IS NOT NULL. We can create SQL that will pull rows if a column's value is NULL. For example:

```
mysql> SELECT acc_id, password FROM acc WHERE password IS NULL;
+---------+----------+
| acc_id  | password |
+---------+----------+
| 1034067 | NULL     |
+---------+----------+
1 row in set (0.00 sec)

mysql> SELECT acc_id, password FROM acc WHERE password = NULL;
Empty set (0.00 sec)
```

In the first SQL query, we are telling the database server to return all rows where the password field value is NULL. There is one such row in the table, and it is displayed. The second SQL query does nearly the same thing, but instead it tries to match the password value equal to NULL—no results are found.

What's Next

So where is MySQL going? Well, the current plan is to introduce new functionality under the 4.0 version in separate segments. Expect to see increments like 4.0.1, 4.0.2, and so forth. Several large additions are planned for 4.1, including subselects and stored procedures.

This chapter has attempted to provide a brief but comprehensive introduction to MySQL SQL for those who aren't familiar with it. For more comprehensive information on MySQL SQL, please refer to the extensive documentation available on www.mysql.com. In the next chapter, we take a complete look at the installation of MySQL, Java, and Connector/J to build a development system to be used throughout the remainder of this book.

CHAPTER 4

Installing MySQL, Java, and Connector/J

If you've made it this far, you are ready to begin the process of integrating MySQL, Java, and Connector/J to build applications and sites that provide your users with a bounty of information. In this chapter, we explain how to install MySQL, Java, and Connector/J on your system. We cover both Linux and Windows, and for the most part, we show the basic installation that works on 99 percent of the environments out there. If these instructions don't work, you will need to turn to the product documentation.

Installing MySQL

You can find the MySQL database system at http://www.mysql.com under the downloads section of the site. Several different downloads are available, as shown in Figure 4.1.

On the right-hand side of the MySQL Web page, you can see two major sections: Production and Development. The Production line of products has been thoroughly tested both within and outside MySQL. An organization can comfortably use the Production products in such an environment and be assured of stability and reliability. The Development line of products has been tested within MySQL with MySQL's own baseline tests but the products aren't at the level of production readiness. As you can see, the 4.0.x line of MySQL is currently in the Development stage and isn't recommended yet for production use.

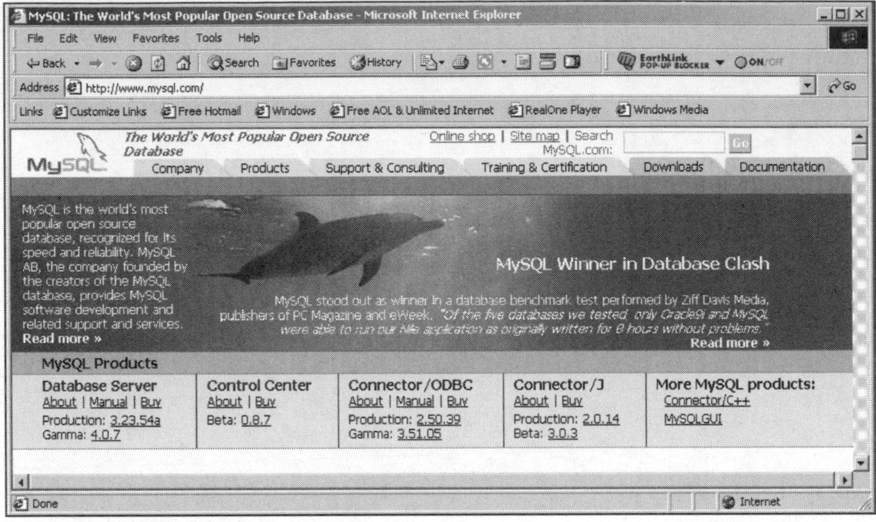

Figure 4.1 The available MySQL downloads.

Looking at the Production MySQL servers, you have two possibilities: MySQL and MySQL-Max. The MySQL download is a basic MySQL server without transaction support table types compiled into the binary. The MySQL-Max download includes support for the BDB table type in some platforms and the InnoDB table type in all platforms. Depending on which Production system you decided to download, you have the option of pulling the version for Windows, Linux, Solaris, and a host of other platforms.

If you are downloading for Windows, you automatically get both the standard MySQL distribution as well as MySQL-Max. If you are downloading the Linux version, MySQL recommends using the RPM file for a clean installation. Note that you will have to download a number of Linux files. You should download the server and client programs files to have an operational development system. After you click on the correct platform version, the installation instructions change.

Linux Installation

For the Linux version of MySQL, you have two different files on your system. One has a name like MySQL-3.23/MySQL-3.23.52-1.i386.rpm, and the other has a name like MySQL-3.23/MySQL-client-3.23.52-1.i386.rpm. Since these are RPM files, they should install without much error on most recent Linux installations. The steps are

1. Install the server: type *rpm -i MySQL-VERSION.i386.rpm.*
2. Install the client tools: type *rpm -i MySQL-client-VERSION.i386.rpm.*

The installation process places all of the code in /var/lib/mysql. In addition, the process makes entries in rc.d/ to automatically start MySQL when the machine boots.

Windows Installation

The MySQL distribution for Windows comes as a zip file and will need to be uncompressed before it can be used. Use WinZip or another tool of your choice to perform the decompression. Once you do, follow these instructions to install the server on a NT/2000/XP box:

1. Log on as the administrator user.
2. Stop the current MySQL if you're performing an upgrade.
    a. Open a command prompt.
    b. If MySQL is running as a service, type *net stop <mysql>* where *<mysql>* is the name of the MySQL server service name (normally the value is *mysql*).
    c. If MySQL is running as an application, change to the /bin directory of the MySQL installation and type *mysqladmin –u root shutdown*.
3. If you are changing from the basic MySQL server to the Max version, you need to remove the service.
4. Locate the setup.exe file of the new installation from the uncompressed files.
5. After MySQL is installed, copy one of the configuration files in the installation directory to the root directory, c:/. If you are using the Max version of MySQL, configure the appropriate InnoDB or BDB options in the configuration file.
6. If you want to install the server as a service, type the command *-mysqld-max-nt- --install* (or *--install-manual* if you don't want Windows to automatically start the service when the machine boots).

If you are installing MySQL on Windows 95, 98, or ME, the server cannot be used as a service and thus you will need to start and stop the server manually. Use the mysqladmin.exe application in the /bin directory to start MySQL.

All Other Installations

It is beyond the scope of this book to provide installation instructions for every platform that MySQL supports. If you need to install MySQL on another platform, download the appropriate distribution and refer to http://www.mysql.com/documentation/mysql/bychapter/manual_Installing.html #Installing for complete instructions.

Testing the MySQL Installation

To determine that MySQL has been installed and is executing correctly, browse to the /bin directory of MySQL and execute the file mysql. You should see information like that shown in Figure 4.2.

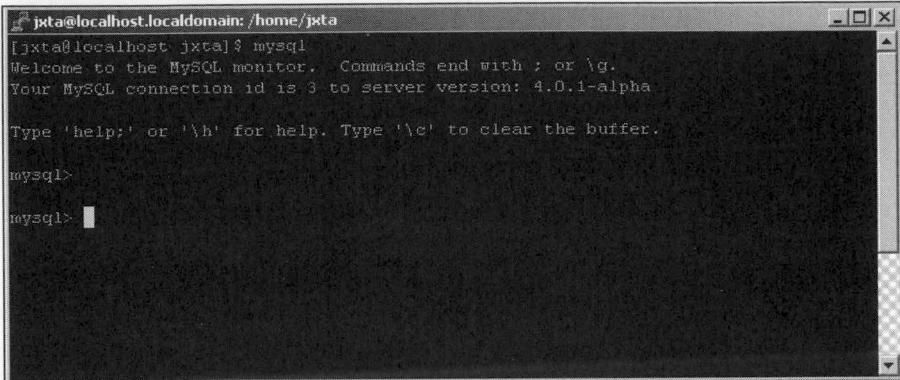

Figure 4.2 Testing MySQL.

Installing Java

Once the MySQL database server is installed, it's time to install Java. You can find the Java software development kit (SDK) at http://java.sun.com/j2se/1.4.1/download.html. When you get to this page, you see downloads for numerous platforms and options for either the Java Runtime Environment (JRE) or SDK. Be sure to grab the SDK so you will be able to write code with Java. For Windows, you will find an EXE file to download. When the file has finished downloading, double-click on it to launch the installation wizard. Just a few clicks through the wizard is all it takes to install Java on Windows. When the Java installation wizard has finished installing Java, add the path to the /bin directory of the installation to the system PATH environment variable. That way, you will have access to the Java tools from a Windows command prompt.

For Linux, you will find both an RPM and a self-extracting BIN file. If you download the RPM file, it will initially include a BIN extension, which you need to remove. Install the RPM with the rpm-I command. If you download the BIN self-extracting file, you need to change the file to have execution permissions with the chmod a+x command. Once permissions are set correctly, just execute the file to install Java.

Full instructions for installing the Windows, Linux, and other environments can be found at http://java.sun.com/j2se/1.4.1/install.html if you run into problems.

Testing the Java Installation

Once Java has been installed, you should test the installation. To do this, create a file called hello.java and add the following code:

```
public class hello {
  public static void main(String[] args) {
    System.out.println("Hello World - It Works");
  }
}
```

Compile the code with the command

```
javac hello.java
```

If you get an error saying the javac command cannot be found, then you will need to check the path to the /bin directory; this means that the system is unable to find the Java compiler in the /bin directory. If things work out correctly, execute the Java with

```
java Hello
```

You should see the text "Hello World—It Works" on your screen. If you don't see this text, check Sun's instructions to correct the installation.

Installing Connector/J

If you refer to Figure 4.1, you see that both the Production and Development areas have downloads available for Connector/J. Clicking on either of the links brings you to the respective page for that particular version of the code. In both cases, two files are available for download: a zip and a tar.gz.

Most of the code in the remainder of this book executes under the Production version of the code, but better performance and many small JDBC support changes are available in the Development 3.0 version. Our test machines used the 3.0 version of Connector/J.

If you download the zip version of the code, we assume you are installing on a Windows box and that the tar/gz version for Linux or another Unix flavor. In either case, you need to uncompress the file to expose both the source code for the driver as well as a JAR file called (in 3.0) mysql-connector-java-3.0.1-beta-bin.jar. This file contains all of the necessary class files for the driver.

There are a few ways to install the driver. The first is to copy the /com and /org files into another directory listed in your classpath. Another option is to add the full path to the JAR file to your CLASSPATH variable. Finally, you can just copy the JAR file to the $JAVA_HOME/jre/lib/ext directory.

On a Windows platform (if you installed SDK1.4.1), the directory is found at /program files/java/j2re1.4.1/lib/ext. Just copy the JAR file to that directory, and the library will be available for applications that execute within the Java Virtual Machine.

On a Linux platform using SDK 1.4.1, the directory where you want to place the JAR file is /usr/java/j2sdk1.4.0/jre/lib/ext.

Testing the Connector/J Installation

Once you've installed both Java and the Connector/J driver, create a test file called test.java and enter the following code into the file:

```
public class test {
  public static void main(String[] args) {
    try {
      Class.forName("com.mysql.jdbc.Driver").newInstance();
      System.out.println("Good to go");
    } catch (Exception E) {
      System.out.println("JDBC Driver error");
    }
  }
}
```

Save and exit the test file and compile it with this command:

```
javac test.java
```

Now execute the code with this command:

```
java test
```

If the Java Virtual Machine was able to find your Connector/J JAR file, you will see the text "Good to go" on the console; otherwise, you will see "JDBC Driver Error". If you get an error, check that the JAR file is in the correct directory and/or check the CLASSPATH variable to be sure the full path to the JAR file has been included. Figure 4.3 shows all of these steps.

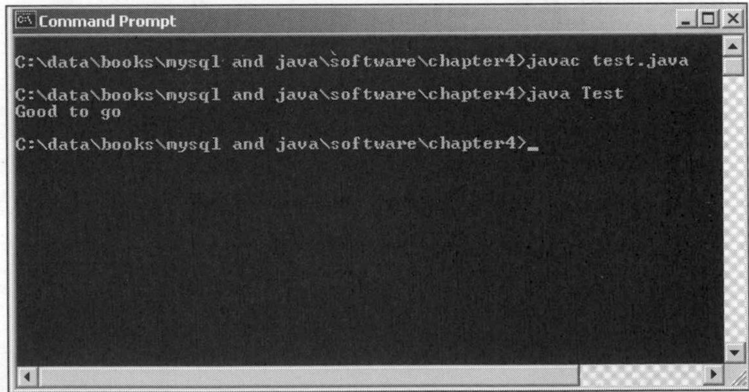

Figure 4.3 Testing the Connector/J driver.

What's Next

Once you have installed all of the applications shown in this chapter, you are ready to start writing all sorts of Java applications that can access a MySQL database. In the next chapter, we begin looking at how to write applications and applets to access MySQL. We explore some of the basic functionality provided in the JDBC specification and implemented in Connector/J.

CHAPTER 5

Using JDBC with Java Applications and Applets

Now that we have a development environment put together, it's time to start writing Java code that will allow access to a MySQL database using the Connector/J JDBC driver. In the remaining chapters of this book, it is our goal to exercise as much of the functionality found in the driver as possible. This chapter covers the basics of instantiating the driver, connecting to the database from Java, executing queries, and handling results. From a Java perspective, we look at doing all of these tasks from both applications and applets utilizing various GUI components to deal with the information transfer from the user to the database and from the database to the user.

Hello World

For the sake of tradition, the first application we build is Hello World. The code in Listing 5.1 creates a Java application and pulls information from a MySQL database.

```
package mysql;
import java.sql.*;

public class Hello {
  Connection connection;
```

Listing 5.1 Hello World. (continues)

```
  private void displaySQLErrors(SQLException e) {
    System.out.println("SQLException: " + e.getMessage());
    System.out.println("SQLState:     " + e.getSQLState());
    System.out.println("VendorError:  " + e.getErrorCode());
  }

  public Hello() {
     try {
       Class.forName("com.mysql.jdbc.Driver").newInstance();
     }
     catch (SQLException e) {
       System.err.println("Unable to find and load driver");
       System.exit(1);
     }
  }

  public void connectToDB() {
     try {
       connection = DriverManager.getConnection(
         "jdbc:mysql://localhost/accounts?user=&password=");
     }
     catch(SQLException e) {
       displaySQLErrors(e);
     }
   }

  public void executeSQL() {
     try {
       Statement statement = connection.createStatement();

       ResultSet rs = statement.executeQuery(
         "SELECT * FROM acc_acc");

       while (rs.next()) {
         System.out.println(rs.getString(1));
       }

       rs.close();
       statement.close();
       connection.close();
     }
     catch(SQLException e) {
       displaySQLErrors(e);
     }
   }

   public static void main(String[] args) {
```

Listing 5.1 Hello World. (continues)

```
        Hello hello = new Hello();

        hello.connectToDB();
        hello.executeSQL();
    }
}
```

Listing 5.1 Hello World. (continued)

Since this is our first code for connecting Java to MySQL through Connector/J, we want to spend a fair amount of time going through it. First, note that this is a traditional Java application that instantiates an object and calls a few methods. When the Hello object is instantiated, the constructor is called to handle any initialization that needs to take place.

Loading the Connector/J Driver

In the constructor, we have placed code that attempts to locate and instantiate our Connector/J JDBC driver. The process begins with the Class.forName method. This method is designed to dynamically load a Java class at runtime. The Java Virtual Machine (JVM) uses the current system classpath (as well as any additional paths defined when the JVM was executed) to find the class passed to the method as a parameter. In our case, the system attempts to find the Driver class found in the com.mysql.jdbc package. In Chapter 4, we placed the Connector/J JAR file in the classpath of the JVM so it could be found. Once it finds the file, the code executes the newInstance() method to instantiate a new object from the Driver class. During the instantiation, the Driver will register itself with a static class called DriverManager, which is responsible for managing all JDBC drivers installed on the current system.

If the JVM is unable to locate the driver, it outputs a message to the console and exits the application. Note that the DriverManager is designed to handle multiple JDBC driver objects just as long as they register with the class. This means that you can write a Java application that connects with more than one type of database system through JDBC. Note that simply loading the JDBC driver for a database doesn't result in any type of connection with the database.

Using DriverManager to Connect to a Database

Once our application object has been created and initialized, the code attempts to build a connection to the database. This is an important step, and therefore we'll spend some time discussing the connection code. If you look in the connectToDB() method in our Hello object, you see that the connection from Java to the database is performed in a single line of code:

```
connection = DriverManager.getConnection(
"jdbc:mysql://localhost/accounts?user=&password=");
```

As you can see, the DriverManager is the catalyst used to create the connection to the database. This is consistent with its job of managing all JDBC drivers. When the getConnection() method is called, the DriverManager needs to decide what JDBC driver to use to connect to the database. Figure 5.1 shows how the DriverManager determines the proper JDBC driver to use with a given connection request.

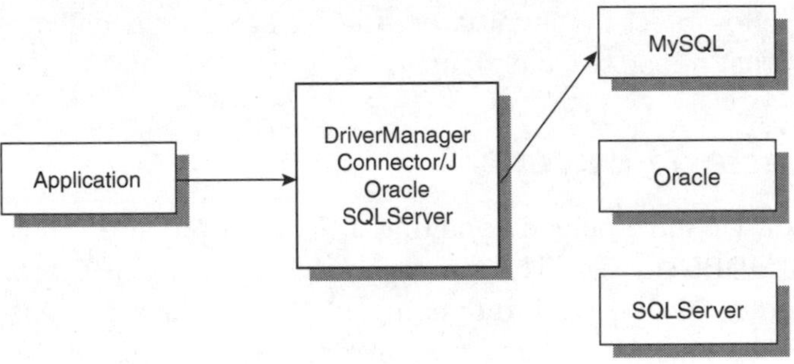

Figure 5.1 Determining the proper driver.

Let's begin our discussion of obtaining a connection to the database by examining the API for the DriverManager.

DriverManager API

DriverManager is a static class that exposes methods for handling connections to a database as well as administrative methods for JDBC drivers. The following methods are those we might be interested in using:

Connection getConnection(String URL)—The DriverManager uses a registered driver in an attempt to build a connection to a specified database.

Connection getConnection(String URL, Properties props)—The DriverManager uses a registered driver in an attempt to build a connection to the specified database using the properties provided in the Properties object.

Connection getConnection(String URL, String username, String password)—The DriverManager uses a registered driver in an attempt to build a connection to the specified database using the provided username and password.

Driver getDriver(String URL)—The method returns a registered driver that will potentially be used to connect to a database with the provided URL.

Enumeration getDrivers()—The method returns all of the currently registered drivers.

int getLoginTimeout()—The method returns the maximum time in seconds that the current DriverManager will wait for a connection to a database.

void setLoginTimeout(int secs)—The method sets the maximum time in seconds that the current DriverManager will wait for a connection to the database.

These methods can be characterized into three groups: driver management, timeout management, and connection management.

Driver Management Methods

Once a driver (or set of drivers) has been registered with a DriverManager, you usually don't have to do anything further with the driver. However, a few methods are available for obtaining and removing drivers from the DriverManager if you need to. A current list of registered drivers can be obtained using code like this:

```
Enumeration e = DriverManager.getDrivers();
while (e.hasMoreElements()) {
  Driver d = (Driver)e.nextElement();
  System.out.println("Driver Major Version = " +
    d.getMajorVersion());
}
```

Once a reference to a driver has been obtained, the deRegisterDriver() method can be used to remove the driver. In almost all cases, you won't need to use any of this information unless you want to remove from the application all JDBC access to a particular database.

Timeout Management Methods

When connecting to a database—whether local or remote to the Java application—the application doesn't know if the database system itself is currently online. There can be situations where a database is down for maintenance or the machine has crashed. A Java application has the option of setting a timeout value for the maximum time that the DriverManager will wait as it attempts to create a connection. The default timeout is 30 seconds before the driver throws a java.net.ConnectException exception. For situations where the database is on a remote machine, the timeout might need to be extended. The following code shows an example of setting a timeout of 90 seconds:

```
DriverManager.setLoginTimeout(90);
```

The setLoginTimeout() method accepts a single integer value representing the maximum timeout in seconds for a connection attempt. If you need to obtain the current timeout setting, use the getLoginTimeout() method. If you use this method without setting the timeout, a value of 0 will be returned, indicating that the system default timeout of 30 seconds should be used.

Connection Management Methods

The meat of the DriverManager object is found in the connection methods. A method called getConnection() is overloaded three times to provide numerous ways of supplying arguments to the DriverManager. The signatures for the methods are as follows:

```
Connection getConnection(String URL);
Connection getConnection(String URL, Properties info);
Connection getConnection(String URL, String user, String password);
```

In all three methods, the primary connection information is found in the first parameter of type URL (which we discuss in the next section). The first overloaded method assumes that all of the information for the connection will be passed in the URL. The second method gets connection options from the Properties parameter. The third method obtains connection information from the URL, but pulls the username and password for the database connection from the method parameters.

Using URL Options in Connector/J

In all of the getConnection() methods, the URL parameter is responsible for providing the DriverManager with information about the type and location of the database with which a connection should be established. From a standards perspective, a URL (Uniform Resource Locator) provides a common way of locating resources found on the Internet. More than likely, you use HTTP URLs every day. A lot of information is transferred in URLs, and that information can be used for Web pages as well as database locations. The general format of a URL is

```
<protocol>:<subprotocol>:<subname>
```

In a URL for a Web page, the protocol is HTTP and there is no subprotocol or subname. In the JDBC world, the protocol is defined as jdbc. The *<subprotocol>* is typically the name of the driver this particular connection URL needs to use, and the *<subname>* is a string representing connection information, such as the source of the database. The Connector/J driver requires that the *<subprotocol>* be defined as *mysql*. So our URL looks like this:

```
jdbc:mysql:<subname>
```

The *<subname>* is a little more complex because it consists of up to three different components. The general format of the *<subname>* is

```
//<host>[:<port>][/<databaseName>]
```

Notice the use of the double slashes just as with an HTTP URL. The *<host>* component is the domain name or IP address of the server hosting the MySQL database application. The *<host>* can be followed by a colon and a port number where the database application accepts connections. The default port in MySQL is 3306; the Connector/J driver will also default to port 3306 if one is not found in the *<subname>*. Finally, the database the driver should begin using when a connection is first made can be added to the *<subname>*. Here are a few examples:

```
jdbc:mysql://localhost
jdbc:mysql://localhost/accounts
jdbc:mysql://192.156.44.3/db_dev
jdbc:mysql://database.company.com/prod
jdbc:mysql://database.company.com:4533/prod
```

In each of the sample URLs, the JDBC driver will be able to determine which host currently is running a MySQL database application, what port to communicate through to the database system, and the initial database.

In addition to specifying the initial database that the application should use for the current connection, the Connector/J driver allows properties to be appended to the driver string. For example, we can specify the username and password to be used with the connection:

```
jdbc:mysql://192.156.44.3/db_dev?user=newuser&password=newpassword
```

The properties are appended to the driver string using the ? and & delimiters. The first property must use the ? delimiter, and all others must use &. Connector/J includes quite a few properties that can be specified on the connection string, as shown in Table 5.1.

Table 5.1 Connection Properties

NAME	DESCRIPTION	DEFAULT
user	The username for the connection.	None
password	The password for the user.	None
autoReconnect	Set to true if the connection should automatically be reconnected.	false
maxReconnects	If autoReconnect=true, represents the total reconnect attempts.	3
initialTimeout	If autoReconnect=true, represents the time to wait (in seconds) between reconnect attempts.	2

Table 5.1 Connection Properties (continued)

NAME	DESCRIPTION	DEFAULT
maxRows	Limits the total number of rows to be returned by a query.	0 (maximum)
useUnicode	If true, the server will use Unicode when returning strings; otherwise, the server attempts to use the character set that is being used on the server.	true
characterEncoding	If useUnicode=true, specifies the encoding to be used.	None
relaxAutoCommit	If relaxAutoCommit=true, then the server allows transaction calls even if the server doesn't support transactions.	false
capitalizeTypeNames	If set to true, type names will be capitalized in DatabaseMetaData results.	false
profileSql	If set to true, queries and timings will be dumped to STDERR.	false
socketTimeout	If > 0 in milliseconds, the driver will drop the connection when the timeout expires and return the SQLState error of 08S01.	0
StrictFloatingPoint	If set to true, the driver will compensate for floating float rounding errors in the server.	false

As you can see, there is quite a bit of information that can be conveyed to the Driver and used for queries to the database.

Using Properties with the Connection

One of the getConnection() methods exposed by the DriverManager allows the use of a Properties object to pass information to the DriverManager. All of the connection parameters shown in Table 5.1 can be placed in a Java Properties object. For example:

```
Properties prop = new Properties();
prop.setProperty("user", "newuser");
prop.setProperty("password", "newpass");
myConnection = getConnection(
  "jdbc:mysql://localhost/accounts", prop);
```

In this code, a Properties object is instantiated and assigned to the prop variable. Using the setProperty() method, the user and password properties are set to values appropriate for the connection. After all of the properties are set, the object is used in a call to create a connection to the database.

Handling Errors

When dealing with connections to external sources, you must know how to handle errors that might occur. Both the JDBC driver and MySQL provide numerous types of errors. As you will see throughout our example program, try/catch blocks are provided to capture SQLException exceptions that are thrown by the Connector/J driver. When a SQLException exception is thrown, a call is made to the displaySQLErrors() method defined as a private method within our object. That method is shown here:

```
private void displaySQLErrors(SQLException e) {
  System.out.println("SQLException: " + e.getMessage());
  System.out.println("SQLState:     " + e.getSQLState());
  System.out.println("VendorError:  " + e.getErrorCode());
}
```

Like Connector/J, JDBC drivers implement three different specification-defined pieces of error information. These are the exception itself, the SQL-State, and a vendor error code. Our method outputs the values of these three components if an error occurs when we're trying to accomplish some JDBC task. For example, if we define a host address for our MySQL database system that doesn't exist, the following is displayed on the console:

```
Unable to connect to host
08S01
0
```

In a production system, we probably want to log the error to an error file and attempt to recover from the error. This might include attempting to connect to another database.

Executing Queries Through Statement Objects

At this point in our code, we have pulled the Connector/J JDBC driver into our application and created a connection to the database. The example code in Listing 5.1 makes a call to an object method called executeSQL(), where the work to pull results from the database occurs. Within this method, the code builds a SQL statement object, executes the SQL, and displays the results.

Building a Statement Object

The first step in getting data from the MySQL database is to build a Statement object. The Statement object is designed to be an intermediary between the database connection and the results found from executing some SQL. When a

Statement object executes a query, it returns a ResultSet object. The default configuration for the Statement object is to return a single ResultSet. If the application needs to work with two different results at the same time, multiple Statement objects will need to be instantiated. As you can see from the API documentation in Appendix B "Databases and Tables", the Statement object has quite a few methods associated with it. Throughout this chapter, we cover most of those methods and how they relate to the MySQL database.

The Statement object to be used in our example code is created from the Connection object using the method createStatement(), as shown here:

```
Statement statement = connection.createStatement();
```

When calling the createStatement() object, you must enclose it within a try/catch block and capture any SQLException exceptions. The Connection object contains three different variations of the createStatement() method:

- **Statement createStatement()**—Instantiates a Statement object to be used for sending queries to the database server.
- **Statement createStatement(int resultSetType, int resultSet Concurrency)**—Instantiates a Statement object to be used for sending queries to the database server using the provided type and concurrency.
- **Statement createStatement(int resultSetType, int resultSetConcurrency, int resultSetHoldabilitiy)**—Instantiates a Statement object to be used for sending queries to the database server using the provided type, concurrency, and holdability.

Three parameters are set for ResultSets when a Statement object is created. These are listed below, and we cover them in more detail when we discuss ResultSet objects:

- ResultSetType—The default is TYPE_SCROLL_INSENSITIVE; the possible values are

    TYPE_FORWARD_ONLY—The ResultSet cursor moves forward.

    TYPE_SCROLL_INSENSITIVE—The cursor may scroll in any direction and is not sensitive to changes.

    TYPE_SCROLL_SENSITIVE—The cursor may scroll in any direction and is sensitive to changes.

- ResultSetConcurrency—This parameter determines whether the ResultSet may be updated in place and the updates automatically applied to the database. The default is CONCUR_READ_ONLY; it is the only option supported by Connector/J.

- ResultSetHoldability—This parameter is not implemented in Connector/J's implementation of createStatement().

When you're using the createStatement() methods, you include the parameters when you're creating a ResultSet or use the defaults as appropriate. In most cases, you use createStatement() without any parameters.

Executing SQL

Now that we have a Statement object, it's time to execute the SQL statements designed to return results for use in our application. The Statement object includes several types of query methods, as shown in Appendix B. In this section, we cover the method executeQuery(), which is designed to execute SQL that will return a result. This means the method expects to execute a SELECT query.

In our example code, the following line sets off the process of retrieving results from the database:

```
ResultSet rs = statement.executeQuery("SELECT * FROM acc_acc");
```

There are a few things you should note about this code. The first is that the SQL query statement is provided to the executeQuery() method as a String. The object passes the query to the database, which in turn executes it. Connector/J doesn't, and shouldn't, make any type of determination on the validity of the SQL being passed by the application. If the database is unable to execute the SQL, a SQLException exception will be thrown. If the command is successful, the executeQuery() method returns a ResultSet object containing the rows from the database.

Ultimately, three outcomes can occur when the executeQuery() method executes. The first is an exception. An exception can occur for many reasons, among them are the following:

- The connection is no longer valid to the database server.
- The SQL has a syntax error in it.
- The currently logged-in user doesn't have permission to the database table used in the SQL.

You need to wrap your executeQuery() in a try/catch block, but it will be a design issue as to which errors you attempt to recover from and which allow the application to fail. There are some database operation errors that you recover from by changing the nature of the operation—you might be able to connect to a secondary database, or limit the results. Other errors may be catastrophic, like being unable to update the database. The second outcome is a ResultSet with results in it. This is the most favorable outcome. The third outcome also produces a ResultSet, but instead the set is empty, which indicates that the query didn't produce any rows from the database.

Displaying Results

The example code takes the ResultSet produced by the execution of our query string and displays the first column of each row. As you see in the next section, the ResultSet object includes a host of methods for manipulating the rows and columns it currently stores.

Using the ResultSet Object

The ResultSet object is the primary storage mechanism for the rows returned from a query on the MySQL database. It is imperative that you have a full understanding of how the object works and how you get our data out of it. Conceptually, the ResultSet object looks like an adjustable two-dimensional array, as you can see in Figure 5.2.

	acc_id	username	password
Internal pointer →			
	1034033	jimmy	hispassw
	1034035	jdoe	does

Figure 5.2 The ResultSet object.

As shown in Figure 5.2, the ResultSet object consists of rows containing data based on the information returned from the database query. The columns of the object are the fields from the database as specified in the query. If the query uses a * in the SELECT, then all of the columns from the database will be represented in the ResultSet. If only a few of the columns are listed in the SELECT, then only those columns will appear in the set.

The ResultSet uses an internal cursor to keep track of what row data should be returned when the application requests data. The default behavior for a ResultSet is to maintain read-only data and allow the internal cursor to move forward through the rows. If the data needs to be used a second time, the cursor will need to be moved to the beginning. When a ResultSet object is first instantiated and filled, the internal cursor is set to a position just before the first row.

A large number of getter methods are available for retrieving data from the ResultSet object. These methods pull data from a specific row/column cell and attempt to convert the data to a Java data type as defined by the getter method. See Chapter 7, "MySQL Type Mapping," for a full discussion on mapping between MySQL, Connector/J, and Java.

Determining the Cursor Position

As we mentioned earlier, when a ResultSet is first instantiated, the internal cursor is positioned just before the first row in the set. You have four methods for monitoring where the cursor is in the set. To determine if it is sitting before the first row, use the method isBeforeFirst(); for example:

```
ResultSet rs = statement.executeQuery("SELECT * FROM acc_acc");
boolean whereIsIt = rs.isBeforeFirst()
```

The isBeforeFirst() method returns a value of true if the internal cursor is sitting before the first row. In our code example, the value returned will be true. The complement to this method is isAfterLast(). When the cursor has been moved beyond all of the rows in the set, the isAfterLast() method returns a value of true.

We can also tell whether the internal cursor has been moved to either the first or the last row of the object. The isFirst() method will return true if the cursor is sitting at the first row, and isLast() returns true if the cursor is sitting on the last row.

Finally, you can use the getRow() method to return the current row number from the ResultSet. If you execute the getRow() method just after getting the ResultSet from the executeQuery() method, the value returned will be 0. Thus, the first actual data row in a ResultSet has a value of 1. This is something to remember when using the methods in the next section to move around the object.

Moving the Cursor

Once you know where the cursor is currently pointing within the set, you can move it anywhere you like. First, let's look at two methods that allow you to move to a specific location within the ResultSet. The first method is based on counting from an absolute position from either the beginning or the end of the rows:

```
boolean absolute(int rows)
```

The absolute() method moves the internal cursor to a specific row in the ResultSet. Thus, the method called rs.absolute(2) moves to the second row in the object. If a value is entered that is outside the bounds of the row count in the ResultSet, a SQLException exception will be thrown. To the method, a positive value indicates that it should count from the beginning of the rows; a negative value indicates that it should count from the end of the rows.

The second method counts based on the current cursor position:

```
boolean relative(int rows)
```

With the relative() method, the system moves the cursor using the current row as a pivot point. A positive parameter moves the internal cursor *X* number of rows from the current position. A negative parameter moves the internal cursor *X* number of rows back from the current position. If a value of 0 is passed to the method, the cursor will not move.

As you might have guessed, using the method absolute(1) will move the cursor to the first row and the method absolute(-1) will move the cursor to the last row. Two methods for doing the same thing are first() and last(). These methods will move the cursor to the first and last rows in the ResultSet, respectively.

It's even possible to move the cursor before the first row as well as after the last row. The beforeFirst() method moves the internal cursor to row 0, which is just before the first row. The method afterLast() moves the cursor to a position just after the last row.

In most cases, though, you probably want to move through the ResultSet one row at a time. Just as we did in our example code in Listing 5.1, the next() method moves the cursor one row ahead at a time. Since the internal cursor starts before the first row, the next() method should be called before any processor starts on the ResultSet. Note that a default ResultSet is a forward-only data type; therefore, only the next() method should be valid. However, Connector/J has implemented the previous() method to work on any ResultSet object. In fact, there is even a prev() method defined in Connector/J for moving the cursor backward.

In the cases of first(), last(), next(), and previous(), the methods all return a Boolean value indicating whether the command was successful. For first() and last(), the methods return false only when the ResultSet object is empty and therefore no first or last row exists. The methods next(), previous(), and Connector/J's prev() return false when there are no longer any valid rows left in the ResultSet. For example, next() returns true until the internal cursor points to the position after the last row.

As you might have noticed, there is no method for determining the size of the ResultSet. We must rely on the Boolean values returned by the methods that move the internal cursor. There is a way to get the total size of a result from the database using a query, but it's a little more complex than the current topics we are discussing. We tackle that one in the next chapter.

Getter Methods

Once the cursor has been set on a particular row, the contents of each column can be obtained. In our example code, we pull the first column—the column starting at 1—using the code

```
System.out.println(rs.getString(1));
```

This code tells the ResultSet to return (as a String) the value located in the first column of the row the internal cursor is currently pointing to. Clearly, the cursor must be pointing to a valid row; otherwise, the getter method will throw a SQLException exception.

Looking at the ResultSet API, you will notice that there are quite a large number of methods for obtaining values from the set. Each method is designed to pull a specific type, such as integer or string. As an example, consider the getString() methods:

```
String getString(int columnIndex);
String getString(String columnName);
```

Both of these methods pull a value from MySQL as a String. Even if the value in MySQL is an integer, the integer will be coaxed into the String type. However, what we really want to consider are the parameters to the method. Notice how one of them is passing an integer and the other is a String. Let's look at an example of how the getters will work based on a real database. One of our sample databases is called accounts, and it contains a table named acc_acc. This table is defined as:

```
acc_id - int
username - varchar
acc_id - int
username - varchar
password - varchar
ts - timestamp
act_ts - timestamp
```

Using the getString() methods, we can pull the value contained in the username column in two different ways. First, we pull the values using some example SQL:

```
ResultSet rs = statement.executeQuery("SELECT * FROM acc_acc");
```

Now we know that the variable rs is a ResultSet and that its internal pointer is set at a position before the first row. To start pulling the data from the set, we need to move the internal pointer to the next row:

```
rs.next();
```

With the internal pointer at the first row in the object, we can output the values in the username column by using the getString() method. Two different methods are available, as shown here:

```
System.out.println(rs.getString(1));
System.out.println(rs.getString("username"));
```

In the first output statement, the column number is used to let the ResultSet object know which column the value should be pulled from. In the second output statement, we use the name of the column as defined in the query. There is hidden meaning in that last sentence. In the query we used—SELECT * FROM acc_acc—we asked for all of the columns from data in the acc_acc table without any row restrictions. The * pulls all of the columns as well as the column names defined in the table. What this means to the ResultSet is that the values can be pulled using the names as declared in the table. Consider the following code:

```
ResultSet rs = statement.executeQuery(
  "SELECT acc_id, username FROM acc_acc");
rs.next();
System.out.println(rs.getString("username"));
System.out.println(rs.getString("password"));
```

The first output line pulls the username value from the ResultSet. We can again use the name of the column as defined in the table since we've asked the database to return both the acc_id and username from the table. The second output line will produce a SQLException exception because no password column is defined in the ResultSet. Finally, consider this code:

```
ResultSet rs = statement.executeQuery(
  "SELECT acc_id, username "User" FROM acc_acc");
rs.next();
System.out.println(rs.getString("User"));
System.out.println(rs.getString("username"));
```

The first output line attempts to pull a column called User from the ResultSet. It will be successful because our SELECT pulled the username column from the table but renamed it as User (which is the column name used in the ResultSet). The second output line in this code example produces a SQLException exception.

Primitive Getters

Connector/J includes getter methods for all of the primitive types defined within a MySQL table. In this section, we present examples for using each of the methods.

Boolean

If you are interested in retrieving a column's value as a Java Boolean value, two methods are available:

```
Boolean getBoolean(int columnIndex)
Boolean getBoolean(String columnName);
```

As we've discussed, the task of the getter method is to pull the value from a table column and attempt to convert it to the intended Java type. For the getBoolean()

methods, the outcome is a Boolean value. Consider a table defined as

```
mysql> describe bool;
+-------+------------+------+-----+---------+-------+
| Field | Type       | Null | Key | Default | Extra |
+-------+------------+------+-----+---------+-------+
| id    | int(11)    | YES  |     | NULL    |       |
| a     | tinyint(1) | YES  |     | NULL    |       |
| b     | int(11)    | YES  |     | NULL    |       |
| c     | varchar(4) | YES  |     | NULL    |       |
| d     | varchar(5) | YES  |     | NULL    |       |
+-------+------------+------+-----+---------+-------+
5 rows in set (0.00 sec)
```

Now see what happens if we put the following data into the table:

```
mysql> select * from bool;
+------+------+------+------+------+
| id   | a    | b    | c    | d    |
+------+------+------+------+------+
|    1 |    1 |    0 | true | f    |
+------+------+------+------+------+
1 row in set (0.00 sec)
```

The data can be pulled with the following Java code:

```
ResultSet rs = statement.executeQuery(
         "SELECT * FROM bool");

while (rs.next()) {
  System.out.println(rs.getString("a") + " " +
rs.getBoolean("a"));
  System.out.println(rs.getString("b") + " " +
rs.getBoolean("b"));
  System.out.println(rs.getString("c") + " " + r
rs.getBoolean("c"));
  System.out.println(rs.getString("d") + " " +
rs.getBoolean("d"));
}
```

Can you guess the output? Here it is:

```
1 true
0 false
true true
f false
```

As you can see, the values within the columns are properly translated into Boolean values.

Byte

If the information in your database needs to be obtained as a raw byte or series of bytes, then the following four methods will be helpful to you:

```
Byte getByte(int columnIndex);
Byte getByte(String columnName);
byte[] getBytes(int columnIndex);
byte[] getBytes(String columnName);
```

In most cases, these methods will not throw an exception because nearly all values in a MySQL column can be returned as bytes.

Double

If the value in a MySQL column is a double or a value that can be converted to a double, then you can use the following two methods to pull that value:

```
double getDouble(int columnIndex);
double getDouble(String columnName);
```

If the value in the MySQL column cannot be converted to a double, a SQLException exception will be thrown with an error value of S1009.

Float

Real or floating-point values can be returned from the MySQL database using these methods:

```
float getFloat(int columnIndex);
float getFloat(String columnName);
```

If the value in the MySQL column cannot be converted to a float, a SQLException exception will be thrown with an error value of S1009. If the strictFloatingPoint property supplied to the Connection object has a value of true, then Connector/J attempts to compensate the returned value for rounding errors that might have occurred in the server.

Int

The MySQL server can handle integer values, and you can use the following two methods to pull their associated value from the database:

```
int getInt(int columnIndex);
int getInt(String columnName);
```

If the strictFloatingPoint property has been set to true in the Connection object, the Connector/J driver attempts to handle rounding errors in the integer values stored on the database. Values that cannot be converted to an integer will throw the SQLException exception.

Long

Longs can be pulled from the database using these methods:

```
long getLong(int columnIndex);
long getLong(String columnName);
```

The Connector/J code attempts to build a long by reading the value from the database as a double and applying a downcast to a long. If the value cannot be converted to a long, the exception SQLException will be thrown.

Short

Since the MySQL database can store shorts, we need to be able to get them out as well. The methods for doing this are

```
short getShort(int columnIndex);
short getShort(String columnName);
```

The short values will be obtained using a downcast from a double. The SQLException exception will be thrown if the value returned cannot be converted to a short.

Closing the Objects

In our example code, we have created many different objects, including ResultSet, Statement, and Connection objects. When we have finished with each of the pieces, they should be closed so that the JVM as well as the Connector/J driver knows that the memory the objects are occupying can be given back to the system.

It is important that we close the objects in the reverse order in which they were opened. This means the ResultSet objects should have their close() method called before we call the Connection object's close(). There will be times when closing the objects in the wrong order can produce a SQLException exception.

With this in mind, a closed connection from Connector/J to the MySQL database server can cause a SQLException to be thrown if any of the methods (such as createStatement()) can be called against it. The Connection object includes a method called isClosed(), which returns a value of true if the current Connection object has lost its link to the database server. In these cases, the Connection object needs to be reconnected with the database server before any additional work can occur on the object.

Making It Real

Well, you may not have found our first example very exciting, so let's expand things a little and make them more useful and powerful, as well as add some graphics. Next we create a GUI that will allow us to see all of the account numbers in our database table, select one, and then display the information associated with the account number on the same GUI. Later in the chapter, we expand the GUI to insert, delete, and update the database information through the GUI. First, we have our initial code, shown in Listing 5.2.

```
import java.awt.*;
import java.awt.event.*;
import javax.swing.*;
import java.sql.*;
import java.util.*;

public class Accounts extends JFrame {

  private JButton getAccountButton;
  private JList   accountNumberList;
  private Connection connection;
  private JTextField accountIDText,
                     usernameText,
                     passwordText,
                     tsText,
                     activeTSText;

  public Accounts() {
    try {
      Class.forName("com.mysql.jdbc.Driver").newInstance();
    } catch (Exception  e) {
      System.err.println("Unable to find and load driver");
      System.exit(1);
    }
  }

  private void buildGUI() {
    Container c = getContentPane();
    c.setLayout(new FlowLayout());

    //Do Account List
    Vector v = new Vector();
    try {
      Statement statement = connection.createStatement();
      ResultSet rs = statement.executeQuery("SELECT acc_id FROM
acc_acc");

      while(rs.next()) {
        v.addElement(rs.getString("acc_id"));
      }
      rs.close();
    } catch(SQLException e) { }
    accountNumberList = new JList(v);
```

Listing 5.2 Our GUI application. (continues)

```
accountNumberList.setVisibleRowCount(2);
JScrollPane accountNumberListScrollPane =
  new JScrollPane(accountNumberList);

//Do Get Account Button
getAccountButton = new JButton("Get Account");
getAccountButton.addActionListener (
  new ActionListener() {
    public void actionPerformed(ActionEvent e) {
      try {
        Statement statement = connection.createStatement();
        ResultSet rs = statement.executeQuery(
         "SELECT * FROM acc_acc WHERE acc_id = "
         + accountNumberList.getSelectedValue());
        if (rs.next()) {
          accountIDText.setText(rs.getString("acc_id"));
          usernameText.setText(rs.getString("username"));
          passwordText.setText(rs.getString("password"));
          tsText.setText(rs.getString("ts"));
          activeTSText.setText(rs.getString("act_ts"));
        }
      } catch(SQLException ee) {}
    }
  }
);

JPanel first = new JPanel();
first.add(accountNumberListScrollPane);
first.add(getAccountButton);

accountIDText = new JTextField(15);
usernameText = new JTextField(15);
passwordText = new JTextField(15);
tsText = new JTextField(15);
activeTSText = new JTextField(15);

JPanel second = new JPanel();
second.setLayout(new GridLayout(5,1));
second.add(accountIDText);
second.add(usernameText);
second.add(passwordText);
second.add(tsText);
second.add(activeTSText);

c.add(first);
c.add(second);
setSize(200,200);
```

Listing 5.2 Our GUI application. (continues)

```
    show();
  }

  public void connectToDB() {
    try {
      connection = DriverManager.getConnection(
        "jdbc:mysql://localhost/accounts");
    } catch(SQLException e) {
      System.out.println("Unable to connect to database");
      System.exit(1);
    }
  }

  private void displaySQLErrors(SQLException e) {
    System.out.println("SQLException: " + e.getMessage());
    System.out.println("SQLState:     " + e.getSQLState());
    System.out.println("VendorError:  " + e.getErrorCode());
  }

  private void init() {
    connectToDB();
  }

  public static void main(String[] args) {
     Accounts accounts = new Accounts();

     accounts.addWindowListener(
       new WindowAdapter() {
         public void windowClosing(WindowEvent e) {
           System.exit(0);
         }
       }
     );

     accounts.init();
     accounts.buildGUI();
  }
}
```

Listing 5.2 Our GUI application. (continued)

The code in Listing 5.2 is designed to illustrate using MySQL and a Java GUI application. Figure 5.3 shows what the GUI looks like when it is first executed. We've broken down the code into a series of methods, which we discuss next.

Our Main Function

Just as in any Java application, our main function instantiates an object of our class type. Notice that our class extends JFrame because we need to provide a GUI with the application. When the object's constructor is called, the Connector/J driver will be located and pulled into the application. Once the object has been created, a windowClosing event is attached to exit the application when the user clicks the window's close button. Two methods are called on the object. The first is init(), which builds a connection to the database, and the second is buildGUI(), which handles the construction of the GUI presentation.

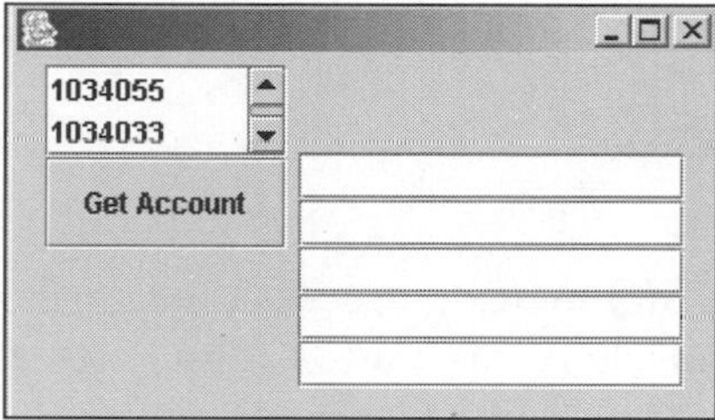

Figure 5.3 Our GUI when first executed.

The init() Method

The init() method is quite simple: It creates a Connection object and attempts to communicate with the MySQL database server. If a connection is successful, an object variable is instantiated to hold the Connection. A try/catch block is used to grab any errors in the connection attempt and to exit the application appropriately.

The buildGUI() Method

The vast majority of the work for the application occurs in the buildGUI() method. In Figure 5.3 you see that we have several GUI components to build and place on the GUI frame. The most important is the list in the upper-left corner, which holds all of the account numbers from our acc_acc table on the MySQL database. A user will click one of these account numbers and click on the Get Account button to pull all of the information for the one account and display it in the text boxes on the screen. Our goal in this discussion isn't to provide details on the use of Java GUI components but to describe how those components interact with Connector/J to pull information from the database.

Building a JList with Account Numbers

Our GUI will contain a JList component, a JButton, and five JTextFields. First, we create the JList with all of the account numbers currently in the acc_acc database table. A JList requires a Model; to populate it we've chosen to use a vector. In the buildGUI() method, the code begins by instantiating a new Vector object. A try/catch block is entered, and SQL code executes a SELECT of just the acc_id column from the acc_acc table. Next, a loop is used to pull each of the acc_id numbers from the ResultSet as a String object. The String is added to the vector. The loop pulls each of the account numbers and places them in the vector. Notice that the catch doesn't do anything with a potential error. This will be fixed in our next iteration of the code.

Once the vector has been populated, the JList component is created using the vector. After the JList is created, the code puts a scroll pane around it so that the user will be able to have scrollbars available to see all of the account numbers in the list.

The Get Account Button

After the JList component, the buildGUI() method creates the GUI's only button, called Get Account. The user will click this button after clicking on an appropriate account number. The code begins by instantiating the button and labeling it, and then moves to the action associated with it. In our code example, we build the event processing code right into the button itself instead of having the application implement the ActionListener interface.

When the user clicks on the Get Account button, its ActionListener() will fire. We want the code to pick up the account number currently selected on the JList control and use the value to pull all of the account information from the MySQL database and place that information in the five JTextField controls.

To accomplish this, a try/catch block is coded with the database control within it. A Statement object is instantiated from the Connection object, and the executeQuery() method is called. The parameter to the executeQuery() method is the SQL string that we want executed against the MySQL database. The full string is

```
ResultSet rs = statement.executeQuery(
  "SELECT * FROM acc_acc WHERE acc_id = "
  + accountNumberList.getSelectedValue());
```

As you can see from the string, we have a SELECT statement that will pull all columns from the database where the acc_id is equal to the current selected value on the JList control. If the query isn't successful, the catch block is called, but there is no error-handling at the moment. If the SQL was successful and there is a result in the ResultSet object, each of the JTextField controls are populated by pulling the database data as String objects using the getString() getter methods.

Creating Text Fields with Account Information

Once the account list and Get Account button have been created, they are added to a panel, which is added to the application frame. After that step, our code creates five JTextField controls to hold the five column values from a row in the acc_acc table. These controls are added to a second panel, which is also added to the application frame.

Once all of the controls have been created and attached to the application, the frame is sized and displayed to the user. At this point, the user can select an account number on the JList control and click on the Get Account button to display the information on the GUI. Figure 5.4 shows an example of what the output will look like when this is performed.

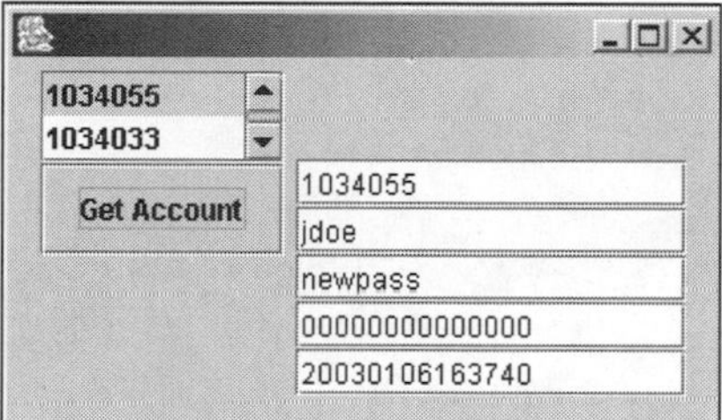

Figure 5.4 Displaying a full record.

Executing a Query with No Results

Up to now, we have been concentrating on pulling information from the database using a SELECT command. Connector/J, SQL, and MySQL also allow information to be inserted and updated as needed. The operations of insert, delete, and update are considered no-result queries because they don't return a ResultSet object after being executed. For this reason, we don't use the executeQuery() method but instead use a method called executeUpdate(). The signature for the method is

```
int executeUpdate(String SQL);
```

The method accepts a single String parameter, which represents the query to be executed. The query shouldn't cause the database server to return a ResultSet, so no SELECTs are allowed. As you can see, the method will return an integer value after the query is performed. This integer represents the total number of rows affected by the query.

The question arises, though, about the actual query statements that do not return a ResultSet. There are quite a few; let's look at the following ones:

- **insert**—Puts a new row into the database table.
- **delete**—Removes a row from the database table.
- **update**—Updates an existing row in the table.
- **drop table**—Removes a complete table from the database.
- **create table**—Builds a new table.
- **alter table**—Changes aspects of the table.

Let's start with the insert query statement. As we already know, the insert command will allow a new row to be put into a database table. We want to expand our GUI program to allow the user to place an account number, username, and password in the appropriate text boxes and click a button to add the information to the table. Listing 5.3 shows the new code. In addition to the insert button, we have expanded the code to put SQL errors into a JTextArea.

```
import java.awt.*;
import java.awt.event.*;
import javax.swing.*;
import java.sql.*;
import java.util.*;

public class Accounts extends JFrame {

  private JButton getAccountButton,
                  insertAccountButton;
  private JList   accountNumberList;
  private Connection connection;
  private JTextField accountIDText,
                     usernameText,
                     passwordText,
                     tsText,
                     activeTSText;
  private JTextArea  errorText;

  public Accounts() {
    try {
      Class.forName("com.mysql.jdbc.Driver").newInstance();
    } catch (Exception  e) {
      System.err.println("Unable to find and load driver");
      System.exit(1);
    }
  }

  private void loadAccounts() {
    Vector v = new Vector();
    try {
      Statement statement = connection.createStatement();
      ResultSet rs = statement.executeQuery(
        "SELECT acc_id FROM acc_acc");

      while(rs.next()) {
        v.addElement(rs.getString("acc_id"));
      }
```

Listing 5.3 Our application for inserting a new row. (continues)

```
      rs.close();
    } catch(SQLException e) {
      displaySQLErrors(e);
    }
    accountNumberList.setListData(v);
  }

  private void buildGUI() {
    Container c = getContentPane();
    c.setLayout(new FlowLayout());
    accountNumberList = new JList();
    loadAccounts();
    accountNumberList.setVisibleRowCount(2);
    JScrollPane accountNumberListScrollPane =
      new JScrollPane(accountNumberList);

    //Do Get Account Button
    getAccountButton = new JButton("Get Account");
    getAccountButton.addActionListener (
      new ActionListener() {
        public void actionPerformed(ActionEvent e) {
          try {
            Statement statement = connection.createStatement();
            ResultSet rs = statement.executeQuery(
              "SELECT * FROM acc_acc WHERE acc_id = "
              + accountNumberList.getSelectedValue());
            if (rs.next()) {
              accountIDText.setText(rs.getString("acc_id"));
              usernameText.setText(rs.getString("username"));
              passwordText.setText(rs.getString("password"));
              tsText.setText(rs.getString("ts"));
              activeTSText.setText(rs.getString("act_ts"));
            }
          } catch(SQLException selectException) {
            displaySQLErrors(selectException);
          }
        }
      }
    );

    //Do Insert Account Button
    insertAccountButton = new JButton("Insert Account");
    insertAccountButton.addActionListener (
      new ActionListener() {
        public void actionPerformed(ActionEvent e) {
          try {
            Statement statement = connection.createStatement();
```

Listing 5.3 Our application for inserting a new row. (continues)

```
          int i = statement.executeUpdate("INSERT INTO acc_acc VALUES(" +
            accountIDText.getText() + ", " +
            "'" + usernameText.getText() + "', " +
            "'" + passwordText.getText() + "', " +
            "0" + ", " +
            "now())");
          errorText.append("Inserted " + i + " rows successfully");
          accountNumberList.removeAll();
          loadAccounts();
        } catch(SQLException insertException) {
          displaySQLErrors(insertException);
        }
      }
    }
  );

  JPanel first = new JPanel(new GridLayout(3,1));
  first.add(accountNumberListScrollPane);
  first.add(getAccountButton);
  first.add(insertAccountButton);

  accountIDText = new JTextField(15);
  usernameText = new JTextField(15);
  passwordText = new JTextField(15);
  tsText = new JTextField(15);
  activeTSText = new JTextField(15);
  errorText = new JTextArea(5, 15);
  errorText.setEditable(false);

  JPanel second = new JPanel();
  second.setLayout(new GridLayout(6,1));
  second.add(accountIDText);
  second.add(usernameText);
  second.add(passwordText);
  second.add(tsText);
  second.add(activeTSText);

  JPanel third = new JPanel();
  third.add(new JScrollPane(errorText));

  c.add(first);
  c.add(second);
  c.add(third);
  setSize(500,500);
  show();
}
```

Listing 5.3 Our application for inserting a new row. (continues)

```
  public void connectToDB() {
    try {
      connection = DriverManager.getConnection(
        "jdbc:mysql://192.168.1.25/accounts
        ?user=spider&password=spider");
    } catch(SQLException connectException) {
      System.out.println("unable to connect to db");
      System.exit(1);
    }
   }

  private void displaySQLErrors(SQLException e) {
     errorText.append("SQLException: " + e.getMessage() + "\n");
    errorText.append("SQLState:      " + e.getSQLState() + "\n");
    errorText.append("VendorError:   " + e.getErrorCode() + "\n");
  }

  private void init() {
    connectToDB();
  }

  public static void main(String[] args) {
     Accounts accounts = new Accounts();

     accounts.addWindowListener(
       new WindowAdapter() {
         public void windowClosing(WindowEvent e) {
           System.exit(0);
         }
       }
     );

     accounts.init();
     accounts.buildGUI();
  }
}
```

Listing 5.3 Our application for inserting a new row. (continued)

Figure 5.5 shows how our GUI should look when it is finished. There are a few differences between the code in Listing 5.2 and that in Listing 5.3. Let's take a look.

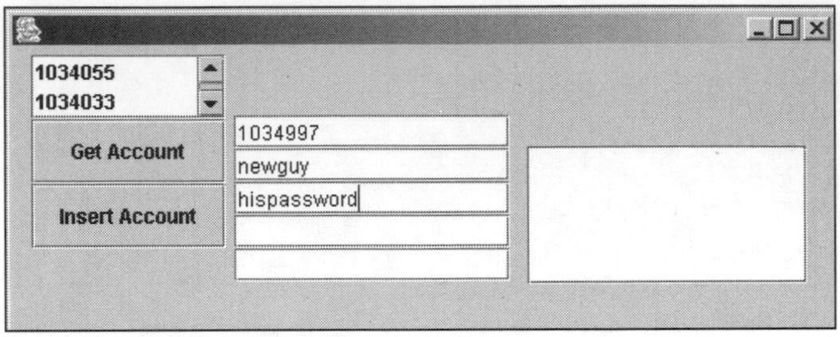

Figure 5.5 Inserting a new row.

The Insert Account Button

By far the largest change between the two applications is the addition of an Insert Account button. First, notice that the format of the button code looks a great deal like that used for the Get Account button. The primary difference is the database code placed in the ActionListener().

The code for inserting a new row into the database requires that the actual values be pulled from each of the top three JTextFields defined to hold the account number, username, and password. The code will first enter a try/catch block and obtain a Statement object. Next, the executeUpdate() method is called using a query string like

```
INSERT INTO acc_acc VALUES(account number, username, password, 0, now)
```

The account number, username, and password are pulled from the appropriate JTextFields using the getText() method. The return value from the execution of the executeUpdate() method is saved and appended to a JTextArea control for error messages. A value of 1 indicates that the insert was successful.

With the new record in the database, the account number JList is out-of-date because it doesn't contain the new account number just inserted. This is where a new method called loadAccounts() comes into play. Once the total number of inserts to the database is put into the JTextArea, a call is made to the removeAll() method of the account number JList control. This wipes out all of the current account numbers. Next, a call is made to loadAccounts(), which queries the database for all current account numbers, places them in a vector, and updates the account number JList control with all of the new accounts. We could have chosen to simply insert the new account number into the account number list, but there might have been updates to the table that didn't come through the GUI. By doing the query again, we pick up all new accounts. Clearly, this is a design decision. If this GUI application is the only way new accounts will be put into the database, then we could just add the account number to the JList and not run another query of the database.

As Figure 5.6 shows, a new record was added to the database with an account number of 1034997. The new account number now appears in the list because of the re-query.

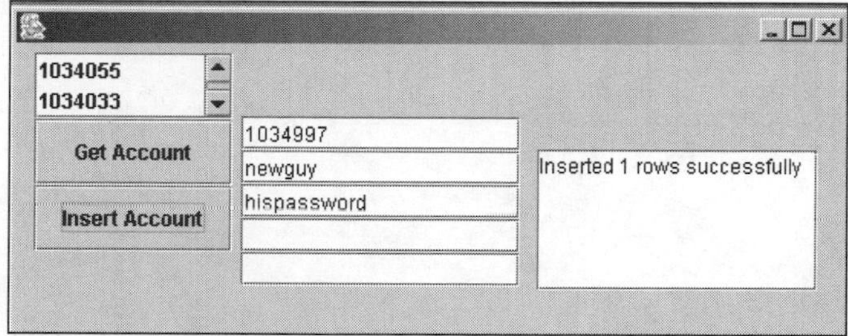

Figure 5.6 Our insert was successful.

Error Notification

As we briefly mentioned in the previous section, this new version of the GUI code includes a JTextArea designed to hold error or notification information for the application. Figure 5.7 shows an example of how error information might look like when placed in the text area. While any of the code can put text into the text area using the append() method, all of the try/catch blocks will call the displaySQLErrors() method to append the SQLException message, SQL-State, and error code information:

```
private void displaySQLErrors(SQLException e) {
   errorText.append("SQLException: " + e.getMessage() + "\n");
  errorText.append("SQLState:     " + e.getSQLState() + "\n");
  errorText.append("VendorError:  " + e.getErrorCode() + "\n");
}
```

Figure 5.7 Error processing.

Deleting Database Rows

Another task that can be accomplished using the updateQuery() method is removing rows from the database. We can add the code in Listing 5.4 to the code in Listing 5.3 to produce an application that can delete rows in the database.

```
//Do Delete Account Button
deleteAccountButton = new JButton("Delete Account");
deleteAccountButton.addActionListener (
  new ActionListener() {
    public void actionPerformed(ActionEvent e) {
      try {
        Statement statement = connection.createStatement();
        int i = statement.executeUpdate(
          "DELETE FROM acc_acc WHERE acc_id = "
          +             accountNumberList.getSelectedValue());
        errorText.append("Deleted " + i + "
          rows successfully");
        accountNumberList.removeAll();
        loadAccounts();
      } catch(SQLException insertException) {
        displaySQLErrors(insertException);
      }
    }
  }
);
```

Listing 5.4 Our Delete Account button code.

The code for the Delete Account button is similar to the code for the Get Account and Insert Account buttons. Most of the work is performed in the ActionListener(). To delete an account, the user selects a value from the account number list control and clicks on the Delete Account button. When this occurs, the ActionListener() is activated. The first step is to create a Statement object and call the executeUpdate() with the query to be executed. The query looks like this:

```
DELETE FROM acc_acc WHERE acc_id = " +
accountNumberList.getSelectedValue()
```

This query tells the database server to find the row or rows where the acc_id column has a value selected from the account number list. The executeUpdate() method executes the query and returns the total number of rows deleted from the database. Figure 5.8 shows the output produced when a row is deleted from the database. In addition to displaying the output, the code refreshes the account number list from the database so that the deleted account number is no longer shown. When the code in Listing 5.4 is added to the application, the first JPanel's GridLayout needs to be changed to 4,1 and the deleteAccountButton needs to be added to the panel. Here's the replacement code:

```
JPanel first = new JPanel(new GridLayout(4,1));
first.add(accountNumberListScrollPane);
first.add(getAccountButton);
```

```
        first.add(insertAccountButton);
        first.add(deleteAccountButton);
```

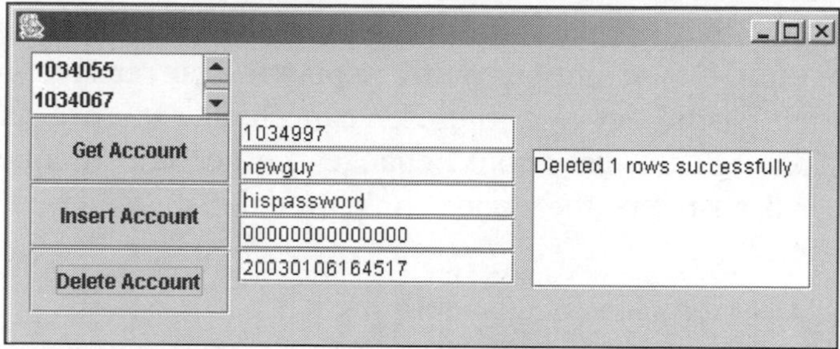

Figure 5.8 We've deleted a row from the database.

Updating Database Rows

The last functionality that we want to add to our GUI application is the update. Once data has been put into the database, it isn't much use if it cannot be pulled from the database or updated to reflect changes in the record. Listing 5.5 contains the code for our update button; add it to the code in Listing 5.3.

```
//Do Update Account Button
updateAccountButton = new JButton("Update Account");
updateAccountButton.addActionListener (
  new ActionListener() {
    public void actionPerformed(ActionEvent e) {
      try {
        Statement statement = connection.createStatement();
        int i = statement.executeUpdate("UPDATE acc_acc " +
          "SET username='" + usernameText.getText() + "', "
            + "password='" + passwordText.getText() + "', "
                + "act_ts = now() "
                + "WHERE acc_id = "
                + accountNumberList.getSelectedValue());
        errorText.append("Updated " + i
          + " rows successfully");
        accountNumberList.removeAll();
        loadAccounts();
      } catch(SQLException insertException) {
        displaySQLErrors(insertException);
      }
    }
  }
);
```

Listing 5.5 The code for updating a record.

As you can see in Listing 5.5, the code for the Delete Account button is similar to the code for the other buttons. The real change is in the ActionListener(). The UPDATE query is a bit more complex from the standpoint of building the actual query. Just as with the other buttons, the user clicks on an account number and clicks on the Get Account button to display the current record. Once the current data has been displayed, the user can change the username and password text. Although the user could change the account number, timestamp, and active timestamp, the code won't pull the data for use in the UPDATE statement.

The actual UPDATE statement is built as follows:

```
UPDATE acc_acc " +
              "SET username='" + usernameText.getText() + "',"
              + "password='" + passwordText.getText() + "', "
              + "act_ts = now() "
              + "WHERE acc_id = "
              + accountNumberList.getSelectedValue());
```

There are a few things to note in the update. First, the username and password are updated based on the values in the appropriate JtextFields. The new values are pulled with the getText() methods. The active timestamp is updated using the MySQL now() function. Finally, we cannot have the code update just any row in the database table. We need to make sure that the update occurs on the record selected by the user. We ensure this by limiting the UPDATE with a WHERE condition on the query. Figure 5.9 shows the original value when the Get Account button is clicked; Figure 5.10 shows the updated record as well as the text indicating that the update was successful.

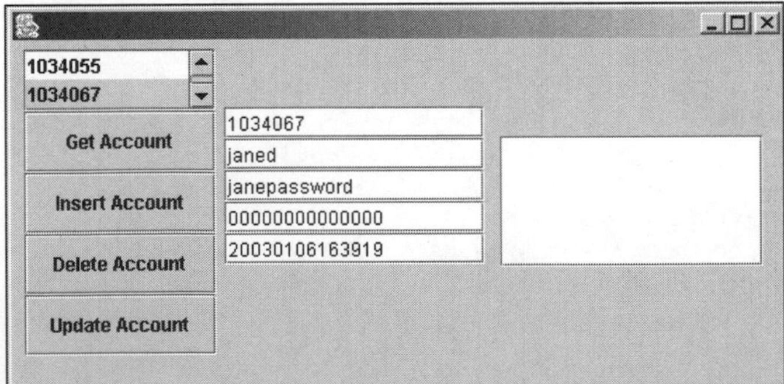

Figure 5.9 Getting the current account.

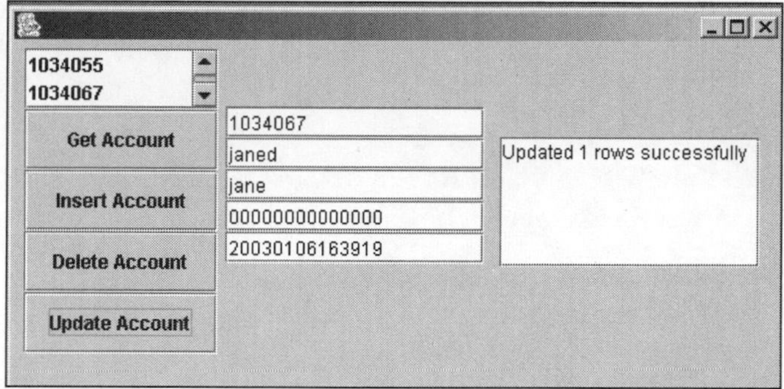

Figure 5.10 Replacing the password text.

CREATE TABLE

If you need to programmatically build a new table for your database, you'll want to use the executeUpdate() method for the simple reason that a ResultSet isn't returned from the execution of the query. An example of using the method to create a new table is

```
Statement statement = connection.createStatement();
int i = statement.executeUpdate(
  "CREATE TABLE acc_new(new_id int, news varchar(64),
   count int, primary key(new_id)");
```

As usual, the code will create a Statement object to execute the query. If the query is successful in creating a new table, the value of i will be 1. If i isn't 1, then more than likely a SQLException exception was thrown, which means the code will need to handle the exception.

DROP TABLE

Another query action that can be performed using the executeUpdate() method is dropping a table. As we've seen, the data within a table can be removed using the DELETE command. In fact, all the data can be removed using the following command:

```
DELETE * FROM acc_acc;
```

This command removes all of the data in the specified table. However, the table that once held the removed data still exists in the database. To remove a table entirely from a database, you need to *drop* the table. The format of the command is

```
DROP TABLE <tablename>
```

Listing 5.6 shows an applet that will obtain all of the tables for the accounts database, display them in a list, and allow a selected table to be removed.

```
import java.awt.*;
import javax.swing.*;
import java.sql.*;
import java.awt.event.*;
import java.util.*;

public class Drop extends JApplet implements ActionListener{

  private Connection connection;
  private JList tableList;
  private JButton dropButton;

  public void init() {
    Connection connection;
    try {
      Class.forName("com.mysql.jdbc.Driver").newInstance();
      connection = DriverManager.getConnection(
        "jdbc:mysql://192.168.1.25/accounts?user=spider&password=spider");
    } catch(Exception connectException) {
      connectException.printStackTrace();}

    Container c = getContentPane();
    tableList = new JList();
    loadTables();
    c.add(new JScrollPane(tableList), BorderLayout.NORTH);

    dropButton = new JButton("Drop Table");
    dropButton.addActionListener(this);
    c.add(dropButton, BorderLayout.SOUTH);
  }

  public void actionPerformed(ActionEvent e) {
    try {
      Statement statement = connection.createStatement();
      ResultSet rs = statement.executeQuery("DROP TABLE "
        + tableList.getSelectedValue());
    } catch (SQLException actionException) {}
  }

  private void loadTables() {
    Vector v = new Vector();
    try {
      Statement statement = connection.createStatement();
      ResultSet rs = statement.executeQuery("SHOW TABLES");
```

Listing 5.6 An applet for dropping tables. (continues)

```
        while(rs.next()) {
          v.addElement(rs.getString(1));
        }
        rs.close();
      } catch(SQLException e) {}
      tableList.setListData(v);
    }
  }
```

Listing 5.6 An applet for dropping tables. (continued)

As Figure 5.11 shows, the applet displays all of the tables in the current database in a list and allows the user to select one of them. Once the user selects a table, the user can click on the Drop Table button to remove the table from the database entirely. Listing 5.6 illustrates how an applet can be used to connect with a MySQL database and obtain information. Most of the code looks just like what we used in the Java applications earlier in the chapter. An applet doesn't have a constructor but instead calls the init() method when it first gets loaded.

One of the pitfalls of using an applet is the need for the Connector/J driver to be installed and included in the classpath for the applet downloaded to the client. Once the driver has been pulled into the JVM where the applet is executing, the SHOW TABLES command is used to return a ResultSet to the applet. Each of the values in the ResultSet are pulled and placed in a JList control.

Once the JList is filled with the tables in the current database, a Drop Table button is placed on the applet GUI as well. Notice that the applet class implements the ActionListener interface. There is an actionPerformed() method in the applet class for handling the click of the Drop Table button.

When the button is clicked, the currently selected table is obtained and added to a DROP TABLE command, which is subsequently sent to the database server.

Disconnecting from the Database

Although not entirely necessary, it is a good idea to disconnect your application from the database in order to allow MySQL to release a resource it is currently using for its connection to your application.

When closing the database, ensure that all of the components currently using a connection are closed first. This means that all ResultSet objects need to be closed, then all Statement objects, and finally, you can close the connection to the database with its close() method.

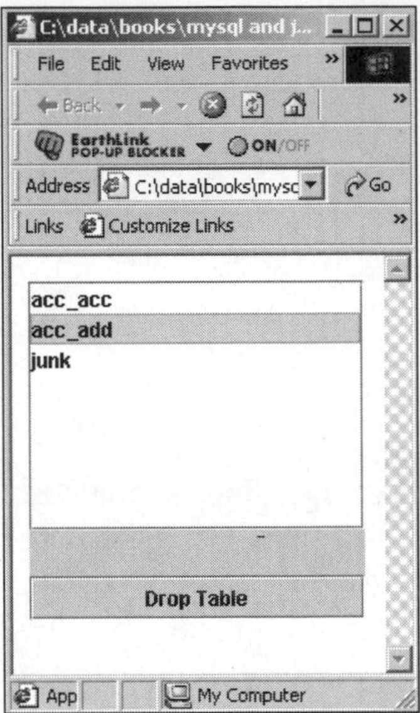

Figure 5.11 Our drop table applet.

Advanced ResultSet Manipulation

One of the most important capabilities we can give our users is the power to move through the data in a database. Users might not know what data they need, or perhaps they don't remember the exact account number. The code in Listing 5.7 adds quite a bit of ResultSet navigation to our original application, as well as the ability to go to a specific record and execute a freehand query.

```
import java.awt.*;
import java.awt.event.*;
import javax.swing.*;
import java.sql.*;
import java.util.*;

public class Accounts extends JFrame {

  private JButton getAccountButton,
                  insertAccountButton,
                  deleteAccountButton,
                  updateAccountButton,
```

Listing 5.7 Our navigatable ResultSet. (continues)

```
                 nextButton,
                 previousButton,
                 lastButton,
                 firstButton,
                 gotoButton,
                 freeQueryButton;
private JList    accountNumberList;
private JTextField accountIDText,
                   usernameText,
                   passwordText,
                   tsText,
                   activeTSText,
                   gotoText,
                   freeQueryText;
private JTextArea  errorText;

private Connection connection;
private Statement  statement;
private ResultSet  rs;

public Accounts() {
  try {
    Class.forName("com.mysql.jdbc.Driver").newInstance();
  } catch (Exception  e) {
    System.err.println("Unable to find and load driver");
    System.exit(1);
  }
}

private void loadAccounts() {
  Vector v = new Vector();
  try {
    rs = statement.executeQuery("SELECT * FROM acc_acc");

    while(rs.next()) {
      v.addElement(rs.getString("acc_id"));
    }
  } catch(SQLException e) {
    displaySQLErrors(e);
  }
  accountNumberList.setListData(v);
}

private void buildGUI() {
  Container c = getContentPane();
  c.setLayout(new FlowLayout());
```

Listing 5.7 Our navigatable ResultSet. (continues)

```
accountNumberList = new JList();
loadAccounts();
accountNumberList.setVisibleRowCount(2);
JScrollPane accountNumberListScrollPane =
 new JScrollPane(accountNumberList);

gotoText = new JTextField(3);
freeQueryText = new JTextField(40);

//Do Get Account Button
getAccountButton = new JButton("Get Account");
getAccountButton.addActionListener (
  new ActionListener() {
    public void actionPerformed(ActionEvent e) {
      try {
        rs.first();
        while (rs.next()) {
          if (rs.getString("acc_id").equals(
            accountNumberList.getSelectedValue()))
            break;
        }
        if (!rs.isAfterLast()) {
          accountIDText.setText(rs.getString("acc_id"));
          usernameText.setText(rs.getString("username"));
          passwordText.setText(rs.getString("password"));
          tsText.setText(rs.getString("ts"));
          activeTSText.setText(rs.getString("act_ts"));
        }
      } catch(SQLException selectException) {
        displaySQLErrors(selectException);
      }
    }
  }
);

//Do Insert Account Button
insertAccountButton = new JButton("Insert Account");
insertAccountButton.addActionListener (
  new ActionListener() {
    public void actionPerformed(ActionEvent e) {
      try {
        Statement statement = connection.createStatement();
        int i = statement.executeUpdate("INSERT INTO acc_acc
          VALUES(" + accountIDText.getText() + ", " +
          "'" + usernameText.getText() + "', " +
          "'" + passwordText.getText() + "', " +
          "0" + ", " + "now())");
```

Listing 5.7 Our navigatable ResultSet. (continues)

```
          errorText.append("Inserted " + i
            + " rows successfully");
          accountNumberList.removeAll();
          loadAccounts();
        } catch(SQLException insertException) {
          displaySQLErrors(insertException);
        }
      }
    }
  );

  //Do Delete Account Button
  deleteAccountButton = new JButton("Delete Account");
  deleteAccountButton.addActionListener (
    new ActionListener() {
      public void actionPerformed(ActionEvent e) {
        try {
          Statement statement = connection.createStatement();
          int i = statement.executeUpdate(
            "DELETE FROM acc_acc WHERE acc_id = " +
            accountNumberList.getSelectedValue());
          errorText.append("Deleted " + i
            + " rows successfully");
          accountNumberList.removeAll();
          loadAccounts();
        } catch(SQLException insertException) {
          displaySQLErrors(insertException);
        }
      }
    }
  );

  //Do Update Account Button
  updateAccountButton = new JButton("Update Account");
  updateAccountButton.addActionListener (
    new ActionListener() {
      public void actionPerformed(ActionEvent e) {
        try {
          Statement statement = connection.createStatement();
          int i = statement.executeUpdate("UPDATE acc_acc " +
            "SET username='" + usernameText.getText() + "', "
            + "password='" + passwordText.getText() + "', "
            + "act_ts = now() " + "WHERE acc_id = "
            + accountNumberList.getSelectedValue());
          errorText.append("Updated " + i
            + " rows successfully");
          accountNumberList.removeAll();
```

Listing 5.7 Our navigatable ResultSet. (continues)

```
          loadAccounts();
        } catch(SQLException insertException) {
          displaySQLErrors(insertException);
        }
      }
    }
  );

  //Do Next Button
  nextButton = new JButton(">");
  nextButton.addActionListener (
    new ActionListener() {
      public void actionPerformed(ActionEvent e) {
        try {
          if (!rs.isLast()) {
            rs.next();
            accountIDText.setText(rs.getString("acc_id"));
            usernameText.setText(rs.getString("username"));
            passwordText.setText(rs.getString("password"));
            tsText.setText(rs.getString("ts"));
            activeTSText.setText(rs.getString("act_ts"));
          }
        } catch(SQLException insertException) {
          displaySQLErrors(insertException);
        }
      }
    }
  );

  //Do Next Button
  previousButton = new JButton("<");
  previousButton.addActionListener (
    new ActionListener() {
      public void actionPerformed(ActionEvent e) {
        try {
          if (!rs.isFirst()) {
            rs.previous();
            accountIDText.setText(rs.getString("acc_id"));
            usernameText.setText(rs.getString("username"));
            passwordText.setText(rs.getString("password"));
            tsText.setText(rs.getString("ts"));
            activeTSText.setText(rs.getString("act_ts"));
          }
        } catch(SQLException insertException) {
          displaySQLErrors(insertException);
        }
      }
```

Listing 5.7 Our navigatable ResultSet. (continues)

```
    }
  );


  //Do last Button
  lastButton = new JButton(">|");
  lastButton.addActionListener (
    new ActionListener() {
      public void actionPerformed(ActionEvent e) {
        try {
          rs.last();
          accountIDText.setText(rs.getString("acc_id"));
          usernameText.setText(rs.getString("username"));
          passwordText.setText(rs.getString("password"));
          tsText.setText(rs.getString("ts"));
          activeTSText.setText(rs.getString("act_ts"));
        } catch(SQLException insertException) {
          displaySQLErrors(insertException);
        }
      }
    }
  );


  //Do first Button
  firstButton = new JButton("|<");
  firstButton.addActionListener (
    new ActionListener() {
      public void actionPerformed(ActionEvent e) {
        try {
          rs.first();
          accountIDText.setText(rs.getString("acc_id"));
          usernameText.setText(rs.getString("username"));
          passwordText.setText(rs.getString("password"));
          tsText.setText(rs.getString("ts"));
          activeTSText.setText(rs.getString("act_ts"));
        } catch(SQLException insertException) {
          displaySQLErrors(insertException);
        }
      }
    }
  );

  //Do gotoButton
  gotoButton = new JButton("Goto");
  gotoButton.addActionListener (
    new ActionListener() {
```

Listing 5.7 Our navigatable ResultSet. (continues)

```
      public void actionPerformed(ActionEvent e) {
        try {
          rs.absolute(Integer.parseInt(gotoText.getText()));
          accountIDText.setText(rs.getString("acc_id"));
          usernameText.setText(rs.getString("username"));
          passwordText.setText(rs.getString("password"));
          tsText.setText(rs.getString("ts"));
          activeTSText.setText(rs.getString("act_ts"));
        } catch(SQLException insertException) {
          displaySQLErrors(insertException);
        }
      }
    }
  );

  //Do freeQueryButton
  freeQueryButton = new JButton("Execute Query");
  freeQueryButton.addActionListener (
    new ActionListener() {
      public void actionPerformed(ActionEvent e) {
        try {
          if (freeQueryText.getText().toUpperCase().
            indexOf("SELECT") >= 0) {
            rs = statement.executeQuery(
              freeQueryText.getText());
            if (rs.next()) {
              accountIDText.setText(rs.getString("acc_id"));
              usernameText.setText(rs.getString("username"));
              passwordText.setText(rs.getString("password"));
              tsText.setText(rs.getString("ts"));
              activeTSText.setText(rs.getString("act_ts"));
            }
          } else {
            int i = statement.executeUpdate(
              freeQueryText.getText());
            errorText.append("Rows affected = " + i);
            loadAccounts();
          }
        } catch(SQLException insertException) {
          displaySQLErrors(insertException);
        }
      }
    }
  );


  JPanel first = new JPanel(new GridLayout(5,1));
```

Listing 5.7 Our navigatable ResultSet. (continues)

```
    first.add(accountNumberListScrollPane);
    first.add(getAccountButton);
    first.add(insertAccountButton);
    first.add(deleteAccountButton);
    first.add(updateAccountButton);

    accountIDText = new JTextField(15);
    usernameText = new JTextField(15);
    passwordText = new JTextField(15);
    tsText = new JTextField(15);
    activeTSText = new JTextField(15);
    errorText = new JTextArea(5, 15);
    errorText.setEditable(false);

    JPanel second = new JPanel();
    second.setLayout(new GridLayout(6,1));
    second.add(accountIDText);
    second.add(usernameText);
    second.add(passwordText);
    second.add(tsText);
    second.add(activeTSText);

    JPanel third = new JPanel();
    third.add(new JScrollPane(errorText));

    JPanel fourth = new JPanel();
    fourth.add(firstButton);
    fourth.add(previousButton);
    fourth.add(nextButton);
    fourth.add(lastButton);
    fourth.add(gotoText);
    fourth.add(gotoButton);


    JPanel fifth = new JPanel();
    fifth.add(freeQueryText);

    c.add(first);
    c.add(second);
    c.add(third);
    c.add(fourth);
    c.add(fifth);
    c.add(freeQueryButton);
    setSize(500,500);
    show();
  }
```

Listing 5.7 Our navigatable ResultSet. (continues)

```
  public void connectToDB() {
    try {
      connection = DriverManager.getConnection(
        "jdbc:mysql://localhost/accounts");
      statement = connection.createStatement();
      statement.setMaxRows(5);
      statement.setFetchSize(2);
    } catch(SQLException connectException) {
      System.out.println(connectException.getMessage());
      System.out.println(connectException.getSQLState());
      System.out.println(connectException.getErrorCode());
      System.exit(1);
    }
   }

  private void displaySQLErrors(SQLException e) {
    errorText.append("SQLException: " + e.getMessage() + "\n");
    errorText.append("SQLState:     " + e.getSQLState() + "\n");
    errorText.append("VendorError:  " + e.getErrorCode()
      + "\n");
  }

  private void init() {
    connectToDB();
  }

  public static void main(String[] args) {
     Accounts accounts = new Accounts();

     accounts.addWindowListener(
       new WindowAdapter() {
         public void windowClosing(WindowEvent e) {
           System.exit(0);
         }
       }
     );

     accounts.init();
     accounts.buildGUI();
  }
}
```

Listing 5.7 Our navigatable ResultSet. (continued)

Figure 5.12 shows an example of the new GUI for our application. At the bottom of the GUI are four buttons for moving through records in the ResultSet and displaying the appropriate text in the text fields. There is also a text field/Goto button combination for entering an absolute row value and allowing the user to click the Goto button and display the absolute row. Finally, there is a text field for a freehand query and a related button to execute the query in the line. Errors will be displayed in the error text area.

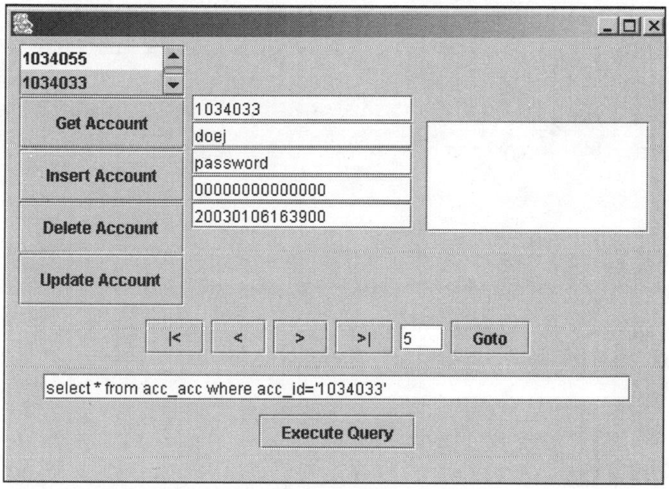

Figure 5.12 The new GUI for our application.

In order to implement this GUI, we changed the loadAccounts() method so that a global Statement and ResultSet object is created. When the loadAccounts() method is called, instead of just pulling the account number from the database we pull all of the fields. That way, we have access to the entire result within the application. By keeping the ResultSet local to the object, we ensure that all of the buttons will have access to it.

All of the buttons and text fields are created and added to the GUI using two additional panels. We explain the code for each button next.

One Step Forward

When the user clicks on the forward button on the GUI, the system executes the following code:

```
if (!rs.isLast()) {
 rs.next();
 accountIDText.setText(rs.getString("acc_id"));
```

```
    usernameText.setText(rs.getString("username"));
    passwordText.setText(rs.getString("password"));
    tsText.setText(rs.getString("ts"));
    activeTSText.setText(rs.getString("act_ts"));
  }
```

At this point, loadAccount() is called. This method obtains the next row in the ResultSet and displays it in the text fields—we hope without any errors occurring. To obtain the next row in the set, the next() method is called to move the internal pointer forward. However, we don't want to do this if the internal pointer is currently sitting on the last row of the set. That is the reason we have the if(!rs.isLast()) condition in the code. We can move the internal pointer forward as long as we aren't on the last row. After the internal pointer is moved forward, the information in the current row is displayed.

One Step Back

The back button should move the internal pointer to the previous row in the ResultSet and display the current information. Instead of using isLast(), the code uses a condition like if (!isFirst()) to make sure that the pointer isn't sitting on the first row.

Fast-Forward to the End

If we want to move the end of the rows, we click on the >| button. There isn't any checking involved here—just a call to rs.last() and code that displays the values in the row. In a production system, though, we would need to check whether the ResultSet object was empty.

Rewind to the Beginning

We can easily move to the beginning of the ResultSet by clicking on the |< button. The code will execute a rs.first() method and display the current row values.

Goto Record

We might also want to provide our users with the ability to jump to a specific record. This is done with the absolute() method associated with the ResultSet object. When the user clicks on the Goto button, the code pulls the current text in the text field next to the button. The String value from the text field is converted to an integer and used in the rs.absolute() method call. If an error doesn't occur, the values in the current row are displayed. All sorts of error detection must take place in the code for this type of functionality so that the user enters a proper value.

Freehand Query

Finally, we've added a large JTextField control that allows the user to type in a freehand query statement and execute it by clicking on the Execute Query button. The current code is actually somewhat smart in that will try to determine whether the query is a SELECT command or some other type. If the command is a SELECT, the String in the JTextField is used in an executeQuery() method call and a ResultSet object is returned. Otherwise, an executeUpdate() method call is made and the total number of rows affected is displayed in the error text area.

Obviously, giving a user this kind of power could backfire. Users could execute the DROP TABLE acc_acc command and wipe out all of the account number records. Or they could build new tables and all sorts of other "bad" things.

Batches

A new feature in the JDBC specification is the use of batches. The idea is to provide a mechanism where a large number of updates can be performed in a group with the hopes of better performance from the driver and database server. The Statement class offers the following methods that support batches:

- **oid clearBatch()**—Clears the current batch queue.
- **void addBatch(String SQL)**—Adds the SQL string to the batch queue.
- **int[] executeBatch()**—Executes the batch queue.

Batching works by creating a Statement object and adding SQL to the batch queue. In most cases, the batched queries will be inserts and updates. For example:

```
Statement statement = connection.createStatement();
statement.addBatch("UPDATE acc_acc SET acc_id = 10394443
  where  acc_id = 1034034");
statement.addBatch("UPDATE acc_acc SET password = 'password'");
statement.addBatch("INSERT INTO acc_acc VALUES(1034009,
  'newuser', 'password', 0, now()");
```

Once all of the updates have been batched together, they can be executed with a single statement:

```
int[] results = statement.executeBatch()
```

The Connector/J driver will execute each of the updates in the batch regardless of whether or not the previous update was successful. One of the keys to the batch update is the integer array returned as a result. If all of the updates are successful, the array will include the count of affected rows for each of the updates in the same order they were added to the batch queue.

If the row value in the result array is 0 or greater, then the update was successfully executed. However, a value of 0 probably means the update didn't do anything to the database. A value of SUCCESS_NO_INFO means that the update was successfully executed but that the server was unable to determine the total number of rows affected. A value of EXECUTE_FAILED means that the MySQL server rejected the query or that the query failed during execution.

In addition to the result array, the executeBatch() method will throw the BatchUpdateException exception if any of the queries fail. The exception won't be thrown, though, until all of the batched queries have had a chance to execute. Once the batch has been executed, it is a good idea to call statement.clearBatch() before adding more updates to the queue.

Limiting Results

The Statement object contains several methods for controlling the total number of results to be returned from a query against the database. Two of the methods are

```
setMaxRows()
setFetchSize()
```

The setMaxRows() method will specify the total number of rows that can be returned from a single query against a database. The default value is 0, meaning the driver should return as many rows as possible based on the supplied query. If you don't want the driver to return all of the possible rows at once, you might use the setFetchSize() method to limit the number of rows the driver will pull at a time. However, Connector/J doesn't support the use of the setFetchSize() method, nor does it support pulling subsets of data from the database. Connector/J will always retrieve all possible rows from the MySQL database when a query is executed. This behavior is based on the mechanism of the MySQL database server itself and isn't limited by the driver.

The idea behind the fetch size is to allow an application to execute a query against the database and process smaller subsets of data at a time. If there are 2 million rows in a result, the application might want to process only 1000 at a time. The driver would theoretically pull the first 1000 rows and when the application tried to access row 1001, the driver would automatically go back to the database for the additional rows.

When this feature of the specification comes up, the first question is usually "Why would you be returning a 2 million row result in the first place?" At this point, two options can be floated as alternatives. The first is to use the LIMIT clause available in the SELECT command. Not only can you limit the number of rows returned, but you can also specify an offset so you get rows 1 through 1000, then 1001 through 2000, and so on. The MySQL database server can optimize the use of the LIMIT clause for better performance.

The second option is to build a small class that will keep track of the LIMIT clause for you and just return ResultSets in the new ranges when a method like getNextSet() is called.

Database Warnings and Exceptions

In all of the code we have created up to this point, we have included try/catch blocks to handle any SQLException exceptions that are thrown by Connector/J in response to a database error. When an exception is thrown, the developer knows that a major error has occurred on the database, a connection, or a resultset. Additional information can be gathered from the database and Connector/J components known as *warnings*. A warning is an error but is not substantial enough to trigger an exception. An example would be the loss of precision when pulling a value that is a MySQL type and converting it to a Java type.

Warnings are provided by the Connection, ResultSet, and Statement objects but aren't "thrown" automatically. The warnings are kept in a queue, and the queue is cleared using this method:

```
void clearWarnings()
```

If your application wants to keep track of or deal with all exceptions and warnings, the clearWarnings() method should be used before any work is done with any of the three object types mentioned previously. After the operation occurs—such as ResultSet rs = statement.executeQuery();—the getWarnings() method is called on the Statement object to see if any warnings were produced when the executeQuery() method was executed. The format of the getWarnings() method is as follows:

```
public SQLWarning getWarnings()
```

A return value of null indicates there are no more warnings. Once a SQLWarning method has been obtained, the following methods can be used to display its contents. Notice that the methods are the same ones used in a SQLException. The reason is the SQLWarning is a derived class from SQLException.

```
String getMessage();
String getSQLState();
int getErrorCode();
```

Since SQLWarnings are chained together, use the following code to get the next warning in the chain:

```
SQLWarning warning = statement.getWarnings();
SQLWarning nextWarning = warning.getNextWarning();
```

What's Next

In this chapter, we covered the basic Connector/J functionality. We showed you how to use the various Connector/J methods from both Java applications and applets. In the next chapter, we expand our Connector/J coverage to the more complex functionality, such as using PreparedStatements, manipulating time/date data types, and creating updatable ResultSets.

CHAPTER 6

Achieving Advanced Connector/J Functionality with Servlets

In the previous chapter, we looked at using Connector/J, MySQL, and Java applications to access data from a database. Users of these applications typically access the program from their desktop. If you are designing a Web-based application with Java, either you are developing an Enterprise JavaBeans (EJB) system (which we discuss in Chapter 11, "EJBs with MySQL"), or you are using a servlet or a Java ServerPage (JSP). In this chapter, we explore how to access the database from both a servlet and a JSP page. To demonstrate how to use a servlet, we develop an application for including fingerprint images into the account application from the previous chapter. We also create a servlet and associated HTML for viewing the images from the Web.

Servlets

Building servlets is one of the most powerful uses of Java in the Internet arena. Servlets are basically server-side components that can be executed by browsing to them, calling them in an HTML form, or including them in a JSP page. Since the components execute on the server and are written in Java, they make great candidates for database access. Listing 6.1 shows a generic servlet that has the ability to access a MySQL database using the Connector/J driver. Unlike with an applet, we are able to produce HTML for clients without requiring them to have the driver on their local machine.

```
import java.io.*;
import java.sql.*;
import javax.servlet.*;
import javax.servlet.http.*;

public class JDBCServlet extends HttpServlet {

  public void doGet(HttpServletRequest inRequest,
    HttpServletResponse outResponse)
    throws ServletException, IOException {

    PrintWriter out = null;
    Connection connection = null;
    Statement statement;
    ResultSet rs;

    outResponse.setContentType("text/html");
    out = outResponse.getWriter();

    try {
      Class.forName("com.mysql.jdbc.Driver");

      connection = DriverManager.getConnection(
        "jdbc:mysql://localhost/acc_id");
      statement = connection.createStatement();

      rs = statement.executeQuery(
        "SELECT acc_id FROM acc_acc");

      out.println(
        "<HTML><HEAD><TITLE>Account Numbers</TITLE></HEAD>");
      out.println("<BODY>");
      out.println("<UL>");

      while (rs.next()) {
        out.println("<LI>" + rs.getString("acc_id"));
      }

      out.println("</UL>");
      out.println("</BODY></HTML>");

      rs.close();
      statement.close();
      connection.close();
    }
    catch(ClassNotFoundException e) {
```

Listing 6.1 Our basic servlet/JDBC code. (continues)

```
      out.println("Driver Error"); }
    catch(SQLException e) {
      out.println("SQLException: " + e.getMessage());
    }
  }

  public void doPost(HttpServletRequest inRequest,
    HttpServletResponse outResponse)
    throws ServletException, IOException {
    doGet(inRequest, outResponse);
  }
}
```

Listing 6.1 Our basic servlet/JDBC code. (continued)

When building servlets, you have to follow a specific format defined in the Java specification. The servlet class will extend HTTPServlet and more than likely will have two methods, called doGet() and doPost(). These methods handle the GET and POST HTTP message types. It is common practice to implement the doGet() method and have doPost() call doGet() so they will be handling the same data.

The servlet code within doGet() begins by setting the response type to text/html, which lets the client browser know that the information passed from the servlet should be rendered using an HTML processor. The servlet could return a different type of format if needed.

Next we enter a try/catch block and start the process of connecting to the database and obtaining data to return to the user. Since a servlet is a Java process, we need Connector/J loaded so that we have the driver necessary for accessing MySQL. The servlet uses the Class.forName() method to load the driver (just as all of the applications did in the previous chapter). Notice however, that the NewInstance() method isn't called on the driver once it's loaded. The servlet performs this operation itself.

After the driver is loaded, all of the code to obtain information from the database is the same as we saw in the previous chapter. A Connection object is instantiated from the DriverManager, a Statement object is created from the Connection object, and finally, a ResultSet object is built when the executeQuery() method is executed against the Statement object. When this process completes, a loop is used to move through the ResultSet and builds an HTML document for passing to the client browser. Lastly, all of the pieces in the process are closed and the HTML is passed to the browser.

NOTE

The code used to obtain database results within the servlet is exactly the same as the code used in a Java application or applet. Therefore, you'll find it easy to build Java and MySQL applications.

DataSource Connections

When using Java servlets and eventually beans, you have an alternative way of obtaining information about the connection to the MySQL database. The alternative is to use a DataSource and Java Naming and Directory Interface (JNDI). JNDI provides a way to set specific physical database information on the application server instead of placing the information directly in the application. The application in Listing 6.1 obtains a connection to the database server with this code:

```
Class.forName("com.mysql.jdbc.Driver");
connection = DriverManager.getConnection(
        "jdbc:mysql://localhost/acc_id");
statement = connection.createStatement();
```

As you can see, the application is very specific about the database to be accessed. With JNDI, we place information about the database connection into the application server's configuration file. For example:

```
<resource-ref>
  <res-ref-name>jdbc/AccountsDB</res-ref-name>
  <res-type>javax.sql.DataSource</res-type>
  <init-param driver-name="com.mysql.jdbc.Driver"/>
  <init-param url="jdbc:mysql://192.168.1.25/accounts"/>
  <init-param user="spider"/>
  <init-param password="spider"/>
  <init-param max-connections="20"/>
  <init-param max-idle-time="30"/>
</resource-ref>
```

This information begins with the name of the resource, jdbc/AccountsDB; the class to use when the resource is needed, DataSource; the driver name; the URL for locating the database; and then some information about the parameters to be passed to the driver when it is instantiated. To obtain this connection information from an application, replace the previous connection statements with the following:

```
Context ctx = new InitialContext();
DataSource ds = (DataSource)ctx.lookup("java:comp/env/jdbc/AccountsDB");
connection = ds.getConnection();
```

This code begins by getting the configuration context surrounding this application. Next, the resource reference name is looked up in the context. Finally, a connection is instantiated from the DataSource object returned from the context lookup. At this point, all the code to obtain Statement objects and execute queries is the same.

Execution Environment

So how do you actually execute the servlet code? You will need to have an application server available on which you will put the servlet source code. Numerous servers are available, including Resin, Tomcat, and BOSS, among others. In this chapter, we execute all of the examples using the Resin application server.

Databases

This chapter goes beyond the basics of using Connector/J with MySQL. Therefore, we need to add another database and table to our growing database system. We assume that you have created the databases in the previous chapter. Our new database is called identification, and you build it with this command:

```
create database identification;
```

The schema for a table called thumbnail is as follows:

thumb_id – int—A unique record indicator for the table.

acc_id – int—A foreign key for the acc_acc table.

pic – blob—Represents the binary data for a fingerprint.

sysobject – blob—A serialized Java object for a fingerprint.

ts – timestamp—The timestamp value; 0 indicates current.

acc_ts – timestamp—The last update time.

Build the table with this command:

```
create table thumbnail (
thumb_id int not null,
acc_id int not null,
pic blob,
sysobject blob,
ts timestamp,
act_ts timestamp,
primary key(thumb_id, acc_id, ts));
```

You can download the sample database code from the book's Web site at http://wiley.com/gradecki/mysqljava.

PreparedStatements

As you know from reading the chapter introduction, one of the applications we want to build is a servlet/HTML combination that will allow a remote user to obtain information from the database for each of the accounts in our database. Our code should display all of the account information from the acc_acc table as well as from the acc_add table. Eventually, we plan to tie in the new thumbnail table we just created. In order to use the new application, users will need to use a browser and browse to an initial HTML page, where they will be prompted to enter an account number and click on a submit button. Then, a servlet will be contacted and used to obtain results from the database and will return the results to the client browser. Figure 6.1 shows what we are talking about. After looking at Figure 6.1, scan through the code in Listings 6.2 and 6.3 to see an example of what the code looks like.

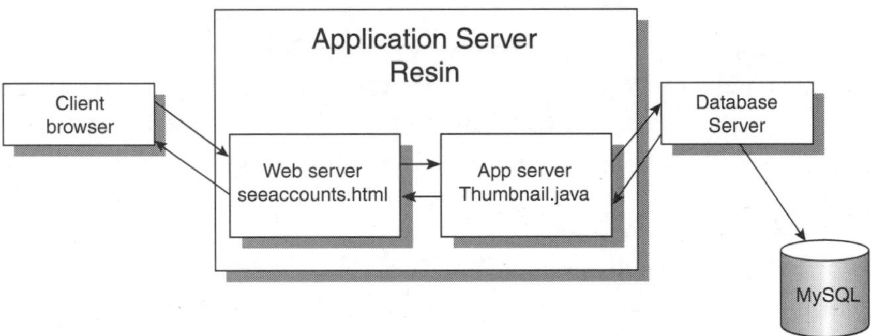

Figure 6.1 Our servlet/HTML.

```
<HTML>
<BODY>
<TITLE>See Account Information</TITLE>
Enter account number to view:<BR>
<form
  action="http://localhost:8080/ca/SeeAccount"
  method="post">
  <input name="account">
  <input type="submit" name="submit" value="submit">
</form>
</BODY>
</HTML>
```

Listing 6.2 Our example HTML.

```
import java.io.*;
import java.sql.*;
import javax.servlet.*;
import javax.servlet.http.*;

public class SeeAccount extends HttpServlet {

  public void doGet(HttpServletRequest inRequest,
    HttpServletResponse outResponse)
    throws ServletException, IOException {

    PrintWriter out = null;
    Connection connection = null;
    PreparedStatement statement = null;
    ResultSet rs,
              rs2;

    try {
      outResponse.setContentType("text/html");
      out = outResponse.getWriter();

      Class.forName("com.mysql.jdbc.Driver");
      connection = DriverManager.getConnection(
       "jdbc:mysql://localhost/accounts");

      if (connection != null) {
       if (inRequest.getParameter("submit").equals("submit")) {
          statement = connection.prepareStatement(
            "SELECT * FROM acc_acc " +
            "LEFT JOIN acc_add " +
            "on acc_acc.acc_id = acc_add.acc_id " +
            "WHERE acc_acc.acc_id = ? AND acc_acc.ts = 0");
          if (statement != null) {
            statement.setInt(1, Integer.parseInt(
              inRequest.getParameter("account")));
            rs = statement.executeQuery();

            if (!rs.next()) {
              out.println("<HTML>No Account Found for # " +
                inRequest.getParameter("account") + "</HTML>");
            } else {
              out.println("<HTML><HEAD><TITLE>Thumbnail
                Identification Record</TITLE></HEAD>");
              out.println("<BODY>");
              out.println("Account Information:<BR>");
              out.println("<table>");
              out.println("<form method='UpdateAccount'
```

Listing 6.3 Our servlet example for PreparedStatements. (continues)

```
          method='post'>");
        out.println("<tr><td>");
        out.println("Account: <input name='acc_id'
          value='" + rs.getString("acc_acc.acc_id") +
          "'><BR>");
        out.println("Name: <input name='username'
          value='" + rs.getString("acc_acc.username") +
          "'><BR>");
        out.println("Address1: <input name='address1'
          value='" + rs.getString("acc_add.address1") +
          "'><BR>");
        out.println("Address2: <input name='address2'
          value='" + rs.getString("acc_add.address2") +
          "'><BR>");
        out.println("Address3: <input name='address3'
          value='" + rs.getString("acc_add.address3") +
          "'><BR>");
        out.println("City: <input name='city' value='" +
          rs.getString("acc_add.city") + "'><BR>");
        out.println("State: <input name='state' value='"
          + rs.getString("acc_add.state") + "'><BR>");
        out.println("Zip: <input name='zip' value='" +
          rs.getString("acc_add.zip") + "'><BR>");
        out.println("<input type='submit' value='update'
          name='submit'>");
        out.println("</form>");
        out.println("</td>");
        out.println("<td>thumbnail");
        out.println("</td></tr>");
        out.println("</table>");
        out.println("</BODY></HTML>");
      }
    } else {
        out.println("<HTML>Statement is NULL</HTML>");
    }
  } else {
    //do update
    statement = connection.prepareStatement(
      "UPDATE accounts.acc_acc SET username = ?
      WHERE accounts.acc_acc.acc_id = ?");
    statement.setString(1, inRequest.getParameter(
      "username"));
    statement.setInt(2, Integer.parseInt(
      inRequest.getParameter("acc_id")));
    int i = statement.executeUpdate();

    statement = connection.prepareStatement("UPDATE
      accounts.acc_add SET address1=?, address2=?, " +
```

Listing 6.3 Our servlet example for PreparedStatements. (continues)

```
            "address3=?, city=?, state=?, zip=? WHERE
            accounts.acc_add.acc_id = ?");

          statement.setString(1, inRequest.getParameter(
            "address1"));
          statement.setString(2, inRequest.getParameter(
            "address2"));
          statement.setString(3, inRequest.getParameter(
            "address3"));
          statement.setString(4, inRequest.getParameter(
            "city"));
          statement.setString(5, inRequest.getParameter(
            "state"));
          statement.setString(6, inRequest.getParameter(
            "zip"));
          statement.setInt(7, Integer.parseInt(
            inRequest.getParameter("acc_id")));
          int j = statement.executeUpdate();

          out.println("<HTML>");
          out.println("Update to acc_acc = " + i + "<BR>");
          out.println("Update to acc_add = " + j + "<BR>");
          out.println("</HTML>");
        }
      } else {
          out.println("<HTML>Connection is NULL</HTML>");
      }
    }
    catch(ClassNotFoundException e) {
      out.println("Driver Error");
    }
    catch(SQLException e) {
      out.println("<HTML>");
      out.println("SQLException: " + e.getMessage());
      out.println("</HTML>");
    }
    catch(Exception e) {
      e.printStackTrace();
    }
  }

  public void doPost(HttpServletRequest inRequest,
    HttpServletResponse outResponse)
    throws ServletException, IOException {
     doGet(inRequest, outResponse);
  }
}
```

Listing 6.3 Our servlet example for PreparedStatements. (continued)

Our example code in Listing 6.2 shows the HTML that the client browser will initially connect with to see an account. The result of the HTML on the client browser is shown in Figure 6.2. When the user puts an account number in the form input line and clicks on the submit button, the servlet in Listing 6.3 is activated and the information shown in Figure 6.3 is returned to the user. In addition to allowing the user to see the information in the database, the code lets the user change the information. After putting in new information using the edit lines displayed in Figure 6.3, the user clicks on the update button. The same servlet in Listing 6.3 is called, and the different code is executed to update both the acc_acc and acc_add tables. Figure 6.4 shows the output when the tables are successfully updated.

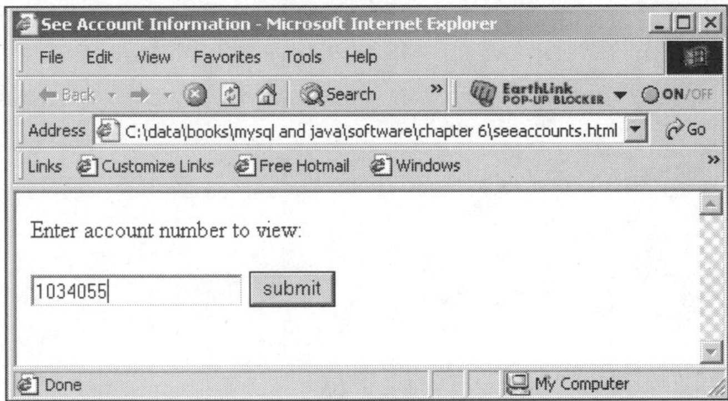

Figure 6.2 Our initial HTML Web page.

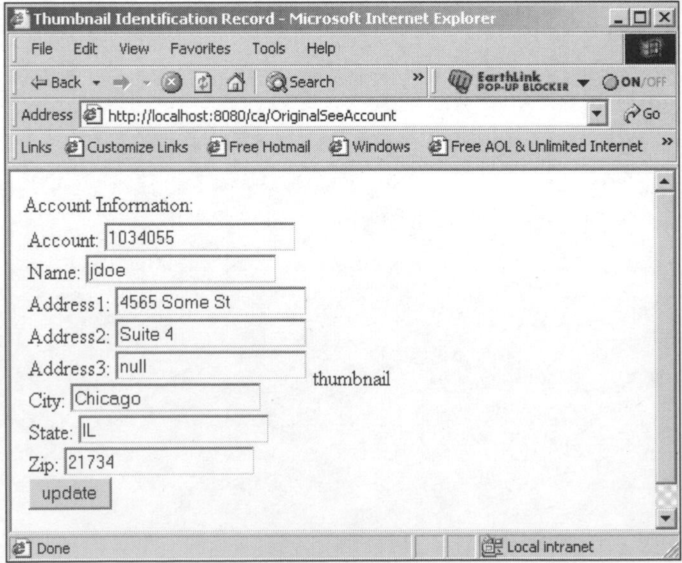

Figure 6.3 Information is returned from our database.

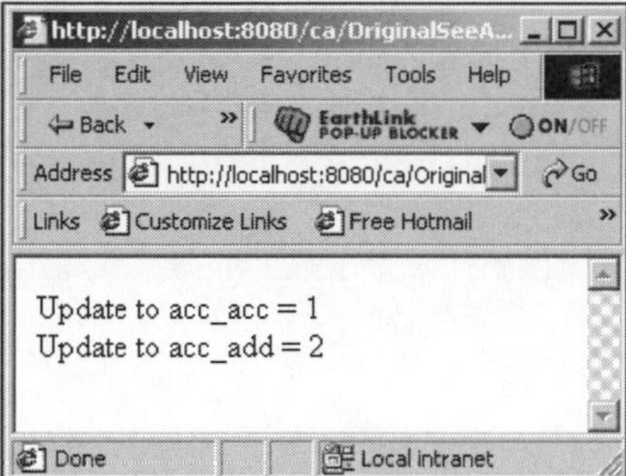

Figure 6.4 The update was successful.

Connecting to the Database

Look at Figures 6.3 and 6.4 carefully, and you will notice that we need to get information from both the acc_acc and acc_add tables in order to present the necessary information on the return HTML page. Fortunately, both of those tables are defined within the accounts database on our MySQL server. So we will be connecting to the server and changing or USEing the accounts database. The full connection code is found in two statements:

```
Class.forName("com.mysql.jdbc.Driver");
connection = DriverManager.getConnection(
 "jdbc:mysql://localhost/accounts");
```

Determining the Submit Type

After the connection to the database is made, we need to determine what the user wants our servlet to be doing. As we mentioned previously, the servlet will be able to display the information from a specific account as well as update the information changed by the user. If users want to see account information, they click on the submit button when the HTML from Listing 6.2 is displayed. Looking back at that HTML, you see the following tag:

```
<input type="submit" name="submit" value="submit">
```

This tag will display the submit button, name it submit, and provide a value of submit when it is clicked. Now let's skip ahead in our servlet code and pull out the following code:

```
out.println("<input type='submit' value='update' name='submit'>");
```

The servlet displays all of the account information within a form that allows the user to change the information. At the bottom of the form is a submit button, but this button displays a value of *update* when it is clicked. Our servlet can use this information to determine what it is supposed to be doing.

The following line of code makes the determination:

```
if (inRequest.getParameter("submit").equals("submit")) {
```

After a connection to the database is made and the connection is valid, the servlet executes this line of code. The parameter called submit relates to either button displayed to the user: the first submit button for getting the account information or the submit button for updating the information. The value of the submit parameter is compared to the text "submit". If a match is made, the code after the IF statement is executed; otherwise, the code after an ELSE is executed.

Displaying Data

The code just after the IF statement displayed in the previous section handles all of the tasks necessary to display the account information to the user. The code begins by creating a new type of statement called a PreparedStatement. As you might have guessed, when we access the MySQL database for the account information, we are going to limit the data returned using the account number entered by the user. We need a WHERE clause like this:

```
WHERE acc_id = 1034055 and ts = 0
```

This WHERE clause will cause the database server to return information for records only in which the acc_id is 1034055 and the ts field is 0. In the previous chapter, we built this WHERE clause using code like this:

```
"WHERE acc_id = " + <somevariable> + " and ts = 0"
```

While this works, there will be cases later in this chapter where we want to insert binary data into the query for updating. SQL, Connector/J, and MySQL all support a Statement object called PreparedStatement. This statement gives us the ability to use placeholders within the query and replace them with actual values using statements that place the data into the query in the proper format. For example, our WHERE clause could be written as follows:

```
"WHERE acc_id = ? and ts = 0"
```

The ? character is the placeholder and is counted as placeholder number 1. Before showing you how to use the PreparedStatement, let's create an object of its type first. The code in our servlet is

```
statement = connection.prepareStatement(
"SELECT *
FROM acc_acc
LEFT JOIN acc_add
  on acc_acc.acc_id = acc_add.acc_id
WHERE acc_acc.acc_id = ? AND acc_acc.ts = 0");
```

Notice that there is a join in this code; we ignore that fact until the "Joins" section later in this chapter. A PreparedStatement is created using the Connection object and a call to the method prepareStatement(String). Unlike with the

Statement object, we place our query into the call to prepareStatement using the ? placeholder in all of the places we need to fill with data at a later point. The query can contain any number of placeholders, and they are counted with the leftmost placeholder having a value of 1.

Once the PreparedStatement has been allocated, it's time to fill in the accounts number. We accomplish this with the following code:

```
statement.setInt(1,
Integer.parseInt(inRequest.getParameter("account")));
```

The JDBC specification defines a large set of set<type> methods against a PreparedStatement object to fill all of the placeholders. In the statement above, the method fills the first placeholder with the integer value associated with the account parameter returned from the <form> HTML found in Listing 6.2. Using the placeholders means that we needn't concern ourselves with creating a large query string using smaller strings. In addition, we don't need to worry about formatting the actual value being passed to the database server.

Once all of the parameters have been filled, the query is executed with the code

```
rs = statement.executeQuery();
```

Once the query returns the ResultSet, we need to build the HTML that will be passed back to the client browser as a result of its initial request. Earlier in the servlet code, a call was made to obtain a PrintWriter object:

```
out = outResponse.getWriter();
```

The PrintWriter object is directly associated with the Response object passed back to the client browser. Anything that we write in the PrintWriter object will be passed back to the browser. Since we have already told the system that the response will be HTML, we need to put HTML tags into the object.

The first code we encounter after the ResultSet is obtained from our query is a check to ensure that there are results from the query. The code looks like this:

```
if (!rs.next()) {
  out.println("<HTML>No Account Found for # " +
    inRequest.getParameter("account") + "</HTML>");
} else {
```

Because we need to move to the next row in the ResultSet, we check the return value of a call to rs.next(). If the command is successful, then we know there was at least one result in the set (we don't handle multiple rows in this example code). Otherwise, the account wasn't in the database, so we return a small HTML page to the client to let them know the account wasn't found.

If the account was found, we start the process of building the HTML page found in Figure 6.3. The HTML page consists of a little text and a <FORM> with the account information. Refer to Listing 6.3 for all of the HTML passed to the client to build the page. All of the values returned from the ResultSet are obtained with the familiar rs.getString() method and used to build the various tags necessary for the client. Once the HTML is created, the page is automatically returned to the client's browser by the servlet. Once the page is displayed, the user can review the information and possibly change it.

Updating Data

If the user finds information that is wrong for the displayed account, he or she can make changes right in the Web form returned from the servlet. As Figure 6.3 shows, users can click on the update button when they have finished making necessary changes. When the button is clicked, the action associated with the form is triggered and our servlet is called again. This time, the condition that determines which button was clicked evaluates to false and the ELSE code executes.

The real power of PreparedStatement objects is found within the code that updates the database. When you're updating the database, your first step is to build the UPDATE query using a PreparedStatement. In our code there are two updates: one to the acc_acc table and another to the acc_add table. The code to update acc_acc is as follows:

```
statement = connection.prepareStatement(
"UPDATE acc_acc
SET username = ?
WHERE acc_acc.acc_id = ?");

statement.setString(1, inRequest.getParameter("username"));
statement.setInt(2, Integer.parseInt(
inRequest.getParameter("acc_id")));

int i = statement.executeUpdate();
```

The code starts with building the actual PreparedStatement object and putting the necessary placeholders into the query. As you can see, the UPDATE to acc_acc includes two placeholders. The first is the username, and the second is the account number we are updating. The setString(int, String) method pulls the username value from the <form> parameter called username and replaces the first placeholder with that value. The method replaces the second placeholder with the account number passed from the form as well. Then, a call is made to executeUpdate(). Our code records the return value from executeUpdate() in a variable for display to the client browser.

NOTE

Notice that our code calls executeQuery() when the PreparedStatement is using a SELECT; executeUpdate() is called when the PreparedStatement is using INSERT, UPDATE, or DELETE—just like when you're using a Statement object.

Here's the code for updating acc_add:

```
statement = connection.prepareStatement(
"UPDATE acc_add
SET address1=?, address2=?, address3=?,
city=?, state=?, zip=? WHERE acc_add.acc_id = ?");

statement.setString(1, inRequest.getParameter("address1"));
statement.setString(2, inRequest.getParameter("address2"));
statement.setString(3, inRequest.getParameter("address3"));
statement.setString(4, inRequest.getParameter("city"));
statement.setString(5, inRequest.getParameter("state"));
statement.setString(6, inRequest.getParameter("zip"));
statement.setInt(7, Integer.parseInt(inRequest.getParameter("acc_id")));

int j = statement.executeUpdate();
```

As you can see, this code is quite complex. It contains a total of seven placeholders. (See how much easier it is to include placeholders and to replace them accordingly compared with building a large string with "" and +.) We use setString() and setInt() methods to replace each of the values in the query with the actual values pulled from the <form> parameters.

Finally, the query is executed and the update count returned. Both of the update counts are displayed to users, letting them know the appropriate tables have been updated. Here's the code that accomplishes this:

```
out.println("<HTML>");
out.println("Update to acc_acc = " + i + "<BR>");
out.println("Update to acc_add = " + j + "<BR>");
out.println("</HTML>");
```

Using Placeholders in a Loop

Another benefit of using placeholders and a PreparedStatement object is the ability to perform a large number of updates through a loop. For example, let's assume we have an array filled with the account numbers for a particular update. Not all of the account numbers are represented in the array, so we cannot perform a mass update. Instead, we can use a loop and a PreparedStatement:

```
int updateCount = 0;
statement = connection.prepareStatement(
```

```
"UPDATE acc_acc
SET password='null'
WHERE ts = 0 and acc_id = ?");

for (int i=0;i<accounts.length;i++) {
 statement.setInt(accounts[i]);
 updateCount += statement.executeUpdate();
}
```

This code contains a PreparedStatement with an UPDATE statement that sets the password field to null. The UPDATE query uses a placeholder for the account number in the WHERE clause. If we have just three accounts to update, we wouldn't need a loop or even a PreparedStatement. However, if our account array holds 15,000 accounts, we have the perfect solution. Our code loops through all of the accounts in the array, places them in the statement, and executes it. When we are all done with the code, the updateCount variable should be the same as accounts.length.

Using Placeholders in PreparedStatement

The JDBC specification defines setter functions for replacing a placeholder in a PreparedStatement. It defines functions for all of the data types stored in database fields. The following is a list of those methods. (We note when a method is not implemented by Connector/J.)

void setArray(int i, java.sql.Array anArray)—Not implemented; sets an Array parameter.

void setBlob(int i, java.sql.Blob aBlob)—Sets a BLOB parameter.

void setCharacterStream(int parameterIndex, java.io.Reader reader, int length)—If the database type is a LONGVARCHAR and Data is Unicode, the amount of data will be very large, and using setCharacterStream() allows it to be stored properly.

void setClob(int i, java.sql.Clob aClob)—Sets a CLOB parameter.

void setDate(int parameterIndex, java.sql.Date ADate, java.util.Calendar Cal)—Sets a parameter to a java.sql.Date value.

void setNull(int parameterIndex, int sqlType, java.lang.String Arg)—Sets a parameter to SQL NULL.

void setRef(int i, java.sql.Ref aRef)—Not implemented; sets a REF parameter.

void setTime(int parameterIndex, java.sql.Time aTime, java.util.Calendar Cal)—Sets a parameter to a java.sql.Time value.

void setAsciiStream(int parameterIndex, java.io.InputStream aStream, int length)—If the database type is a LONGVARCHAR and the data is ASCII, the amount of data will be very large, and using setCharacter-Stream() allows it to be stored properly.

void setBigDecimal(int parameterIndex, java.math.BigDecimal aBD)—Sets a parameter to a java.lang.BigDecimal.

void setBinaryStream(int parameterIndex, java.io.InputStream X, int length)—If the database type is a LONGVARBINARY, the amount of data will be very large, and using setBinaryStream() allows it to be stored properly.

void setBoolean(int parameterIndex, boolean aBoolean)—Sets a parameter to a Java Boolean value.

void setByte(int parameterIndex, byte aByte)—Sets a parameter to a Java byte value.

void setBytes(int parameterIndex, byte[] aByteArray)—Sets a parameter to a Java array of bytes.

void setDate(int parameterIndex, java.sql.Date aDate)—Sets a parameter to a java.sql.Date.

void setDouble(int parameterIndex, double aDouble)—Sets a parameter to a Java double value.

void setFloat(int parameterIndex, float aFloat)—Sets a parameter to a Java float value.

void setInt(int parameterIndex, int anInt)—Sets a parameter to a Java int value.

void setLong(int parameterIndex, long aLong)—Sets a parameter to a Java long value.

void setNull(int parameterIndex, int sqlType)—Sets a parameter to SQL NULL.

void setObject(int parameterIndex, java.lang.Object anObject, int targetSqlType, int scale)—Sets the value of a parameter using an object.

void setObject(int parameterIndex, java.lang.Object anObject, int targetSqlType)—Sets the value of a parameter using an object.

void setObject(int parameterIndex, java.lang.Object anObject)—Sets the value of a parameter using an object.

void setShort(int parameterIndex, short aShort)—Sets a parameter to a Java short value.

void setString(int parameterIndex, java.lang.String aString)—Sets a parameter to a Java String value.

void setTime(int parameterIndex, java.sql.Time aTime)—Sets a parameter to a java.sql.Time.

void setTimestamp(int parameterIndex, java.sql.Timestamp aTS)—Sets a parameter to a java.sql.Timestamp.

void setTimestamp(int parameterIndex, java.sql.Timestamp aTS, java.util.Calendar Cal)—Sets a parameter to a java.sql.Timestamp value.

void setUnicodeStream(int parameterIndex, java.io.InputStream aStream, int length)—If the database type is a LONGVARVHAR, the amount of data will be very large, and using setUnicodeStream() allows it to be stored properly.

Using setObject/setBytes

Before we move away from the PreparedStatement object, let's look at using some of the getter methods with larger pieces of data than an integer. In this section, we examine both the setBytes() and setObject() methods. The code in Listing 6.4 implements a Java console application designed to import a fingerprint image into the identification.thumbnail database table. In addition, the code builds an ID object for use by other applications. The code for the ID class appears in Listing 6.5.

```
import java.sql.*;
import java.io.*;

public class Thumbnail {
  Connection connection;
  PreparedStatement statement;

  public Thumbnail() {
     try {
       Class.forName("com.mysql.jdbc.Driver").newInstance();
       connection = DriverManager.getConnection(
         "jdbc:mysql://localhost/identification");
     }
     catch (Exception  e) {
       System.err.println("Unable to find and load driver");
       System.exit(1);
     }
  }

  public void doWork(String[] args) {
```

Listing 6.4 Our update code with objects and bytes. (continues)

```
    try {
     File f = new File(args[2]);
     Byte[] bytes = new byte[(int)f.length()];

     FileInputStream fs = new FileInputStream(f);
     BufferedInputStream bis = new BufferedInputStream(fs);
     bis.read(bytes);

     ID id = new ID();
     id.nail_id = Integer.parseInt(args[0]);
     id.acc_id = Integer.parseInt(args[1]);

     statement = connection.prepareStatement(
       "INSERT INTO thumbnail VALUES(?,?,?,?, 0, now())");

     statement.setInt(1, id.nail_id);
     statement.setInt(2, id.acc_id);
     statement.setBytes(3, bytes);
     statement.setObject(4, id);

     int i = statement.executeUpdate();
     System.out.println("Rows updated = " + i);

     bis.close();
     fs.close();
     statement.close();
     connection.close();
    } catch(Exception e) {
      e.printStackTrace();
    }
  }

  public static void main(String[] args) {
    Thumbnail nail = new Thumbnail();
    nail.doWork(args);
  }
}
```

Listing 6.4 Our update code with objects and bytes. (continued)

```
import java.io.Serializable;

public class ID implements Serializable {

  public int nail_id;
  public int acc_id;
```

Listing 6.5 Our ID class code. (continues)

```
    public byte[] bytes;

    public ID() {
    }
}
```

Listing 6.5 Our ID class code. (continued)

If you look back at some of the earlier figures in this chapter, you will find there is a placeholder for a fingerprint graphic. In the servlet code, the text string "thumbnail" is output in the rightmost part of a table because our identification.thumbnail table didn't have any graphic data in it. The code in Listing 6.4 allows us to put a .jpg file into the table.

NOTE

There is some debate about whether binary data such as images should be stored in a database. Some believe that binary data should reside in a separate file and that the database should include only a link to that file. As with most computer science topics, it all depends on the application, so we won't get involved in the debate here.

Listing 6.4 is a command-line-based Java application that accepts three parameters, as in this example:

```
java Thumbnail 4001 1034033 nail1.jpg
```

The first parameter is the thumb_id value, the second is acc_id, and the third is the name of a binary file in the JPEG format. The code takes that file and places it in the thumbnail table using the associated thumb and account IDs. The heart of our code is found in the doWork() method.

The code begins by creating a File object associated with the filename. If the file isn't found, an exception is thrown. Next, our code creates a byte array based on the full size of the file found on the local hard drive. To bring in the contents of the file, a FileInputStream is associated with a BufferedInputStream. The read() method is called and the contents of the file are loaded into the byte array.

In the same example, we illustrate how to use the setObject() method, so we need to instantiate a new object based on the ID class found in Listing 6.5. The nail_id and acc_id methods are populated with the thumb_id and acc_id values passed in from the command line. A PreparedStatement object is created based on the INSERT query statement needed to put data into the table. Here is the statement:

```
statement = connection.prepareStatement(
"INSERT INTO thumbnail VALUES(?,?,?,?, 0, now())");
```

Notice there are four placeholders. The placeholders are replaced with our data using these commands:

```
statement.setInt(1, id.nail_id);
statement.setInt(2, id.acc_id);
statement.setBytes(3, bytes);
statement.setObject(4, id);
```

You've already seen the first two commands, but setBytes() and setObject() are new. You typically use the setBytes() method when you've defined a BLOB data type for a table field. The code behind setBytes() properly prepares the bytes of information for insertion into the table.

The goal of the setObject() method is the serialization of an object for insertion into the database. In order for the method to work properly, the object to be stored must be based on a class that implements serialization, as does the ID class shown in Listing 6.5. An application that wants to use the object can retrieve it using getObject() and cast it to the proper class type.

After all of the data has been inserted into the PreparedStatement object, the executeUpdate() method is called, and the fingerprint and its associated object are stored in the database for later retrieval.

Getting BLOBs

Now that we have a fingerprint in our database, we need to remove it and allow the user to see it along with all of the account information. Add the following code to the servlet just before the code that builds the reply HTML for a submit request:

```
statement2 = connection.prepareStatement(
"SELECT pic
INTO DUMPFILE 'nail" + inRequest.getParameter("account")
+ ".jpg' FROM identification.thumbnail WHERE acc_id = "
+ inRequest.getParameter("account"));
```

This code will SELECT the pic columns from the identification.thumbnail table and dump the contents to a file (with a name like nail1034033.jpg) on the database server. By adding the following code to the HTML, we ensure that the user sees the contents of the file from the database rather than the work thumbnail:

```
out.println("<td><img src='../images/nail"
  + inRequest.getParameter("account") + ".jpg'>");
```

The HTML code uses the <img src> tag to locate the file and display its contents on the client's browser. However, if your database server isn't on the same machine as your Web or application server, this won't work. This is because the database server is typically hidden from the client, which means the client won't be able to "link" to the file dumped from the database.

The solution is to remove the earlier statement and replace it with this:

```
FileOutputStream fo = new FileOutputStream("./doc/images/nail"
+ inRequest.getParameter("account") + ".jpg");

BufferedOutputStream bos = new BufferedOutputStream(fo);
bos.write(rs.getBytes("thumbnail.pic"));
bos.close();
```

This code creates a FileOutputStream object and opens a file on the Web server using the nail<account number>.jpg format. This file will be visible to the client browser. Next, our code builds a BufferOutputStream to stream the bytes from the code rs.getBytes("thumbnail.pic") to the file. The getBytes() method pulls the fingerprint JPEG file from the database in the same manner that setBytes() replaced the file in the database. If you look back at our original query for the servlet, you can see that we don't pull any data from the identification.thumbnail database table, so we have to change the query. The new query is as follows:

```
statement = connection.prepareStatement(
"SELECT *, thumbnail.pic
FROM accounts.acc_acc " + "LEFT JOIN accounts.acc_add
on accounts.acc_acc.acc_id = accounts.acc_add.acc_id "
+ "LEFT JOIN identification.thumbnail on
accounts.acc_acc.acc_id = identification.thumbnail.acc_id "
+ "WHERE accounts.acc_acc.acc_id = ?
AND accounts.acc_acc.ts = 0");
```

Our new query pulls data from the acc_acc, acc_add, and thumbnail tables using a join (which we discuss in the next section). Once all of the data is present, the code places a fingerprint file on the Web server and builds an appropriate <img src> tag for viewing the file. We've shown the result in Figure 6.5.

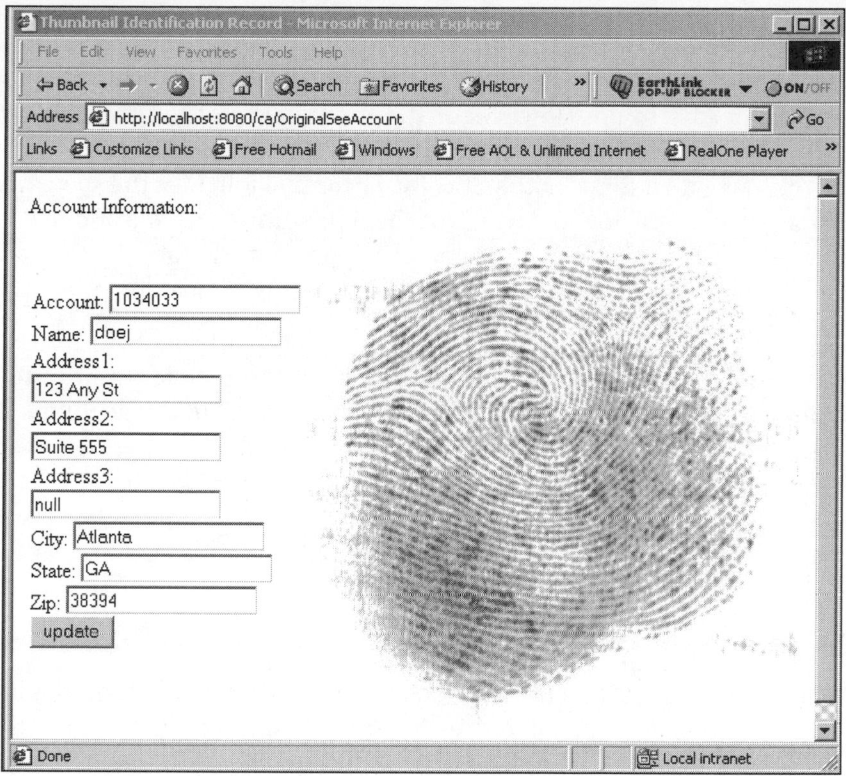

Figure 6.5 Full Identification Information for an Account.

Joins

In our original servlet code earlier in this chapter, we included a SELECT query that used a join to find data in both the acc_acc and acc_add tables. The query was:

```
SELECT * FROM acc_acc

LEFT JOIN acc_add on acc_acc.acc_id = acc_add.acc_id

WHERE acc_acc.acc_id = ? AND acc_acc.ts = 0
```

To enable our users to view information from a specific account, we need to do several things. First we must make sure that the account exists in acc_acc, the primary account table. We accomplish this with the following query:

```
SELECT * FROM acc_acc

WHERE acc_acc.acc_id = ? AND acc_acc.ts = 0
```

If the account exists, we want to pull in any information that might exist in the acc_add table for this account. This can be accomplished using the query

```
SELECT * FROM acc_add
WHERE acc_add.acc_id = ?
```

If we execute the first query and an account exists, executing the second query is probably safe to do. However, if the first query doesn't return a result, we don't want to run the second query. We could use IF conditions to achieve this, but a join will do it for us automatically. The initial join tells the system to return a single result, which will have all of the fields from acc_acc and acc_add, and rows only where the account number is found in the acc_id of the acc_acc table. The result will be either a ResultSet object with no data rows or an object with data from both tables.

In the previous section, we expanded our join to include a third table called thumbnail. This table is unique because it isn't found in the accounts database but in the identification database.

```
SELECT *, thumbnail.pic FROM accounts.acc_acc
LEFT JOIN accounts.acc_add
on accounts.acc_acc.acc_id = accounts.acc_add.acc_id
LEFT JOIN identification.thumbnail
on accounts.acc_acc.acc_id = identification.thumbnail.acc_id
WHERE accounts.acc_acc.acc_id = ? AND accounts.acc_acc.ts = 0
```

In this new join, we take the previous join and add a left join on the identification.thumbnail database table. We also specify that we want to pull the thumbnail.pic row along with the rows in acc_acc and acc_add. The join won't occur unless the account number exists in the acc_acc table. The result of the join provides all the data needed to display the file to the user. These joins demonstrate that Connector/J, Java, and MySQL can pull data in just about any fashion for your application.

Updatable ResultSets

All of the applications we have written thus far have handled the issue of updating data within the database using the UPDATE query statement. In many cases, this is the only option. However, suppose we have an application that first executes a SELECT query that pulls data from the table, displays the information, and then allows the user to make changes. In this case, we can use a feature of the JDBC specification called *updatable ResultSets*. This feature allows us to change the data within the ResultSet itself and execute a single method to cause the new data to be sent to the database. We can also use these ResultSets to insert new rows as well as delete rows we aren't interested in.

The code in Listing 6.6 is a combination of code from Chapter 5 (that let us view and modify the account information) and the code for handling a fingerprint. What makes this application unique is the use of updatable ResultSets.

```
import java.awt.*;
import java.awt.event.*;
import javax.swing.*;
import java.sql.*;
import java.util.*;
import java.awt.geom.AffineTransform;
import java.awt.image.BufferedImage;
import java.io.*;


public class IDlook extends JFrame {

  private JButton getAccountButton,
                  updateAccountButton,
                  insertAccountButton,
                  nextButton,
                  previousButton,
                  lastButton,
                  firstButton;
  private JList   accountNumberList;
  private JTextField accountIDText,
                     nailFileText,
                     thumbIDText;
  private JTextArea  errorText;

  private Connection connection;
  private Statement  statement;
  private ResultSet rs;
  private ImageIcon icon = null;
  private ImageIcon iconThumbnail = null;
  JLabel photographLabel;



  public IDlook() {
    try {
      Class.forName("com.mysql.jdbc.Driver").newInstance();
    } catch (Exception  e) {
      System.err.println("Unable to find and load driver");
      System.exit(1);
    }
  }

  private void loadAccounts() {
    Vector v = new Vector();
    try {
      rs = statement.executeQuery("SELECT * FROM thumbnail");

      while(rs.next()) {
        v.addElement(rs.getString("acc_id"));
```

Listing 6.6 Using updatable ResultSets. (continues)

```
      }
    } catch(SQLException e) {
      displaySQLErrors(e);
    }
    accountNumberList.setListData(v);
  }

  private void buildGUI() {
    Container c = getContentPane();
    c.setLayout(new FlowLayout());

    accountNumberList = new JList();
    loadAccounts();
    accountNumberList.setVisibleRowCount(2);
    JScrollPane accountNumberListScrollPane =
      new JScrollPane(accountNumberList);

    //Do Get Account Button
    getAccountButton = new JButton("Get Account");
    getAccountButton.addActionListener (
      new ActionListener() {
        public void actionPerformed(ActionEvent e) {
          try {
            rs.beforeFirst();
            while (rs.next()) {
              if (rs.getString("acc_id").
               equals(accountNumberList.getSelectedValue()))
                break;
            }
            if (!rs.isAfterLast()) {
              accountIDText.setText(rs.getString("acc_id"));
              thumbIDText.setText(rs.getString("thumb_id"));

              icon = new ImageIcon(rs.getBytes("pic"));
              createThumbnail();
              photographLabel.setIcon(iconThumbnail);
            }
          } catch(SQLException selectException) {
            displaySQLErrors(selectException);
          }
        }
      }
    );

    //Do Update Account Button
    updateAccountButton = new JButton("Update Account");
    updateAccountButton.addActionListener (
      new ActionListener() {
        public void actionPerformed(ActionEvent e) {
          try {
```

Listing 6.6 Using updatable ResultSets. (continues)

```
          byte[] bytes = new byte[50000];
          FileInputStream fs =
            new FileInputStream(nailFileText.getText());
          BufferedInputStream bis =
            new BufferedInputStream(fs);
          bis.read(bytes);

          rs.updateBytes("thumbnail.pic", bytes);
          rs.updateRow();
          bis.close();

          accountNumberList.removeAll();
          loadAccounts();
        } catch(SQLException insertException) {
          displaySQLErrors(insertException);
        } catch(Exception generalE) {
          generalE.printStackTrace();
        }
      }
    }
);

//Do insert Account Button
insertAccountButton = new JButton("Insert Account");
insertAccountButton.addActionListener (
  new ActionListener() {
    public void actionPerformed(ActionEvent e) {
      try {
        File f = new File(nailFileText.getText());
        byte[] bytes = new byte[(int)f.length()];
        FileInputStream fs =
          new FileInputStream(f);
        BufferedInputStream bis =
          new BufferedInputStream(fs);
        bis.read(bytes);

        rs.moveToInsertRow();
        rs.updateInt("thumb_id",
          Integer.parseInt(thumbIDText.getText()));
        rs.updateInt("acc_id",
          Integer.parseInt(accountIDText.getText()));
        rs.updateBytes("pic", bytes);
        rs.updateObject("sysobject", null);
        rs.updateTimestamp("ts", new Timestamp(0));
        rs.updateTimestamp("act_ts", new Timestamp(
          new java.util.Date().getTime()));
        rs.insertRow();
        bis.close();

        accountNumberList.removeAll();
```

Listing 6.6 Using updatable ResultSets. (continues)

```
          loadAccounts();
        } catch(SQLException insertException) {
          displaySQLErrors(insertException);
        } catch(Exception generalE) {
          generalE.printStackTrace();
        }
      }
    }
  );

  photographLabel = new JLabel();
  photographLabel.setHorizontalAlignment(JLabel.CENTER);
  photographLabel.setVerticalAlignment(JLabel.CENTER);
  photographLabel.setVerticalTextPosition(JLabel.CENTER);
  photographLabel.setHorizontalTextPosition(JLabel.CENTER);

  JPanel first = new JPanel(new GridLayout(4,1));
  first.add(accountNumberListScrollPane);
  first.add(getAccountButton);
  first.add(updateAccountButton);
  first.add(insertAccountButton);

  accountIDText = new JTextField(15);
  thumbIDText = new JTextField(15);
  errorText = new JTextArea(5, 15);
  errorText.setEditable(false);

  JPanel second = new JPanel();
  second.setLayout(new GridLayout(2,1));
  second.add(thumbIDText);
  second.add(accountIDText);

  JPanel third = new JPanel();
  third.add(new JScrollPane(errorText));

  nailFileText = new JTextField(25);

  c.add(first);
  c.add(second);
  c.add(third);
  c.add(nailFileText);
  c.add(photographLabel);


  setSize(500,500);
  show();
}

public void connectToDB() {
  try {
```

Listing 6.6 Using updatable ResultSets. (continues)

```
      connection = DriverManager.getConnection(
        "jdbc:mysql://localhost/Identification");
      statement = connection.createStatement(
        ResultSet.TYPE_SCROLL_INSENSITIVE,
                   ResultSet.CONCUR_UPDATABLE);

    } catch(SQLException connectException) {
      System.out.println(connectException.getMessage());
      System.out.println(connectException.getSQLState());
      System.out.println(connectException.getErrorCode());
      System.exit(1);
    }
  }

  private void displaySQLErrors(SQLException e) {
    errorText.append("SQLException: " + e.getMessage() + "\n");
    errorText.append("SQLState:     " + e.getSQLState()+"\n");
    errorText.append("VendorError:  " + e.getErrorCode()+"\n");
  }

  private void init() {
    connectToDB();
  }

  private void createThumbnail() {
    int maxDim = 350;
    try {
      Image inImage = icon.getImage();

      double scale =
       (double)maxDim/(double)inImage.getHeight(null);
      If (inImage.getWidth(null) > inImage.getHeight(null)) {
        scale = (double)maxDim/(double)inImage.getWidth(null);
      }

      int scaledW = (int)(scale*inImage.getWidth(null));
      int scaledH = (int)(scale*inImage.getHeight(null));

      BufferedImage outImage = new BufferedImage(scaledW,
        scaledH, BufferedImage.TYPE_INT_RGB);

      AffineTransform tx = new AffineTransform();

      if (scale < 1.0d) {
        tx.scale(scale, scale);
      }

      Graphics2D g2d = outImage.createGraphics();
      g2d.drawImage(inImage, tx, null);
      g2d.dispose();
```

Listing 6.6 Using updatable ResultSets. (continues)

```
      iconThumbnail = new ImageIcon(outImage);
    } catch (Exception e) {
      e.printStackTrace();
    }
  }

  public static void main(String[] args) {
    IDlook id = new IDlook();

    id.addWindowListener(
      new WindowAdapter() {
        public void windowClosing(WindowEvent e) {
          System.exit(0);
        }
      }
    );

    id.init();
    id.buildGUI();
  }
}
```

Listing 6.6 Using updatable ResultSets. (continued)

Figure 6.6 shows an example of the application we want to build. The user is able to select an account number in the combo box and click on the Get Account button. The code pulls information from the thumbnail table and displays the thumb_id, the acc_id, and the fingerprint image. The user is able to change the fingerprint image by placing a file path in the text field above the image and clicking on the Update Account button. To insert a new row into the table, the user simply enters new thumb_id, acc_id, and fingerprint image file values into the appropriate text fields and clicks on the Insert Account button.

The overall makeup of our application is the same as that in the previous chapter, where we created a GUI and used JPanels to hold the various controls. The real work is found in the code for the buttons. First, though, let's look at the code within the loadAccounts() method. The loadAccounts() method pulls all of the data from the thumbnail table using this query:

```
rs = statement.executeQuery("SELECT * FROM thumbnail");
```

The result of the executeQuery() method is a ResultSet object. Since we want to use updatable ResultSets, we have to build the Statement object in a little different format. Here's the code:

```
      statement = connection.createStatement(
  ResultSet.TYPE_SCROLL_INSENSITIVE,
             ResultSet.CONCUR_UPDATABLE);
```

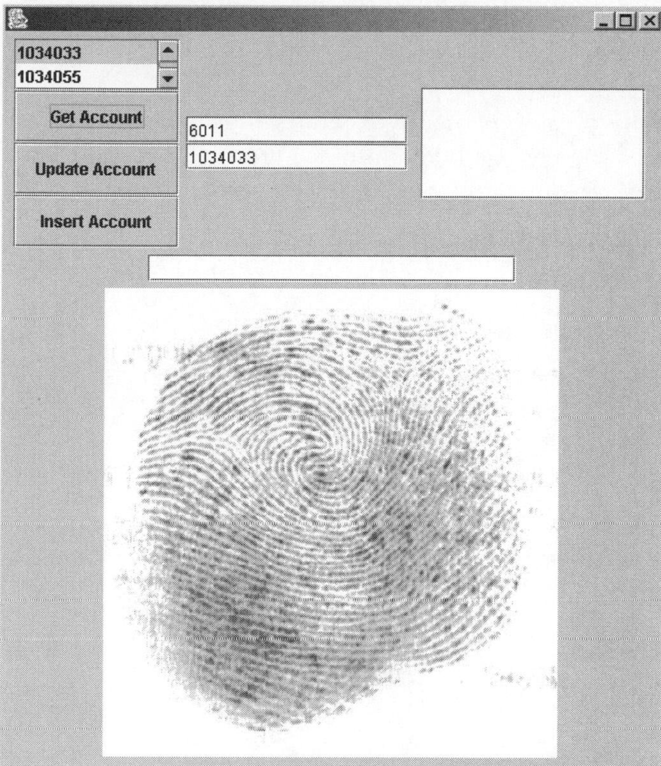

Figure 6.6 Our initial account.

By using the ResultSet.CONCUR_UPDATABLE flag, we tell the Statement object to always return a ResultSet object that we can change on the fly and to send those changes back to the database. Therefore, when the executeQuery() method gets executed, the system-wide ResultSet can be updated as needed. Updates to the ResultSet will occur via the update button or the insert button.

The Update Button Code

When a user clicks on the update button, the system assumes the user wants to change the fingerprint image kept in the database. Our code inserts the new image path in the nailFileText JTextField, pulls the image file, opens it, and places its contents in a byte array. You'll recall that in our previous applications, we created an UPDATE query using a PreparedStatement, inserted the new image bytes into the statement, and updated the database.

However, since we have an updatable ResultSet, we can use a series of methods called update<type> to place new values into the ResultSet. The update methods all work on the current row of the ResultSet, so we need to be sure the internal pointer is sitting on a data row and not before or after a row. The code used for the fingerprint image is:

```
rs.updateBytes("thumbnail.pic", bytes);
```

Once all of the fields in the ResultSet have been updated, our code calls the updateRow() method. For example:

```
rs.updateRow();
```

The Connector/J driver automatically executes the appropriate query to the database and places the changed data into it. Figure 6.7 shows how the application looks when the user wants to update the current record.

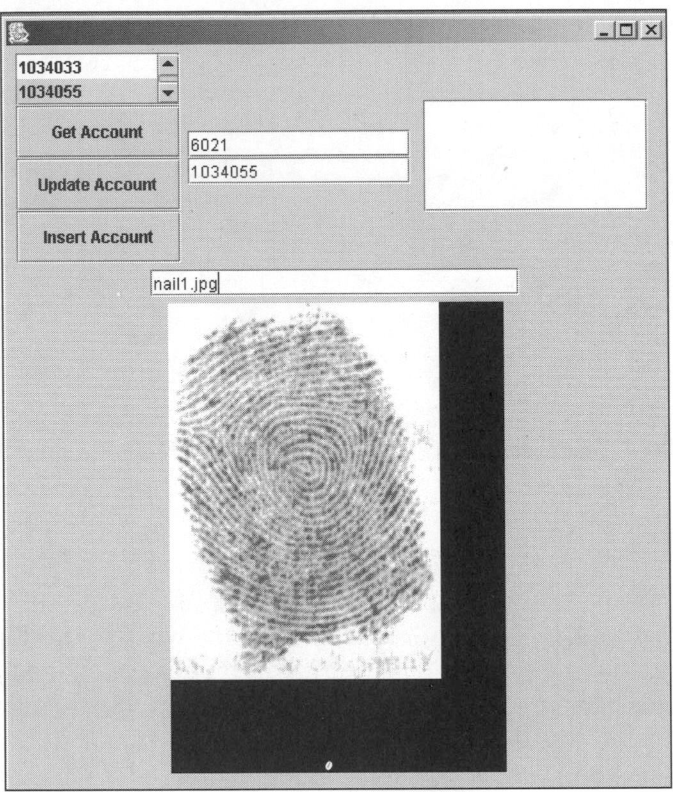

Figure 6.7 A second account getting a new picture.

The Insert Button Code

To add a new record to the database, the user enters thumb_id and acc_id values, as well as the fingerprint image path, into the appropriate text fields. After the user clicks on the insert button, the system attempts to find the fingerprint image and begins updating the ResultSet. However, since we are inserting a new row into the ResultSet, we don't want to change any of the current rows. We must let the ResultSet know that we need a new row put into the object so we can update it and send the information to the database.

We can use the moveToInsertRow() method to insert the new row into the object. For example:

```
rs.moveToInsertRow();
```

This method inserts a row into the ResultSet object and moves the internal pointer to the new row. Now the code can use the update<type> methods to put the new values into the row. The methods used are as follows:

```
rs.updateInt("thumb_id",Interger.parseInt(thumbIDText.getText()));
rs.updateInt("acc_id",  Integer.parseInt(accountIDText.getText()));
rs.updateBytes("pic", bytes);
rs.updateObject("sysobject", null);
rs.updateTimestamp("ts", new Timestamp(0));
rs.updateTimestamp("act_ts", new Timestamp( new java.util.Date().get-
Time()));
```

Notice that we have used the Int, Bytes, Object, and Timestamp update methods to place the appropriate values into the row. Finally, our code places the new row in the database with the command

```
rs.insertRow();
```

Figure 6.8 shows our application when the user enters new values into the fields and the record is inserted into the database.

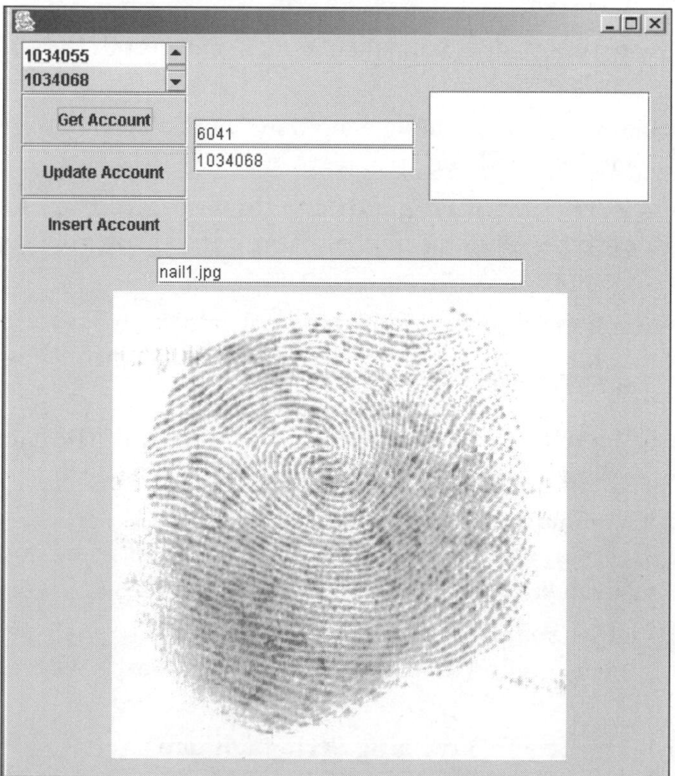

Figure 6.8 A second account with a new picture.

Update Methods

The following methods are available to you when you're using updatable ResultSets. We've indicated methods that aren't implemented in Connector/J.

void cancelRowUpdates()—If you make calls to the various update<type> methods, you can reverse the changes by executing this method. However, if you call updateRow(), the changes will be made to the database.

void deleteRow()—Deletes the row in the ResultSet where the internal pointer is currently pointing.

void insertRow()—Inserts the current row into the database with values updated in the ResultSet.

void moveToInsertRow()—Moves the internal pointer to a new row, which can be updated and inserted into the database.

void refreshRow()—Pulls data from the database for the current row in the ResultSet. The row cannot be a newly created insert row.

boolean rowDeleted()—Not implemented in Connector/J. Determines if this row has been deleted.

boolean rowInserted()—Not implemented in Connector/J. Determines if the current row has been inserted.

boolean rowUpdated()—Not implemented in Connector/J. Determines if the current row has been updated.

void updateAsciiStream(int columnIndex, java.io.InputStream aStream, int length)— Allows a column in the current row to be updated using a Stream. Assumes the data is ASCII-based.

void updateAsciiStream(java.lang.String columnName, java.io.InputStream aStream, int length)—Allows a column in the current row to be updated using a Stream. Assumes the data is ASCII-based.

void updateBigDecimal(int columnIndex, java.math.BigDecimal aBigDecimal)—Allows a column to be updated with a BigDecimal value.

void updateBigDecimal(java.lang.String columnName, java.math.BigDecimal aBigDecimal)—Allows a column to be updated with a BigDecimal value.

void updateBinaryStream(int columnIndex, java.io.InputStream aStream, int length)—Allows a column to be updated with a Binary Stream.

void updateBinaryStream(java.lang.String columnName, java.io.InputStream aStream, int length)—Allows a column to be updated with a BinaryStream.

void updateBoolean(int columnIndex, Boolean aBoolean)—Allows a column to be updated with a Boolean.

void updateBoolean(java.lang.String columnName, Boolean aBoolean)—Allows a column to be updated with a Boolean.

void updateByte(int columnIndex, byte aByte)—Updates a column with a single byte value.

void updateByte(java.lang.String columnName, byte aByte)—Updates a column with a single byte value.

void updateBytes(int columnIndex, byte[] aByteArray)—Updates a column with an array of bytes.

void updateBytes(java.lang.String columnName, byte[] aByteArray)—Updates a column with an array of bytes.

void updateCharacterStream(int columnIndex, java.io.Reader aStream, int length)—Allows a column to be updated using a character stream.

void updateCharacterStream(java.lang.String columnName, java.io.Reader aStream, int length)—Allows a column to be updated using a character stream.

void updateDate(int columnIndex, java.sql.Date aDate)—Allows a column to be updated with a Date value.

void updateDate(java.lang.String columnName, java.sql.Date aDate)—Allows a column to be updated with a Date value.

void updateDouble(int columnIndex, double aDouble)—Allows a column to be updated with a double.

void updateDouble(java.lang.String columnName, double aDouble)—Allows a column to be updated with a double.

void updateFloat(int columnIndex, float aFloat)—Updates a column using a Float value.

void updateFloat(java.lang.String columnName, float aFloat)—Updates a column using a Float value.

void updateInt(int columnIndex, int aInt)—Updates a column with an Int value.

void updateInt(java.lang.String columnName, int aInt)—Updates a column with an Int value.

void updateLong(int columnIndex, long aLong)—Updates a column with a long value.

void updateLong(java.lang.String columnName, long aLong)—Updates a column with a long value.

void updateNull(int columnIndex)—Places a null value in the specified column.

void updateNull(java.lang.String columnName)—Places a null value in the specified column.

void updateObject(int columnIndex, java.lang.Object anObject)—Places a serialized object into the specified column.

void updateObject(int columnIndex, java.lang.Object anObject, int scale)—Places a serialized object into the specified column.

void updateObject(java.lang.String columnName, java.lang.Object anObject)—Places a serialized object into the specified column.

void updateObject(java.lang.String columnName, java.lang.Object anObject, int scale)—Places a serialized object into the specified column.

void updateRow()—Updates the changed values for the correct row into the database.

void updateShort(int columnIndex, short aShort)—Allows a column to be updated with a short value.

void updateShort(java.lang.String columnName, short aShort)—Allows a column to be updated with a short value.

void updateString(int columnIndex, java.lang.String aString)—Updates a column with a String value.

void updateString(java.lang.String columnName, java.lang.String aString)—Updates a column with a String value.

void updateTime(int columnIndex, java.sql.Time aTime)—Updates a column with a Time value.

void updateTime(java.lang.String columnName, java.sql.Time aTime)—Updates a column with a Time value.

void updateTimestamp(int columnIndex, java.sql.Timestamp aTS)—Updates a column with a Timestamp value.

void updateTimestamp(java.lang.String columnName, java.sql.Timestamp aTS)—Updates a column with a Timestamp value.

Manipulating Date/Time Types

The listing for inserting a new row into the fingerprint database includes code that inserts a timestamp value into the row. When developers need to access time, data, and timestamp values in a ResultSet, they can use the getDate(), getTime(), and getTimestamp() methods, which we examine next. Most of the methods perform some level of conversion from the MySQL column type to the Java data type. We cover these mappings in detail in the next chapter.

Methods for Retrieving a Value as a Date Type

The getDate() method attempts to pull the specified column from the MySQL table as a java.sql.Date data type. As shown in the next chapter, the MySQL data types of Date, Timestamp, and Year will all map to the Date data type. The following values will result in a null:

Null

```
0000-00-00
0000-00-00 00:00:00
00000000000000
```

If the value in the column is fewer than 10 characters and not a type Null, Year, Date, or Timestamp, an error will be returned. In Connector/J, the getDate(int columnIndex, Calendar cal) method maps to getDate(int columnIndex).

```
Date getDate(int columnIndex)
Date getDate(int columnIndex, Calendar cal)
Date getDate(String columnName)
Date getDate(String columnName, Calendar cal)
```

Methods for Retrieving a Value as a Time Type

The java.sql.Time data type can be obtained from a column using the getTime() method. The MySQL data types appropriate for the Time data type are Timestamp, DATETIME, and other values that match a length of 5 or 8. The system attempts to convert the values as best as possible. A null is represented as

Null

```
0000-00-00
0000-00-00 00:00:00
00000000000000
```

The methods with a Calendar parameter map to the methods without such values.

```
Time getTime(int columnIndex)
Time getTime(int columnIndex, Calendar cal)
Time getTime(String columnName)
Time getTime(String columnName, Calendar cal)
```

Methods for Retrieving a Value as a Timestamp Type

The getTimestamp() method converts fields of the type Year, Timestamp, and Date. A null is represented as

```
Null
0000-00-00
0000-00-00 00:00:00
00000000000000
```

The methods with a Calendar parameter map to the methods without such values.

```
Timestamp getTimestamp(int columnIndex)
Timestamp getTimestamp(int columnIndex, Calendar cal)
Timestamp getTimestamp(String columnName)
Timestamp getTimestamp(String columnName, Calendar cal)
```

Handling BLOB and CLOB

In our examples, we have been using an array of bytes to handle the fingerprint image as it was placed in the database. There is another way to handle the use of large amounts of binary and character data. The BLOB and CLOB are SQL-defined data types designed to handle these large data types. As we discuss in the next chapter, the BLOB type can be used with several MySQL types, including:

- INYBLOB
- BLOB
- MEDIUMBLOB
- LONGBLOB

Likewise, the CLOB type can be used with the following MySQL types:

- TINYTEXT
- TEXT
- MEDIUMTEXT
- LONGTEXT

Connector/J and MySQL can work with BLOBs and CLOBs using four different methods. The methods

```
Blob getBlob(int i)
Blob getBlob(String colName)
```

retrieve the value of the designated column in the current row of this ResultSet object as a BLOB object in the Java programming language. The methods

```
Clob getClob(int i)
Clob getClob(String colName)
```

retrieve the value of the designated column in the current row of this ResultSet object as a CLOB object in the Java programming language.

Once data has been stored in a BLOB or CLOB field in the database, it can be removed and manipulated in a CLOB or BLOB object. For example, when the code in Listing 6.6 pulled the fingerprint image from the database, it used the getBytes() method. While this is valid, the data could more correctly be returned as a BLOB object. One reason for doing this is the driver might be written to implement streaming of the data from the database to the BLOB object. This means the system will pull the data in segments as needed rather than pulling all of the data at once. Currently, the Connector/J driver doesn't stream the data but pulls the data all at once. This doesn't mean that you cannot use the BLOB object.

Previously, the code to pull the fingerprint image was

```
accountIDText.setText(rs.getString("acc_id"));
thumbIDText.setText(rs.getString("thumb_id"));
icon = new ImageIcon(b.getBytes(rs.getByte("pic"));
```

To pull the data as a BLOB or CLOB, we'd use this code:

```
accountIDText.setText(rs.getString("acc_id"));
thumbIDText.setText(rs.getString("thumb_id"));
Blob b = rs.getBlob("pic");

icon = new ImageIcon(b.getBytes(1L, (int)b.length()));
```

By pulling the data as a BLOB or CLOB, you can take advantage of several methods defined in each class. The methods available in the BLOB are

InputStream getBinaryStream()—Returns a stream that can be used to manipulate the bytes associated with the BLOB.

byte[] getBytes(long pos, int length)—Returns a byte array copied from the bytes associated with the BLOB starting at a specific position and that has the specified length.

long length()—Returns the number of bytes in the BLOB value designated by this BLOB object.

long position(Blob pattern, long start)—Returns the position value where the specific *pattern* of bytes is located in the bytes represented by the BLOB object.

long position(byte[] pattern, long start)—Not implemented in Connector/J. Returns the position value where the specific *pattern* of bytes is located in the bytes represented by the BLOB object.

OutputStream setBinaryStream(long pos)—Not implemented in Connector/J. Returns a BinaryStream used to set the bytes associated with the BLOB object.

int setBytes(long pos, byte[] bytes)—Not implemented in Connector/J.

int setBytes(long pos, byte[] bytes, int offset, int len)—Not implemented in Connector/J. Writes a series of bytes to the BLOB object using the specified position with the data bytes, the offset, and total bytes to copy.

void truncate(long len)—Not implemented. Truncates the bytes associated with the BLOB object to the length specified.

If you have a CLOB object, the methods available are

InputStream getAsciiStream()—Not implemented by Connector/J. Returns a stream to access the internal String.

Reader getCharacterStream()—Returns a character stream to access the internal String.

String getSubString(long pos, int length)—Returns a copy of the String associated with the CLOB starting at the specified position and having the specified length.

long length()—Returns the total number characters represented by the CLOB.

long position(Clob searchstr, long start)—Retrieves the character position at which the specified substring searchstr appears in the SQL CLOB value represented by this CLOB object.

long position(String searchstr, long start)—Retrieves the character position at which the specified substring searchstr appears in the SQL CLOB value represented by this CLOB object.

OutputStream setAsciiStream(long pos)—Returns a stream that can be used to get ASCII values for the internal String.

Writer setCharacterStream(long pos)—Not implemented by Connector/J. Retrieves a stream that can be used to set the internal String.

int setString(long pos, String str)—Not implemented by Connector/J. Writes the specified String to the internal String represented by the CLOB.

int setString(long pos, String str, int offset, int len)—Not implemented by Connector/J. Writes the specified String to the internal String represented by the CLOB.

void truncate(long len)—Not implemented. Truncates the bytes associated with the CLOB object to the length specified.

Using Streams to Pull Data

Just as we can pull large amounts of data from a database using getBytes() or getBlob(), we can also attach a stream to a ResultSet column. For example, we can pull the bytes from the table and put them into an output file. Here's the code to accomplish that:

```
int b;
InputStream bis = rs.getBinaryStream("pic");
FileOutputStream f = new FileOutputStream("pic.jpg");
while ( (b = bis.read()) >= 0 ) {
  f.write(b);
}
f.close();
bis.close();
```

The code starts by creating an InputStream for the pic column found in our thumbnail table. Next, the code creates a FileOutputStream object and assigns it to the pic.jpg file on the local hard drive. Next, a loop is created to systematically read values from the InputStream and write to the FileOutputStream. The InputStream associated with the ResultSet column can be used anywhere a Java method allows an InputStream.

The methods available are

InputStream getAsciiStream(int columnIndex)—Associates an InputStream with the specified column. The Connector/J driver calls getBinary Stream() when this method is called.

InputStream getAsciiStream(String columnName)—Associates an InputStream with the specified column. The Connector/J driver calls get BinaryStream() when this method is called.

InputStream getBinaryStream(int columnIndex)—Associates an InputStream with the specified column.

InputStream getBinaryStream(String columnName)—Associates an InputStream with the specified column.

Reader getCharacterStream(int columnIndex)—Associates a Reader object stream with the specified column.

Reader getCharacterStream(String columnName)—Associates a Reader object stream with the specified column.

Handling ENUM

The MySQL database server allows you to create a database table column using the ENUM type. For example, we might have table defined and filled with data as shown in Figure 6.9.

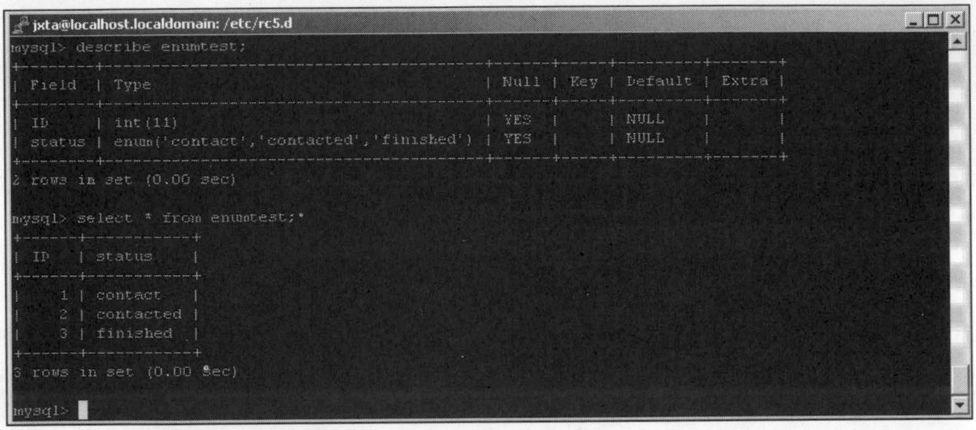

```
jxta@localhost.localdomain: /etc/rc5.d
mysql> describe enumtest;
+--------+----------------------------------------+------+-----+---------+-------+
| Field  | Type                                   | Null | Key | Default | Extra |
+--------+----------------------------------------+------+-----+---------+-------+
| ID     | int(11)                                | YES  |     | NULL    |       |
| status | enum('contact','contacted','finished') | YES  |     | NULL    |       |
+--------+----------------------------------------+------+-----+---------+-------+
2 rows in set (0.00 sec)

mysql> select * from enumtest;
+------+-----------+
| ID   | status    |
+------+-----------+
|    1 | contact   |
|    2 | contacted |
|    3 | finished  |
+------+-----------+
3 rows in set (0.00 sec)

mysql>
```

Figure 6.9 An ENUM table and data.

As you can see in Figure 6.9, the MySQL data type is an ENUM type and not a String. However, no method is available for pulling an ENUM from the ResultSet directly. In most cases, the data will be pulled as a String using the getString("status") method. If your application needs to know all of the possible values that could be stored in the ENUM but you don't want to hard-code the values, you can use the following code to extract the values:

```
ResultSet rs = statement.executeQuery(
"SHOW COLUMNS FROM enumtest LIKE 'status'");
```

This code will produce a ResultSet with the following information in it:

```
+-------+-----------------------+----+---+--------+-------+
|Field  |Type                   |Null|Key| Default | Extra |
+-------+-----------------------+----+---+--------+-------+
|status |enum('contact',        |    |   |        |       |
|       |'contacted', 'finished')| YES|   | NULL   |       |
+-------+-----------------------+----+---+--------+-------+
1 row in set (0.00 sec)
```

Now we need to pull out the String, parse for the ENUM types, and keep them in an array. Here's some example code:

```
try {
  statement = connection.createStatement();
  ResultSet rs = statement.executeQuery(
    "SHOW COLUMNS FROM enumtest LIKE 'status'");

  rs.next();
  String enums = rs.getString("Type");
  System.out.println(enums);
  int position = 0, count = 0;
  String[] availableEnums = new String[10];
```

```
      while ((position = enums.indexOf("'", position)) > 0) {
        int secondPosition = enums.indexOf("'", position+1);
        availableEnums[count++] = enums.substring(
          position+1, secondPosition);

        position = secondPosition+1;
        System.out.println(availableEnums[count-1]);
      }

      rs.close();
      statement.close();
      connection.close();
     } catch(Exception e) {
      e.printStackTrace();
     }
```

The code starts by getting the definition of the ENUM column within the table and pulling out the string for the type. Next, a loop is set up to match the single quotes of the ENUM values. Each pair of single quotes is found, and the string within the quotes is placed in a String array.

Using Connector/J with JavaScript

Not everyone is comfortable using servlets for building Web-based applications. In these cases, a Web developer might turn to JavaScript as a tool for database access. The code in Listing 6.7 accesses a remote database and displays the thumb_id, the acc_id, and a thumbnail version of the fingerprint image stored in the database.

```
<%@ page import='java.sql.*, javax.sql.*, java.io.*' %>
<HTML>
<HEAD>
<TITLE>View Images</TITLE>
</HEAD>
<BODY>
<%
    Class.forName("com.mysql.jdbc.Driver").newInstance();

    Connection connection = DriverManager.getConnection(
      "jdbc:mysql://localhost/identification");
    Statement statement = connection.createStatement();
    ResultSet rs = statement.executeQuery("SELECT * FROM thumbnail");
%>
<UL>
```

Listing 6.7 JavaScript database access. (continues)

```
<%
  while (rs.next()) {
%>
  <LI>
<%
    FileOutputStream fo =
new FileOutputStream("./doc/images/nail"
+ rs.getString("acc_id") + ".jpg");
    BufferedOutputStream bos = new BufferedOutputStream(fo);
    bos.write(rs.getBytes("pic"));
    bos.close();

    out.println(rs.getString("thumb_id") + " " +
                rs.getString("acc_id") + "<img
src='../images/nail" +
                rs.getString("acc_id") + ".jpg' width=50
height=100>");
  }
%>
  </UL>
</BODY>
</HTML>
```

Listing 6.7 JavaScript database access. (continued)

Figure 6.10 shows an example of what the client browser displays when it accesses the JavaScript in Listing 6.7. One of the most important differences between an applet and a Java application is the use of the <@ tag to pull in the Java libraries needed for the code. As with all JavaScript code, the server-side script must be found in the <% %> tags. The code begins with the familiar loading of the Connector/J driver.

You might recall that we did this sort of thing in the applet code in Chapter 5, but it required the driver to be found on the client. This is not the case with JavaScript because the JavaScript code executes on the server instead of on the client.

After the driver is loaded, a connection is made to the MySQL database and the appropriate SQL is executed to pull all of the data from the identification table. The code creates a loop to build file-based versions of the fingerprint image data on the server. Then, HTML code is created to display the values of the thumb_id and acc_id columns as well as a link to the fingerprint image on the server.

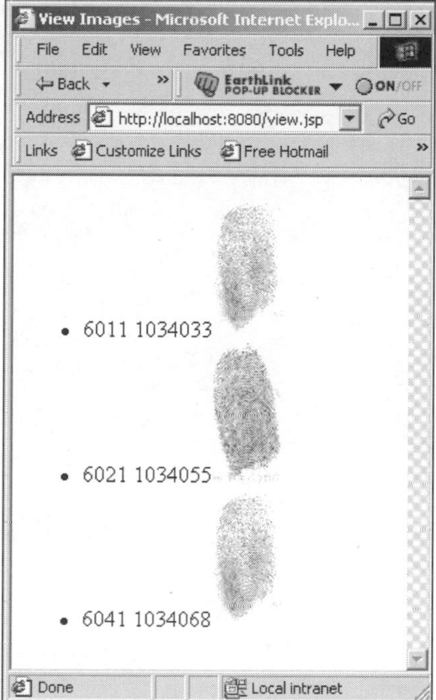

Figure 6.10 Output from our JavaScript.

What's Next

In this chapter, we provided you with the tools necessary to build servlets that access the MySQL database server. We explored using PreparedStatements, joins, updatable ResultSets, and many other advanced topics. In the next chapter, we look at how Connector/J handles the transition of data from the MySQL database.

CHAPTER 7

MySQL Type Mapping

In the previous two chapters, we introduced techniques for interacting with a data source, such as MySQL, using the Java programming language. One issue that complicates such interaction is that of mapping column types. As is the case with many data source implementations, MySQL does not strictly adhere to any particular standard when it comes to the definitions and naming of SQL column types. Since it is not practical for the JDBC API to directly support all possible implementation choices with regard to SQL column types, the API attempts to "abstract away" the differences. This abstraction is centered on the java.sql.Types class, which defines a set of constants that identify generic SQL types; these types are referred to as JDBC types.

The JDBC types serve as a sort of middle ground between Java client code and a MySQL server. On the Java side, each JDBC type is associated with a specific Java type. On the MySQL side—or more specifically within the Connector/J implementation—each MySQL type is associated with a specific JDBC type. Thus, MySQL types can be mapped to Java types, and vice versa, with the help of the JDBC types. In this chapter, we detail these mappings, providing a type summary, the associated JDBC type, and the corresponding Java type for each MySQL column type. We break the column types into three groups for our discussion: character, date and time, and numeric.

Character Column Types

The character column types, summarized in Table 7.1, are characterized by the fact that each defines values consisting of an arbitrary sequence of characters. With the exception of SET and ENUM, the types differ primarily in allowable size and the manner in which they are compared; the SET and ENUM types correspond to groups of character type values (strings) that define the allowable values for a column.

Table 7.1 Character Column Types

MYSQL TYPE	JDBC TYPE	JAVA TYPE
CHAR	CHAR	String
VARCHAR	VARCHAR	String
TINYTEXT	LONGVARCHAR	String
TEXT	LONGVARCHAR	String
MEDIUMTEXT	LONGVARCHAR	String
LONGTEXT	LONGVARCHAR	String
TINYBLOB	LONGVARBINARY	byte[]
BLOB	LONGVARBINARY	byte[]
MEDIUMBLOB	LONGVARBINARY	byte[]
LONGBLOB	LONGVARBINARY	byte[]
SET	VARCHAR	String
ENUM	VARCHAR	String

CHAR

The MySQL CHAR column type represents a fixed-length character sequence container. The length is specified by the column definition and must be in the range 0 to 255 (a length of 0 is not supported prior to MySQL version 3.23). Column values are right-padded with spaces where the number of characters is less than the defined length; trailing spaces are stripped upon retrieval.

The CHAR column type maps to the CHAR JDBC type, which in turn corresponds to a Java String. The recommended ResultSet getter method for retrieving CHAR types is getString().

VARCHAR

The MySQL VARCHAR type represents a variable-length character sequence container. An upper limit on the allowable length is specified by the column definition and must be in the range 0 to 255 (a length of 0 is not supported prior to MySQL version 4.0.2). All trailing space is stripped from column values before insertion, which is contrary to the ANSI SQL specification.

The VARCHAR type maps to the VARCHAR JDBC type, which in turn corresponds to a Java String. The recommended ResultSet getter method for retrieving VARCHAR types is getString().

TINYTEXT

The MySQL TINYTEXT type represents a variable-length character sequence container capable of holding up to 255 characters. Column values of type TINYTEXT are stored as is, with no padding, stripping, or character substitution. Comparison and sorting of TINYTEXT values is performed in a case-insensitive manner.

The TINYTEXT type maps to a LONGVARCHAR JDBC type, which in turn corresponds to a Java String. The recommended ResultSet getter methods for retrieving TINYTEXT types are getAsciiStream() and getCharacterStream().

TEXT

The MySQL TEXT type represents a variable-length character sequence container capable of holding up to 65,535 characters. Column values of type TEXT are stored as is, with no padding, stripping, or character substitution. Comparison and sorting of TEXT values is performed in a case-insensitive manner.

The TEXT type maps to a LONGVARCHAR JDBC type, which in turn corresponds to a Java String. The recommended ResultSet getter methods for retrieving TEXT types are getAsciiStream() and getCharacterStream().

MEDIUMTEXT

The MySQL MEDIUMTEXT type represents a variable-length character sequence container capable of holding up to 16,777,215 characters. Column values of type MEDIUMTEXT are stored as is, with no padding, stripping, or character substitution. Comparison and sorting of MEDIUMTEXT values is performed in a case-insensitive manner.

The MEDIUMTEXT type maps to a LONGVARCHAR JDBC type, which in turn corresponds to a Java String. The recommended ResultSet getter methods for retrieving MEDIUMTEXT types are getAsciiStream() and getCharacterStream().

LONGTEXT

The MySQL LONGTEXT type represents a variable-length character sequence container capable of holding up to 4,294,967,295 characters. Column values of type LONGTEXT are stored as is, with no padding, stripping, or character substitution. Comparison and sorting of LONGTEXT values is performed in a case-insensitive manner.

The LONGTEXT type maps to a LONGVARCHAR JDBC type, which in turn corresponds to a Java String. The recommended ResultSet getter methods for retrieving MEDIUMTEXT types are getAsciiStream() and getCharacterStream().

TINYBLOB

The MySQL TINYBLOB type represents a variable-length character sequence container capable of holding up to 255 characters. Column values of type TINYBLOB are stored as is, with no padding, stripping, or character substitution. Comparison and sorting of TINYBLOB values is performed in a case-sensitive manner.

The TINYBLOB type maps to a LONGVARBINARY JDBC type, which in turn corresponds to a Java byte array (i.e., byte[]). The recommended ResultSet getter method for retrieving TINYBLOB types is getBinaryStream().

BLOB

The MySQL BLOB type represents a variable-length character sequence container capable of holding up to 65,535 characters. Column values of type BLOB are stored as is, with no padding, stripping, or character substitution. Comparison and sorting of BLOB values is performed in a case-sensitive manner.

The BLOB type maps to a LONGVARBINARY JDBC type, which in turn corresponds to a Java byte array (i.e., byte[]). The recommended ResultSet getter method for retrieving BLOB types is getBinaryStream().

MEDIUMBLOB

The MySQL MEDIUMBLOB type represents a variable-length character sequence container capable of holding up to 16,777,215 characters. Column values of type MEDIUMBLOB are stored as-is, with no padding, stripping, or character substitution. Comparison and sorting of MEDIUMBLOB values is performed in a case-sensitive manner.

The MEDIUMBLOB type maps to a LONGVARBINARY JDBC type, which in turn corresponds to a Java byte array (i.e., byte[]). The recommended ResultSet getter method for retrieving MEDIUMBLOB types is getBinaryStream().

LONGBLOB

The MySQL LONGBLOB type represents a variable-length character sequence container capable of holding up to 4,294,967,295 characters. Column values of type LONGBLOB are stored as is, with no padding, stripping, or character substitution. Comparison and sorting of LONGBLOB values is performed in a case-sensitive manner.

The LONGBLOB type maps to a LONGVARBINARY JDBC type, which in turn corresponds to a Java byte array (i.e., byte[]). The recommended ResultSet getter method for retrieving LONGBLOB types is getBinaryStream().

SET

The MySQL SET type represents a character sequence container capable of holding a subset of the fixed-character sequences specified by an associated column definition. Comma delimiters are used for SET values that contain more than one member. A SET value may consist of at most 64 members.

The SET type maps to a VARCHAR JDBC type, which in turn corresponds to a Java String. The recommended ResultSet getter method for retrieving SET types is getString().

ENUM

The MySQL ENUM type represents a character sequence container capable of holding exactly one character sequence selected from those specified by an associated column definition. A column of type ENUM may specify up to 65,535 distinct values, any one of which may be taken on by an ENUM value inserted into the corresponding column.

The ENUM type maps to a VARCHAR JDBC type, which in turn corresponds to a Java String. The recommended ResultSet getter method for retrieving ENUM types is getString().

Using Character Types

The code in Listing 7.1 demonstrates the use of character column types. Statement and PreparedStatement objects are used to create and populate a table that stores character types. The table is then queried, the column values extracted, and the results written to the standard output. Since TINYTEXT, MEDI-

UMTEXT, and LONGTEXT differ from TEXT only in terms of maximum length, only the TEXT type is presented in the example. Likewise, BLOB serves to demonstrate the use of TINYBLOB, MEDIUMBLOB, and LONGBLOB.

```
try
{
  String createSql = "CREATE TABLE jmCharacter ("
                   + "jmChar CHAR(80), jmVarchar VARCHAR(80), "
                   + "jmText TEXT, jmBlob BLOB, "
                   + "jmSet SET('red','green','blue'), "
                   + "jmEnum ENUM('true','false'))";

  Statement stmt = conn.createStatement();

  stmt.execute( createSql );

  String charValue = "This is a CHAR";
  String varcharValue = "This is a VARCHAR";
  String textValue = "This is a TEXT";
  String blobString = "This is a BLOB";
  byte[] blobValue = blobString.getBytes();
  String setValue = "blue,green";
  String enumValue = "true";

  String insertSql = "INSERT INTO jmCharacter "
                   + "VALUES (?,?,?,?,?,?)";

  PreparedStatement pstmt = conn.prepareStatement( insertSql );

  pstmt.setString( 1, charValue );
  pstmt.setString( 2, varcharValue );
  pstmt.setString( 3, textValue );
  pstmt.setBytes( 4, blobValue );
  pstmt.setString( 5, setValue );
  pstmt.setString( 6, enumValue );

  pstmt.execute();

  ResultSet results = stmt.executeQuery( "SELECT * from jmCharacter" );

  results.next();

  // Extract CHAR and VARCHAR values
  charValue = results.getString( "jmChar" );
  System.out.println( "jmChar    : " + charValue );
  varcharValue = results.getString( "jmVarchar" );
  System.out.println( "jmVarchar: " + varcharValue );
```

Listing 7.1 Using character columns types. (continues)

```
    // Extract TEXT value from InputStream
    InputStream textStream = results.getAsciiStream( "jmText" );
    BufferedReader textReader =
               new BufferedReader( new InputStreamReader( textStream ) );
    textValue = textReader.readLine();

    while ( textValue != null )
    {
      System.out.println( "jmText   : " + textValue );
      textValue = textReader.readLine();
    }

    textReader.close();

    // Extract BLOB value from InputStream
    InputStream blobStream = results.getBinaryStream( "jmBlob" );
    DataInputStream dataStream = new DataInputStream( blobStream );

    dataStream.readFully( blobValue );
    System.out.println( "jmBlob   : " + new String( blobValue ) );

    dataStream.close();

    // Extract SET and ENUM values
    setValue = results.getString( "jmSet" );
    System.out.println( "jmSet    : " + setValue );
    enumValue = results.getString( "jmEnum" );
    System.out.println( "jmEnum   : " + enumValue );
  }
  catch( IOException ioX )
  {
    System.err.println( ioX );
  }
  catch( SQLException sqlX )
  {
    System.err.println( sqlX );
  }
```

Listing 7.1 Using character columns types. (continued)

Date and Time Column Types

Not surprisingly, the date and time column types, summarized in Table 7.2, provide for the handling of information related to dates and times. The important thing to note about these types is that they place a strict limit on the format used to represent dates and times, saving MySQL the need to understand the multitude of formats currently in use throughout the world.

Table 7.2 Date and Time Column Types

MYSQL TYPE	JDBC TYPE	JAVA TYPE
DATE	DATE	java.sql.Date
TIME	TIME	java.sql.Time
DATETIME	TIMESTAMP	java.sql.Timestamp
YEAR	DATE	java.sql.Date
TIMESTAMP	TIMESTAMP	java.sql.Timestamp

DATE

The MySQL DATE type represents a container that holds a calendar date of form YYYY-MM-DD, where YYYY is a four-digit year, MM is a two-digit month, and DD is a two-digit day. The supported date range is 1000-01-01 through 9999-12-31.

The DATE type maps to a DATE JDBC type, which in turn corresponds to java.sql.Date. The recommended ResultSet getter method for retrieving DATE types is getDate().

TIME

The MySQL TIME type represents a container that holds an elapsed time of form (h)hh:mm:ss, where (h)hh is a two- or three-digit hour, mm is a two-digit minute, and ss is a two-digit second. The supported time range is –838:59:59 to 838:59:59.

The TIME type maps to a TIME JDBC type, which in turn corresponds to java.sql.Time. The recommended ResultSet getter method for retrieving TIME types is getTime().

DATETIME

The MySQL DATETIME type represents a container that combines a calendar date and clock time using the format YYYY-MM-DD hh:mm:ss. The format of the date portion is the same as that used for the DATE type. The format of the time portion differs from that of the TIME type in that it is limited to values appropriate to a 24-hour day. The supported range of dates and times is 1000-01-01 00:00:00 through 9999-12-31 23:59:59.

The DATETIME type maps to a TIMESTAMP JDBC type, which in turn corresponds to java.sql.Timestamp. The recommended ResultSet getter method for retrieving DATETIME types is getTimestamp().

YEAR

The MySQL YEAR type represents a container that holds a calendar year in one of two formats, depending on how the associated column is defined. By default, the format is a four-digit year that may take on values ranging from 1901 through 2155; additionally, the value 0000 is valid. The format may also be specified as a two-digit year, in which case the values 70 through 69 correspond to the years 1970 through 2069.

The YEAR type maps to a DATE JDBC type, which in turn corresponds to java.sql.Date. The recommended ResultSet getter method for retrieving YEAR types is getDate().

TIMESTAMP

The MySQL TIMESTAMP type represents a container that holds a calendar date and clock time of form YYYYMMDDhhmmss, where YYYY is a four-digit year, MM is a two-digit month, DD is a two-digit day, hh is a two-digit hour, mm is a two-digit minute, and ss is a two-digit second. The supported range is 1970-01-01 00:00:00 through sometime in the year 2037.

The TIMESTAMP type maps to a TIMESTAMP JDBC type, which in turn corresponds to java.sql.Timestamp. The recommended ResultSet getter method for retrieving TIMESTAMP types is getTimestamp().

Using Date and Time Types

The code in Listing 7.2 demonstrates the use of date and time column types. Statement and PreparedStatement objects are used to create and populate a table that stores date and time types. The table is then queried, the column values extracted, and the results written to the standard output. Though more sophisticated processing is certainly possible, this example simply manipulates, or uses directly, the string representations of the java.sql.Time, java.sql.Date, and java.sql.Timestamp classes in order to generate output in a standard format.

```
try
{
  String createSql = "CREATE TABLE jmDateAndTime ("
                   + "jmDate DATE, jmTime TIME, "
                   + "jmDatetime DATETIME, jmYear YEAR, "
                   + "jmTimestamp TIMESTAMP)";

  Statement stmt = conn.createStatement();

  stmt.execute( createSql );

  java.sql.Date dateValue = java.sql.Date.valueOf( "1969-07-20" );
  java.sql.Time timeValue = java.sql.Time.valueOf( "18:37:29" );
  Timestamp datetimeValue = Timestamp.valueOf( "2000-12-31 23:59:59" );
  java.sql.Date yearValue = java.sql.Date.valueOf( "1972-01-01" );
  Timestamp timestampValue = Timestamp.valueOf( "2001-02-03 04:05:06" );

  String insertSql = "INSERT INTO jmDateAndTime "
                   + "VALUES (?,?,?,?,?)";

  PreparedStatement pstmt = conn.prepareStatement( insertSql );

  pstmt.setDate( 1, dateValue );
  pstmt.setTime( 2, timeValue );
  pstmt.setTimestamp( 3, datetimeValue );
  pstmt.setDate( 4, yearValue );
  pstmt.setTimestamp( 5, timestampValue );

  pstmt.execute();

  ResultSet results = stmt.executeQuery( "SELECT * from jmDateAndTime" );

  results.next();

  // Extract DATE and TIME values
  dateValue = results.getDate( "jmDate" );
  System.out.println( "jmDate     : " + dateValue.toString() );
  timeValue = results.getTime( "jmTime" );
  System.out.println( "jmTime     : " + timeValue.toString() );

  // Extract DATETIME value
  datetimeValue = results.getTimestamp( "jmDatetime" );
  String datetimeStr = datetimeValue.toString();
  StringTokenizer datetimeTok = new StringTokenizer( datetimeStr, "." );
  System.out.println( "jmDatetime : " + datetimeTok.nextToken() );

  // Extract YEAR value
```

Listing 7.2 Using date and time columns types. (continues)

```
   yearValue = results.getDate( "jmYear" );
   String yearStr = yearValue.toString();
   StringTokenizer yearTok = new StringTokenizer( yearStr, "-" );
   System.out.println( "jmYear      : " + yearTok.nextToken() );

   // Extract TIMESTAMP value
   timestampValue = results.getTimestamp( "jmTimestamp" );
   String timestampStr = timestampValue.toString();
   StringTokenizer timestampTok =
                         new StringTokenizer( timestampStr, "-:. " );
   StringBuffer timedateBuf = new StringBuffer( 14 );
   timedateBuf.append( timestampTok.nextToken() ); // Year
   timedateBuf.append( timestampTok.nextToken() ); // Month
   timedateBuf.append( timestampTok.nextToken() ); // Day
   timedateBuf.append( timestampTok.nextToken() ); // Hour
   timedateBuf.append( timestampTok.nextToken() ); // Minute
   timedateBuf.append( timestampTok.nextToken() ); // Second
   System.out.println( "jmTimestamp: " + timedateBuf.toString() );
 }
 catch( SQLException sqlX )
 {
   System.err.println( sqlX );
 }
```

Listing 7.2 Using date and time columns types. (continued)

Numeric Column Types

The numeric column types, summarized in Table 7.3, provide a means for handling integer and floating point values of differing size. It is important to note that, by default, MySQL integer types are signed. The column type mappings discussed in the following sections assume this default and are not necessarily valid where a column type is defined with an unsigned attribute. In such cases, using the mapping for the next largest type is typically a reasonable approach, given that the Java language does not support unsigned types.

Table 7.3 Numeric Column Types (continues)

MYSQL TYPE	JDBC TYPE	JAVA TYPE
TINYINT	TINYINT	byte
SMALLINT	SMALLINT	short
MEDIUMINT	INTEGER	int

Table 7.3 Numeric Column Types (continued)

MYSQL TYPE	JDBC TYPE	JAVA TYPE
INT	INTEGER	int
BIGINT	BIGINT	long
FLOAT	REAL	float
DOUBLE	DOUBLE	double
DECIMAL	DECIMAL	java.math.BigDecimal

TINYINT

The MySQL TINYINT type represents the smallest available integer type. Values of this type require one byte of storage and may take on values in the range –128 to 127 (0 to 255 if unsigned). MySQL aliases for this type include BIT and BOOL.

The TINYINT type maps to a TINYINT JDBC type, which in turn corresponds to a Java byte. The recommended ResultSet getter method for retrieving TINYINT types is getByte(). If the column type is modified by the unsigned attribute, consider using the MySQL SMALLINT mapping.

SMALLINT

The MySQL SMALLINT type represents a small integer type. Values of this type require two bytes of storage and may take on values in the range –32768 to 32767 (0 to 65535 if unsigned).

The SMALLINT type maps to a SMALLINT JDBC type, which in turn corresponds to a Java short. The recommended ResultSet getter method for retrieving SMALLINT types is getShort(). If the column type is modified by the unsigned attribute, consider using the MySQL MEDIUMINT or INT mapping.

MEDIUMINT

The MySQL MEDIUMINT type represents an intermediate size integer type. Values of this type require three bytes of storage and may take on values in the range –8388608 to 8388607 (0 to 16777215 if unsigned).

The MEDIUMINT type maps to an INTEGER JDBC type, which in turn corresponds to a Java int. The recommended ResultSet getter method for retrieving MEDIUMINT types is getInt(). Since a Java int is a four-byte type, this mapping is also appropriate where the column type is modified by the unsigned attribute.

INT

The MySQL INT type represents the basic integer type. Values of this type require four bytes of storage and may take on values in the range –2147483648 to 2147483647 (0 to 4294967295 if unsigned). The MySQL INTEGER type is an alias for this type.

The INT type maps to an INTEGER JDBC type, which in turn corresponds to a Java int. The recommended ResultSet getter method for retrieving INT types is getInt(). If the column type is modified by the unsigned attribute, consider using the MySQL BIGINT mapping.

BIGINT

The MySQL BIGINT type represents the largest integer type. Values of this type require eight bytes of storage and may take on values in the range –9223372036854775808 to 9223372036854775807 (0 to 18446744073709551615 if unsigned).

The BIGINT type maps to a BIGINT JDBC type, which in turn corresponds to a Java long. The recommended ResultSet getter method for retrieving BIGINT types is getLong(). Use of unsigned BIGINT column types is not generally recommended since any arithmetic involving such types is susceptible to overflow and truncation errors.

FLOAT

The MySQL FLOAT type represents the smaller of two available floating-point types. Values of this type require four bytes of storage and allow values of –3.402823466E+38 to –1.175494351E-38, 0, and 1.175494351E-38 to 3.402823466E+38.

The FLOAT type maps to a REAL JDBC type, which in turn corresponds to a Java float. The recommended ResultSet getter method for retrieving FLOAT types is getFloat(). Note that the JDBC FLOAT type corresponds to an eight-byte floating-point value, rather than a four-byte type.

DOUBLE

The MySQL DOUBLE type represents the larger of two available floating-point types. Values of this type require eight bytes of storage and allow values of –1.7976931348623157E+308 to –2.2250738585072014E-308, 0, and 2.2250738585072014E -308 to 1.7976931348623157E+308. MySQL aliases for this type include REAL and DOUBLE PRECISION.

The DOUBLE type maps to a DOUBLE JDBC type, which in turn corresponds to a Java double. The recommended ResultSet getter method for retrieving DOUBLE types is getDouble().

DECIMAL

The MySQL DECIMAL type represents a general numeric value. It differs from the other numeric column types in that the value is stored as a sequence of characters; in a sense, it might be considered a very specialized character column type. MySQL aliases for this type include DEC and NUMERIC.

The DECIMAL type maps to a DECIMAL JDBC type, which in turn corresponds to java.math.BigDecimal. The recommended ResultSet getter method for retrieving DECIMAL types is getBigDecimal().

Using Numeric Types

The code in Listing 7.3 demonstrates the use of numeric column types. Statement and PreparedStatement objects are used to create and populate a table that stores numeric types. The table is then queried, the column values extracted, and the results written to the standard output.

```
try
{
  String createSql = "CREATE TABLE jmNumeric ("
                   + "jmTinyint TINYINT, jmSmallint SMALLINT, "
                   + "jmMediumint MEDIUMINT, jmInt INT, "
                   + "jmBigint BIGINT, "
                   + "jmFloat FLOAT, jmDouble DOUBLE, "
                   + "jmDecimal DECIMAL(10,3))";

  Statement stmt = conn.createStatement();

  stmt.execute( createSql );

  byte tinyintValue = 16;
  short smallintValue = 4096;
  int mediumintValue = 1048576;
  int intValue = 268435456;
```

Listing 7.3 Using numeric column types. (continues)

```
    long bigintValue = 8589934592L;
    float floatValue = 3.3E+38F;
    double doubleValue = 1.7E+308;
    BigDecimal decimalValue = new BigDecimal( "1234567.890" );

    String insertSql = "INSERT INTO jmNumeric "
                     + "VALUES (?,?,?,?,?,?,?,?,?)";

    PreparedStatement pstmt = conn.prepareStatement( insertSql );

    pstmt.setByte( 1, tinyintValue );
    pstmt.setShort( 2, smallintValue );
    pstmt.setInt( 3, mediumintValue );
    pstmt.setInt( 4, intValue );
    pstmt.setLong( 5, bigintValue );
    pstmt.setFloat( 6, floatValue );
    pstmt.setDouble( 7, doubleValue );
    pstmt.setBigDecimal( 8, decimalValue );

    pstmt.execute();

    ResultSet results = stmt.executeQuery( "SELECT * from jmNumeric" );

    results.next();

    // Extract TINYINT, SMALLINT, MEDIUMINT, INT, and BIGINT values
    tinyintValue = results.getByte( "jmTinyint" );
    System.out.println( "jmTinyint  : " + tinyintValue );
    smallintValue = results.getShort( "jmSmallint" );
    System.out.println( "jmSmallint : " + smallintValue );
    mediumintValue = results.getInt( "jmMediumint" );
    System.out.println( "jmMediumint: " + mediumintValue );
    intValue = results.getInt( "jmInt" );
    System.out.println( "jmInt      : " + intValue );
    bigintValue = results.getLong( "jmBigint" );
    System.out.println( "jmBigint   : " + bigintValue );

    // Extract FLOAT and DOUBLE values
    floatValue = results.getFloat( "jmFloat" );
    System.out.println( "jmFloat    : " + floatValue );
    doubleValue = results.getDouble( "jmDouble" );
    System.out.println( "jmDouble   : " + doubleValue );

    // Extract DECIMAL value
    decimalValue = results.getBigDecimal( "jmDecimal" );;
    System.out.println( "jmDecimal  : " + decimalValue.toString() );
}
```

Listing 7.3 Using numeric column types. (continues)

```
catch( SQLException sqlX )
{
  System.err.println( sqlX );
}
```

Listing 7.3 Using numeric column types. (continued)

What's Next

In this chapter, we gave you an overview of the details involved in mapping data types between Java and MySQL. We discussed mappings that provide the information you need to safely insert and extract MySQL column values using Java client code. In the next chapter, we turn our attention to the important topic of database transactions.

CHAPTER 8

Transactions and Table Locking with Connector/J

Data integrity is one of the most important concepts you have to grasp when writing applications that manipulate a database. It is vital that the information in the database remain consistent and accurate. While there may be times when only a single application is reading information from the database and making updates, more than likely multiple users as well as multiple applications use the database at the same time. This means that two people might be updating a customer's record at the same time, which means that the data from the updates is mixed. Or one application might be updating a value in a record at the time that another application is reading the same record and inserting another row. In these types of situations, the database data can become "dirty"—in other words, it won't accurately model the real world. In this chapter, we look at the concept of transactions and table locking within MySQL and how you can use Connector/J to support database data integrity.

Understanding the Problem

Before we get into the technical information necessary to support transactions, let's look at an example to fully illustrate the problem caused by multiple simultaneous database accesses. Consider the acc_acc table, where an account's username and password is stored. The most active row is designated by the ts field with a value of 0. If a user changes his or her password, you don't update the row in the database; instead, you inactivate the current row by setting the ts field equal to the current time. A new row is then inserted into the database with the same information as the inactive row, except the password is new and the act_ts field contains the current time. The act_ts of the new row links the row with the previously changed row. Now, you can easily store the current time; thus, you can update the old row with ts = current time and simply insert the new row. It doesn't seem as if a transaction is necessary.

However, consider that once the current row is updated with ts = current time, there will be no active rows for the account. If another application tries to access the account, an empty set is returned. You cannot insert the new row first because then there would be two rows with a ts field equal to 0. After updating the current row, you expect the new row to be inserted right away—which means there will be a short time when a ts=0 row isn't available for the account.

But what happens if the application's database connection fails or the query is bad? The account wouldn't have a ts=0 row available. By using a transaction, you tell the system that all of the operations within the transaction need to complete successfully; otherwise, the transaction should fail and the system should roll back all of the changes to the previous values. In our example later in this chapter, we explore several scenarios where transactions are needed to maintain integrity.

Under the covers, the code that implements transactions must lock the appropriate database table at some level. The locking keeps other applications from accessing the data in the table. The most inflexible locking occurs at the table level. This means if we execute an update like UPDATE acc_acc, the system will lock the entire acc_acc table and not allow any access to the data. A better solution is to lock only the row or rows where the update needs to occur. As we see in the next section, table types are available in MySQL for row-level transaction locking.

MySQL's Transaction Table Types

Originally, the MySQL database server didn't support transaction tables. With the addition of the BDB table type from sleepycat.com and InnoDB from innodb.com, MySQL allows data to be updated in atomic operations to help eliminate the problems we've been discussing. In this section, we provide a brief overview of the table types and how they are used in MySQL.

The InnoDB Table Type

The InnoDB table type, provided by www.innodb.com, is actually its own database back end glued to MySQL. The system provides full transaction support along with crash recovery. When a transaction write occurs, InnoDB will set a lock at a row level only. It also gives you the ability to perform SELECT queries that don't need to lock the table. As a complete system, InnoDB has been optimized for performance and large data support. According to Innobase Oy (www.innodb.com), InnoDB has worked well in situations with over 1 terabyte of data stored using the table type.

The InnoDB table type is available in MySQL-Max distributions. If you are using or have downloaded a source distribution, you must compile in InnoDB support with the –with-innodb Configure flag. In addition, you should make available several InnoDB table options in the my.cnf MySQL configuration file. The example configuration files supplied with the binary distribution include the following options and values:

```
innodb_data_file_path = ibdata1:1000M
innodb_data_home_dir = c:\ibdata
innodb_log_group_home_dir = c:\iblogs
innodb_log_arch_dir = c:\iblogs
set-variable = innodb_mirrored_log_groups=1
set-variable = innodb_log_files_in_group=3
set-variable = innodb_log_file_size=5M
set-variable = innodb_log_buffer_size=8M
innodb_flush_log_at_trx_commit=1
innodb_log_archive=0
set-variable = innodb_buffer_pool_size=16M
set-variable = innodb_additional_mem_pool_size=2M
set-variable = innodb_file_io_threads=4
set-variable = innodb_lock_wait_timeout=50
```

Here's a description of these variables:

innodb_data_file_path—The path appended to the innodb_data_home_dir directory where the data files should be placed along with the minimum/maximum file sizes.

innodb_data_home_dir—The home directory for InnoDB tables. If this directory is not specified, the data directory defined for MySQL is used.

innodb_log_group_home_dir—The path to InnoDB log files.

innodb_log_arch_dir—The path to archived InnoDB log files if archiving is used.

innodb_mirrored_log_groups—The total number of mirrored log files.

innodb_log_files_in_group—The total number of log files to use in a rotation.

innodb_log_file_size—The total size of the log file group.

innodb_log_buffer_size—The size of the buffer used for InnoDB before writing to the log.

innodb_flush_log_at_trx_commit—If set to 1, a commit causes the transaction information to be flushed to the log.

innodb_log_archive—Set to a value of 0 as archiving occurs within MySQL.

innodb_buffer_pool_size—The size of the various InnoDB caches.

innodb_additional_mem_pool_size—The size of the InnoDB cache for ancillary information.

innodb_file_io_threads—The total number of threads used to handle I/O.

innodb_lock_wait_timeout—The time (in seconds) that InnoDB waits for a lock before automatically rolling back a transaction.

As these variables show, MySQL devotes a good deal of attention to the log files. The reason for this is that the logs are used for transaction and recovery support and are vital to the operation of the InnoDB table type. For this reason, the logs should be located on a drive other than the drive where the actual data is stored.

The BDB Table Type

The BDB table type, supplied by www.sleepycat.com, also provides transaction and crash recovery support. For the most part, BDB is a less advanced system than InnoDB, but it still provides full support for transactions. You must make the appropriate configuration changes on source distributions by using the –with-bdb Configure option.

Once you've installed the BDB table type, make the following values available in the MySQL configuration file:

bdb-home—The base directory for BDB tables. Typically, this will be the same as the MySQL data directory.

bdb-logdir—The directory used for log files; it should be different from the directory used for tables.

bdb_cache_size—The cache size; 384MB is the value provided in sample configuration files.

bdb_max_lock—The total number of locks allowed in the system; 100000 is the value provided in the sample configuration files.

Converting to Transactional from Nontransactional

If you have a table that is based on a nontransactional table type and you want to use transactions, you have to convert the table type to either InnoDB or BDB. There are several ways to accomplish this task.

The first is using the ALTER TABLE command. For example, if you have a table named acc_acc that you want to convert to InnoDB or BDB, use this format:

```
ALTER TABLE acc_acc TYPE = InnoDB
```

The system handles the conversion of the table automatically. However, the InnoDB documentation states that you should not convert a MyISAM table type in this manner. Here's a safer method:

1. Create a new destination table with columns identical to the source table but use a table type of InnoDB or BDB.
2. Copy the records from the source table to the destination table. The command to do this is

   ```
   INSERT INTO destinationTable SELECT * FROM sourceTable
   ```

3. Rename the source table.
4. Rename the destination table to the source table's previous name.

Performing Transactions in MySQL

Whether you use InnoDB or BDB, transaction handling in a database adds a high degree of integrity to the database. In the remainder of this chapter, we discuss how to activate transactions with the autocommit variable, and we examine various queries which can take advantage of transactions.

Using the autocommit Variable

The MySQL database server—and just about all database systems that support transactions—use a variable called autocommit to determine how updates to the database should be handled. By default, autocommit is set to a value of true or 1, which indicates that all updates (insert, update, delete, and so forth) should be automatically committed to the database. In Figure 8.1, we show a SELECT performed on the acc_acc table looking at acc_id 1034546. Notice the ts field has a value other than 0. We use an UPDATE query to change the value of ts to 0, thus activating the row. When we execute the SELECT query again, we see that the ts field has been successfully changed. The value of 0 has been permanently written to the database table, and the previous value for the ts field has been lost and cannot be replaced outside a database restore.

Now we can change the value of autocommit to 0 or false in order to activate the concept of transactions. Figure 8.2 shows an example of SQL we entered using the MySQL administration tool. As the figure shows, the autocommit variable is set to 0. The beginning of the transaction is indicated by using either BEGIN or BEGIN WORK or a SQL command.

```
mysql> select * from acc_acc where acc_id = '1034546';
+---------+----------+----------+----------------+----------------+
| acc_id  | username | password | ts             | act_ts         |
+---------+----------+----------+----------------+----------------+
| 1034546 | jjmyers  | ime      | 20030106171727 | 00000000000000 |
+---------+----------+----------+----------------+----------------+
1 row in set (0.00 sec)

mysql> update acc_acc set ts = 0 where acc_id = '1034546';
Query OK, 1 row affected (0.00 sec)
Rows matched: 1  Changed: 1  Warnings: 0

mysql> select * from acc_acc where acc_id = '1034546';
+---------+----------+----------+----------------+----------------+
| acc_id  | username | password | ts             | act_ts         |
+---------+----------+----------+----------------+----------------+
| 1034546 | jjmyers  | ime      | 00000000000000 | 00000000000000 |
+---------+----------+----------+----------------+----------------+
1 row in set (0.00 sec)

mysql>
```

Figure 8.1 Here, autocommit is set to true.

Next, we perform a SELECT to show the fields for acc_id = 1034546. Notice the value of the password field. We perform an UPDATE query to change the value of the password and perform a SELECT right after the UPDATE to verify that the password has been changed. However, at this point we notice the password is wrong, so we execute a rollback SQL command. The rollback cancels the UPDATE—which we verify by executing another SELECT query to show the password has been changed back to its original value.

The autocommit variable is valid only against transactional table types. If an UPDATE query is performed against a nontransactional table, the autocommit variable value is ignored and the UPDATE is made permanent.

```
mysql> set autocommit=0;
Query OK, 0 rows affected (0.00 sec)

mysql> select * from acc_acc where acc_id = '1034546';
+---------+----------+----------+----------------+----------------+
| acc_id  | username | password | ts             | act_ts         |
+---------+----------+----------+----------------+----------------+
| 1034546 | jjmyers  | ime      | 20030106175202 | 00000000000000 |
+---------+----------+----------+----------------+----------------+
1 row in set (0.01 sec)

mysql> update acc_acc set password='mypsw' where acc_id = '1034546';
Query OK, 1 row affected (0.00 sec)
Rows matched: 1  Changed: 1  Warnings: 0

mysql> select * from acc_acc where acc_id = '1034546';
+---------+----------+----------+----------------+----------------+
| acc_id  | username | password | ts             | act_ts         |
+---------+----------+----------+----------------+----------------+
| 1034546 | jjmyers  | mypsw    | 20030106175449 | 00000000000000 |
+---------+----------+----------+----------------+----------------+
1 row in set (0.00 sec)

mysql> rollback;
Query OK, 0 rows affected (0.00 sec)

mysql> select * from acc_acc where acc_id = '1034546';
+---------+----------+----------+----------------+----------------+
| acc_id  | username | password | ts             | act_ts         |
+---------+----------+----------+----------------+----------------+
| 1034546 | jjmyers  | ime      | 20030106175202 | 00000000000000 |
+---------+----------+----------+----------------+----------------+
1 row in set (0.00 sec)

mysql>
```

Figure 8.2 An example of a transaction.

In these examples, we used the MySQL administration tool to show how transactions work. In the next few sections, we illustrate transactions using Java and Connector/J.

Update Transactions

Earlier, we discussed a scenario where you need to update and insert rows that rely on each other. For example, suppose you want to change the ts value on one row and insert a new row with the same value for the act_ts. You aren't necessarily concerned with the timestamp value, but you must take into account the lack of a ts=0 row should the update or insert fail. Consider the following query and row from a test database:

```
mysql> select * from acc_add where acc_id = 1034055;

+--------+---------+----------+----------------+----------------+
| add_id | acc_id  | name     | ts             | act_ts         |
+--------+---------+----------+----------------+----------------+
|  30004 | 1034055 | John Doe | 00000000000000 | 20021015200759 |
+--------+---------+----------+----------------+----------------+
1 row in set (0.00 sec)
```

In this table row, you find a record with a ts value of 0. Let's change the address for this account, 1034055, which means the ts of this row should be non-zero and a new row inserted with the new address. The code in Listing 8.1 shows how you might do this from Java.

```
import java.sql.*;
import java.io.*;

public class Transaction1 {
  Connection connection;

  public Transaction1() {
     try {
       Class.forName("com.mysql.jdbc.Driver").newInstance();
       connection = DriverManager.getConnection(
        "jdbc:mysql://192.168.1.25/accounts?
         user=spider&password=spider");
     }
     catch (Exception  e) {
       System.err.println("Unable to find and load driver");
       System.exit(1);
```

Listing 8.1 A transaction to update/insert rows. (continues)

```
    }
  }

  public void doWork() {
   try {
     java.util.Date now = new java.util.Date();
     connection.setAutoCommit(false);
       Statement statement = connection.createStatement(
         ResultSet.TYPE_SCROLL_INSENSITIVE,
         ResultSet.CONCUR_UPDATABLE);
       ResultSet rs = statement.executeQuery(
         "SELECT * FROM acc_add WHERE acc_id = 1034055
          and ts = 0");

       // set old row ts = current time
       rs.next();
       rs.updateTimestamp("ts", new Timestamp(now.getTime()));
       rs.updateRow();

       rs.moveToInsertRow();
       rs.updateInt("add_id", rs.getInt("add_id"));
       rs.updateInt("acc_id", rs.getInt("acc_id"));
       rs.updateString("name", rs.getString("name"));
       rs.updateString("address1", "555 East South Street");
       rs.updateString("address2", "");
       rs.updateString("address3", "");
       rs.updateString("city", rs.getString("city"));
       rs.updateString("state", rs.getString("state"));
       rs.updateString("zip", rs.getString("zip"));
       rs.updateTimestamp("ts", new Timestamp(0));
       rs.updateTimestamp("act_ts", new Timestamp(now.getTime()));
       rs.insertRow();
      connection.commit();

      rs.close();
      statement.close();
      connection.close();

   } catch(Exception e) {
     try {
       connection.rollback();
     } catch (SQLException error) { }
     e.printStackTrace();
   }
  }

  public static void main(String[] args) {
```

Listing 8.1 A transaction to update/insert rows. (continues)

```
    Transaction1 trans = new Transaction1();
    trans.doWork();
  }
}
```

Listing 8.1 A transaction to update/insert rows. (continued)

When the code in Listing 8.1 executes, the following rows will be found in the acc_add table based on an acc_id of 1034055. Notice the original row is now ts <> 0 and the new row is ts=0.

```
mysql> select * from acc_add where acc_id = 1034055;

+--------+---------+----------+----------------+----------------+
| add_id | acc_id  | name     | ts             | act_ts         |
+--------+---------+----------+----------------+----------------+
|  30004 | 1034055 | John Doe | 20021028221407 | 20021015200759 |
|  30004 | 1034055 | John Doe | 00000000000000 | 20021028221407 |
+--------+---------+----------+----------------+----------------+
2 rows in set (0.00 sec)
```

In order to accomplish this successfully, we need to perform a transaction via the doWork() method. Connector/J handles transactions using several methods found in the Connection object:

- setAutoCommit(Boolean)—Sets MySQL's autocommit variable.
- commit()—Commits all updates since the last commit()/rollback() method call, if any.
- rollback()—Rolls back all updates since the last commit()/rollback() method call, if any.

Our code begins by setting the autocommit variable to false:

```
connection.setAutoCommit(false);
```

We get the current time using the java.util.Date class. This time is used to set the ts field of the current row and the act_ts field of the new row. The code uses an UpdatableResult so the appropriate parameters are passed to the createStatement() method, as shown here:

```
Statement statement = connection.createStatement(
  ResultSet.TYPE_SCROLL_INSENSITIVE,
  ResultSet.CONCUR_UPDATABLE);
```

Next, we execute a query to pull in a row with an acc_id of 1034055 and the ts field equal to 0. Using the time value previously created, our code updates the ts field to the new value and writes back the entire row to the database. Here's the relevant code:

```
rs.next();
rs.updateTimestamp("ts", new Timestamp(now.getTime()));
rs.updateRow();
```

Since we have set autocommit to false, the update won't be made permanent just yet. Now we need to insert the new row with the changed address information. Here's how we do that:

```
rs.moveToInsertRow();
rs.updateInt("add_id", rs.getInt("add_id"));
rs.updateInt("acc_id", rs.getInt("acc_id"));
rs.updateString("name", rs.getString("name"));
rs.updateString("address1", "555 East South Street");
rs.updateString("address2", "");
rs.updateString("address3", "");
rs.updateString("city", rs.getString("city"));
rs.updateString("state", rs.getString("state"));
rs.updateString("zip", rs.getString("zip"));
rs.updateTimestamp("ts", new Timestamp(0));
rs.updateTimestamp("act_ts", new Timestamp(now.getTime()));
rs.insertRow();
```

The key part of this code is setting the ts field to 0 and the act_ts field to the current time. Now the two different updates must be committed to the database. We do this with a call to the commit() method:

```
connection.commit();
```

But what about a rollback? We place the rollback() method in the catch code for the try/catch block surrounding all of the code doing the database manipulation. If any of the code throws an exception, the rollback() method fires and all of the changes are removed from the database table. Our code then displays an error message to let the user know his or her changes weren't recorded.

The SELECT/INSERT Transaction

As the complexity of your application and its associated database increases, you'll inevitably come across situations in which a transaction is necessary to create a snapshot of time: in order to grab a total, a momentary price, or some other changing value. You must identify this changing value in a transaction so it can be read and recorded without other applications trying to change the data. For example, consider the following snippet of Java code:

```
connection.setAutoCommit(false);
Statement statement = connection.createStatement();
ResultSet rs = statement.executeQuery("SELECT MAX(acc_id) FROM
acc_acc");
rs.next();
int acc_id = rs.getString("max(acc_id)");
```

```
statement.executeUpdate(
  "INSERT INTO acc_acc VALUES(" + acc_id + ", 'name',
   'password', 0, " + date);
connection.commit();
```

In this code snippet, we insert a new account into the acc_acc table and we want to know the currently largest acc_id value in the database. Since other applications are trying to add accounts at the same time, we need a way to get the maximum account value and insert the new row before another application does its INSERT. When another application attempts to get the maximum acc_id value and insert a new row, it will have to wait until the current transaction is finished. When it gets a chance to update the database, that application will receive an error because the maximum acc_id has already been used. All applications should be able to recover from this type of situation by either attempting to get the maximum acc_id again or choosing one randomly.

Multiple Table Transactions

If you are entering an entirely new account into the database, you probably need to handle INSERT queries to acc_acc, acc_add, and the thumbnail tables. Transactions can work across tables and databases as well, as the following code shows:

```
connection.setAutoCommit(false);
Statement statement = connection.createStatement();
ResultSet rs = statement.executeQuery("SELECT MAX(acc_id) FROM
acc_acc");
rs.next();

int acc_id = rs.getInt("max(acc_id)") + 1;

statement.executeUpdate(
  "INSERT INTO acc_acc VALUES(" + acc_id + ", 'name',
   'password', 0, " + date);

rs = statement.executeQuery("SELECT MAX(add_id) FROM acc_add");
rs.next();
int add_id = rs.getInt("max(add_id) ") + 1;
statement.executeUpdate(
  "INSERT INTO acc_add VALUES(" + add_id + ", " + acc_id + ",
  'name', 'address1', null, null, 'city', 'state', 'zip', 0,
  date) ";

rs = statement.executeQuery(
  "SELECT MAX(thumb_id) FROM identificaton.thumbnail");
rs.next();
int thumb_id = rs.getInt("max(thumb_id) ") + 1;
statement.executeUpdate(
```

```
    "INSERT INTO identification.thumbnail VALUES(" + thumb_id +
    ", " + acc_id + ", null, null, 0, date) ";

  connection.commit();
```

As you can see, we simply repeat the process of finding the maximum primary key value, incrementing by 1 and INSERTing a new row into the appropriate table. This code updates three different tables before performing a commit. If any of the updates fail, a rollback() call is made in the catch code.

Foreign Key Integrity on Deletes

Finally, if you have to delete rows from a database, keep in mind that MySQL and Connector/J don't yet support the full concept of a foreign key and automatic deletes. In other words, if you remove a row in acc_acc, you also remove the corresponding rows in acc_add and identification.thumbnail. By using transactions, you ensure that the rows are all removed under the umbrella of a single transaction.

Ending a Transaction

In MySQL, executing a commit() method on the Connection method or commit; command at the MySQL administrator prompt causes the transaction to be written to the database permanently. The database server defines other commands that cause a transaction to end in the same manner as a commit. These commands are

- ALTER TABLE
- BEGIN
- CREATE INDEX
- DROP DATABASE
- DROP TABLE
- RENAME TABLE
- TRUNCATE

You can issue any of these commands before an official commit to make the server commit the transaction—just as if you had used the commit command.

Transaction Isolation

In the chapter introduction, we stated that data integrity is an important database concept. Transactions are designed to help with this goal, but when multiple applications are performing transactions concurrently, several problems can arise. Three of the most common problems are dirty reads, phantom reads, and nonrepeatable reads. You can address these issues by setting transaction isolation levels. The isolation levels available in MySQL and supported in Connector/J are as follows:

TRANSACTION_NONE—Puts no restrictions on the read and updates to the database.

TRANSACTION_READ_UNCOMMITTED—Allows uncommitted changes by one transaction to be readable by other transactions.

TRANSACTION_READ_COMMITTED—Makes all updates to a table invisible to all other transactions until a commit is performed.

TRANSACTION_REPEATABLE_READ—Keeps all SELECTs consistent in a single transaction.

TRANSACTION_SERIALIZABLE—Causes all read and updates to operate in a serialized sequence.

You set the various isolation levels by using the setTransactionLevel() method associated with the Connection object. Table 8.1 shows how database performance will be affected.

Table 8.1 Database Isolation Levels Supported in Connector/J

TRANSACTION LEVEL	DIRTY READS	NON-REPEAT-ABLE READS	PHANTOM READS	PER-FORM-ANCE IMPACT
TRANSACTION_NONE	N/A	N/A	N/A	FASTEST
TRANSACTION_READ_UNCOMMITED	Allows	Allows	Allows	FASTEST
TRANSACTION_READ_COMMITED	Prevents	Allows	Allows	FAST
TRANSACTION_REPEATABLE_READ	Prevents	Prevents	Allows	MEDIUM
TRANSACTION_SERIALIZABLE	Prevents	Prevents	Prevents	SLOW

Dirty Reads

A dirty read occurs when incorrect data is read from a row update. Consider the following sequence of commands from two transactions:

Step 1: Database row has ACC_ADD = 4510 and STATE = 'AZ'.

Step 2: Connection1 starts Transaction1 (T1).

Step 3: Connection2 starts Transaction2 (T2).

Step 4: T1 updates STATE = 'IL' for = ACC_ADD = 4510.

Step 5: Database now has STATE = 'IL' for ACC_ADD = 4510.

Step 6: T2 reads STATE = 'IL' for ACC_ADD = 4510.

Step 7: T2 commits transaction using STATE = 'IL'.

Step 8: T1 rolls back the transaction because of some problem.

In this illustration, Transaction2 has read an update in the database that hasn't been committed yet. As it turns out, Transaction1 has a problem with the update and rolls it back—but *after* Transaction2 has already read and updated another row using the "bad" STATE value. To solve this problem, you can use the read_committed, serializable, and repeatable_read isolation levels.

Phantom Reads

In a phantom read, during one transaction new rows are inserted into the database by another transaction. For example:

Step 1: The database has a row ACC_ID = 4510 and ADD_ID = 10.

Step 2: Connection1 starts Transaction1 (T1).

Step 3: Connection2 starts Transaction2 (T2).

Step 4: T1 selects a row with a condition SELECT ACC_ID WHERE ADD_ID = 10.

Step 5: T2 inserts a row with a condition INSERT ACC_ID=4520 WHERE ADD_ID = 10.

Step 6: T2 commits the transaction.

Step 7: Database has two rows with that condition.

Step 8: T1 selects again with a condition SELECT ACC_ID WHERE ADD_ID = 10 and gets two rows instead of one row.

Step 9: T1 commits the transaction.

The problem in this scenario is that Transaction1 will get two rows from the same query. To keep this from occurring, you can use the serializable isolation level.

Nonrepeatable Reads

In a nonrepeatable read situation, one transaction reads a database row and receives two different values because another transaction has updated the row between the reads. For example:

Step 1: A database row has ACC_ADD = 4510 and STATE = 'AZ'.

Step 2: Connection1 starts Transaction1 (T1).

Step 3: Connection2 starts Transaction2 (T2).

Step 4: T1 reads STATE = 'AZ' for ACC_ADD = 4510.

Step 5: T2 updates STATE = 'IL' for ACC_ADD = 4510.

Step 6: T2 commits the transaction.

Step 7: The database row has ACC_ADD = 4510 and STATE = 'IL'.

Step 8: T1 reads STATE = 'IL' for ACC_ADD = 4510.

Step 9: T1 commits the transaction.

In this example, Transaction1 reads a STATE value AZ initially and then read the state value IL; however, it should only see a value of AZ when the SELECTs are performed in the same transaction. To solve this problem, use the repeatable_read isolation level.

Table Locking

In our discussion of the SELECT/INSERT transaction, we described a situation in which a transaction works to keep new duplicate records from being inserted into the database. Even if two or more applications get the same maximum acc_id, they will be unable to complete the INSERT successfully because the primary key will be violated with the duplicate acc_id values.

What if we could do another trick and block the SELECT so that no other application would be able to do the SELECT until after the transaction? Consider this variation of the SELECT/INSERT code:

```
connection.setAutoCommit(false);
Statement statement = connection.createStatement();
statement.executeUpdate("LOCK TABLES acc_acc WRITE");
ResultSet rs = statement.executeQuery("SELECT MAX(acc_id) FROM
acc_acc");
rs.next();
int acc_id = rs.getInt("max(acc_id)") + 1;
statement.executeUpdate(
  "INSERT INTO acc_acc VALUES(" + acc_id + ", 'name',
   'password', 0, " + date);
connection.commit();
statement.executeUpdate("UNLOCK TABLES");
```

In this new code, we have added two additional queries. The first one is

```
statement.executeUpdate("LOCK TABLES acc_acc WRITE");
```

This query causes the MySQL database server to lock the acc_acc table for writing—which also blocks all SELECTs except for the current connection. When this query executes, the server throws a database lock on the acc_acc table for all other connections to the server. No other connection will be able to work with the table until the code executes the following statement:

```
statement.executeUpdate("UNLOCK TABLES");
```

This query unlocks the database lock on acc_acc and allows other blocking applications access to the database table. Clearly the act of locking a database table can have interesting side effects on the other applications waiting to work with the table. The worst situation that can occur is that the current application crashes and the lock isn't released on the acc_acc table—which causes the system to come to a halt.

When using a SELECT/INSERT transaction and the SELECT is vital to the INSERT, you either have to lock the table where the SELECT occurs or handle the errors that occur when the application attempts to insert a duplicate primary key into the database.

What's Next

Multiple users as well as multiple applications typically use a database at the same time—which means that updates can occur at the same time other applications are accessing the same database and tables. Transactions allow an application to modify data without interference from those other applications. In extreme cases, the application can lock an entire table and not allow writes or reads.

In the next chapter, we explain how you can access the additional information provided by database and ResultSet metadata.

CHAPTER 9

Using Metadata

The information stored in a database table isn't always everything you need when developing an application. If you are writing a servlet that will be used to remotely administer the database, you might like to know about current database features, what databases are defined, and other information. The JDBC specification and Connector/J provide access to several methods that allow an application to access information about the database as well as information about a ResultSet object. In this chapter, we cover some of the more common and useful methods found in the DatabaseMetaData object. For a complete listing, refer to Appendix C.

Many of the methods allow arguments for determining which databases and tables the methods should return information from. In these cases, you can use the full string name of the table, or you can use string patterns in which the % character is used to match 0 or more characters and the underscore (_) is used to match one character.

Using Database Metadata

Connector/J provides information about the database server behind a connection by using the DatabaseMetaData object. This object is designed to provide information in five major areas:

- General Source Information
- Feature Support

- Data Source Limits
- SQL Objects Available
- Transaction Support

The code in Listing 9.1 provides a glimpse at some of the methods in each of these five areas. The current JDBC specification and Connector/J implement hundreds of attributes and methods in the DatabaseMetaData object, and we can't cover all of them here. See Appendix B to learn about all the attributes and methods.

```
import java.io.*;
import java.sql.*;
import javax.servlet.*;
import javax.servlet.http.*;
import javax.naming.*;
//import javax.naming.spi.ObjectFactory;
import javax.sql.DataSource;

public class DatabaseInfo extends HttpServlet {

  public void doGet(HttpServletRequest inRequest,
    HttpServletResponse outResponse)
    throws ServletException, IOException {

    PrintWriter out = null;
    Connection connection = null;
    Statement statement;
    ResultSet rs;

      outResponse.setContentType("text/html");
      out = outResponse.getWriter();

    try {
      Context ctx = new InitialContext();
      DataSource ds =
(DataSource)ctx.lookup("java:comp/env/jdbc/AccountsDB");
      connection = ds.getConnection();

      DatabaseMetaData md = connection.getMetaData();
      statement = connection.createStatement();

      out.println("<HTML><HEAD><TITLE>
        Database Server Information</TITLE></HEAD>");
      out.println("<BODY>");
```

Listing 9.1 A database metadata example. (continues)

```
      out.println("<H1>General Source Information</H1>");
      out.println("getURL() - " + md.getURL() + "<BR>");
      out.println("getUserName() - " + md.getUserName() +
"<BR>");
      out.println("getDatabaseProductVersion - "
        + md.getDatabaseProductVersion() + "<BR>");
      out.println("getDriverMajorVersion - "
        + md.getDriverMajorVersion() + "<BR>");
      out.println("getDriverMinorVersion - "
        + md.getDriverMinorVersion() + "<BR>");
      out.println("nullAreSortedHigh - "
        + md.nullsAreSortedHigh() + "<BR>");

      out.println("<H1>Feature Support</H1>");

      out.println("<H1>Data Source Limits</H1>");
      out.println("getMaxRowSize - " + md.getMaxRowSize() + "<BR>");
      out.println("getMaxStatementLength - "
        + md.getMaxStatementLength() + "<BR>");
      out.println("getMaxTablesInSelect - "
        + md.getMaxTablesInSelect() + "<BR>");
      out.println("getMaxConnections - "
        + md.getMaxConnections() + "<BR>");
      out.println("getMaxCharLiteralLength - "
        + md.getMaxCharLiteralLength() + "<BR>");

      out.println("<H1>SQL Object Available</H1>");
      out.println("getTableTypes()<BR><UL>");
      rs = md.getTableTypes();
      while (rs.next()) {
        out.println("<LI>" + rs.getString(1));
      }
      out.println("</UL>");

      out.println("getTables()<BR><UL>");
      rs = md.getTables("accounts", "", "%", new String[0]);
      while (rs.next()) {
        out.println("<LI>" + rs.getString("TABLE_NAME"));
      }
      out.println("</UL>");

      out.println("<H1>Transaction Support</H1>");
      out.println("getDefaultTransactionIsolation() - "
        + md.getDefaultTransactionIsolation() + "<BR>");
      out.println("dataDefinitionIgnoredInTransactions() - "
        + md.dataDefinitionIgnoredInTransactions() + "<BR>");
```

Listing 9.1 A database metadata example. (continues)

```
        out.println("<H1>General Source Information</H1>");
        out.println("getMaxTablesInSelect - "
          + md.getMaxTablesInSelect() + "<BR>");
        out.println("getMaxColumnsInTable - "
          + md.getMaxColumnsInTable() + "<BR>");
        out.println("getTimeDateFunctions - "
          + md.getTimeDateFunctions() + "<BR>");
        out.println("supportsCoreSQLGrammar - "
          + md.supportsCoreSQLGrammar() + "<BR>");

        out.println("getTypeInfo()<BR><UL>");
        rs = md.getTypeInfo();
        while (rs.next()) {
          out.println("<LI>" + rs.getString(1));
        }
        out.println("</UL>");

        out.println("</BODY></HTML>");
      } catch (Exception e) {
       e.printStackTrace();
      }
    }

    public void doPost(HttpServletRequest inRequest,
      HttpServletResponse outResponse)
      throws ServletException, IOException {
      doGet(inRequest, outResponse);
    }
  }
```

Listing 9.1 A database metadata example. (continued)

When the code in Listing 9.1 executes, it displays five different areas of information, as we explained earlier. Figures 9.1, 9.2, and 9.3 show the values displayed when the code executes against a test machine running MySQL 4.0.

Getting the Object

As the code in Listing 9.1 shows, the DatabaseMetaData object is obtained using code like the following:

```
DatabaseMetaData md = connection.getMetaData();
```

Since the DatabaseMetaData object isn't related to a statement or a query, you can request the object using the getMetaData() method once you've established a connection to a MySQL database.

Figure 9.1 Output from our database metadata example.

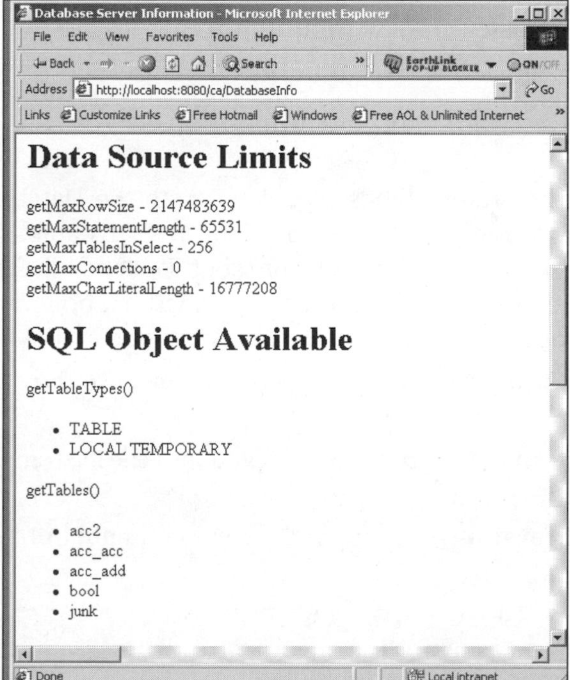

Figure 9.2 Additional output from the metadata example.

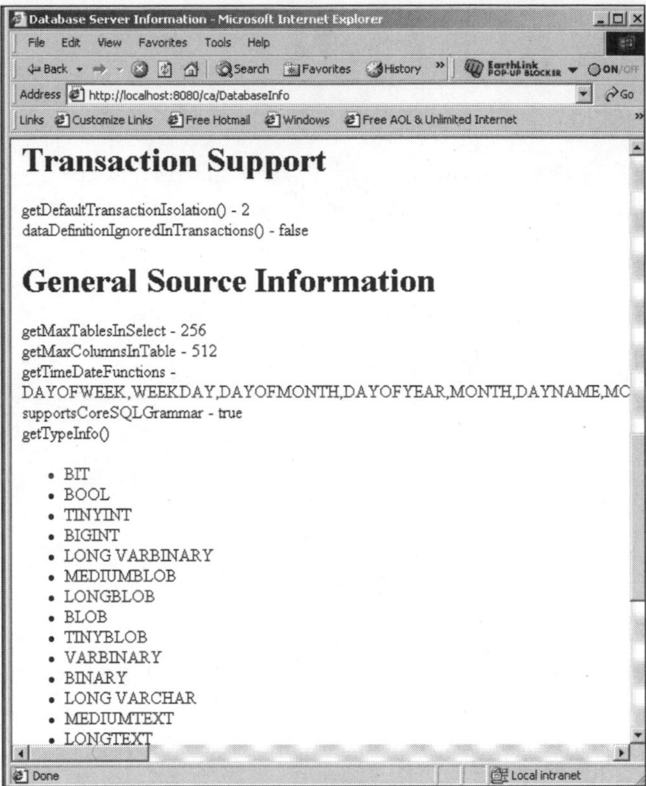

Figure 9.3 The final two areas of output.

General Source Information

The General Source Information methods associated with the DatabaseMetaData object are designed to give information about the MySQL database server in general and are not specific to one database or table. The code in Listing 9.1 details just six of the many methods that provide information about the server. Figure 9.1 shows the output generated from the following size methods:

getURL()—Returns a string with the URL used to connect to the database server.

getUserName()—Returns the current user logged into the system on this connection.

getDatabaseProductVersion()—Returns the version number of the database server.

getDriverMajorVersion()—Returns the major version number of the JDBC driver—Connector/J in our case.

getDriverMinorVersion()—Returns the minor version number of the JDBC driver.

nullsAreSortedHigh()—Returns a true/false value indicating whether nulls will be sorted before or after the data.

getTimeDateFunctions()—Returns all of the time/data functions available on the server.

getTypeInfo()—Returns a ResultSet object with all of the possible types supported by the database server. The code to extract the information is

```
rs = md.getTypeInfo();
while (rs.next()) {
  out.println("<LI>" + rs.getString(1));
}
```

Feature Support

Some of the more useful parts of the DatabaseMetaData object are the methods associated with features supported on the server. Figure 9.1 shows the output of the example methods:

supportsAlterTableWithDropColumn()—Returns true/false if the server supports the ALTER TABLE command with a drop column.

supportsBatchUpdates()—Returns true/false if the driver and server support batch updates.

supportsTableCorrelationNames()—Returns true/false if the database server supports correlation names.

supportsPositionedDelete()—Returns true/false if the server supports positioned DELETE commands.

supportsFullOuterJoins()—Returns true/false if the server supports full nested outer joins.

supportsStoredProcedures()—Returns true/false if the server supports stored procedures.

supportsMixedCaseQuotedIdentifiers()—Returns true/false if identifiers can be mixed case when quoted.

supportsANSI92EntryLevelSQL()—Returns true/false if the server supports the entry-level SQL for ANSI 92.

supportsCoreSQLGrammar()—Returns true/false if the server supports core ODBC SQL grammar.

What makes these methods useful is the fact that your application can execute different code based on the support provided by the MySQL and Connector/J. You could write your application to support older versions of the database as well as the cutting-edge development version by keeping track of the features supported.

Data Source Limits

Figure 9.2 shows the output generated for the chosen methods under Data Source Limits. These methods provide information on the total number of specified elements that will be returned or allowed. The examples methods are

getMaxRowSize()—Returns the maximum number of bytes allowed in a row.

getMaxStatementLength()—Returns the maximum length of a statement.

getMaxTablesInSelect()—Returns the maximum number of tables that can appear in a SELECT.

getMaxColumnsInTable()—Returns the maximum number of columns that can be defined in a table.

getMaxConnections()—Returns the maximum number of concurrent connections currently defined.

getMaxCharLiteralLength()—Returns the maximum number of characters allowed in a literal.

SQL Object Available

The SQL Object Available methods are designed to give you information about table types and other information about the actual SQL objects in the database server. Figure 9.2 shows an example of the output generated from these methods:

getTableTypes()—Returns a ResultSet object with all of the table types available on the current server.

getTables(database, schema, table, types)—Returns all of the tables in a given database, having a specific schema, narrowed by table and type. The schema parameter is ignored in Connector/J. The code for the call looks like this:

```
rs = md.getTables("accounts", "", "%", new String[0]);
while (rs.next()) {
  out.println("<LI>" + rs.getString("TABLE_NAME"));
}
```

The result returned by the getTables() method has the following columns available: TABLE_CAT, TABLE_SCHEM, TABLE_NAME, TABLE_TYPE, REMARKS, TYPE_CAT, TYPE_SCHEM, TYPE_NAME, SEL_REFERENCING_COL_NAME, and REF_GENERATION.

Transaction Support

Transaction support is new to MySQL and Connector/J, and the DatabaseMetaData object includes a few methods for determining transaction support, as shown in Figure 9.3. The two methods are:

getDefaultTransactionIsolation()—Returns the default transaction isolation. Possible values are TRANSACTION_NONE, TRANSACTION_READ_UNCOMMITTED, TRANSACTION_READ_COMMITTED, TRANSACTION_REPEATABLE_READ, and TRANSACTION_SERIALIZABLE.

dataDefinitionIgnoredInTransactions()—Returns true/false indicating whether data definition changes are ignored in a transaction.

The ResultSet Metadata

The database metadata provides fairly consistent data concerning the server itself. We can also use the ResultSet metadata. Each time a query is made against the database, all of the data is stored in the appropriate data structures within the object. Along with the data, we can also obtain information about the specific columns returned by the query.

The ResultSet object includes a method with the signature

```
ResultSetMetaData getMetaData();
```

This method returns a ResultSetMetaData object containing a dozen or so methods that return all kinds of information about the columns returned in the result. Let's look at two different applications that show the majority of the available methods.

Getting Column Information

In all of the applications to this point, we have assumed and hard-coded the columns in the query that we know exist in the database table. If we have an application that allows the user to enter a query or if the structure of the database changes often, we might want to rely on the database itself to provide information about the columns. The code in Listing 9.2 uses the ResultSetMetaData object's methods to determine column information.

```
import java.io.*;
import java.sql.*;
import javax.servlet.*;
import javax.servlet.http.*;
import javax.naming.*;
import javax.sql.DataSource;

public class SeeAccount extends HttpServlet {
```

Listing 9.2 A ResultSet metadata example. (continues)

```
  public void doGet(HttpServletRequest inRequest,
    HttpServletResponse outResponse)
    throws ServletException, IOException {

    PrintWriter out = null;
    Connection connection = null;
    Statement statement = null;

    ResultSet rs;

    try {
      outResponse.setContentType("text/html");
      out = outResponse.getWriter();

      Context ctx = new InitialContext();
      DataSource ds = (DataSource)ctx.lookup(
        "java:comp/env/jdbc/AccountsDB");
      connection = ds.getConnection();

      statement = connection.createStatement();
      rs = statement.executeQuery("SELECT * FROM acc_acc");
      ResultSetMetaData md = rs.getMetaData();

      out.println("<HTML><HEAD><TITLE>
        Thumbnail Identification Record</TITLE></HEAD>");
      out.println("<BODY>");
      out.println("Account Information:<BR>");
      while (rs.next()) {
        for (int i=1;i<=md.getColumnCount();i++) {
                   out.println(md.getColumnName(i) + " : "
                     + rs.getString(i) + "<BR>");
        }
        out.println("<HR>");
      }
      out.println("</BODY></HTML>");
    } catch(Exception e) {
      e.printStackTrace();
    }
  }

  public void doPost(HttpServletRequest inRequest,
    HttpServletResponse outResponse)
    throws ServletException, IOException {
     doGet(inRequest, outResponse);
  }
}
```

Listing 9.2 A ResultSet metadata example. (continued)

Looking at the servlet in Listing 9.2, you can see that it executes a query to pull back rows from the acc_acc table. Once the query has been executed, we obtain the metadata from the ResultSet using this code:

```
ResultSetMetaData md = rs.getMetaData();
```

To show how to use the metadata, use the following code:

```
        while (rs.next()) {
          for (int i=1;i<=md.getColumnCount();i++) {
                    out.println(md.getColumnName(i) + " : " +
  rs.getString(i) + "<BR>");
          }
          out.println("<HR>");
    }
```

The outer loop is designed to move through each of the rows in the ResultSet object. In the past, we have displayed the information by pulling each of the field values using the name of the column or a value. For example:

```
out.println("acc_id = " + rs.getString("acc_id"));
```

Instead, let's use some of the information returned by the DatabaseMetaData object. First, we create an inner loop that cycles through all of the fields in the result. Without the metadata, there is no way to obtain this information. However, with the metadata we can make a call to the getColumnCount() method. This method returns the total number of columns in the ResultSet. Obviously, the column count will differ based on the actual query.

We could list all of the columns as long as we always know the query. While this is going to be the case in most applications, let's list all of the columns using the getColumnCount(). Since we are going to display all of the column values, it would be nice to display the actual column name. We can obtain the column name from the metadata by using the getColumnName() method. This method accepts the column number, starting at 1, and returns a string with the column name.

The column name value will be the string value used in the query. For example, if the SELECT query uses a * to obtain all of the columns in the specified query, the getColumnName() method returns the column names defined by the table. If you change the query and include functions or aliases, those strings are returned. If you create a query to pull the account number from the acc_acc table but want the column name to be "Account Number" instead of acc_id, use this query:

```
SELECT acc_id "Account Number" FROM acc_acc
```

The getColumnName() method returns the "Account Number" string. Our code displays the column name followed by the value in the column. The results of the code are shown in Figure 9.4. The DatabaseMetaData object includes a method called getColumnLabel() that we can also use to display a suggested column name such as “Account Number”.

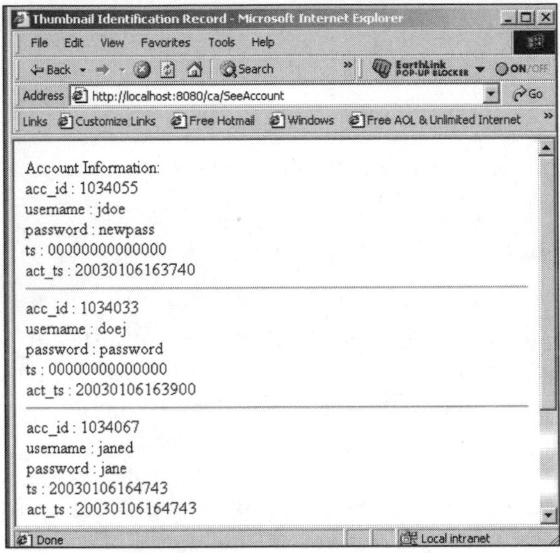

Figure 9.4 The ResultSet output.

Other ResultSet Metadata

In addition to determining the total number of columns in a ResultSet object and the name of the columns, the DatabaseMetaData object includes other methods for finding out information about each column value. Consider the code in Listing 9.3.

```
      out.println("<HTML><HEAD><TITLE>
Thumbnail Identification Record</TITLE></HEAD>");
      out.println("<BODY>");
      out.println("Account Information:<BR>");
      out.println("<table>");
      out.println("<tr><td>");
      for (int i=1;i<=md.getColumnCount();i++) {
        out.println("Column #" + i + "<BR>");
        out.println("getColumnName : "
          + md.getColumnName(i) + "<BR>");
        out.println("getColumnClassName : "
          + md.getColumnClassName(i) + "<BR>");
        out.println("getColumnDisplaySize : "
          + md.getColumnDisplaySize(i) + "<BR>");
```

Listing 9.3 Code for obtaining other metadata information. (continues)

```
            out.println("getColumnType : "
              + md.getColumnType(i) + "<BR>");
            out.println("getTableName : "
              + md.getTableName(i) + "<BR>");
            out.println("<HR>");
        }
```

Listing 9.3 Code for obtaining other metadata information. (continued)

Let's execute this code against the acc_acc and acc_add tables; we show part of the output in Figure 9.4. Four primary ResultSetMetaData methods are used:

- getColumnClassName(int)
- getColumnDisplaySize(int)
- getColumnType(int)
- getTableName(int)

For each of the columns in the ResultSet object, we want to display specific information about the data held in the column and characteristics of the code. The first piece of information displayed for each column is the name of the column. Next, we display the name of the java.sql type the column is capable of containing by using the getColumnClassName(int) method.

As you can see in Figure 9.5, the values pulled from the method will be in the form of java.sql.type—such as java.sql.Integer or java.sql.String. If you aren't sure how to pull data from a table column, you can use this method:

```
String dataType = md.getColumnClassName(i);
if (dataType.indexOf("Integer") > 0)
 int intData = rs.getInt(i);
else if (dataType.indexOf("Timestamp") > 0)
 Timestamp tsData = rs.getTimestamp(i)
else
 String stringData = rs.getString(i);
```

Our code compares the data type string pulled from the column against various types. If it finds a match, the code uses a specific getType() method to obtain the data in the column. After displaying the class name for the column, we display the maximum size of the data in the column by using the method getColumnDisplaySize(int). The value returned is the maximum size of the data in the field—not necessarily the real size of the data. Next, we display the column type by using the getColumnType(int) method. The value returned is related to the class type of the column and can be used to dictate how the data should be handled within the application. Finally, we use the getTableName(int) method to display the name of the table in which the column resides. If the initial query uses a join, the strings displayed may be different since the columns will be from different tables.

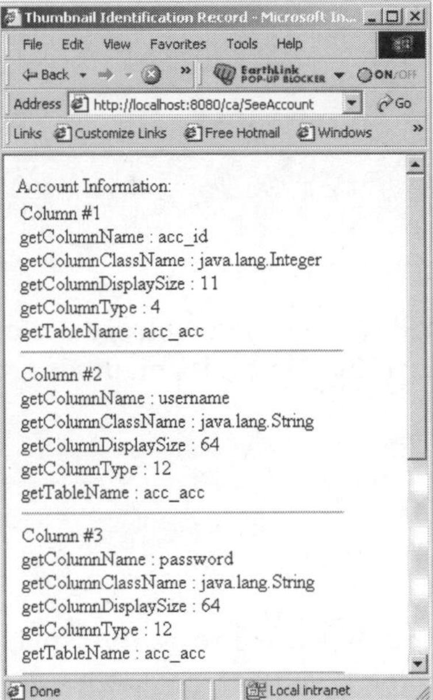

Figure 9.5 More ResultSet information.

What's Next

In this chapter, we covered both the DatabaseMetaData and ResultSetMetaData objects. We showed how you can obtain the information from both the database and the result set, and we examined several ways to use the data. In the next chapter, we cover how to use connection pooling within your applications and servlet code.

CHAPTER 10

Connection Pooling with Connector/J

When an application connects to the database server, it can query for results, perform transactions, and change the data as needed. When it finishes all of its work, the application closes the connection. If the application needs more data, it can make a new connection and perform additional queries. Each time the application needs data, it opens a connection and then closes the connection when it finishes. This process is time-consuming and uses resources.

A savvy developer will notice the connection to the database server is being constantly opened and closed—so the developer ensures that the connection to the database server is opened when the application starts and closed when the application finishes. Such an approach might work for a simple application executing on a single client machine, but what if the application is being used by 50 call-center employees? Should the database server have 50 constant connections to the client applications? Probably not.

The solution is to use a connection pool, which automatically handles connections to the database and allocates them to applications as needed. The application will think it is opening a new connection, but it will actually be reusing one previously opened. In this chapter, we discuss the concepts behind JDBC's implementation of a connection pool. We also examine third-party connection pool software for use with the DriverManager, and we describe how to use connection pools with an application server.

What Is a Connection Pool?

A *connection pool* is a cache of database connections that can be reused by one or more applications. The pool creates connections to the database as needed (until reaching a specified maximum count) and keeps those connections open for use by any application that needs to obtain data from the database. Figure 10.1 shows how the connection pool looks to the system.

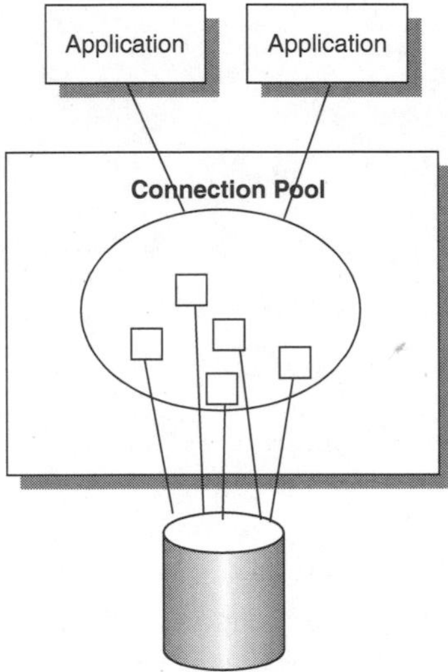

Figure 10.1 The connection pool.

To see how the connection pool aids in the execution of multiple applications to the same database, consider the following example. Two servlets are executing on a server, and they need access to the database. Each of the applications will (independently of each other) create a connection to the database, execute their queries, and close the connection. Regardless of whether the two applications build their connections at the same time or sequentially, two connections are created and destroyed. If the system uses a connection pool, each of the applications can ask the pool for a connection to the database instead of creating their own.

If this is the first time a request is being made to a connection to the database, the connection pool creates the physical connection and passes it to the requesting application. When the application closes the connection, the pool doesn't physically close the connection to the database but keeps it open in the event that another application needs it. When a second application needs the database, it makes its request of the connection pool. The connection pool returns the same connection it had created for the first application. The second application doesn't have to wait for the physical connection to be opened. Over time, the savings created by using a connection pool can be great.

In the event the first application hasn't closed its connection to the database when the second application needs it, the connection pool opens another physical connection. Typically, the connection pool keeps a specified number of physical connections open to the database as needed. If there are only a couple applications making requests of the pool, only a couple of physical connections are needed.

As you'll see in the next two sections, connection pools are created in different ways depending on whether you are using a DataSource object or the DriverManager to connect to the database server.

Pooling with DataSource

When a Java application server is used to handle the execution of code—like a servlet, for example—the connection to the database is handled through a DataSource and a JNDI entry. The marriage of an application server and JDBC allows for the creation of connection pools behind the scene. From the application's standpoint, there isn't any difference between getting a normal connection to the database and a connection pooled in a cache.

To activate the connection pool functionality, look at the JNDI entry found in the application server's configuration file. Here's the entry we find from Chapter 6 when we first looked at writing servlets that needed database access:

```
<resource-ref>
  <res-ref-name>jdbc/AccountsDB</res-ref-name>
  <res-type>javax.sql.DataSource</res-type>
  <init-param driver-name="org.gjt.mm.mysql.Driver"/>
  <init-param url="jdbc:mysql://localhost:3306/accounts"/>
  <init-param user=""/>
  <init-param password=""/>
  <init-param max-connections="20"/>
  <init-param max-idle-time="30"/>
</resource-ref>
```

For connection pools, the element we want to concentrate on is <res-type>. This element tells the application server which class should be used to implement the associated resource. When we weren't using connection pooling, we used the DataSource class. The <init-param> max-connections element told the class how many concurrent connections could be made to the database at any given time. The JDBC specification for connection pooling uses a different class, called javax.sql.ConnectionPoolDataSource. The class replaces DataSource, as shown in the following <res-type> element:

```
<res-type>javax.sql.ConnectionPoolDataSource</res-type>
```

To support the ConnectionPoolDataSource, the specification defines a few new parameters, as shown in Table 10.1.

Table 10.1 ConnectionPoolDataSrouce Parameters

PROPERTY NAME	TYPE	DESCRIPTION
maxStatements	int	The maximum number of statements to pool; 0 means to disable.
initialPoolSize	int	The initial size of the pool when created.
minPoolSize	int	The minimum number of physical connections that should be established on pool creation. 0 means that the system should create pools as needed.
maxPoolSize	int	The maximum number of physical connections. 0 means no maximum.
maxIdleTime	int	The maximum number of seconds a connection remains in the pool unused. 0 means no limit.

In order to exhibit the maximum control over the connection pool, use all of the properties in Table 10.1. Note that the application server is allowed to use different property names for those listed, so you should consult your application server documentation to determine the exact property names. For example, the following configuration is used in the Resin application server:

```
<resource-ref>
  <res-ref-name>jdbc/AccountsDB</res-ref-name>
  <res-type>javax.sql.ConnectionPoolDataSource</res-type>
  <init-param driver-name="org.gjt.mm.mysql.Driver"/>
  <init-param url="jdbc:mysql://localhost:3306/accounts"/>
  <init-param user=""/>
  <init-param password=""/>
  <init-param max-connections="20"/>
  <init-param max-idle-time="30"/>
  <init-param max-active-time="1"/>
  <init-param max-pool-time="1"/>
  <init-param connection-wait-time="1"/>
</resource-ref>
```

From this <resource-ref> element we see that

- The connection pool will have a maximum size of 20 connections.

- A connection can be idle for 30 minutes.
- The active time of a connection is one hour.
- The maximum time an idle connection can remain in the pool is one hour.
- A connection will wait for one minute before timing out.

To show how to use the connection pool from a servlet, consider the code in Listing 10.1.

```
import java.io.*;
import java.sql.*;
import javax.servlet.*;
import javax.servlet.http.*;
import javax.naming.*;

import javax.sql.DataSource;

public class SeeAccount extends HttpServlet {

  public void doGet(HttpServletRequest inRequest,
    HttpServletResponse outResponse)
    throws ServletException, IOException {

    PrintWriter out = null;
    Connection connection = null;
    Statement statement = null;
    ResultSet rs;

    outResponse.setContentType("text/html");
    out = outResponse.getWriter();

    try {
      Context ctx = new InitialContext();
      DataSource ds = (DataSource)ctx.lookup(
        "java:comp/env/jdbc/AccountsDB");
      connection = ds.getConnection();


      statement = connection.createStatement();
      rs = statement.executeQuery("SELECT acc_id FROM acc_acc");

      if (!rs.next()) {
        out.println("<HTML>No Account Found</HTML>");
      } else {
        out.println("<HTML><HEAD><TITLE>
```

Listing 10.1 Our connection pool servlet. (continues)

```
        Connection Pool Test</TITLE></HEAD>");
      out.println("<BODY>");
      out.println(rs.getString("acc_id") + "<br>");
      out.println("</BODY></HTML>");
    }
  }
  catch(Exception e) {
    e.printStackTrace();
  }
}

public void doPost(HttpServletRequest inRequest,
  HttpServletResponse outResponse)
  throws ServletException, IOException {
   doGet(inRequest, outResponse);
}
}
```

Listing 10.1 Our connection pool servlet. (continued)

The code in Listing 10.1 outputs a list of all account numbers in the acc_acc table. This isn't very interesting on the surface, but it shows that the code itself doesn't need to change when you use a connection pool; the application server handles the details.

To see how the connection pool reacts with multiple connections, let's create an HTML page that builds a table of calls to the servlet. Listing 10.2 shows the HTML code, and Figure 10.2 shows the output from the HTML page. Figure 10.3 shows the process list from MySQL as a result of the HTML.

```
<!DOCTYPE HTML PUBLIC "-//W3C//DTD HTML 4.0 Frameset//EN">
<HTML>
<HEAD><TITLE>Servlet Connection Pooling: A Test</TITLE></HEAD>

<!-- Causes 25 near simultaneous requests for same servlet. -->

<FRAMESET ROWS="*,*,*,*,*" BORDER=0 FRAMEBORDER=0 FRAMESPACING=0>
  <FRAMESET COLS="*,*,*,*,*">
    <FRAME SRC="/ca/JDBCServlet">
    <FRAME SRC="/ca/JDBCServlet">
    <FRAME SRC="/ca/JDBCServlet">
```

Listing 10.2 Our connection pool test HTML code. (continues)

```
    <FRAME SRC="/ca/JDBCServlet">
    <FRAME SRC="/ca/JDBCServlet">
  </FRAMESET>
  <FRAMESET COLS="*,*,*,*,*">
    <FRAME SRC="/ca/JDBCServlet">
    <FRAME SRC="/ca/JDBCServlet">
    <FRAME SRC="/ca/JDBCServlet">
    <FRAME SRC="/ca/JDBCServlet">
    <FRAME SRC="/ca/JDBCServlet">
  </FRAMESET>
  <FRAMESET COLS="*,*,*,*,*">
    <FRAME SRC="/ca/JDBCServlet">
    <FRAME SRC="/ca/JDBCServlet">
    <FRAME SRC="/ca/JDBCServlet">
    <FRAME SRC="/ca/JDBCServlet">
    <FRAME SRC="/ca/JDBCServlet">
  </FRAMESET>
  <FRAMESET COLS="*,*,*,*,*">
    <FRAME SRC="/ca/JDBCServlet">
    <FRAME SRC="/ca/JDBCServlet">
    <FRAME SRC="/ca/JDBCServlet">
    <FRAME SRC="/ca/JDBCServlet">
    <FRAME SRC="/ca/JDBCServlet">
  </FRAMESET>
  <FRAMESET COLS="*,*,*,*,*">
    <FRAME SRC="/ca/JDBCServlet">
    <FRAME SRC="/ca/JDBCServlet">
    <FRAME SRC="/ca/JDBCServlet">
    <FRAME SRC="/ca/JDBCServlet">
    <FRAME SRC="/ca/JDBCServlet">
  </FRAMESET>
</FRAMESET>

</HTML>
```

Listing 10.2 Our connection pool test HTML code. (continued)

As Figure 10.3 shows, the connection pool needs to open more than the initial 10 connections. Once the connections have finished executing, they will sit in the pool for 30 seconds. All of the connections over 10 will be closed, and the remaining connections will be left open for other applications that need the database.

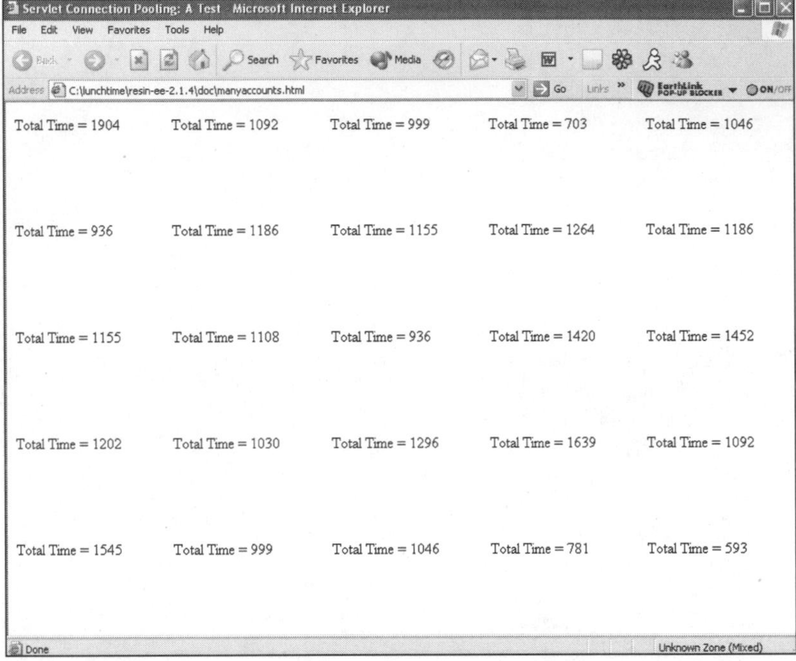

Figure 10.2 The output from our connection pool test.

```
mysql> show processlist;
+----+--------+-----------+----------+---------+------+-------+------------------+
| Id | User   | Host      | db       | Command | Time | State | Info             |
+----+--------+-----------+----------+---------+------+-------+------------------+
|  4 | joeg   | localhost | NULL     | Sleep   | 365  |       | NULL             |
|  8 | ODBC   | localhost | NULL     | Query   | 0    | NULL  | show processlist |
| 11 | nobody | localhost | accounts | Sleep   | 1    |       | NULL             |
| 12 | nobody | localhost | accounts | Sleep   | 1    |       | NULL             |
+----+--------+-----------+----------+---------+------+-------+------------------+
4 rows in set (0.00 sec)

mysql> show processlist;
+----+--------+-----------+----------+---------+------+-------+------------------+
| Id | User   | Host      | db       | Command | Time | State | Info             |
+----+--------+-----------+----------+---------+------+-------+------------------+
|  4 | joeg   | localhost | NULL     | Sleep   | 367  |       | NULL             |
|  8 | ODBC   | localhost | NULL     | Query   | 0    | NULL  | show processlist |
| 11 | nobody | localhost | accounts | Sleep   | 1    |       | NULL             |
| 12 | nobody | localhost | accounts | Sleep   | 0    |       | NULL             |
+----+--------+-----------+----------+---------+------+-------+------------------+
4 rows in set (0.00 sec)
```

Figure 10.3 The process list from MySQL.

Pooling with the DriverManager

When you're using DataSource, using a connection pool is a piece of cake. Just a change to the application server configuration file, and suddenly all of your applications that use the database will be part of a connection pool and see some level of performance increase. But what if you are using a Java application that is living outside an application server?

Java applications will use the DriverManager to build connections to the database. By default, the JDBC driver doesn't support connection pooling. The JDBC specification provides interfaces that can be implemented by an application server to give connection pooling functionality. There are no such interfaces for the DriverManager side of things. For applications, you need to provide your own connection pool. Fortunately, this isn't a big deal. In fact, we cover just one of many different libraries already created to handle connection pools. A simple Web search for JDBC MySQL Connection Pool will reveal many of them. Here are links to three of them:

- http://opensource.devdaily.com/ddConnectionBrokerDocs.shtml
- http://homepages.nildram.co.uk/~slink/java/DBPool/
- http://developer.java.sun.com/developer/onlineTraining/Programming/JDC-Book/conpool.html

DDConnectionBroker

The first link is to the DDConnectionBroker package designed to work with MySQL and an associated JDBC driver like Connector/J. On the page you will find a link to download a JAR file called DDConnectionBroker.jar. Place this JAR file in your CLASSPATH.

The JAR file includes code for a ConnectionPool with an API defined as:

```
DDConnectionBroker DDConnectionBroker(
String driver,           // JDBC Driver
String url,          // URL Connection String
String username,          // username to access the database
String password,          // password to access the database
int minConnections,          // minimum number of connections
int maxConnections,          // maximum number of connections
int timeout,          // timeout for idle connections in pool
int leaseTime,          // amount of time an application gets
String logFile          // place to see the output from the
pool
)
Connection getConnection()
freeConnection(Connection)
```

That's it! The key to the DDConnectionBroker connection pool class is the constructor. As you can see, we define the number of connections allowed in the pool, the amount of time an idle connection will remain in the pool (in milliseconds), and the total time an application may keep the connection (in milliseconds).

Listing 10.3 shows how the DDConnectionBroker pool can be used with our simple application.

```
import java.io.*;
import java.sql.*;

public class Pool {

  public static void main(String[] args)  {
    new Pool();
  }

  public Pool()  {
    setUp();

    try {
      broker = new DDConnectionBroker("com.mysql.jdbc.Driver",

"jdbc:mysql://localhost/accounts",
                                      "",
                                      "",
                                      2,
                                      10,
                                      5000,
                                      120000,
                                      "c:\temp");
    }
    catch (SQLException se) {
      System.err.println( se.getMessage() );
      System.err.println( "Could not construct a broker,
quitting." );
      System.exit(-1);
    }

    Connection connection = null;
    try {
      connection = broker.getConnection();

      Statement statement = connection.createStatement();
      ResultSet rs = statement.executeQuery("SELECT acc_id FROM
acc_acc");
      while ( rs.next() ) {
        System.out.println(rs.getString("acc_id"));
      }
    } catch (SQLException se) {
      System.err.println( " an SQLException: "
        + se.getMessage() );
    } finally {
      try {
        broker.freeConnection( connection );
```

Listing 10.3 Using DDConnectionBroker with our application. (continues)

```
        } catch (Exception e) {
          System.err.println( "an exception trying to free
Connection: "
            + e.getMessage() );
        }
      }
    }
  }
```

Listing 10.3 Using DDConnectionBroker with our application. (continued)

As you can see from the listing, we create an object of the DDConnectionBroker class with all of the information necessary to access our database. The connection to the database is requested from the DDConnectionBroker object, the connection is used, and then freed.

In a larger application, the connection pool could be instantiated to be used throughout the entire code. That way, all connections to the database would come from the pool and not from code that would create individual connections to the database.

What's Next

In this chapter, we discussed how connection pools work. We included examples for using connection pools in both application server-based code and independent Java applications where third-party software is used to build the pool. In the next chapter, we discuss how to use Connector/J with Enterprise JavaBeans.

CHAPTER 11

EJBs with MySQL

When data is contained in a database, there is always an immediate need to extract that data and present it to the user. One of the most powerful aspects of a Web site is the ability to grant clients and customers easy and immediate access to your data. This convenience for your customers, however, represents a drastic increase in complexity for the database developer. Now you must be concerned with new levels of database connectivity, security, and transaction processing. Enterprise Java Beans is one solution to these issues. In this chapter we look at writing EJBs, under the Resin application server, which have the ability to access a database.

Multi-tier Architecture

In the early days of software development, the most common way for a user to access data was through a terminal connected to a mainframe. When PCs came into production, they were commonly connected to either the mainframe or a file server. This interaction is typically called *client/server*. The client machine accesses the server when it needs information or has an update to perform.

With the development of the Web and more intensive applications, a three-layer, or three-tier, architecture was developed. As Figure 11.1 shows, a three-tier architecture consists of a presentation tier, a business tier, and a database tier.

Figure 11.1 The three-tier architecture.

The presentation, or client, tier is where the user interacts with the system. The user enters information to update or perform queries. The client tier sends the request to the business tier, where rules and logic are applied to the user's request. The business tier connects with the database to satisfy the user requests. The client tier is never allowed to access the database directly; instead, it must always communicate with the business tier.

As you might expect, the business tier handles the load for the entire system. The business tier will typically do the following:

- Handle requests from the client
- Process the requests
- Connect with the database and retrieve/update data
- Send results back to the client

As the complexity of applications has increased, the business tier has started to become a bottleneck. To help alleviate some of the processing needed on the business tier, a fourth tier has been added, as shown in Figure 11.2.

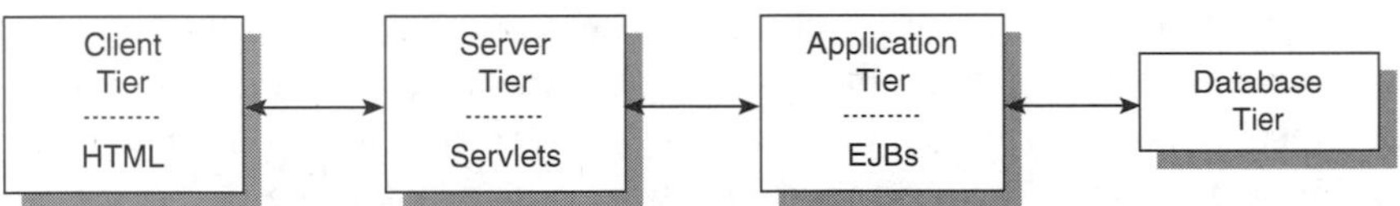

Figure 11.2 The four-tier architecture.

The four-tier architecture splits the functionality of the business tier into two separate areas. The first is a service tier where, for instance, a Web server, application server, and associated servlets are hosted. The servlets are the first component to respond to a request from the client. The servlet provides code for handling the business rules and logic necessary for the clients to be productive. Now instead of the servlet going directly to the database, it makes calls to Enterprise JavaBeans (EJBs) executing on a third tier. The EJBs communicate with the fourth tier, the database. In a large enterprise, the tiers are positioned to handle large volumes of requests.

When the designers of a system want to use the four-tier design with servlets and EJBs, but the enterprise isn't large enough for a four-tier system, they can combine the servlets and EJBs in the middle tier until they need the fourth.

Using Beans

As we mentioned earlier, an EJB is a component, and as such it cannot "live" on its own and must be part of an application. The bean exposes a defined interface, including methods that can be called, and invokes a particular response from it. A bean has the option of doing the work behind the exposed methods itself, or it might instantiate or call other beans to complete the necessary task.

To accomplish all that the bean needs to do, it must live within an environment called a *container*. The container is responsible for managing all of the beans, including such functionality as security and transactions. To take full advantage of the container, the EJB must be defined using a predefined Sun specification.

EJB Types

The specification for EJBs defines two types: *session* and *entity*. When you read the abundance of information available on beans, you commonly find that the types are broken down into the *active* type, or session, and the *passive* type, or entity. Let's look at each type before we start writing EJBs to interact with MySQL.

Session Beans

A session bean is designed to handle business processes as prescribed by the logic in the application. If we code in the three-tier architecture, the session bean contains that part of the servlet that handles all of the functionality needed to fulfill a client's request. When the bean is working on behalf of a request for our new second-tier servlet, it is considered active. The session bean continues to be active until it finishes with its current request. When the request is finished, the bean becomes inactive and waits to handle another request.

All session beans are designed to work on a request from a single client at a time. There is no multitasking in the beans. If another client needs to obtain information from the database, it has to either wait for the current bean to finish its work or the servlet has to instantiate a new session bean.

The session bean derives its name from the idea that the single bean should be available to handle all of the operations needed by a client during the client's session. This might be a single request from the database or it could be a group of transactions. With this in mind, let's break down the session bean into two categories. The *stateless* session bean is used to handle a single request against the database; a *stateful* session bean will "stay around" as long as the client needs attention.

Entity Beans

If you've followed us through the book to this chapter, you are well aware that using Java and MySQL requires you to write SQL. It might be nice to develop our applications in a manner that doesn't require as much SQL as we've seen. An entity bean is a component that allows us to model the data in our database using an object-oriented view.

The object-oriented view of the database is represented as entity beans for each of the tables. For our examples so far, we'd create entity beans for the acc_acc, acc_add, and acc_cert tables. Just like session beans, the entity bean lives in a container. One of the most important jobs the container has in respect to entity beans is making sure the data in the bean is consistent with the data in the database. This is especially true since the entity bean allows more than one client to access it at a time.

The EJB Environment

EJBs are designed against a strict specification developed by Sun. This specification and its interfaces are defined in the Java 2 Platform Enterprise Edition (J2EE). J2EE is an extension to the base Java implementation called J2SE, or Java 2 Platform Standard Edition. Within J2EE are the APIs needed for the development of EJBs as well as a reference implementation for using beans like an EJB container.

What an EJB Looks Like

As we start our discussion of using EJB and Connector/J to access data in a MySQL database, let's look at the pieces defined in the J2EE specification for Enterprise JavaBeans.

The Bean

All beans are required to implement the interface

```
public interface javax.ejb.EnterpriseBean extends
java.io.Serializable {}
```

Within the implementation is the logic required by the application for this bean. If the bean is a session, it generally includes the methods and code necessary for implementing functionality. If the bean is an entity bean, the code models the data in the database. This commonly consists of the columns of the table this bean represents.

The Remote Interface

Insulating the developer from the issues of networking programming as much as possible was one of the priorities established during the development of the EJB specification. When you consider the four-tier architecture, you realize that quite a bit of network programming could be involved since the servlet must communicate with the beans and the beans with the database.

To keep the network programming isolated, the EJB specification uses the concept of a proxy object, which works as an external interface to the bean. The proxy object accepts requests from the client and routes them through the container to the bean. The proxy object, also called the remote interface, must include all of the methods exposed by the bean because it is the primary component all clients will deal with. Further, the remote interface must implement EJBObject, defined as

```
public interface EJBObject extends Remote {
 public EJBHome getEJBHome() throws RemoteException;
 public Object getPrimaryKey() throws RemoteException;
 public void remove() throws RemoteException, RemoveException;
 public Handle getHandle() throws RemoteException;
 boolean isIdentical(EJBObject obj) throws RemoteException;
}
```

The container uses the methods defined here to manage the bean. In addition to these methods, the developer adds ones that will be exposed by the bean to external clients. Figure 11.3 shows an example of our bean.

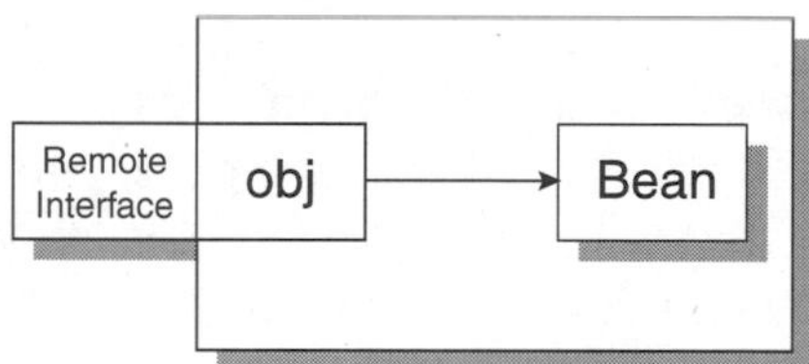

Figure 11.3 A sample bean and its external interface.

The Home Interface

With the remote interface in place, the specification defines another object proxy, called the home interface. The home interface is used to find and create an EJB. The home interface is a proxy object, just like the remote interface, as shown in Figure 11.4.

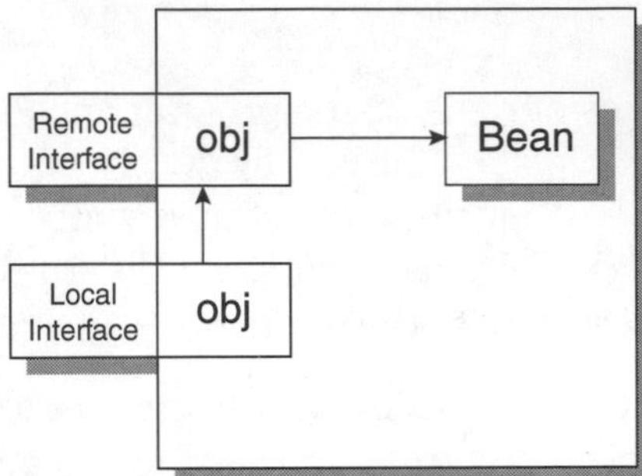

Figure 11.4 The home interface proxy object.

When an application needs access to a particular bean, it uses the home interface to obtain a reference to the object. The home interface acts as a factory and either returns a previously instantiated bean that is inactive or creates a new one as needed. The J2EE specification defines the following interface to be implemented by the bean:

```
public interface <example>Home extends EJBHome {
      <example> create(<parameters>) throws RemoteException,
CreateException;
}
```

This interface is used for each of the beans in the system, and the <example> placeholder is replaced by the name of the bean. The developers of the bean place as many create() methods as necessary using appropriate parameters.

Deployment Information

One of the last parts needed for the successful creation of an EJB is deployment information. This information typically consists of management, persistence, execution, and security requirements. In the section "Application Server Configuration," we provide an example of deployment information.

The JAR/WAR File

Finally, all of the components of the bean are packaged together into a JAR or Web archive (WAR) file. It should be noted that exactly which components are added to the JAR/WAR file is specific to the application server used to contain the bean.

The Application Server

We've mentioned a couple times that the bean must live in a container. Connector/J doesn't provide this container, and a simple Web server doesn't either.

What you need is a Java application server. The application server is designed to act as the container for the beans and in many cases provides for the execution of servlets and traditional HTML files. The examples provided in this chapter are all centered around Resin, available at www.caucho.com.

It is important to understand the environment where a bean will be deployed because some servers provide helper packages for writing EJBs as well as determine specifically how to deploy the EJB.

Application Server Configuration

In this chapter, we develop both session and entity beans. The beans have the ability to access the MySQL database through the Connector/J driver. In order for the EJBs to access MySQL, we have to create a <resource-ref> just as we did when building servlets. In Resin, we have the ability to create both global and localized resource references to the database. Listing 11.1 contains an example of a <resource-ref> element used for the various beans listed in this chapter.

```
<resource-ref>
  <res-ref-name>jdbc/AccountsDB</res-ref-name>
  <res-type>javax.sql.DataSource</res-type>
  <init-param driver-name="com.mysql.jdbc.Driver"/>
  <init-param url="jdbc:mysql://192.168.1.25/accounts"/>
  <init-param user="spider"/>
  <init-param password="spider"/>
  <init-param max-connections="20"/>
  <init-param max-idle-time="30"/>
</resource-ref>
```

Listing 11.1 Our <resource–ref> element.

We named our resource reference AccountsDB to indicate that the reference will be connecting to the Accounts database. All of the other parameters are provided as needed for the specific MySQL database. Of particular concern is the driver name, which must be the Connector/J driver.

Next in Listing 11.2 we create a reference in the local web.xml file associated with the application being built so that the beans will have access to the database.

```
<resource-ref>
    <res-ref-name>java:comp/env/cmp</res-ref-name>
    <class-name>com.caucho.ejb.EJBServer</class-name>
```

Listing 11.2 The web.xml file. (continues)

```
    <init-param data-source="java:comp/env/jdbc/ca"/>
  </resource-ref>

</web-app>
```

Listing 11.2 The web.xml file. (continued)

The Role of the Servlet

Before we move into developing beans, we need to say a few words about the role of the servlet when using EJBs. In the past, the servlet has done all of the work involved in handling a client's request. When we use beans, the servlet still plays an important role—as an intermediary between the client and the beans.

The client still makes requests of the servlet, but now the servlet becomes responsible for gathering all of the form information passed from the client and structuring the output generated from the data obtained from the beans.

Entity Beans

Of the session and entity bean types, the entity EJB is where the primary interaction occurs between the application and the database. The entity bean is designed to directly model a database table and allow the Java programmer to interact with the table using traditional object-oriented principles. In this section, we describe how to build an entity bean for one of our example tables.

We are going to model the acc_acc table, which is defined as

acc_id—int

username—varchar

password—varchar

ts—timestamp

act_ts—timestamp

To model this table, we begin by creating the bean.java file. Listing 11.3 contains the required class definition.

```
import javax.ejb.*;
public abstract class AccountRecordBean
```

Listing 11.3 AccountRecordBean.java. (continues)

```
    extends com.caucho.ejb.AbstractEntityBean {
    public abstract String getUsername();
    public abstract String getPassword();
    public abstract String getTS();
    public abstract String getAct_TS();

    public abstract void setUsername(String username);
    public abstract void setPassword(String password);

    public abstract int getAcc_id();

    public abstract void setTS(String time);
    public abstract void setAct_TS(String time);
}
```

Listing 11.3 AccountRecordBean.java. (continued)

One of the first things to notice in the code is the class signature. The name of the class is AccountRecordBean. You'll recall from our earlier discussion that the bean.java file is always preceded with the name of the session or the entity name. In the case of an entity bean, the table should be referenced. The signature also extends a Resin-specific interface called AbstractEntityBean. This is a helper interface that keeps the amount of method-defining necessary to a minimum. Next, all of the columns in the table are defined in terms of both getter and setter methods. We also define the create() method.

The methods defined in the AccountRecordBean class are both the setter and getter type. The first five are getter methods. The most important of these is getAcc_id(). This method is used by the system as well as the developer to obtain the rows in the table using the primary key, which happens to be acc_id.

The other four getter methods return the username, password, ts, and act_ts columns values as String objects. When an entity EJB is instantiated, you are able to access the specific column values using the getter methods. When it's time to make changes to the data in the table, setter methods are necessary. Four methods are listed for all of the columns in the table except the acc_id. We don't allow the developer to set the acc_id because this is a primary key and must be managed by the bean itself.

The bean is instantiated using the create() method, which calls the ejbCreate() method defined in this class. When the create() method defined in the home interface is called, a username and a password are supplied as parameters. The parameters are passed to the ejbCreate() method for use in the creation of the row in the database table.

When the method is called, the system automatically creates a row in the database using an autogenerated acc_id. The supplied username and password are set as well as the ts and act_ts columns. Note that none of the getter and setter methods are defined beyond the signature. The entity bean automatically generates code to return the column values. With the bean created, we must define the home interface. Listing 11.4 defines the code for the home interface.

```
import javax.ejb.*;

public interface AccountRecordHome extends EJBLocalHome {
  AccountRecord findByPrimaryKey(int value)
    throws FinderException;

  AccountRecord create(String username, String password)
    throws CreateException;
}
```

Listing 11.4 AccountRecordHome.java.

The home interface defines two primary methods for entity beans. The first is called findByPrimaryKey(). This method is used by the system and developer to return a table row based on the primary key and the getAcc_id() method defined within the bean class code. Next, we need to have a create() method, as mentioned earlier. The ejbCreate() method is used by the system, but the create() method defined in the home interface is called by a developer who needs another row in the database table. Notice that there is no code defined since the system automatically creates the code to call the appropriate ejbCreate() method.

With the bean and home interfaces complete, the last interface we need is the local one. Listing 11.5 shows the interface.

```
import javax.ejb.*;

public interface AccountRecord extends EJBLocalObject {
  String getPassword();
  String getUsername();
  String getTS();
  String getAct_TS();
  int getAcc_id();
```

Listing 11.5 AccountRecord.java. (continues)

```
    void setUsername(String username);
    void setPassword(String password);
    void setTS(String time);
    void setAct_TS(String time);
}
```

Listing 11.5 AccountRecord.java. (continued)

As you can see, the local interface looks very similar to the home interface. The interface consists of the getter and setter methods necessary for changing and obtaining data from the database. Next, we need to let the Resin application server know about the entity bean. For our purposes, the entity bean allows only local access because the session beans that access the entity beans are located on the same server.

The Resin server needs the bean information located in a file with an .ejb extension. Listing 11.6 shows the entry in an EJB file for the entity bean.

```
<entity>
      <ejb-name>AccountRecordBean</ejb-name>
      <local-home>AccountRecordHome</local-home>
      <local>AccountRecord</local>
      <ejb-class>AccountRecordBean</ejb-class>

      <persistence-type>Container</persistence-type>
      <reentrant>True</reentrant>

      <prim-key-class>int</prim-key-class>
      <primkey-field>acc_id</primkey-field>

      <abstract-schema-name>accountTable</abstract-schema-name>
      <sql-table>acc_acc</sql-table>

      <cmp-field><field-name>acc_id</field-name></cmp-field>
      <cmp-field><field-name>username</field-name></cmp-field>
      <cmp-field><field-name>password</field-name></cmp-field>
      <cmp-field><field-name>ts</field-name></cmp-field>
      <cmp-field><field-name>act_ts</field-name></cmp-field>
  </entity>
```

Listing 11.6 Our EJB file.

The EJB file is broken up into several sections. The first is the definition of the interfaces and the classes that make up those interfaces. The second is the entity bean configuration, which consists of two elements defining the persistence type and specifying whether the bean is re-entrant. The third section contains all of the information about the database table the entity bean is related to.

In this section, the first part is the definition of the primary key in the table and its type. The acc_acc table uses an int column called acc_id for the primary key. Next, the code defines the table the entity bean is associated with using an internal name and the SQL table. Finally, the code defines all of the columns in the table using the <field-name> element.

Session Beans

To show how the entity bean is used along with MySQL, let's build a session bean that will use the entity bean. Listing 11.7 shows the session bean class we want to use.

```
import javax.ejb.*;
import java.rmi.*;
import com.caucho.ejb.*;
import javax.naming.*;
import javax.servlet.*;

public class AccountBean extends AbstractSessionBean {

  private AccountRecordHome home;

  public void ejbCreate() {
    try {
      Context cmp = (Context) new InitialContext().lookup(
        "java:comp/env/cmp");

      home = (AccountRecordHome) cmp.lookup("AccountRecordBean");
    } catch (NamingException e) {
      e.printStackTrace();
    }
  }

  public boolean createAccount(String username, String password)
{
    try {
      home.create(username, password);
      return true;
    } catch ( CreateException e) {
      return false;
    }
  }
}
```

Listing 11.7 AccountBean.java.

The session bean contains the ejbCreate() method called when the session bean is instantiated, as well as other methods needed by the bean. Let's start with the ejbCreate() method, which has the single task of finding the home interface for the AccountRecordBean entity bean. This is accomplished in a two-step process. The first step is to locate the system's bean container using the lookup() method associated with the Context object. Once the container is found, a lookup method is used against it to find the "AccountRecordBean" entry. The system looks in the EJB file for a bean with the passed value. The home interface is returned and stored in a private attribute for later use.

The primary goal of the Account session bean is to create a new account on the system. The new account is created in the database by calling the create() method against our AccountRecordBean's home interface, passing in the supplied username and password as shown in the createAccount() method.

We've defined the remote interface in Listing 11.8.

```
import java.rmi.*;
import javax.ejb.*;

public interface Account extends EJBObject {
  boolean createAccount(String username, String password)
    throws RemoteException;
}
```

Listing 11.8 Account.java.

The only method we expose is the createAccount() method. The method requires two parameters for the username and password. The local interface is shown in Listing 11.9.

```
public interface AccountLocal extends javax.ejb.EJBLocalObject {
  public boolean createAccount(String username, String password);
}
```

Listing 11.9 AccountLocal.java.

Since the only exposed method is createAccount(), the local interface has only a single method. The remote and local home interfaces appear in Listings 11.10 and 11.11, respectively.

```
import javax.ejb.*;
import java.rmi.*;
```

Listing 11.10 AccountHome.java. (continues)

```
public interface AccountHome extends EJBHome {
  Account create() throws RemoteException, CreateException;
}
```

Listing 11.10 AccountHome.java. (continued)

```
public interface AccountLocalHome extends javax.ejb.EJBLocalHome
{
  AccountLocal create() throws javax.ejb.CreateException;
}
```

Listing 11.11 AccountLocalHome.java.

Both of the home interfaces simply expose the create() methods, which are used to instantiate a session bean.

Using the Beans

At this point, we have defined both an entity and a session bean. The session bean exposes a single method called createAccount(username, password). This method is designed to create a new account and place the information in the database. The session bean uses an AccountRecordBean EJB to actually place the row into the table. Notice, though, that we didn't write any SQL for INSERTing the new row into the database. The entity beans are designed specifically to keep the developer from worrying about SQL and data access.

Listing 11.12 shows the servlet we use to access the session and entity beans.

```
import java.io.*;
import javax.servlet.*;
import javax.servlet.http.*;
import javax.naming.*;
import javax.ejb.*;
import test.*;


public class caHandler extends HttpServlet {
  private AccountLocalHome accountHome = null;

  public void init()
    throws ServletException
```

Listing 11.12 The support servlet. (continues)

```
  {
    try {
      Context cmp = (Context) new InitialContext().lookup(
       "java:comp/env/cmp");

      accountHome = (AccountLocalHome) cmp.lookup("AccountBean");
    } catch (NamingException e) {
      e.printStackTrace();
    }
  }

  public void doGet(HttpServletRequest req, HttpServletResponse
res)
    throws IOException, ServletException {

    PrintWriter out = res.getWriter();
    res.setContentType("text/html");

    if (req.getParameter("submit").equals("new")) {
      out.println("Thank you for requesting a new account with
our site.");
      try {
        if (accountHome == null) {
          out.println("We are sorry but your request failed");
        } else {
          AccountLocal account = accountHome.create();
          if (account.createAccount(
            req.getParameter("username"),
            req.getParameter("password"))) {
            out.println("Your Account was created
successfully<BR>");
          } else {
            out.println("We are sorry but your request
failed<BR>");
          }
        }
      } catch(Exception e) {
        out.println("We are sorry but your request failed<BR>");
      }

    }
  }

  public void doPost(HttpServletRequest req, HttpServletResponse
res)
    throws IOException, ServletException {
    doGet(req, res);
  }
}
```

Listing 11.12 The support servlet. (continued)

When the servlet is called by the HTML shown in Listing 11.13, the init() method fires if this is the first time the servlet has been used. Within init(), we obtain the home interface to the Account session bean described earlier. We aren't instantiating a new bean at this point; we are just getting a reference to the home interface. The real work occurs in the doGet() method, where the home interface is used to obtain a new Account bean object with this statement:

```
AccountLocal account = accountHome.create();
```

Once the Account bean has been created, we can use it to create a new account on the database. The code to do this is:

```
account.createAccount(req.getParameter("username"),
  req.getParameter("password"))
```

The code makes a call to createAccount(String, String), which is the one exposed method for the Account EJB. When the method is called, the createAccount() method, as described earlier, creates an AccountRecord bean using the supplied username and password. This is subsequently inserted into the database. Throughout this entire process, we didn't write any SQL because the EJB did all of the work for us. This is the fundamental goal of container-managed persistence.

```
<HTML>
<BODY>
<TITLE>Certificate Authorization</TITLE>
<BR>
To create a new account, please enter a desired username/password
combination:<BR>
<form action="http://localhost:8080/ca/caHandler" method="post">
  Username: <input name="username"><BR>
  Password: <input name="password" type="password"><BR>
  <input type="submit" name="submit" value="new">
</form>
</BODY>
</HTML>
```

Listing 11.13 The HTML for the servlet.

Adding a Query

We can add capability to the entity bean by using the <query> element in the EJB file and adding a new method to the home interface. Listing 11.14 shows the addition to the home interface code.

```
import javax.ejb.*;

public interface AccountRecordHome extends EJBLocalHome {
  AccountRecord findByPrimaryKey(int value)
    throws FinderException;

  AccountRecord create(String username, String password)
    throws CreateException;

  AccountRecord findByUsernamePassword(String username, String
password)
    throws FinderException;
}
```

Listing 11.14 AccountRecordHome.java.

The findByUsernamePassword(String, String) method is a finder method for use by the developer. The code for the method is located in the EJB file, as shown in Listing 11.15.

```
<query>
  <query-method>
    <method-name>findByUsernamePassword</method-name>
  </query-method>
  <ejb-ql>SELECT o FROM accountTable o
    WHERE o.username=?1 AND o.password=?2</ejb-ql>
</query>
```

Listing 11.15 Our query code.

In the EJB file, a <method-name> element is used to define a new finder method. The method uses the EJB-QL language to define a SQL statement that will be used. The username and password parameters passed to the finder method are used directly in the query. Using this new query functionality, we can add code like the following to the servlet and access an account already in the database:

```
try {
      AccountRecord account = accountHome.findByUsernamePassword(user-
name, password);
      If (account != null)
        out.println("Your account ID is " +
account.getAcc_id());
} catch (Exception e) {
      return "error - not found";
}
```

This code uses the findByUsernamePassword() query from the home interface. The result of the query is either a newly created AccountRecord bean populated with the appropriate row from the database or a null.

Bean-Managed Persistence

The entity bean we created earlier in the chapter is built using container-managed persistence (CMP). This means that the container does all of the work of creating the bean, obtaining data for it, finding a row based on the primary key, and so forth. CMP is the preferred method for designing beans because you don't have to deal with the details of SQL. If, however, you want to use an entity bean that needs to be implemented using an uncommon storage back end or that has some other oddity, use bean-managed persistence (BMP) instead. In BMP, the bean is responsible for handling its data.

For BMP, you must write code in four major methods (and one optional):

ejbCreate()—Called when a create() method call is made against the home interface.

ejbPostCreate()—Called after the bean is created.

ejbLoad()—Loads data from the persistent store into the bean.

ejbStore()—Stores the bean into a persistent store.

ejbPostCreate()—Called after the bean is created.

In addition to these methods, you have to write the code for ejbFind() methods relating to any find() methods located in the home interface. In our CMP bean, the findByPrimaryKey() method has to have a corresponding ejbFindByPrimaryKey() method that will return the primary key of a bean based on some criteria.

To write a BMP EJB, we need to change the <persistence-type> element in the EJB file from container to bean. We must also remove all of the <cmp-field> entries since we will be managing the fields. Next, we add code for each of the methods. The skeleton for the BMP bean is

```
import javax.ejb.*;

public abstract class AccountRecordBean
  extends com.caucho.ejb.AbstractEntityBean {
  int acc_id;
  String username;
  String password;
  Timestamp ts;
  Timestamp act_ts;
```

```
    public int ejbCreate(String username, String password)
      throws CreateException, RemoteException {
    }

    public void ejbPostCreate(String course, String instructor) {
    }

    public int ejbLoad() throws RemoteException {
    }

    public int ejbStore()throws RemoteException {
    }

    public int ejbRemove()throws RemoteException {
    }

    public String findByPrimaryKey() throws RemoteException {
    }

  }
```

ejbCreate()

We can use the ejbCreate() method when we want to insert a new row into the database. To accomplish this, we need to access the database, check to see if the row already exists, and either insert a row into the table or throw an exception. The code might look like this:

```
    public int ejbCreate(String username, String password)
      throws CreateException, RemoveException {
        InitialContext ctx = new InitialContext();
        DataSource ds = (DataSource)
              ctx.lookup( "java:comp/env/jdbc/AccountsDB" );
        Connection conn = ds.getConnection();
        PreparedStatement stmt = conn.prepareStatement(
             "SELECT * FROM acc_acc WHERE username=? and password=?" );
        stmt.setString( 1, username );
              stmt.setString(2, password);
        ResultSet rs = stmt.executeQuery();
        duplicateKey = rs.next();
        rs.close();
        stmt.close();
        if ( ! duplicateKey ) {
           stmt = conn.prepareStatement(
              "INSERT INTO acc_acc (null, ?, ?, ? ,?)");
           stmt.setString( 1, username );
           stmt.setString( 2, password );
                    stmt.setTimestamp(null);
                    stmt.setTimestamp(new Timestamp(new
  Date().getDate()));
```

```
            stmt.executeUpdate();
            stmt.close();
        }
        conn.close();
    } catch (Exception ex) {
        throw new java.rmi.RemoteException( "ejbCreate Error", ex );
    }
    if ( duplicateKey )
        throw new javax.ejb.DuplicateKeyException();
    return null;

    }
```

As the preceding code shows, we are responsible for doing all of the database work in a bean-managed persistence mode.

ejbLoad()

In the ejbLoad() method, the code has to load all of the fields for the row associated with a particular primary key. For example:

```
public void ejbLoad()
  throws java.rmi.RemoteException
{
    boolean found = false;
    try {
        InitialContext ctx = new InitialContext();
        DataSource ds = (DataSource)
            ctx.lookup( "java:comp/env/jdbc/AccountsDB" );
        Connection conn = ds.getConnection();
        PreparedStatement stmt = conn.prepareStatement(
              "SELECT username FROM acc_acc WHERE acc_id=?");
        stmt.setString( 1, acc_id );
        ResultSet rs = stmt.executeQuery();
        if ( rs.next()) {
            found = true;
            username = rs.getString(2);
           password = rs.getString(3);
           ts = rs.getTimestamp(4);
           act_ts = re.getTimestamp(5);
        }
        rs.close();
        stmt.close();
        conn.close();
    } catch (Exception ex) {
        throw new java.rmi.RemoteException( "ejbLoad Error", ex );
    }
    if ( ! found )
        throw new java.rmi.RemoteException( "Bean not found" );
  }
```

In this code, the database table is checked for a row with a specific acc_id value. If a match is found, all of the bean's attributes are set based on the returned row; otherwise, an exception is thrown.

ejbStore()

The ejbStore() method is responsible for placing the bean's information back into the database table. This isn't an INSERT into the table, but an UPDATE of a previously created row. The code might look like this:

```
public void ejbStore()
  throws java.rmi.RemoteException
{
    boolean found = false;
    try {
        InitialContext ctx = new InitialContext();
        DataSource ds = (DataSource)
            ctx.lookup( "java:comp/env/jdbc/AccountsDB" );
        Connection conn = ds.getConnection();
        PreparedStatement stmt = conn.prepareStatement(
              "UPDATE acc_acc set username=?, password=?,
                ts=? act_ts =?WHERE acc_id=?");
        stmt.setString( 1, username );
        stmt.setString( 2, password );
        stmt.setTimestamp( 3, ts );
        stmt.setTimestamp 4, act_ts );
        stmt.setInt( 5, acc_id );
        if (stmt.executeUpdate() <= 0) {
          throw new java.rmi.RemoteException( "Bean not found" );
        }

        stmt.close();
        conn.close();
    } catch (Exception ex) {
        throw new java.rmi.RemoteException( "ejbLoad Error", ex );
    }
}
```

This code performs an UPDATE on the database table using the values stored in the attributes of the bean.

ejbRemove()

The ejbRemove() method is designed to delete the rows from the database for the table based on the current acc_id of the bean. The code looks like this:

```
public void ejbRemove()
  throws java.rmi.RemoteException
{
```

```
        boolean found = false;
        try {
            InitialContext ctx = new InitialContext();
            DataSource ds = (DataSource)
                ctx.lookup( "java:comp/env/jdbc/AccountsDB" );
            Connection conn = ds.getConnection();
            PreparedStatement stmt = conn.prepareStatement(
                  "DELETE FROM acc_acc WHERE acc_id=?");
            stmt.setInt( 1, acc_id );

            stmt.close();
            conn.close();
        } catch (Exception ex) {
            throw new java.rmi.RemoteException( "ejbLoad Error", ex );
        }
    }
```

ejbFindByPrimaryKey()

The ejbFindByPrimaryKey() method returns a String representation of the primary key for the current bean. The code checks to make sure the row exists in the table before returning the account id. The code for the method is

```
public String findByPrimaryKey() throws RemoteException {
   try {
      InitialContext ctx = new InitialContext();
      DataSource ds = (DataSource)
          ctx.lookup( "java:comp/env/jdbc/AccountsDB" );
      Connection conn = ds.getConnection();
      PreparedStatement stmt = conn.prepareStatement(
            "SELECT username FROM acc_acc WHERE acc_id=?");
      stmt.setString( 1, acc_id );
      ResultSet rs = stmt.executeQuery();
      if ( rs.next()) {
                  rs.close();
                  stmt.close();
                  conn.close();
        return ""+acc_id;
      } else {
        throw new java.rmi.FinderException(
          "findByPrimaryKey Error", ex );
      }
   } catch (Exception ex) {
      throw new java.rmi.RemoteException( "ejbLoad Error", ex );
   }
}
```

Setter/Getter Methods

You need to implement all of the setter/getter methods defined in the CMP bean in the BMP bean, but you have to set/get the attributes of the bean yourself.

Once all of the methods have been placed in the bean, there will be no noticeable difference between the CMP and the BMP beans.

What's Next

In this chapter, we presented a simple example of how to build an entity bean that will access data in a MySQL database using the Connector/J driver. In the next chapter, we build a MySQL database interface.

CHAPTER 12

Building a General Interface for MySQL

In previous chapters, we have explored many of the elements involved in bringing MySQL and Java together to address database-related needs. In this chapter, we shift our focus to building a general database application. For the sake of maximizing both generality and potential usefulness, we will build a graphical interface for MySQL. Such an application offers ample opportunity to demonstrate a number of Java's strengths, both in terms of the language itself and its ability to work with data sources via the JDBC API.

The application we present in this chapter is built around the notion of database tasks. Over the course of development, we introduce four such tasks. The first provides information about the underlying JDBC driver and database product, including names and version numbers. The second provides an interface for executing arbitrary SQL queries. The third provides the user with information regarding the column definitions for a given table. Finally, we define a task that allows the user to insert a new row into an existing table. Along the way, we also develop a number of utility classes that support extensibility by simplifying input, output, task delegation, exception handling, and session initiation. Given our focus, the user interface is of course less refined than it might be for a production application. Furthermore, depending on user needs, the individual tasks might lack a degree of functionality (e.g., meaningful handling of binary data); however, the application should convey some of what is possible and provide a foundation for developing and implementing more sophisticated tasks.

Tasks

With the exception of the most generic of interfaces, the range of operations you might need to carry out on a data source is so diverse that attempting to capture all of them in a single application is impractical. While generic interfaces certainly have their place, they tend to require more knowledge and experience on the part of the user. By moving away from a generic interface, you find it becomes easier to tailor operations to specific user tasks.

It is the notion of specific user tasks that drives the design of our MySQL interface. However, if the interface is to remain generally useful, it is important that the task code not be tied too tightly to framework of the interface. Unless the addition and removal of tasks is straightforward, an interface that is useful for one user might very well be useless for another. An obvious approach to addressing this issue involves viewing tasks as removable modules and building a framework in support of such modules. While it is not within the scope of this chapter to build a complete, full-featured framework for such modules, the example application does provide one possible approach to developing such a framework.

Accepting that our interface is to be built around task modules, the obvious question becomes one of what constitutes a task. From the user's perspective, a task is some useful unit of work; whether that corresponds to retrieving a trivial piece of information from the database or carrying out a complex transaction depends on the needs of a particular user. From the perspective of our interface design, a task is an entity that has a name, a delegate class, and a flag indicating whether it is currently enabled. The name is a simple task identifier used by interface components that must deal with task identity. The delegate class represents the type of the object to which task completion is delegated. The enabled flag provides a technique for specifying whether the task is to be considered active by the interface. This task definition is captured and encapsulated by the TaskDefinition class shown in Listing 12.1.

```
package mysqljava;

public class TaskDefinition
{
  public TaskDefinition( String name,
                         Class delegate, boolean enabled )
  {
```

Listing 12.1 The class representing task modules. (continues)

```
    this.name = name;
    this.delegate = delegate;
    this.enabled = enabled;
  }

  public String getName()
  {
    return (name);
  }

  public Class getDelegate()
  {
    return (delegate);
  }

  public boolean isEnabled()
  {
    return (enabled);
  }

  private String name;
  private Class delegate;
  private boolean enabled;
}
```

Listing 12.1 The class representing task modules. (continued)

Holding to the goal of simple task addition and removal, defined tasks are provided through a configuration file containing entries like the following:

```
mysqljava.DbInfo:enabled:Database Info
mysqljava.ShowColumns:disabled:Show Columns
mysqljava.SqlQuery:disabled:SQL Query
mysqljava.InsertRow:disabled:Insert Row
```

Each entry consists of three colon-delimited fields. The first field specifies the fully qualified name of the delegate class. The second field is the flag indicating whether the task should be considered active. The final field is the name associated with the task. These are simply textual representations of the fields encapsulated by our TaskDefinition class. How these fields are used to support pluggable modules should become clear in later sections. For now, take a look at Listing 12.2 to see how the configuration file is processed to generate a task list. Given an InputStreamReader representing a configuration file, an object of type Tasks parses the task definition entries, converts the fields to appropriate types, creates corresponding TaskDefinition objects, and makes the task list available via an Enumeration.

```
package mysqljava;

import java.io.*;
import java.util.*;

public class Tasks
{
  public Tasks( InputStreamReader taskS )
  {
    readTasks( taskS );
  }

  public int getTaskCount()
  {
    return (taskDefs.size());
  }

  public Enumeration getTasks()
  {
    return (taskDefs.elements());
  }

  private void readTasks( InputStreamReader taskS )
  {
    try
    {
      BufferedReader reader = new BufferedReader( taskS );

      String taskLine;

      while ( (taskLine = reader.readLine()) != null )
      {
        addTaskDefinition( taskLine );
      }
    }
    catch( IOException ioX )
    {
      System.err.println( "Failed to fully parse task file: "
                          + ioX );
    }
  }

  private void addTaskDefinition( String taskLine )
  {
    StringTokenizer taskTok = new StringTokenizer( taskLine,
```

Listing 12.2 The class representing the list of defined tasks modules. (continues)

```
DELIM );

    if ( taskTok.countTokens() != TOKEN_NUM )
    {
      System.err.println( "Invalid task definition: "
                          + taskLine );
      return;
    }

    Class taskClass = null;
    String taskClassName = taskTok.nextToken();

    try
    {
      taskClass = Class.forName( taskClassName );
    }
    catch( ClassNotFoundException cnfX )
    {
      System.err.println( "Class '" + taskClassName
                        + "' not found: " + cnfX );
      return;
    }

    boolean taskEnabled = false;

    if ( taskTok.nextToken().equalsIgnoreCase( "enabled" ) )
    {
      taskEnabled = true;
    }

    String taskName = taskTok.nextToken();

    TaskDefinition def = new TaskDefinition( taskName,
                                             taskClass,
                                             taskEnabled );

    taskDefs.add( def );
  }

  private Vector taskDefs = new Vector();

  final static int TOKEN_NUM = 3;
  final static String DELIM = ":";
}
```

Listing 12.2 The class representing the list of defined tasks modules. (continued)

SQL Exceptions

One common feature shared by most of the JDBC API methods is that they make use of the SQLException class, either directly or indirectly, through derived exception classes. As such, it is worth a little upfront effort to provide some generalized SQLException processing. For the purposes of our sample application, we limit ourselves to a single message-processing method. This method, defined in our SqlExceptionReader class, is shown in Listing 12.3.

In addition to the functionality inherited from the java.lang.Exception, SQLException provides a SQLState code, a vendor-specific exception code, and the ability to chain additional SQLException objects. The readException() method of SqlExceptionReader extracts the additional fields, stepping through the exception chain if necessary, and builds an exception message containing the available information.

```
package mysqljava;

import java.sql.*;


public class SqlExceptionReader
{
  public static String readException( SQLException sqlX )
  {
    StringBuffer msg = new StringBuffer( 1024 );
    SQLException nextX;
    int exceptionNumber = 0;

    do
    {
      ++exceptionNumber;

      msg.append( "Exception " + exceptionNumber + ": \n" );
      msg.append( "  Message: " + sqlX.getMessage() + "\n" );
      msg.append( "  State  : " + sqlX.getSQLState() + "\n" );
      msg.append( "  Code   : " + sqlX.getErrorCode() + "\n" );
    }
    while ( (nextX = sqlX.getNextException()) != null );

    return (msg.toString());
  }
}
```

Listing 12.3 A class for reading SQLExceptions.

MySQL Connections

Since a data source connection is a prerequisite for any task involving communication with a database, it makes sense to capture the required connection data in a common class. We do this with the ConnectionData class shown in Listing 12.4. This class represents a host name and port, a database name, and a username and password. Accessors for username and password are provided, along with an accessor that returns a MySQL-compatible URL of the form

```
jdbc:mysql://hostname:port/database_name
```

Perhaps more useful is the class's buildConnection() method, which uses the contained URL data, username, and password to obtain and return a Connection object. As is seen in the listing, we opted to use the DriverManager approach to obtaining a Connection object. Depending on your environment, it might make more sense to obtain Connection objects from a source implementing the DataSource or ConnectionPoolDataSource interfaces specified in the javax.sql package.

```
package mysqljava;

import java.sql.*;

public class ConnectionData
{
  public ConnectionData( String hostName,
                         String dbName,
                         String port,
                         String username,
                         String password )
  {
    this.hostName = hostName;
    this.dbName = dbName;
    this.port = port;
    this.username = username;
    this.password = password;
  }

  public String getUsername()
  {
    return (username);
  }

  public String getPassword()
```

Listing 12.4 The class used for establishing database connections. (continues)

```
  {
    return (password);
  }

  public String getUrl()
  {
    String url = "jdbc:mysql://" + hostName
               + ":" + port + "/" + dbName;

    return (url);
  }

  public Connection buildConnection()
  {
    try
    {
      Class.forName( "com.mysql.jdbc.Driver" );
    }
    catch( ClassNotFoundException cnfX )
    {
      cnfX.printStackTrace( System.err );
      return (null);
    }

    try
    {
      Connection conn = DriverManager.getConnection(
                                    getUrl(),
                                    getUsername(),
                                    getPassword() );


      return (conn);
    }
    catch( SQLException sqlX )
    {
      System.out.println(
              SqlExceptionReader.readException( sqlX ) );
      return (null);
    }
  }

  private String hostName;
  private String dbName;
  private String port;
  private String username;
  private String password;
}
```

Listing 12.4 The class used for establishing database connections. (continued)

The Task Delegate

In defining the interface's view of a task, we introduced the notion of a *task delegate*. As implied by the name, this is an entity to which the interface delegates responsibility for task execution, whatever that might involve. The delegate might in turn hand over responsibility for portions of the task to other entities; however, a major design goal is that our interface need not be concerned with what happens after it has dispatched the task. In working toward this goal, we introduce the TaskDelegate Java interface shown in Listing 12.5. This is a Java language interface that must be implemented by any class that is to serve as a task delegate. When a delegate's execute() method is invoked, the caller is responsible for providing an appropriate session object. The method's return value indicates only whether the task is successfully dispatched; this does not necessarily correspond to successful task execution.

While TaskDelegate is trivial in appearance, it is an important piece of our design. In addition to explicitly stating the method(s) that delegates must support, it allows the interface to treat all task delegate objects as instances of type TaskDelegate, regardless of the underlying object type. This allows our interface to rely on polymorphism for proper dispatch and simplifies the process of obtaining delegate instances via Java's reflection facilities. The net result is that our interface is capable of dispatching tasks in a straightforward manner without any knowledge of the task's implementation, aside from the name of its delegate class.

```
package mysqljava;

import java.sql.*;

public interface TaskDelegate
{
  public boolean execute( Connection conn );
}
```

Listing 12.5 The task delegate interface.

The Task Manager

Access to defined tasks begins with the task manager. This is a graphical interface that supports task selection and input of database connection parameters. Figure 12.1 shows a task manager with four defined tasks. Our task manager consists of two primary pieces. The first, and more interesting of the two, is the

TaskPanel class shown in Listing 12.6. The second is the TaskManager class shown in Listing 12.7.

The TaskPanel class, with the help of its three inner classes, provides the bulk of the task management interface. The inner classes include ConnectionPane, TaskPane, and TaskHandler, which are responsible for connection parameter input, task selection, and task dispatch, respectively. The ConnectionPane simply provides for input of the information required by our ConnectionData class, namely a host name and port, a database name, and a username and password. The TaskPane provides a set of buttons for task selection. The number of buttons, and the manner in which they are named, is based on the task list that is loaded when the application is launched; in other words, the buttons correspond to the enabled tasks specified in the configuration file. The TaskHandler class is an ActionListener responsible for handling ActionEvents associated with the buttons on the TaskPane.

When a user clicks on a task button, the TaskHandler requests the ConnectionData object associated with the ConnectionPane and attempts to build a connection with the specified database. If it obtains a valid Connection object, it then requests the task list and iterates through the list looking for a TaskDefinition object with a name that matches that provided by the task button. If a matching TaskDefinition is located, reflection is used to obtain an instance of the corresponding delegate class. The delegate object is then cast to a TaskDelegate since that is known to be a least common denominator for all delegate classes. Finally, the TaskDelegate execute() method is used to dispatch the task.

The second piece of our task manager, the TaskManager class, is the application driver. It parses the configuration file, builds the task list, and provides the main application frame and menu bar. By default, it expects to find a configuration file named tasks.conf; however, an alternate configuration file may be provided via the command line.

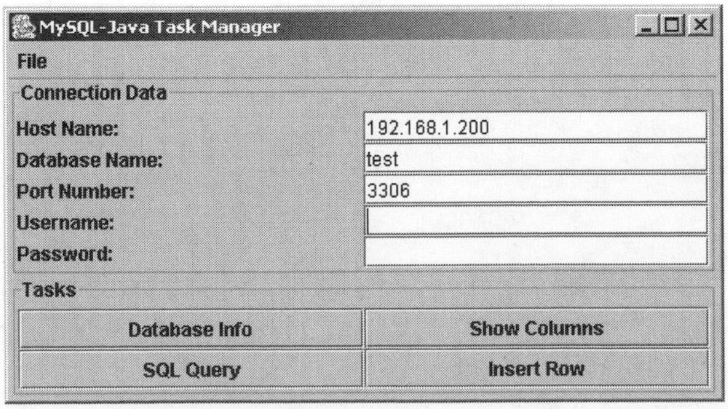

Figure 12.1 The task manager.

```
package mysqljava;

import java.awt.*;
import java.awt.event.*;
import java.sql.*;
import java.util.*;
import javax.swing.*;
import javax.swing.border.*;

public class TaskPanel extends JPanel
{
  public TaskPanel( Tasks taskList )
  {
    this.taskList = taskList;

    setLayout( new BorderLayout() );

    connPane = new ConnectionPane();
    connPane.setBorder( new TitledBorder( "Connection Data" ) );

    taskPane = new TaskPane();
    taskPane.setBorder( new TitledBorder( "Tasks" ) );

    add( connPane, BorderLayout.NORTH );
    add( taskPane, BorderLayout.SOUTH );
  }

  private Tasks taskList;

  private ConnectionPane connPane;
  private TaskPane taskPane;

  class ConnectionPane extends JPanel
  {
    ConnectionPane()
    {
      setLayout( new GridLayout( 5, 2 ) );

      add( hostNameLabel );
      add( hostNameField );
      add( dbNameLabel );
      add( dbNameField );
      add( portNumberLabel );
      add( portNumberField );
      add( usernameLabel );
      add( usernameField );
      add( passwordLabel );
```

Listing 12.6 The task manager's TaskPanel component. (continues)

```
    add( passwordField );
  }

  ConnectionData getConnectionData()
  {
    String password =
                 new String( passwordField.getPassword() );

    ConnectionData data = new ConnectionData(
                              hostNameField.getText(),
                              dbNameField.getText(),
                              portNumberField.getText(),
                              usernameField.getText(),
                              password );


    return (data);
  }

  private JLabel hostNameLabel = new JLabel( "Host Name:" );
  private JLabel dbNameLabel= new JLabel( "Database Name:" );
  private JLabel portNumberLabel =
                           new JLabel( "Port Number:" );
  private JLabel usernameLabel = new JLabel( "Username:" );
  private JLabel passwordLabel = new JLabel( "Password:" );

  private JTextField hostNameField = new JTextField( 20 );
  private JTextField dbNameField = new JTextField( 20 );
  private JTextField portNumberField =
                           new JTextField( "3306", 6 );
  private JTextField usernameField = new JTextField( 20 );
  private JPasswordField passwordField =
                              new JPasswordField( 20 );
}

class TaskPane extends JPanel
{
  TaskPane()
  {
    int taskCount = TaskPanel.this.taskList.getTaskCount();

    int rows = ((taskCount % COLS) == 0)
             ? (taskCount / COLS)
             : ((taskCount / COLS) + 1);


    setLayout( new GridLayout( rows, COLS ) );
```

Listing 12.6 The task manager's TaskPanel component. (continues)

```
    taskButtons = new JButton[taskCount];

    TaskHandler handler = new TaskHandler();

    Enumeration tasks = taskList.getTasks();

    int task = 0;

    while ( tasks.hasMoreElements() )
    {
      TaskDefinition taskDef =
                    (TaskDefinition)(tasks.nextElement());

      if ( ! taskDef.isEnabled() )
      {
        continue;
      }

      String taskName = taskDef.getName();
      taskButtons[task] = new JButton( taskName );
      taskButtons[task].addActionListener( handler );
      add( taskButtons[task++] );
    }
  }

  private JButton[] taskButtons;

  final static int COLS = 2;
}

class TaskHandler implements ActionListener
{
  public void actionPerformed( ActionEvent ae )
  {
    ConnectionData connData = connPane.getConnectionData();

    Connection conn = connData.buildConnection();

    if ( conn == null )
    {
      String msg = "Could not build connection. Check\n"
                 + "provided connection data and verify\n"
                 + "server availability.";
      JOptionPane.showMessageDialog(
                             TaskPanel.this, msg,
                             "Connection Failure",
```

Listing 12.6 The task manager's TaskPanel component. (continues)

```
                                JOptionPane.ERROR_MESSAGE );

  return;
}

String taskName = ae.getActionCommand();

Enumeration tasks = taskList.getTasks();

boolean dispatched = false;

while ( tasks.hasMoreElements() )
{
  TaskDefinition taskDef =
                (TaskDefinition)(tasks.nextElement());

  if ( ! taskDef.isEnabled() )
  {
    continue;
  }

  if ( taskName.equals( taskDef.getName() ) )
  {
    try
    {
      Class delegateClass = taskDef.getDelegate();
      Object delegateObject = delegateClass.newInstance();
      TaskDelegate delegate = (TaskDelegate)delegateObject;

      dispatched = delegate.execute( conn );

      if ( ! dispatched )
      {
        String msg = "Could not execute task: "
                   + taskDef.getName();
        JOptionPane.showMessageDialog(
                                TaskPanel.this, msg,
                                "Task Failure",
                                JOptionPane.ERROR_MESSAGE );

      }
    }
    catch( InstantiationException iX )
    {
      String msg = "Failed to instantiate "
                 + "delegate for task: "
                 + taskDef.getName();
```

Listing 12.6 The task manager's TaskPanel component. (continues)

```
          JOptionPane.showMessageDialog(
                                     TaskPanel.this, msg,
                                     "Task Failure",
                                     JOptionPane.ERROR_MESSAGE );

        }
        catch( IllegalAccessException iaX )
        {
          String msg = "Cound not access delegate for task: "
                     + taskDef.getName();
          JOptionPane.showMessageDialog(
                                     TaskPanel.this, msg,
                                     "Task Failure",
                                     JOptionPane.ERROR_MESSAGE );

        }

        break;
      }
    }

    if ( ! dispatched )
    {
      try
      {
        conn.close();
      }
      catch( SQLException sqlX ) {}
    }
  }
 }
}
```

Listing 12.6 The task manager's TaskPanel component. (continued)

```
package mysqljava;

import java.io.*;
import java.awt.*;
import java.awt.event.*;
import javax.swing.*;
import java.sql.*;
```

Listing 12.7 The task manager's TaskManager component. (continues)

```
public class TaskManager extends JFrame
{
  TaskManager( Tasks taskList )
  {
    super( "MySQL-Java Task Manager" );

    this.taskList = taskList;

    buildGui();

    pack();
    setVisible( true );
  }

  private void buildGui()
  {
    fileMenu.add( fileExit );
    menuBar.add( fileMenu );
    setJMenuBar( menuBar );

    frameContainer.setLayout( new BorderLayout() );
    frameContainer.add( new TaskPanel( taskList ) );
    setContentPane( frameContainer );

    addWindowListener( new WindowHandler() );
    fileExit.addActionListener( new MenuHandler() );
  }

  private JPanel frameContainer = new JPanel();

  private JMenuBar menuBar = new JMenuBar();
  private JMenu fileMenu = new JMenu( "File" );
  private JMenuItem fileExit = new JMenuItem( "Exit" );

  private Tasks taskList;

  class WindowHandler extends WindowAdapter
  {
    public void windowClosing( WindowEvent we )
    {
      System.exit( 0 );
    }
  }

  class MenuHandler implements ActionListener
  {
```

Listing 12.7 The task manager's TaskManager component. (continues)

```
    public void actionPerformed( ActionEvent ae )
    {
      if ( ae.getActionCommand().equals( "Exit" ) )
      {
        System.exit( 0 );
      }
    }
  }

  public static void main( String[] args )
  {
    String configFileName = "tasks.conf";

    if ( args.length == 1 )
    {
      configFileName = args[0];
    }

    File configFile = new File( configFileName );

    if ( ! configFile.exists() || ! configFile.canRead() )
    {
      System.err.println( "Can't read config file '"
                          + configFileName + "'" );
      System.exit( 1 );
    }

    FileReader configReader = null;

    try
    {
      configReader = new FileReader( configFile );
    }
    catch( FileNotFoundException fnfX ) {}

    Tasks taskList = new Tasks( configReader );

    try
    {
      configReader.close();
    }
    catch( IOException ioX ) {}

    TaskManager ex = new TaskManager( taskList );
  }
}
```

Listing 12.7 The task manager's TaskManager component. (continued)

Task Results

Since an application concerned with database-related tasks is almost certain to generate at least some results that are best displayed in table format, we now turn to addressing that need. Through its Swing package, Java provides elegant support for rendering tables, and we take advantage of that fact here. We start by extending Java's AbstractTableModel class, as shown in Listing 12.8. Our derived class, ResultsTableModel, assumes a Vector representation of table data. The constructor expects that each element of a supplied Vector is an array of Strings, with the first containing the column names and each subsequent element representing one row of data. Responsibility for ensuring appropriate String representations for each data element rests with the entity instantiating the ResultsTableModel object.

```
package mysqljava;

import java.util.*;
import javax.swing.table.*;

public class ResultsTableModel extends AbstractTableModel
{
  ResultsTableModel( Vector results )
  {
    columnNames = (String[])(results.get( 0 ));
    results.remove( 0 );

    int rowCount = results.size();
    tableData = new String [rowCount][];

    for ( int i = 0; i < rowCount; ++i )
    {
      tableData[i] = (String[])(results.get( i ));
    }
  }

  public String getColumnName( int colIndex )
  {
    return (columnNames[colIndex]);
  }

  public int getColumnCount()
  {
    return (columnNames.length);
  }
```

Listing 12.8 The model used for displaying results in table format. (continues)

```
  public int getRowCount()
  {
    return (tableData.length);
  }

  public Object getValueAt( int rowIndex, int colIndex )
  {
    return (tableData[rowIndex][colIndex]);
  }

  private String[] columnNames;
  private String[][] tableData;
}
```

Listing 12.8 The model used for displaying results in table format. (continued)

With a model in place for our table data, we next turn to displaying that data. Responsibility for constructing and populating the table rests with our ResultsTablePanel class, which is shown in Listing 12.9. Although somewhat limited in functionality, it gets the job done. Columns are sized based on the anticipated display length of their respective column names, and the resulting table is placed in a scroll pane. A great deal more can be done with Java tables; however, plumbing the depths of table support is beyond the scope of this book.

```
package mysqljava;

import java.util.*;
import java.awt.*;
import javax.swing.*;
import javax.swing.table.*;

public class ResultsTablePanel extends JPanel
{
  public ResultsTablePanel( Vector results )
  {
    ResultsTableModel model = new ResultsTableModel( results );
    JTable resultsTable = new JTable( model );

    resultsTable.setAutoResizeMode( JTable.AUTO_RESIZE_OFF );

    setColumnWidths( resultsTable );
```

Listing 12.9 The results table panel. (continues)

```
    JScrollPane resultsPane = new JScrollPane( resultsTable );

    Dimension viewPortSize =
                    new Dimension( PORT_WIDTH, PORT_HEIGHT );

    resultsTable.setPreferredScrollableViewportSize(
                                          viewPortSize );

    add( resultsPane );
  }

  private void setColumnWidths( JTable table )
  {
    TableCellRenderer renderer =
                 table.getTableHeader().getDefaultRenderer();

    for ( int i = 0; i < table.getColumnCount(); ++i )
    {
      TableColumn column = table.getColumnModel().getColumn( i );

      Object headerValueObj = column.getHeaderValue();

      Component headerComp =
         renderer.getTableCellRendererComponent( table,
                                                 headerValueObj,
                                                 false, false,
                                                 -1, i );


      column.setPreferredWidth(
                       headerComp.getPreferredSize().width );
    }
  }

  final static private int PORT_WIDTH  = 600;
  final static private int PORT_HEIGHT = 400;
}
```

Listing 12.9 The results table panel. (continued)

The final component provided for displaying task results is the ResultsFrame class shown in Listing 12.10. As the name implies, this class provides a frame into which a results panel can be inserted. There is no requirement that the panel contain a table; anything that extends Java's JPanel is acceptable. In addition to the provided panel, the class adds a generic button for closing the results frame.

```
package mysqljava;

import java.awt.*;
import java.awt.event.*;
import javax.swing.*;

public class ResultsFrame extends JFrame
{
  public ResultsFrame( String title, JPanel resultsPanel )
  {
    super( title );

    buildGui( resultsPanel );

    pack();
    setVisible( true );
  }

  private void buildGui( JPanel resultsPanel )
  {
    frameContainer.setLayout( new BorderLayout() );

    frameContainer.add( resultsPanel, BorderLayout.NORTH );

    closeButton.addActionListener( new CloseHandler() );
    frameContainer.add( closeButton, BorderLayout.SOUTH );
    setContentPane( frameContainer );
  }

  private JPanel frameContainer = new JPanel();

  private JButton closeButton = new JButton( "Close" );

  class WindowHandler extends WindowAdapter
  {
    public void windowClosing( WindowEvent we )
    {
      we.getWindow().dispose();
    }
  }

  class CloseHandler implements ActionListener
  {
    public void actionPerformed( ActionEvent ae )
    {
      ResultsFrame.this.dispose();
    }
  }
}
```

Listing 12.10 A general-purpose results frame.

The Database Information Task

We now have the requisite components in place for support of a simple database task, so let's turn our attention to the creation of such a task. As with most applications, access to version information is often useful when determining feature support or reporting problems. Providing a version string for our interface would be a trivial addition, but what about accessing version data for an underlying MySQL server? Or for the JDBC driver that is communicating with the server? This sounds like a task waiting to happen.

The DbInfo class shown in Listing 12.11 serves as the task delegate for our database information task. As required, it implements the TaskDelegate interface and provides a definition of that interface's execute() method. The findDbInfo() method, which does the real database-related work, uses the provided Connection object to obtain a DatabaseMetaData object. The DatabaseMetaData object is in turn used to obtain the information we are after. In particular, the metadata object is used to acquire name and version strings for the database product and the JDBC driver; as a bonus, we also throw in the individual major and minor version numbers for the JDBC driver.

After acquiring the database information, our code combines that information with the appropriate column names, and packages everything up in a Vector. The Vector is used to instantiate a ResultsTablePanel, which is then inserted into a ResultsFrame and displayed for the user. An example of the results frame is shown in Figure 12.2.

```
package mysqljava;

import java.util.*;
import java.sql.*;

public class DbInfo implements TaskDelegate
{
  public DbInfo() {}

  public boolean execute( Connection conn )
  {
    if ( findDbInfo( conn ) )
    {
      ResultsTablePanel results =
                      new ResultsTablePanel( resultsTable );

      new ResultsFrame( "Database Information", results );
```

Listing 12.11 The database information task delegate. (continues)

```
        return (true);
      }

      return (false);
    }

    private boolean findDbInfo( Connection conn )
    {
      String[] columnNames = new String [COLS];

      columnNames[0] = "DB Product Name";
      columnNames[1] = "DB Product Version";
      columnNames[2] = "Driver Name";
      columnNames[3] = "Driver Version String";
      columnNames[4] = "Driver Major Version";
      columnNames[5] = "Driver Minor Version";

      resultsTable.add( columnNames );

      try
      {
        DatabaseMetaData metaData = conn.getMetaData();

        String[] values = new String [COLS];
        values [0] = metaData.getDatabaseProductName();
        values [1] = metaData.getDatabaseProductVersion();
        values [2] = metaData.getDriverName();
        values [3] = metaData.getDriverVersion();
        values [4] = String.valueOf(
                            metaData.getDriverMajorVersion() );
        values [5] = String.valueOf(
                            metaData.getDriverMinorVersion() );

        resultsTable.add( values );
      }
      catch( SQLException sqlX )
      {
        System.out.println(
                    SqlExceptionReader.readException( sqlX ) );

        return (false);
      }

      return (true);
    }
```

Listing 12.11 The database information task delegate. (continues)

```
    private Vector resultsTable = new Vector();

    private final static int COLS = 6;
}
```

Listing 12.11 The database information task delegate. (continued)

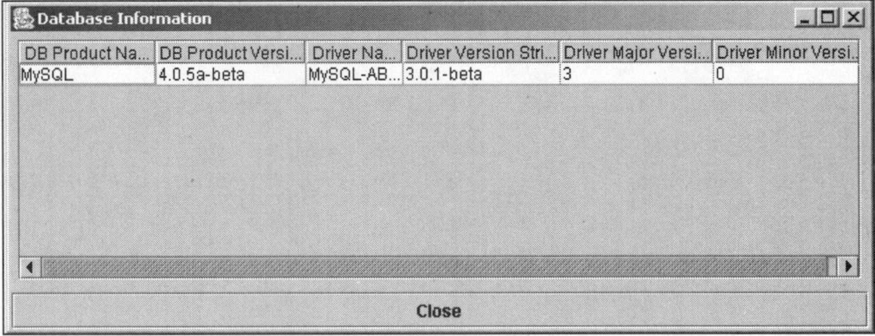

Figure 12.2 The database information task results frame.

User Input for Tasks

Without providing the user with the opportunity to supply additional input parameters, we limit the number of useful tasks that can be supported by our interface. As such, we take this opportunity to add the PromptFrame class shown in Listing 12.12. This class is much like our ResultsFrame class, with the main distinguishing feature being additional flexibility with regard to frame's button. In the case of the PromptFrame, the instantiating object specifies the button's name and associated action handler. This provides support for both custom prompts and cases where the required information necessitates multiple prompts.

```
package mysqljava;

import java.awt.*;
import java.awt.event.*;
import javax.swing.*;

public class PromptFrame extends JFrame
```

Listing 12.12 A general frame class for user input panels. (continues)

```
{
  public PromptFrame( String title,
                      String promptLabel,
                      JPanel promptPanel,
                      ActionListener promptHandler )
  {
    super( title );

    buildGui( promptLabel, promptPanel, promptHandler );

    pack();
    setVisible( true );
  }

  private void buildGui( String promptLabel,
                         JPanel promptPanel,
                         ActionListener promptHandler )
  {
    frameContainer.setLayout( new BorderLayout() );

    frameContainer.add( promptPanel, BorderLayout.NORTH );

    JButton promptButton = new JButton( promptLabel );
    promptButton.addActionListener( promptHandler );
    promptButton.addActionListener( new CloseHandler() );
    frameContainer.add( promptButton, BorderLayout.SOUTH );
    setContentPane( frameContainer );
  }

  private JPanel frameContainer = new JPanel();


  class WindowHandler extends WindowAdapter
  {
    public void windowClosing( WindowEvent we )
    {
      we.getWindow().dispose();
    }
  }

  class CloseHandler implements ActionListener
  {
    public void actionPerformed( ActionEvent ae )
    {
      PromptFrame.this.dispose();
    }
  }
}
```

Listing 12.12 A general frame class for user input panels. (continued)

The SQL Query Task

Returning to the issue of task definitions, we pick up with a task that supports freeform SQL queries. Again the task delegate, named SqlQuery and shown in Listing 12.13, implements the TaskDelegate interface and provides the required definition of execute(). In this case the delegate also implements the ActionListener interface so that it can pass itself to a PromptFrame and serve as the event handler for the prompt's button. Figure 12.3 shows our first use of the PromptFrame class, where the user is being prompted for a SQL query.

Once the query is submitted, the delegate's action event handler passes the real work off to the handleQuery() method. This method begins by creating a Statement object using the provided Connection object. The Statement object is then used to execute the specified SQL query, returning the query results as a ResultSet object. The column names associated with the return rows are obtained by requesting the ResultSetMetaData object associated with the ResultSet. Finally, we step through the ResultSet, extracting the column values for each row.

Since the goal is simply to display the results, we use the ResultSet getString() method to extract all column values, regardless of their defined type. Since getString() is defined for and does the right thing with all JDBC types supported by MySQL, this is a valid approach. If it were necessary to actually manipulate the retrieved values, the recommended accessors, as defined in Chapter 7, would be more appropriate.

As with the database information task, the results are placed in a Vector, that Vector is used to instantiate a ResultsTablePanel, and the results are finally displayed in a ResultsFrame. Figure 12.4 shows sample results from the SQL query task.

```
package mysqljava;

import java.sql.*;
import java.util.*;
import java.awt.*;
import java.awt.event.*;
import javax.swing.*;

public class SqlQuery implements TaskDelegate, ActionListener
{
  public SqlQuery() {}
```

Listing 12.13 The SQL query task delegate. (continues)

```
public boolean execute( Connection conn )
{
  this.conn = conn;

  new PromptFrame( "SQL Query Input",
                  QUERY_CMD, queryPanel, this );

  return (true);
}

public void actionPerformed( ActionEvent ae )
{
  if ( ae.getActionCommand().equals( QUERY_CMD ) )
  {
    Vector results = handleQuery( queryPanel.getQuery() );

    if ( results != null )
    {
      ResultsTablePanel table =
                        new ResultsTablePanel( results );

      new ResultsFrame( "SQL Query Results", table );
    }
  }
}

private Vector handleQuery( String query )
{
  Vector results = new Vector();

  try
  {
    Statement stmt = conn.createStatement();
    ResultSet rows = stmt.executeQuery( query );

    ResultSetMetaData metaData = rows.getMetaData();

    int columnCount = metaData.getColumnCount();

    String[] columnNames = new String [columnCount];

    for ( int i = 0; i < columnCount; ++i )
    {
      columnNames[i] = metaData.getColumnName( (i + 1) );
    }

    results.add( columnNames );
```

Listing 12.13 The SQL query task delegate. (continues)

```
      while ( rows.next() )
      {
        String[] values = new String [columnCount];

        for ( int i = 0; i < columnCount; ++i )
        {
          values[i] = rows.getString( (i + 1) );
        }

        results.add( values );
      }

    }
    catch( SQLException sqlX )
    {
      results = null;

      String msg = "Failed to execute query.\n"
                 + SqlExceptionReader.readException( sqlX );

      JOptionPane.showMessageDialog( queryPanel, msg,
                                     "Query Failure",
                                     JOptionPane.ERROR_MESSAGE );

    }

    return (results);
  }

  private Connection conn = null;
  private QueryPanel queryPanel = new QueryPanel();

  private final static int ROWS = 10;
  private final static int COLS = 50;
  private final static String QUERY_CMD = "Run Query";

  class QueryPanel extends JPanel
  {
    QueryPanel()
    {
      setLayout( new BorderLayout() );
      add( new JLabel( "SQL Query:" ), BorderLayout.NORTH );
      sqlArea.setRows( ROWS );
      sqlArea.setColumns( COLS );
      sqlArea.setLineWrap( true );
      add( sqlArea, BorderLayout.SOUTH );
```

Listing 12.13 The SQL query task delegate. (continues)

```
    }

    String getQuery()
    {
      return (sqlArea.getText());
    }

    private JTextArea sqlArea = new JTextArea();
  }
}
```

Listing 12.13 The SQL query task delegate. (continued)

Figure 12.3 A prompt frame used by the SQL query task.

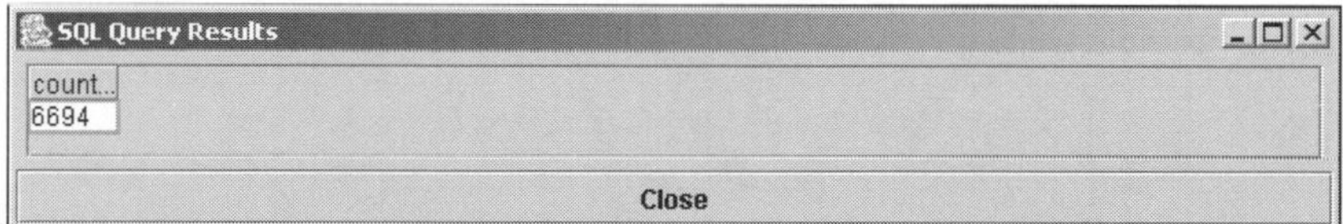

Figure 12.4 The SQL task results frame.

The Show Columns Task

For administrative and development purposes, access to a table's column definitions is often useful. It is just this type of access that our next task supports. As you can see in Listing 12.14, the implementation of the ShowColumns delegate follows the same pattern used for the SQL query task. The TaskDelegate and ActionListener interfaces are implemented, the execute() method is defined, and a PromptFrame is used to obtain additional input from the user—a table name in this case. The database-related work is handed off to the handleLookup() method, and the results are displayed as a table.

As with the database information task, the information we are after is available through a DatabaseMetaData object. In this case, we invoke the Database-

MetaData getColumns() method, which returns a ResultSet object whose rows define each column in the corresponding table; the "%" pattern provided as the fourth parameter to getColumns() matches any column name. For each column, we obtain the name, MySQL type, column size, and JDBC type code; in addition, we extract a value that indicates whether a column accepts a NULL value.

Since the JDBC type is provided as integer code, its readability leaves something to be desired. To address this issue, the JDBC type code is mapped to a corresponding type name using the JdbcTypes class shown in Listing 12.15. This class is just a thin wrapper around a HashMap that provides a mapping between the names and codes defined by the java.sql.Types class. Figure 12.5 shows a sample of the results generated by this task.

```
package mysqljava;

import java.sql.*;
import java.util.*;
import java.awt.*;
import java.awt.event.*;
import javax.swing.*;

public class ShowColumns implements TaskDelegate, ActionListener
{
  public ShowColumns() {}

  public boolean execute( Connection conn )
  {
    this.conn = conn;

    new PromptFrame( "Table Name", SHOW_CMD, tablePanel, this );

    return (true);
  }

  public void actionPerformed( ActionEvent ae )
  {
    if ( ae.getActionCommand().equals( SHOW_CMD ) )
    {
      Vector results = handleLookup( tablePanel.getTableName() );

      if ( results != null )
      {
        ResultsTablePanel table =
                                new ResultsTablePanel( results );
```

Listing 12.14 The show columns task delegate. (continues)

```
        new ResultsFrame( "Table Columns", table );
      }
    }
  }

  private Vector handleLookup( String tableName )
  {
    Vector results = new Vector();

    try
    {
      DatabaseMetaData metaData = conn.getMetaData();

      String[] columnNames = new String [TABLE_COLS];
      columnNames[0] = "Name";
      columnNames[1] = "MySQL Type";
      columnNames[2] = "Size";
      columnNames[3] = "Is Nullable";
      columnNames[4] = "JDBC Type Code";
      columnNames[5] = "JDBC Type Name";

      results.add( columnNames );

      ResultSet colData = metaData.getColumns( null, null,
                                               tableName, "%" );
      while ( colData.next() )
      {
        String[] values = new String [TABLE_COLS];
        values[0] = colData.getString( "COLUMN_NAME" );
        values[1] = colData.getString( "TYPE_NAME" );
        values[2] = String.valueOf(
                       colData.getInt( "COLUMN_SIZE" ) );
        values[3] = colData.getString( "IS_NULLABLE" );

        int jdbcTypeCode = colData.getShort( "DATA_TYPE" );
        values[4] = String.valueOf( jdbcTypeCode );
        values[5] = JdbcTypes.getName( jdbcTypeCode );

        results.add( values );
      }
    }
    catch( SQLException sqlX )
    {
      results = null;

      String msg = "Failed to lookup columns.\n"
                 + SqlExceptionReader.readException( sqlX );
```

Listing 12.14 The show columns task delegate. (continues)

```
      JOptionPane.showMessageDialog( tablePanel, msg,
                                     "Show Columns Failure",
                                     JOptionPane.ERROR_MESSAGE );
    }

    return (results);
  }

  private Connection conn = null;
  private TablePanel tablePanel = new TablePanel();

  private final static int TABLE_COLS = 6;
  private final static String SHOW_CMD = "Show Columns";

  class TablePanel extends JPanel
  {
    TablePanel()
    {
      setLayout( new BorderLayout() );
      add( new JLabel( "Table Name: " ), BorderLayout.WEST );
      tableNameField.setColumns( FIELD_COLS );
      add( tableNameField, BorderLayout.EAST );
    }

    String getTableName()
    {
      return (tableNameField.getText());
    }

    private JTextField tableNameField = new JTextField();

    private final static int FIELD_COLS = 20;
  }
}
```

Listing 12.14 The show columns task delegate. (continued)

```
package mysqljava;

import java.util.*;
import java.sql.*;

public class JdbcTypes
```

Listing 12.15 The JDBC type map. (continues)

```
{
  private final static int CAPACITY = 41;

  private static HashMap codeToName;

  static
  {
    codeToName = new HashMap( CAPACITY );

    codeToName.put( new Integer( Types.ARRAY ), "ARRAY" );
    codeToName.put( new Integer( Types.BIGINT ), "BIGINT" );
    codeToName.put( new Integer( Types.BINARY ), "BINARY" );
    codeToName.put( new Integer( Types.BIT ), "BIT" );
    codeToName.put( new Integer( Types.BLOB ), "BLOB" );
    codeToName.put( new Integer( Types.CHAR ), "CHAR" );
    codeToName.put( new Integer( Types.CLOB ), "CLOB" );
    codeToName.put( new Integer( Types.DATE ), "DATE" );
    codeToName.put( new Integer( Types.DECIMAL ), "DECIMAL" );
    codeToName.put( new Integer( Types.DISTINCT ), "DISTINCT" );
    codeToName.put( new Integer( Types.DOUBLE ), "DOUBLE" );
    codeToName.put( new Integer( Types.FLOAT ), "FLOAT" );
    codeToName.put( new Integer( Types.INTEGER ), "INTEGER" );
    codeToName.put( new Integer( Types.JAVA_OBJECT ),
                    "JAVA_OBJECT" );
    codeToName.put( new Integer( Types.LONGVARBINARY ),
                    "LONGVARBINARY" );
    codeToName.put( new Integer( Types.LONGVARCHAR ),
                    "LONGVARCHAR" );
    codeToName.put( new Integer( Types.NULL ), "NULL" );
    codeToName.put( new Integer( Types.NUMERIC ), "NUMERIC" );
    codeToName.put( new Integer( Types.OTHER ), "OTHER" );
    codeToName.put( new Integer( Types.REAL ), "REAL" );
    codeToName.put( new Integer( Types.REF ), "REF" );
    codeToName.put( new Integer( Types.SMALLINT ), "SMALLINT" );
    codeToName.put( new Integer( Types.STRUCT ), "STRUCT" );
    codeToName.put( new Integer( Types.TIME ), "TIME" );
    codeToName.put( new Integer( Types.TIMESTAMP ),
                    "TIMESTAMP" );
    codeToName.put( new Integer( Types.TINYINT ), "TINYINT" );
    codeToName.put( new Integer( Types.VARBINARY ),
                    "VARBINARY" );
    codeToName.put( new Integer( Types.VARCHAR ), "VARCHAR" );
  }

  static public String getName( int jdbcType )
  {
    return ((String)(codeToName.get( new Integer( jdbcType ) )));
  }
}
```

Listing 12.15 The JDBC type map. (continued)

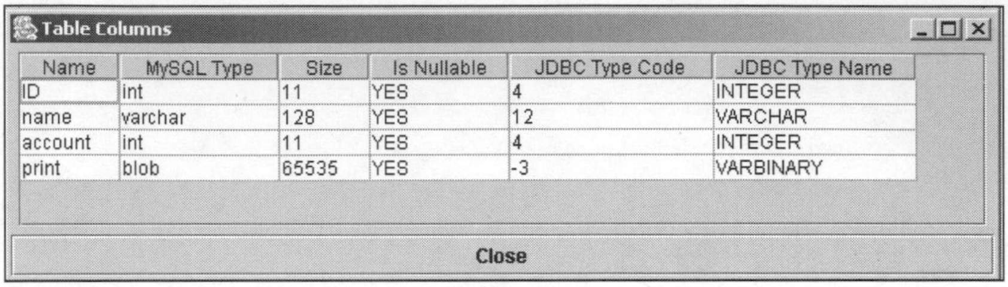

Table Columns

Name	MySQL Type	Size	Is Nullable	JDBC Type Code	JDBC Type Name
ID	int	11	YES	4	INTEGER
name	varchar	128	YES	12	VARCHAR
account	int	11	YES	4	INTEGER
print	blob	65535	YES	-3	VARBINARY

Close

Figure 12.5 The show columns task results frame.

The Insert Row Task

For our last example, we take a look at a task that modifies a database rather than simply retrieving information. The approach taken in implementing the delegate for this task, as shown in Listing 12.16, differs in a couple of ways from that used for previous tasks. First, the user is prompted for input twice, once to obtain the table name and once to obtain the row values. Second, since an insert doesn't generate output appropriate for display in a table, simple dialog boxes are used to present the result.

When the task is initiated, a PromptFrame is used to request the name of the table into which a row is to be inserted. With the table name in hand, the delegate uses the same technique presented for the show columns task to obtain the column names associated with the table. This step is handled by the getColumnNames() method. The column names are then used as labels for a second PromptFrame that requests the values to be entered in the new row; an example of this frame is shown in Figure 12.6.

Once the user submits the row values, the getValuesAsSql() method is invoked to generate the relevant portion of the SQL insert statement. Construction of the insert statement is then completed and passed to the insertRow() method. This method creates a Statement object from the provided Connection object and invokes the Statement's executeUpdate() method, passing the SQL insert statement generated from the user's input. Finally, a dialog box indicating the result of the attempted insert operation is presented to the user.

```
package mysqljava;

import java.sql.*;
```

Listing 12.16 The insert row task delegate. (continues)

```
import java.util.*;
import java.awt.*;
import java.awt.event.*;
import javax.swing.*;

public class InsertRow implements TaskDelegate, ActionListener
{
  public InsertRow() {}

  public boolean execute( Connection conn )
  {
    this.conn = conn;

    new PromptFrame( "Table Name", SELECT_CMD,
                     tablePanel, this );

    return (true);
  }

  public void actionPerformed( ActionEvent ae )
  {
    String cmd = ae.getActionCommand();

    if ( cmd.equals( SELECT_CMD ) )
    {
      tableName = tablePanel.getTableName();
      String[] columnNames = getColumnNames();

      if ( columnNames != null )
      {
        valuePanel = new ValuePanel( columnNames );
        new PromptFrame( "Row Value Input",
                         INSERT_CMD, valuePanel, this );
      }
    }
    else
    if ( cmd.equals( INSERT_CMD ) )
    {
      String insertSql = "INSERT INTO " + tableName
                       + " " + valuePanel.getValuesAsSql();

      insertRow( insertSql );
    }
  }

  private String[] getColumnNames()
  {
```

Listing 12.16 The insert row task delegate. (continues)

```
    String xMsg = "";
    Vector columnNames = new Vector();

    try
    {
      DatabaseMetaData metaData = conn.getMetaData();

      ResultSet colData = metaData.getColumns( null, null,
                                               tableName, "%" );

      while ( colData.next() )
      {
        columnNames.add( colData.getString( "COLUMN_NAME" ) );
      }

      if ( columnNames.size() == 0 )
      {
        columnNames = null;
      }
    }
    catch( SQLException sqlX )
    {
      columnNames = null;

      xMsg = SqlExceptionReader.readException( sqlX );

    }

    if ( columnNames == null )
    {
      String msg = "Failed to access table ("
                 + tableName + ")\n" + xMsg;
      JOptionPane.showMessageDialog( tablePanel, msg,
                                     "Insert Row Failure",
                                     JOptionPane.ERROR_MESSAGE );
      return (null);
    }
    else
    {
      return ((String[])(columnNames.toArray( new String [0] )));
    }
  }

  private void insertRow( String insertSql )
  {
    try
    {
```

Listing 12.16 The insert row task delegate. (continues)

```
        Statement stmt = conn.createStatement();

        int count = stmt.executeUpdate( insertSql );

        if ( count != 1 )
        {
          String msg = "Row insert failed. Returned "
                     + count + ".";

          JOptionPane.showMessageDialog(
                                     null, msg,
                                     "Insert Failure",
                                     JOptionPane.ERROR_MESSAGE );

        }
        else
        {
          String msg = "Row insert successful.";

          JOptionPane.showMessageDialog(
                               null, msg,
                               "Insert Success",
                               JOptionPane.INFORMATION_MESSAGE );

        }
      }
      catch( SQLException sqlX )
      {
        String msg = "Failed to insert row.\n"
                   + SqlExceptionReader.readException( sqlX );

        JOptionPane.showMessageDialog( null, msg,
                                       "Insert Failure",
                                       JOptionPane.ERROR_MESSAGE );
      }
    }

    private String tableName = null;
    private Connection conn = null;
    private ValuePanel valuePanel = null;
    private TablePanel tablePanel = new TablePanel();

    private final static String SELECT_CMD = "Select Table";
    private final static String INSERT_CMD = "Insert Row";

    class TablePanel extends JPanel
    {
```

Listing 12.16 The insert row task delegate. (continues)

```
  TablePanel()
  {
    setLayout( new BorderLayout() );
    add( new JLabel( "Table Name: " ), BorderLayout.WEST );
    tableNameField.setColumns( FIELD_COLS );
    add( tableNameField, BorderLayout.EAST );
  }

  String getTableName()
  {
    return (tableNameField.getText());
  }

  private JTextField tableNameField = new JTextField();

  private final static int FIELD_COLS = 20;
}

class ValuePanel extends JPanel
{
  ValuePanel( String[] columnNames )
  {
    int columnCount = columnNames.length;

    setLayout( new GridLayout( columnCount, 2 ) );

    valueFields = new JTextField [columnCount];

    for ( int i = 0; i < columnCount; ++i )
    {
      add( new JLabel( columnNames[i] + ":" ) );
      valueFields[i] = new JTextField( FIELD_COLS );
      add( valueFields[i] );
    }

    this.columnNames = columnNames;
  }

  String getValuesAsSql()
  {
    StringBuffer cols = new StringBuffer( "(" );
    StringBuffer vals = new StringBuffer( "VALUES(" );

    boolean isFirst = true;

    for ( int i = 0; i < columnNames.length; ++i )
```

Listing 12.16 The insert row task delegate. (continues)

```
        {
          String value = valueFields[i].getText();

          if ( value.length() == 0 )
          {
            continue;
          }

          if ( ! isFirst )
          {
            cols.append( "," );
            vals.append( "," );
          }
          else
          {
            isFirst = false;
          }

          cols.append( columnNames[i] );
          vals.append( "\"" ).append( value ).append( "\"" );
        }

      cols.append( ")" );
      vals.append( ")" );

      return (cols.toString() + " " + vals.toString());
    }

    private String[] columnNames;
    private JTextField[] valueFields;

    private final static int FIELD_COLS = 20;
  }
}
```

Listing 12.16 The insert row task delegate. (continued)

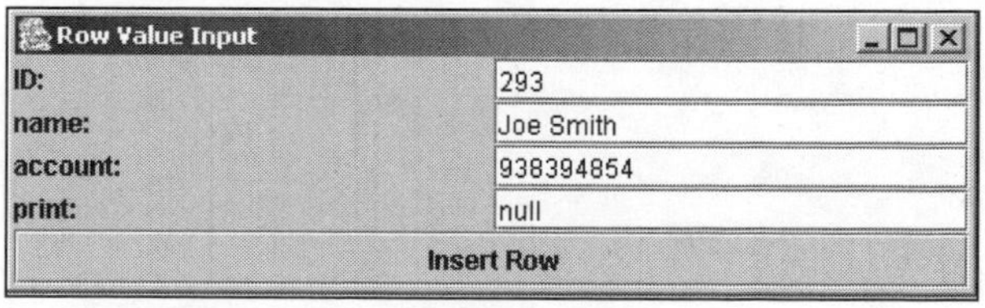

Figure 12.6 The insert row task prompt frame.

What's Next

In this chapter, we detailed the development of a real-world application for accessing MySQL databases using the Java programming language. Okay, maybe calling it a real-world application is going a bit far. There is a distinct lack of bells and whistles, error checking is minimal, and we have taken a few shortcuts. However, the example does provide some insight into ways in which Java and MySQL can combine to address real-world problems. In the next chapter, we turn our attention to the topic of database administration.

CHAPTER 13

Database Administration

MySQL is a comprehensive relational database management system and must be managed to achieve optimal functionality. Some of the issues that you need to understand include how to add users and set up permissions, how to import large amounts of data into various tables, when and how to make backups, and how to replicate data, among other functions. This chapter provides you with a guide to database administration in a development or staging environment. For a production-level system, we recommend that you use a professional database administrator.

Using the mysql Administration Application

One of the most important tools available to the developer is the command-line interface called simply *mysql*, which is located in the /bin directory of both the Unix and Windows systems. mysql is both an interactive and noninteractive application that gives you complete control over the MySQL database server and its related tables.

You start the application in interactive mode by issuing the following command within a terminal window or command prompt:

```
mysql --user=<username> --password=<password> database
```

Replace *<username>* and *<password>* with either a previously defined user in the database or the root user. If you're executing the mysql application as the root user under Unix or as Administrator under Windows, you need only the mysql application name. You append the database name to the command line, which has the same effect as executing the use <database> command. If the application is in the path of the current user or the system, the output shown in Figure 13.1 will be generated.

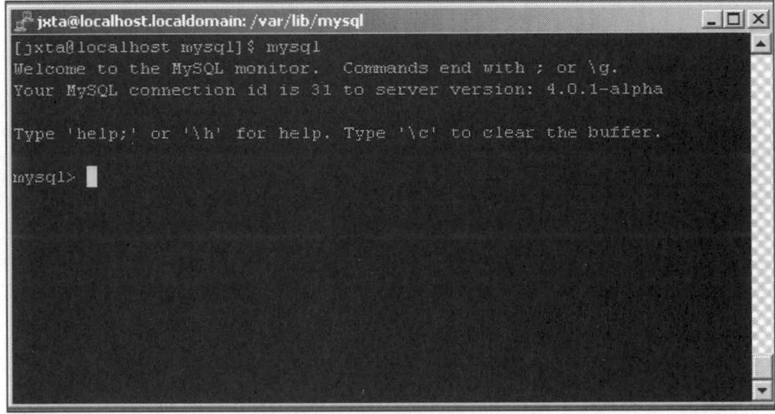

Figure 13.1 The mysql application output.

The application allows any type of SQL to be entered at the command line. All SQL must end with the ; character to indicate the end of a statement. For example, we can query all of the rows in our acc_acc database and display the results in the application. Figure 13.2 shows an example of this query and the resulting output.

To quit the application, enter the exit command. We use the mysql application in most of the sections remaining in this chapter.

```
jxta@localhost.localdomain: /var/lib/mysql
mysql> use accounts;
Reading table information for completion of table and column names
You can turn off this feature to get a quicker startup with -A

Database changed
mysql> select * from acc_acc;
+---------+----------+----------+----------------+----------------+
| acc_id  | username | password | ts             | act_ts         |
+---------+----------+----------+----------------+----------------+
| 1034055 | jdoe     | newpass  | 00000000000000 | 20030106163740 |
| 1034033 | doej     | password | 00000000000000 | 20030106163900 |
| 1034067 | janed    | jane     | 20030106164743 | 20030106164743 |
| 1034546 | jjmyers  | ime      | 20030106175202 | 00000000000000 |
+---------+----------+----------+----------------+----------------+
4 rows in set (0.00 sec)

mysql>
```

Figure 13.2 Using mysql to query our database.

Managing Users and Permissions

Once the MySQL server has been installed, you must immediately change the password for the root user as well as add new users to the server. Adding a new user involves adding an access configuration to the server as well as assigning permissions that allow the user access to specific databases, tables, and columns.

The MySQL database server automatically creates a database called mysql when you install the server. Within this database are four primary tables for holding user and permission information:

- columns_priv—Defines column-level privileges.
- db—Defines database-level privileges.
- tables_priv—Defines table-level privileges.
- user—Defines the users that can connect to the server.

The MySQL server defines a combination of commands that you can use to add users and privileges to the server, as we discuss later in this chapter.

Changing Root

Once you've installed MySQL, changing the root password to the database application should be one of your next steps. The root user has complete authority over the system, just like the root user in Unix or the Administrator in Windows. The database installs the root user but does not set the password. We can see this by using a simple SELECT, as shown here:

```
mysql> use mysql;
Database changed
mysql> select user, password, host from user where user =
'root';
+------+----------+-----------+
| user | password | host      |
+------+----------+-----------+
| root |          | localhost |
| root |          | %         |
+------+----------+-----------+
2 rows in set (0.00 sec)
```

As you can see, the password is blank for the root user, and it creates a big security hole. To solve this problem, we need to assign a password. The following SQL entered into the mysql application will do the trick:

```
mysql> UPDATE user SET password=PASSWORD('<password>') WHERE
user = 'root';
```

This code updates the user table and sets the password field equal to an encrypted password specified by the *<password>* placeholder in those rows where the user field is equal to root. Once the field has been updated, it's a good idea to flush the change by using the command

```
mysql> FLUSH PRIVILEGES;
```

Adding Users

Adding users to a MySQL database can be accomplished in two ways. The first involves using the SQL command INSERT to place rows into one or more of the database tables we discussed earlier. Because the process of giving privileges can span all of the tables, except host, the MySQL database server provides a command called GRANT that allows you to easily add users and give them privileges. Here's the format of the GRANT command:

```
GRANT <privileges> (columns)
ON <db>
TO <user>
IDENTIFIED BY <password>
WITH GRANT OPTION
```

You replace the *<privileges>* placeholder with a comma-delimited string consisting of the following specifiers as needed:

ALTER—Allows the user to alter tables

CREATE—Allows the user to create databases and tables

DELETE—Allows the user to delete table rows

DROP—Allows the user to drop databases

INDEX—Allows the user to create/drop indexes

INSERT—Allows the user to insert rows

SELECT—Allows the user to select rows

UPDATE—Allows the user to update rows

FILE—Allows the user access to files on a local server

PROCESS—Allows the user to view process information or kill threads

RELOAD—Allows the user to flush logs, privileges, and caches

SHUTDOWN—Allows the user to shut down the database server

ALL—Gives the user all privileges

USAGE—Gives the user no privileges

You replace the (*columns*) placeholder with a comma-delimited list of columns in the database that will affected by the privileges. This option allows you to limit a user to specified columns in a database.

The <*db*> placeholder indicates the level to which the privileges affect the databases in the server. As our examples in this section show, the value can be all databases, or you can specify certain databases or a single database with limited columns.

The <*user*> and <*password*> placeholders indicate the username/password combination the new user will use to connect. The <*user*> placeholder is a username@host combination that allows connections to be limited to specific domain or IP addresses. You can substitute a wildcard using the character % in place of the host to give wider access to the system. A "" value can be used in place of the username to give any user from a host access to the database.

The WITH GRANT OPTION gives the new user the ability to grant privileges to new and existing users within the server. Use this option sparingly.

Consider a user john, who needs to access the MySQL server from his office PC, which has an IP address of 192.168.1.45. You don't want to give john administrative access to the system but want to allow him to insert, delete, and so forth on all of the various tables. To do this, use the following GRANT command:

```
mysql> GRANT SELECT, INSERT, UPDATE
ON *.*
TO john@192.168.1.45
IDENTIFIED BY "rudy"
```

This grant gives john basic access to all of the databases in the system. You could limit him to one database:

```
mysql> GRANT SELECT, INSERT, UPDATE
ON accounts.*
TO john@192.168.1.45
IDENTIFIED BY "rudy"
```

By using accounts.* in the ON clause, you ensure that john has access only to the tables in the accounts database. We could further restrict him to specific columns:

```
mysql> GRANT SELECT, INSERT, UPDATE (acc_id, username)
ON accounts.acc_acc
TO john@192.168.1.45
IDENTIFIED BY "rudy"
```

Here, john will be allowed to see only the acc_id and username columns of the accounts.acc_acc table. Suppose you must add another user, jim, who will have more privileges as well as require access from many machines:

```
mysql> GRANT ALL ON *.* TO jim@"%" IDENTIFIED BY "jimmy"
```

The user jim will have access to the server from any host and will be allowed full privileges. Obviously, there are many different combinations that you can create using the GRANT command.

There may be times when you have to remove a privilege from a user. In this case, you use the REVOKE command, which has this format:

```
REVOKE privileges (columns)
ON <database>
FROM <user >
```

For example, let's revoke UPDATE privileges from john:

```
mysql> REVOKE UPDATE ON *.* FROM john@192.168.1.45
```

If john will be going on vacation for two weeks and you don't want to leave his account open, but you don't want to delete him from the server, you can revoke all privileges:

```
mysql> REVOKE ALL ON *.* FROM john@192.168.1.45_
```

If during those two weeks, John decides to leave the company, you need to remove him from the database. That way, even if john doesn't have privileges he can still connect to the database. The command to remove john from the database is as follows:

```
mysql> DELETE FROM user WHERE User="john" and Host = "192.168.1.45";
mysql> flush privileges;
```

This command deletes the row defined for john in the user table, and MySQL no longer permits him to connect.

Limiting Resources

If you have chosen to use MySQL 4.0.2 or greater, you have the ability to limit users and processes to the amount of resources they are capable of using. The resources that can be limited include

- Queries per hour
- Updates per hour
- Connections per hour

You limit resources by specifying user/host values in a user table. These resources are not limited by default. You can define each of the limits by either an integer indicating per-hour rates or by a value such as 5 (which would allow five 5 connections per hour).

You apply limits by using the GRANT command or remove them using REVOKE. For example, suppose you have a user named smith who connects from host 192.168.1.4. You can limit smith to 30 queries per hour with this command:

```
mysql> GRANT ('smith', '192.168.1.4') WITH MAX_QUERIES_PER_HOUR 30;
```

Notice that here the GRANT command is a little different than when used to grant privileges to a user. To limit all of the available resources, use the command

```
mysql> GRANT ('smith', '192.168.1.4') WITH
            MAX_QUERIES_PER_HOUR 30
            MAX_UPDATES_PER_HOUR 60
            MAX_CONNECTIONS_PER_HOUR 10;
```

Several things should be noted:

- If any of the limits are reached, the user's connection is terminated and further connections are refused.
- The system keeps track of the user's usage of the three resources. To flush the values for an individual user, issue the GRANT command with one or all of the MAX_ clauses. To flush all users, use the commands FLUSH PRIVILEGES, FLUSH USER_RESOURCES, or mysqladmin reload.
- The resource limits are activated when the first GRANT command is used that assigns limits to any one user.

Configuring the Query Cache

The MySQL server includes a query cache that keeps track of recent queries by users in the system. The cache is kept in memory and is regulated based on the number and size of the queries hitting the database. By default, the query cache isn't activated when the MySQL server is first executed. The best way to configure the query cache is to enter appropriate values in the MySQL configuration file, my.cnf. The arguments available are as follows:

- query_cache_limit—Specifies the limit for cached results; the default is 1MB.
- query_cache_size—Specifies the memory for the query cache; the default is 0, which means the cache is disabled.
- query_cache_type—Specifies the cache type:

  0—Cache is off.

  1—Cache is on; no SELECT SQL_NO_CACHE queries are cached.

  2—Cache is on; only cache SELECT SQL_CACHE queries are cached.

To see the current status of the cache, execute the command SHOW STATUS to display a result like the following in the mysql application:

```
mysql> SHOW STATUS LIKE "Qcache%";
+-------------------------+-------+
| Variable_name           | Value |
+-------------------------+-------+
| Qcache_queries_in_cache | 30    |
| Qcache_inserts          | 5     |
| Qcache_hits             | 8     |
| Qcache_not_cached       | 57    |
| Qcache_free_memory      | 5434  |
| Qcache_free_blocks      | 254   |
| Qcache_total_blocks     | 6532  |
+-------------------------+-------+
7 rows in set (0.00 sec)
```

Because the query cache is based in memory, it can become fragmented. Eventually the cache may not allow a query to be changed because a slot big enough for the query is not available. You can defragment the cache by issuing the command FLUSH QUERY CACHE. This command consolidates the queries in the cache and frees up larger blocks of space for future queries. The FLUSH TABLES command also defragments the query cache. To remove all queries in the query cache, issue the RESET QUERY CACHE command.

Forcing a Cache

When you execute a query, MySQL evaluates whether or not the query should be cached. Some of the criteria for a query include its size and the current state of the cache; also the MySQL manual defines several functions that aren't cached. If you want to be sure that one of your queries is cached, add the SQL_CACHE clause to the SELECT command. For example:

```
SELECT SQL_CACHE * from acc_acc;
```

If you have another query that you want to make sure isn't cached, use the SQL_NO_CACHE clause:

```
SELECT SQL_NO_CACHE * from acc_cert;
```

The cache determines whether a new query is in the cache by performing a byte-by-byte comparison. In other words, the cache is case-sensitive since the system will compare the byte values of the query versus the cache.

Understanding Log Files

The MySQL server automatically generates several log files, including

- An error log
- A general log
- A binary log
- A slow query log

Error Logs

All of the logs for the MySQL database server are located in the defined data directory such as /mysql/data. The server writes any errors that it finds during boot into an error log file called <*hostname*>.err on Unix and mysql.err on Windows. The contents of the file look something like this:

```
[jxta@localhost mysql]$ cat localhost.localdomain.err
020602 16:26:04  mysqld started
020602 16:26:09  InnoDB: Started
/usr/sbin/mysqld: ready for connections
020604  0:00:55  /usr/sbin/mysqld: Normal shutdown

020604  0:00:55  InnoDB: Starting shutdown...
020604  0:00:59  InnoDB: Shutdown completed
020604  0:00:59  /usr/sbin/mysqld: Shutdown Complete

020604 00:00:59  mysqld ended

020630 21:39:38  mysqld started
InnoDB: Database was not shut down normally.
InnoDB: Starting recovery from log files...
InnoDB: Starting log scan based on checkpoint at
InnoDB: log sequence number 0 43902
020630 21:39:42  InnoDB: Started
/usr/sbin/mysqld: ready for connections
020702 20:10:37  mysqld started
```

It is a good idea to examine the contents of the error file, even when users haven't reported problems. The error file is the first place the server starts to record errors.

General Logs

If you are having difficulties with a client connecting with the database, you can activate a general log when the mysql executable starts. You activate the general log by using the command-line option –log. For example:

```
mysqld -log[=filename]
```

When the server executes, it will by default log all connections and queries to a file called <*hostname*>.log.

Binary Logs

The binary log is used by the MySQL server to record all updates made to the database. Since this is a binary log, it isn't designed for troubleshooting, but instead provides a simple mechanism for master/slave replication. The slave database can read the binary log to determine what updates have occurred on the master. You activate the log by using the –log-bin command-line prompt or through the configuration file.

Slow Query Logs

If you start the server with the command-line option –log-slow-queries, the system creates a log file that holds all queries that take longer than long_query_time to execute. If you suspect that queries are taking a long time to execute, examine this log.

Maintaining Your Tables

To keep your tables in the best condition possible, it's a good idea to run through a check periodically. The CHECK TABLE command works on both MyISAM and InnoDB tables. The format of the command is

```
CHECK TABLE tbl_name[,tbl_name...] [option [option...]]
```

Options include the following:

- QUICK—Doesn't check for bad links.
- FAST—Checks only improperly closed tables.
- MEDIUM—Checks deleted links.
- EXTENDED—Performs a full key lookup for 100-percent consistency.
- CHANGED—Checks only tables that have changed since the last check.

Figure 13.3 shows an example of executing CHECK TABLE on the acc_acc table.

In this example, an extended check is made against the acc_acc table. Any errors in the table are listed as rows in the result set shown. The last row is always the final diagnostic report. The goal is for the Msg_text column to have a value of OK. If the value isn't OK, that means you have to execute the REPAIR TABLE command.

To check the table outside the mysql application tool, use the myisamchk utility. For example:

```
myisamchk acc_acc.myi
```

```
jxta@localhost.localdomain: /var/lib/mysql

mysql> check table acc_acc extended;
+-----------------+-------+----------+----------+
| Table           | Op    | Msg_type | Msg_text |
+-----------------+-------+----------+----------+
| accounts.acc_acc | check | status   | OK       |
+-----------------+-------+----------+----------+
1 row in set (0.02 sec)

mysql>
```

Figure 13.3 Executing a check on a table.

Figure 13.4 shows the output generated by myisamchk when executed against the acc_acc table.

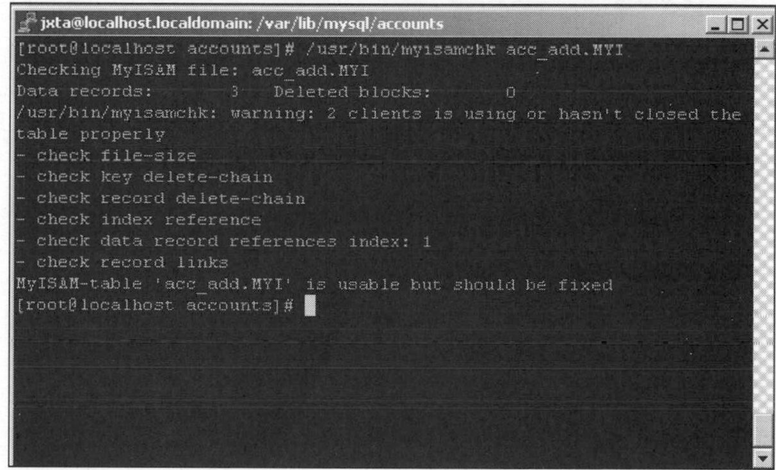

Figure 13.4 An example using myisamchk.

The utility performs the same basic check as the CHECK TABLE command, but from a command-line starting point. There are numerous options for the utility, which you can find in the MySQL manual.

Repairing Tables

If either of the table-checking mechanisms suggest that there is a problem with one of your MyISAM tables, you must use the REPAIR TABLE to bring the table into consistency. If the repairs need to be made from the command line or in a batch situation, you can use the myisamchk application. Figure 13.5 shows an example of running the application using the –r flag.

```
jxta@localhost.localdomain: /var/lib/mysql/accounts
[root@localhost accounts]# /usr/bin/myisamchk acc_add.MYI
Checking MyISAM file: acc_add.MYI
Data records:        3   Deleted blocks:        0
/usr/bin/myisamchk: warning: 2 clients is using or hasn't closed the
table properly
- check file-size
- check key delete-chain
- check record delete-chain
- check index reference
- check data record references index: 1
- check record links
MyISAM-table 'acc_add.MYI' is usable but should be fixed
[root@localhost accounts]# /usr/bin/myisamchk -r acc_add.MYI
- recovering (with sort) MyISAM-table 'acc_add.MYI'
Data records: 3
- Fixing index 1
[root@localhost accounts]#
```

Figure 13.5 Using myisamchk to repair a table.

It is also possible to repair the table using the REPAIR TABLE command. Figure 13.6 shows an example of using the command along with the EXTENDED options. There is a QUICK repair option as well.

```
jxta@localhost.localdomain: /var/lib/mysql/accounts

mysql> repair table acc_add extended;
+------------------+--------+----------+----------+
| Table            | Op     | Msg_type | Msg_text |
+------------------+--------+----------+----------+
| accounts.acc_add | repair | status   | OK       |
+------------------+--------+----------+----------+
1 row in set (0.03 sec)

mysql>
```

Figure 13.6 Using the REPAIR TABLE command.

Backing Up and Restoring Your Database

Once a database has been put into use, it is always a good idea to make backups on a prepared schedule. The MySQL database server holds all of the data in a series of files located on a local or network driver. Figure 13.7 shows the files used to contain the acc_acc, acc_add, and acc_cert tables we've used throughout the book.

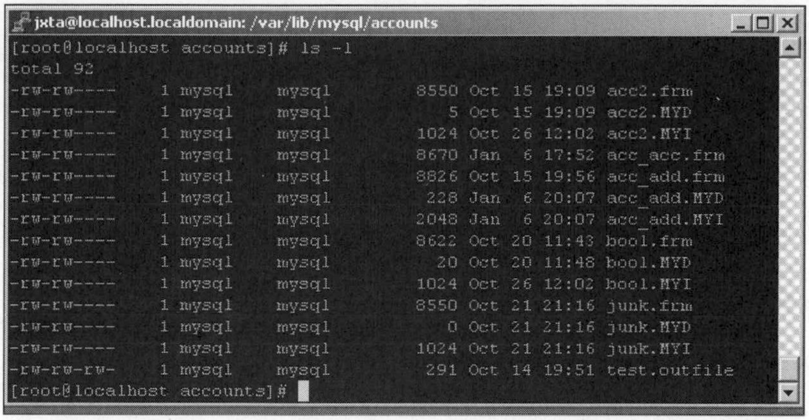

```
jxta@localhost.localdomain: /var/lib/mysql/accounts
[root@localhost accounts]# ls -l
total 92
-rw-rw----    1 mysql    mysql       8550 Oct 15 19:09 acc2.frm
-rw-rw----    1 mysql    mysql          5 Oct 15 19:09 acc2.MYD
-rw-rw----    1 mysql    mysql       1024 Oct 26 12:02 acc2.MYI
-rw-rw----    1 mysql    mysql       8670 Jan  6 17:52 acc_acc.frm
-rw-rw----    1 mysql    mysql       8826 Oct 15 19:56 acc_add.frm
-rw-rw----    1 mysql    mysql        228 Jan  6 20:07 acc_add.MYD
-rw-rw----    1 mysql    mysql       2048 Jan  6 20:07 acc_add.MYI
-rw-rw----    1 mysql    mysql       8622 Oct 20 11:43 bool.frm
-rw-rw----    1 mysql    mysql         20 Oct 20 11:48 bool.MYD
-rw-rw----    1 mysql    mysql       1024 Oct 26 12:02 bool.MYI
-rw-rw----    1 mysql    mysql       8550 Oct 21 21:16 junk.frm
-rw-rw----    1 mysql    mysql          0 Oct 21 21:16 junk.MYD
-rw-rw----    1 mysql    mysql       1024 Oct 21 21:16 junk.MYI
-rw-rw-rw-    1 mysql    mysql        291 Oct 14 19:51 test.outfile
[root@localhost accounts]#
```

Figure 13.7 The acc_* table data files.

As you can see in the figure, the data files are located in the data directory under a subdirectory called accounts, which is the database where the tables are defined. All three of these tables are MyISAM tables, and as such, three files are defined per table. Other table types store data in other directories and files, as we discuss briefly in a later section.

From what we see in the figure and know about MySQL, the easiest way to back up a database that uses MyISAM tables is to follow these steps:

1. Stop the server.
2. Copy the files to another medium.
3. Restart the database.

If you don't have the luxury of stopping the database, you have to do a couple of extra steps. The most important thing is to make sure that no writes occur to the database tables you are backing up. Here are the steps to follow when you cannot shut down the database:

1. Lock the tables with a read lock using the command

   ```
   mysql>LOCK TABLES <tables to backup> READ.
   ```

2. Flush any pending updates using the command

   ```
   mysql> FLUSH TABLES.
   ```

3. Back up the table using only one of the following methods:

   Copy the files manually.

   Use the command mysql> SELECT * INTO OUTFILE "*filename*" FROM <*table*>.

Use the command mysql> BACKUP TABLE *<table>* TO *<path>*.

Use the command mysqldump --opt *<database>* > *<file>*.

Use the command mysqlhotcopy *<database>* *<path>*.

Release the table locks using the command – mysql>UNLOCK TABLES;.

Let's look at what these steps are accomplishing. First, we need to keep in mind that our database server is still executing and that both reads and updates could be occurring. We need to make sure that no write occurs to the tables once we start to copy the data. We accomplish this by issuing the LOCK TABLES command. For example, let's lock the acc_acc table using the following command, which won't allow any updates to occur:

```
mysql> LOCK TABLES acc_acc READ;
```

Next, we need to flush all of the caches associated with the table so that any pending actions are taken care of:

```
mysql> FLUSH TABLES acc_acc;
```

The select table is now ready to be backed up, and as shown in step 3, there are quite a few options available. Let's discuss each of them in order.

The first backup option is to copy the files manually, which is the easiest of the options. With this option and MyISAM files, you just copy all of the files associated with the table. The second option is to issue the command SELECT * INTO OUTFILE "*filename*" FROM *<table>*. With this option, you create a file with all of the data from the table arranged in a grid format. Typically, you use this option when transferring table data from the database to another application like Microsoft Excel; it isn't the best backup option.

The third choice, the BACKUP TABLE command, works only with MyISAM tables. The command copies the .frm and .myd files to the specified path. The index file(s) won't be copied since you can recover them from the data files. The command is designed to move the least amount of data necessary to ensure complete backup of data.

The fourth option, the command mysqldump --opt *<database>* > *<file>*, backs up an entire database to a specified file. The file will not only include data, but also the SQL commands necessary to reproduce the data on another MySQL server or even another database system entirely. Figure 13.8 shows an example of using mysqldump.

The last option is to use the command mysqlhotcopy *<database>* *<path>*. The mysqlhotcopy command makes a very quick backup of the specified database using a Perl script, and you must execute it from the same machine as the database.

```
jxta@localhost.localdomain: /var/lib/mysql/accounts
[root@localhost accounts]# mysqldump accounts acc_acc > acc.sql
[root@localhost accounts]# cat acc.sql
-- MySQL dump 8.19
--
-- Host: localhost    Database: accounts
---------------------------------------------------------
-- Server version       4.0.1-alpha

--
-- Table structure for table 'acc_acc'
--

CREATE TABLE acc_acc (
  acc_id int(11) NOT NULL default '0',
  username varchar(64) default NULL,
  password varchar(64) default NULL,
  ts timestamp(14) NOT NULL,
  act_ts timestamp(14) NOT NULL
) TYPE=InnoDB;

/*!40000 ALTER TABLE acc_acc DISABLE KEYS */;

--
-- Dumping data for table 'acc_acc'
--


INSERT INTO acc_acc VALUES (1034055,'jdoe','newpass',00000000000000,20030106163740);
INSERT INTO acc_acc VALUES (1034033,'doej','password',00000000000000,20030106163900);
INSERT INTO acc_acc VALUES (1034067,'janed','jane',20030106164743,20030106164743);
INSERT INTO acc_acc VALUES (1034546,'jjmyers','ime',20030106175202,00000000000000);

/*!40000 ALTER TABLE acc_acc ENABLE KEYS */;

[root@localhost accounts]#
```

Figure 13.8 Using mysqldump.

Restoring Data

We hope you never need to use a database backup, but there may be times when data is corrupted. In these cases, you have to restore your data. We have seen several ways to back up a MySQL database. There are basically three ways to recover the backed-up data:

1. Copy the files.
2. Use the mysql application.
3. Use the RESTORE TABLE command.

If you used one of the backup options where the database files were just copied to another location, you can restore your data by stopping the database, copying the files into the correct data directory, and restarting the server.

If you saved your data using the mysqldump command, you can "replay" the SQL commands in the backup files into the current mysql server with the command

```
mysql database < <file>
```

Before using this command, though, rename the current database to a backup name and then import the old data into the server.

You can use the RESTORE TABLE command if you used the BACKUP TABLE command to back up your data. The format of the command is

```
RESTORE TABLE <database> FROM <path>
```

If you don't rename the database table to be written, you'll get an error.

InnoDB Table Types

Although the MyISAM table type is the most commonly used type in MySQL, we need to cover two others in our backup discussion: InnoDB and BDB. First, let's look at the InnoDB table type. There are two possible ways to back up the InnoDB tables: performing a binary backup or using a tool called InnoDB Hot Backup.

In the binary backup, it is assumed you can shut down the database server. Follow these steps:

1. Shut down MySQL.
2. Copy the InnoDB files to an appropriate backup medium.

   All data files are located in the /idbata directory.

   Log files are typically located in /mysql/data – ib_logfile_x.
3. Copy the current my.cnf file to the backup medium.
4. Use mysqldump to periodically create readable versions of the database data.

If you don't have the option of shutting down your database server to make the backups of the InnoDB tables, you can use a tool called InnoDB Hot Backup to do the work. The tool is available at www.innodb.com/hotbackup.html.

The Hot Backup tool is designed to make a copy of your InnoDB tables without locking the database or causing any other type of interrupt to its normal operation. In other words, you get a snapshot of the data in your tables at a moment in time. Of course, any additional updates to the table after the snapshot won't be part of the backup. You can request a 30-day evaluation of InnoDB Hot Backup at the URL we've provided or purchase a license.

BDB Table Types

The other transaction table type used in MySQL is BDB, and it provides an alternative to InnoDB. The best way to make a backup of BDB tables is to use a binary process:

1. Stop the MySQL database server.
2. Copy all files with the <*table*>.db name.
3. Copy all log files with the name log.*dddddd* located in the data directory of MySQL—typically <install dir>/mysql/data.

What's Next

This chapter has provided a glimpse into some of the functions that a developer might need to accomplish while using a MySQL database as a back-end storage device for Java. In the next chapter, we look at some of the most popular optimization techniques to get the most from your MySQL database as well as Connector/J and Java.

CHAPTER 14

Performance and Tuning

During the development of an application that spends a good part of its execution accessing a database, you must create a balance to achieve the optimal working environment. In this chapter, we look at some of the performance numbers associated with using Connector/J versions 3.0 and 2.1, how to tune MySQL for performance, and hints for getting the most out of JDBC.

Connector/J 3.0 Performance

From an overall performance perspective, we want to determine how well the driver (both 3.0 and 2.1) can insert new rows into the database, select those same rows, and update one of the columns in each row. The code in Listing 14.1 does the performance work. The test is against a table defined using the following create table command:

```
mysql> create table product(id int auto_increment primary key,
                            string varchar(32),
                            test double,
                            supplier varchar(128),
                            ts timestamp,
                            value int);
```

```
import java.sql.*;
import java.util.Date;
import java.text.DateFormat;

public class Performance{
  Connection connection;

  public Performance() {
     try {
       Class.forName("com.mysql.jdbc.Driver").newInstance();
     } catch (Exception e) {
       System.err.println("unable to load driver");
     }
    try {
       connection = DriverManager.getConnection(
        "jdbc:mysql://192.168.1.25/products?user=spider&password=spider");
     }
     catch(SQLException e) {
         System.out.println("SQLException: " + e.getMessage());
         System.out.println("SQLState: " + e.getSQLState());
         System.out.println("VendorError:  " +
           e.getErrorCode());
     }
  }

  public void run() {
    long startTime;

    try {
      PreparedStatement ps = connection.prepareStatement(
        "INSERT INTO product VALUES(null, 'title', 5.54,
        'supplier', null,      ?)");
      startTime = new Date().getTime();
      for (int i=0;i<1000;i++) {
        ps.setInt(1, i);
        ps.executeUpdate();
      }
      System.out.println("INSERT = " + ((new Date().getTime())
        - startTime));

      Statement statement  = connection.createStatement();
      startTime = new Date().getTime();
      ResultSet rs = statement.executeQuery("SELECT * FROM product");
      while (rs.next()) {
      }
      rs.close();
      statement.close();
      System.out.println("SELECT = " + ((new Date().getTime())
```

Listing 14.1 Performance example code. (continues)

```
        - startTime));



      ps = connection.prepareStatement(
        "UPDATE product SET inventory=10 WHERE inventory = ?");
      startTime = new Date().getTime();
      for (int i=0;i<1000;i++) {
        ps.setInt(1, i);
        ps.executeUpdate();
      }
      System.out.println("UPDATE = " + ((new Date().getTime())
        - startTime));

      connection.close();
    } catch(SQLException e) {   }
  }

  public static void main(String[] args) {
    Performance test = new Performance();
    test.run();
  }
}
```

Listing 14.1 Performance example code. (continued)

We executed the code in Listing 14.1 against a MySQL 3.23-52-NT database running on a 1.4GHz Pentium 4 with 512MB of RAM. We executed the client code on the same machine to eliminate any substantial network traffic. When we used the Connector/J 3.01 beta, it took

- 734 milliseconds to insert 1000 rows
- 20 milliseconds to retrieve 1000 rows
- 13,063 milliseconds (13.063 seconds) to update 1000 rows

When we ran MySQL 4.0.4 on a P166 with 256MB of RAM with the client running on a separate machine over a 100MB LAN, it took

- 741 milliseconds to insert 1000 rows
- 50 milliseconds to retrieve 1000 rows
- 12,358 milliseconds (12.358 seconds) to update 1000 rows

Switching to Connector/J 2.1 doesn't change the numbers too much. When we used the 1.4GHz machine, it took

- 726 milliseconds to insert 1000 rows
- 22 milliseconds to retrieve 1000 rows
- 12,645 milliseconds (12.645 seconds) to update 1000 rows

On the P166, the numbers are

- 761 milliseconds to insert 1000 rows
- 40 milliseconds to retrieve 1000 rows
- 12,448 milliseconds (12.448 seconds) to update 1000 rows

Database Tuning

If a system appears to be running slow, the performance of the database should be checked to ensure it is running at an optimal level for the machine it is executing on. In this section we discuss various server options for tuning the database, using RAID, adding indexes, and examining the options from the MySQL Query Optimizer.

Server Options

When installing MySQL for the first time, you can turn to several configuration file examples supplied in the base directory of the install on a Windows machine. One of these configurations is supposed to be copied to the root directory. Although the Unix version does not supply example configuration files, it's worth looking at some of the server parameters set up in these files to see how a small system is configured versus a large system. Table 14.1 shows the various parameters and their values based on intended server size.

Table 14.1 Server Configuration Options

SERVER SIZE	KEY_ BUFFER_ SIZE	MAX_ ALLOWED_ PACKET	THREAD_ STACK	TABLE_ CACHE	SORT_ BUFFER	NET_ BUFFER_ LENGTH	THREAD_ CACHE_ SIZE
Small	16K	1MB	64K	4	64K	2K	NA
Medium	16MB	1MB	NA	64	512K	8MB	
Large	256MB	1MB	256	NA	1MB	64MB	8
Huge	384MB	1MB	512	NA	2MB	128MB	8

As you can see, some of the server parameters change quite drastically. Here are the explanations for each of the parameters:

key_buffer_size—The total memory used for index blocks. This is a shared amount and should be roughly one-fourth of the total memory in the system.

max_allowed_packet—The total size of a message from a client. Packets bigger than this value throw an exception. The value should be as big as the largest amount of data to be passed to the server. This is important if you are using BLOBs since their data can be quite large.

thread_stack—The size of the stack associated with each server thread.

table_cache—The total number of opened tables allowed on the system.

sort_buffer—The size of the sort buffer opened by a thread when the user uses the ORDER BY or GROUP BY clause.

net_buffer_length—The initial length of the buffer where queries will be initially received. This value will grow to max_allowed_packet as needed.

thread_cache_size—The size of the thread cache when server threads are removed to handle a client's request.

Another server parameter that you might want to consider increasing is read_buffer_size. This parameter indicates the size of a buffer opened by a server thread when a query requires a table scan to be performed instead of using an index.

Using RAID

While the server needs memory to perform its various operations and you can configure the server parameters to balance the machine's memory against the needs of the application, the system disks play a vital role in performance.

At a minimum, the disk hardware used to store the database's data should be the fastest possible. This means a high RPM value and a low disk seek. The difference between an 8-millisecond seek and a 10-millisecond seek can be enormous when multiplied over thousands of queries. To further help with the seek issue, we can take advantage of disk stripping and gain some data redundancy at the same time.

Using RAID level 1, we can instruct the server machine's hardware to spread a disk volume across *N* number of drives. When we do this, seeks to the drive to obtain the data saved in MySQL's table files won't always have to be done against a single drive—which means waiting on the read head to seek to the proper disk location. Instead, data will be read from multiple drives, which results in a greater average seek time across all drives.

Optimizing Tables

When you delete rows from a database table, the database server doesn't actually remove the rows, but instead keeps a running list of rows that are currently marked as deleted. As new records are inserted into the table, the deleted rows are reused. If you delete rows that have BLOBs or variable-length data in them, it is a good idea to execute the OPTIMIZE TABLE <*table*> command occasionally to reclaim deleted space and defragment the table. You can use the command on both MyISAM and BDB tables. Note that the table being optimized is locked for the entire execution of the command.

If you need to execute the OPTIMIZE TABLE command from a batch or command line, use the myisamchk application and use the flags

```
myisamchk --quick --check-only-changed --sort-index --analyze
<table>
```

The MySQL Query Optimizer

When performing simple or complex queries with or without joins, the MySQL server invokes a process called the Query Optimizer. This process attempts to formulate the best possible internal query to use when retrieving your data. In most cases, this means that the optimizer will analyze the intended query and attempt to match appropriate indexes against the tables to be accessed. If there are joins in the SQL, the optimizer might change the order to achieve the best performance from the database.

To learn what the Query Optimizer suggests when executing a query, use the EXPLAIN <SQL> command. For example:

```
mysql> explain select * from acc_acc;
+---------+------+---------------+------+---------+------+------+-------+
| table   | type | possible_keys | key  | key_len | ref  | rows | Extra |
+---------+------+---------------+------+---------+------+------+-------+
| acc_acc | ALL  | NULL          | NULL |    NULL | NULL |   12 |       |
+---------+------+---------------+------+---------+------+------+-------+
```

In this example, we are attempting to determine how the server will handle a request to pull all of the rows from a table. In response to the EXPLAIN command, a result set is returned with a number of columns. The columns are

- **table**—The table being accessed.
- **type**—The join to be used for the query. The possible values are:
  - **ALL**—Indicates a table scan.
  - **Index**—Indicates a scan of an index.
  - **Range**—Specifies that a range of rows will be selected from an index.
  - **Ref**—Used in a join when the key isn't a primary key. The selected key is matched to all rows having the same value.
  - **Eq_ref**—Indicates that one row should be read based on multiple previous rows.

- **Const**—Indicates that one matching row will be examined.
- **System**—Indicates that only one matching row in a system table will be examined.

- **possible_keys**—Specifies the indexes MySQL may use to obtain the data. Some of the indexes might not be used due to the order in which multiple tables are accessed in a join situation.
- **key**—The key MySQL used for the query. If null, then no key was used.
- **key_len**—The length of the key chosen.
- **ref**—Specifies that additional columns were used with the key to select rows.
- **rows**—Specifies the total rows to be examined for the query.
- **Extra**—Contains additional information from the optimizer.

We can get a better idea of values placed in the columns with the following example:

```
mysql> explain select acc_id, username from acc_acc;

+---------+-------+----------+---------+---------+------+-----+-------+
| table   | type  | possible |         |         |      |     |       |
|         |       | keys     | key     | key_len | ref  | rows| Extra |
+---------+-------+----------+---------+---------+------+-----+-------+
| acc_acc | index | NULL     | PRIMARY |      72 | NULL |  12 | Using |
|         |       |          |         |         |      |     | index |
+---------+-------+----------+---------+---------+------+-----+-------+
```

In this example, we have asked for only the acc_id and username rows in the table. MySQL will use an index against the primary key to return the rows. Consider another example:

```
mysql> explain select password, username from acc_acc where username
like 'j%';

+---------+------+---------------+------+---------+------+------+-------+
| table   | type | possible_keys | key  | key_len | ref  | rows | Extra |
+---------+------+---------------+------+---------+------+------+-------+
| acc_acc | ALL  | NULL          | NULL |    NULL | NULL |   12 | where |
|         |      |               |      |         |      |      | used  |
+---------+------+---------------+------+---------+------+------+-------+
```

In this example, we added a WHERE clause. Note that the optimizer suggests that it will have to examine all 12 rows of the table primarily because of the like parameter. Now let's see what a join looks like:

```
mysql> explain
  select acc_acc.acc_id, password, username, state, zip
```

```
from acc_acc
left join acc_add on acc_acc.acc_id = acc_add.acc_id
where acc_acc.ts = 0;
```

```
+---------+------+---------------+------+---------+------+------+-------+
| table   | type | possible_keys | key  | key_len | ref  | rows | Extra |
+---------+------+---------------+------+---------+------+------+-------+
| acc_acc | ALL  | NULL          | NULL |    NULL | NULL |   12 | where |
|         |      |               |      |         |      |      |  used |
| acc_add | ALL  | NULL          | NULL |    NULL | NULL |    3 |       |
+---------+------+---------------+------+---------+------+------+-------+
```

Here we are asking for data from two different tables, so the EXPLAIN command displays how it expects to obtain data from each of them. Note that the optimizer expects to perform a table scan on both tables. Since our tables are small, this isn't too big a deal, but if the tables were larger, we might want to have additional indexes available. If we were to expand the previous query to place a condition on the acc_id of the acc_acc table, the system would be able to pull in the primary index and reduce the number of rows to be examined.

Table Indexes

If you have queries against a large table that aren't tied to the primary key of the table, you can improve system performance by using additional indexes. The index is just a data structure stored in the server alongside the database table to allow fast lookups using one or more columns of the table. To create an index, use the command

```
CREATE INDEX <name> on <table>(columns)
```

For example, we might create an index on our acc_add table based on the zipcode column:

```
mysql> CREATE INDEX zipcode ON acc_add(zip)
```

The database server will run through the current table specified and build an index on the current values. As additional rows are added or deleted, the index will adjust accordingly.

It is possible to create indexes based on multiple columns as well. For example:

```
mysql> CREATE INDEX acc_acc_index ON acc_acc(acc_id, ts);
```

The key to building an index is to determine how the data will be queried. Indexes aren't without a cost—they require CPU cycles for maintenance and disk space for storage.

JDBC Tuning

Without getting into the code used to write MySQL's Connector/J driver, we'd like to point out some simple techniques that you can use to obtain data from the database more efficiently. In this section, we describe techniques broken down into these sections:

- Minimizing data requests
- Keeping consistent connections
- Handling statements
- Batching
- Using transactions and locks
- Defining the architecture
- Getting data

Minimizing Data Requests

The use of a database in an application suggests that a relatively large amount of data is needed to provide a certain level of functionality. Just because a database is available doesn't mean the application should always be requesting a large percentage of it. Therefore, it's fair to say that 99 percent of all SQL SELECT statements should pull all of the fields of a table—in other words, there should be no SELECT * clauses.

Of equal importance is how the application uses the data obtained from the database. Let's look at two different situations. The first involves obtaining application configuration data from the database. This data is considered static in relation to other data. In many cases, the data is used to populate drop-down boxes on a GUI or placed in a combo box. The application should be written so that the data is pulled once and reused when the GUI control is needed a second time. If the data isn't available in the application, the application has to execute a query against the data to retrieve the information. This is costly and can be avoided by taking advantage of the memory available in the machine to cache data. In our second situation, the data obtained from the data is volatile, meaning it can be changed frequently in the database. When this is the case, the application cannot cache the data but can certainly limit the data pulled.

Take a moment and think about performing a search on Yahoo! for the text *car*. At the time of this writing, Yahoo! tells us that there are 49,000,000 matches, but more than likely there are even more matches and Yahoo! has just capped the results. Now when you go to Yahoo!, you will see the first 20 matches on the returned page with the option of moving to the next 20 matches. How do you think this application was pulling the matching information back from the database? Do you think all 49,000,000 rows were pulled at once? How about one million or even one thousand? More than likely, only a few hundred matches are pulled from the database. Obviously, the first 20 are pulled, but the system anticipates the user will click through a few pages of results. If the user wants to view matches 2020 through 2040, the application makes a call to the database. The moral here is the application should return only the rows needed by the application (and maybe a small cushion). A large amount of resources are needed to retrieve thousands and millions of rows, and more than likely the application doesn't need all of those rows at the same time.

Keeping Consistent Connections

In order to get data from a MySQL database, the application software must open a connection through Connector/J to the server. With the current 3.0 driver, it takes 280 milliseconds to open that connection. To see the effect that opening the connection has on the client application, consider this snippet of code:

```
startTime = new Date().getTime();
for (int i=0;i<500;i++) {
  connection = DriverManager.getConnection(
    "jdbc:mysql://localhost/products");
  Statement statement  = connection.createStatement();
  ResultSet rs = statement.executeQuery("SELECT * FROM product");

  rs.close();
  statement.close();
  connection.close();
}
System.out.println("SELECT = " + ((new Date().getTime()) -    start-
Time));


startTime = new Date().getTime();
connection = DriverManager.getConnection(
  "jdbc:mysql://localhost/products");
for (int i=0;i<500;i++) {
  Statement statement  = connection.createStatement();
  ResultSet rs = statement.executeQuery("SELECT * FROM product");

  rs.close();
  statement.close();
}
connection.close();
System.out.println("SELECT = " + ((new Date().getTime()) -
startTime));
```

This code attempts to select all of the rows in a test database 500 times. The first test loop opens a new connection for each attempt at the query. The second test loop opens a single connection and executes the 500 queries against the single connection. The results are

- 281 milliseconds to open a single connection
- 9092 milliseconds to open a single connection and execute 500 queries
- 14,028 milliseconds to open a connection with each individual query

The results are very clear. An application should open a single connection to the database server through which all queries can pass. There is one caveat here, though. If the application isn't active in its queries, the database server may close the connection itself. A prudent administrator won't allow applications to hang on to connections for an indefinite period of time. For this reason, our code might have to check for an open connection before executing a query against it.

Fortunately, there is a good solution to the whole connection problem—using a connection pool. With a connection pool, we can "open" a new connection for each query (if we know they won't be executed in fairly quick succession) without the penalty of actually opening the connection—the pool keeps the connections open and provides us with one when needed.

Handling Statements

In the previous section, we looked at the performance effect of repetitive opening and closing of the database connection. As you saw, the effect can be considerable. If your application still needs a boost, you should analyze all updates to the database to see if the Statement object is being used effectively.

Let's consider use of the Statement object versus the PreparedStatement object. As you'll recall, the PreparedStatement object is designed to be kept by the server and allows the client to substitute values in the statement instead of building a new Statement object each time an update to the database is needed. However, PreparedStatement gets its edge when multiple updates are needed using the same query statement. Consider the following code snippet:

```
ps = connection.prepareStatement(
  "UPDATE product SET value=10 WHERE value = ?");
startTime = new Date().getTime();
for (int i=0;i<1000;i++) {
  ps.setInt(1, i);
  ps.executeUpdate();
}
System.out.println("UPDATE = " + ((new Date().getTime())
  - startTime));
```

```
startTime = new Date().getTime();
for (int i=0;i<1000;i++) {
  Statement statement = connection.createStatement();
  statement.executeUpdate("UPDATE product SET value = " + i + "
    where value = " + i);
}
System.out.println("UPDATE = " + ((new Date().getTime())
  - startTime));
```

This code is designed to update 1000 rows in the database. Each code segment is executed independently to perform the appropriate updates. The first snippet of code creates a PreparedStatement object and uses the setInt() method to place an integer value into it before the server executes the query. The object is created only once, and the setInt() method executes 1000 times.

The second loop executes 1000 times, and it creates a new Statement object for each UPDATE of the database. After all of the code is executed and timed, using a PreparedStatement object in the manner shown here the application will see a performance gain of 2 or 3 percent.

Batching

Another insert performance increase can be gained by using the batch features provided in JDBC 3.0 and Connector/J 3.0. Batching eliminates a good deal of the overhead involved in going back and forth between the application, Connector/J, and the database. The batch updates are handled by the driver, and you can expect a performance gain of 3 or 4 percent on average.

Using Transactions and Locking

In the development of your SQL, there will be times when you need transactions to make sure that all of the data is updated in the database correctly. Associated with transactions is the transaction isolation level. Unfortunately, as more extensive isolation levels are used, the cost increases.

At the low end of the scale is the default setting for MySQL and Connector/J, which is TRANSACTION_NONE and autocommit equal to true. Next is TRANSACTION_READ_UNCOMMITTED, which gives a little more control to the application by allowing specific commit and rollback calls.

Next we have TRANSACTION_READ_COMMITTED. This isolation level begins to affect performance because a lock is placed on each row involved in the transaction. The locks remain on the changed rows until the transaction is either committed or rolled back.

Even more expensive is TRANSACTION_REPEATABLE_READ, in which a lock is placed on all rows being read until the transaction is either committed or rolled back.

Finally, the isolation level TRANSACTION_SERIALIZABLE places a lock on the tables being accessed in the transaction, which causes all other server threads that need to access the table to block. It is important to consider all of the isolation levels and what effect they will have on your application's performance.

Defining the Architecture

When an application is under development, it is acceptable and sometimes even desirable to allow each of the developers to have their own database server running on their local machine. As the application begins to be integrated and tested, it is best to move it to an application server and move the database to its own machine. As we discussed earlier, you should tune the MySQL database server to the environment on which it is executing. If additional applications are competing for memory and CPU cycles, the tuning can be difficult.

Getting Data

After a connection is made to a database and the results returned to the application, the values need to be pulled from the ResultSet object. Fortunately, the JDBC specification defined an extensive number of accessor methods of the get<type>() variety to pull values from the object.

The methods are all defined in pairs, like this:

```
getString(int)
getString(String)
```

The current Connector/J implementation of these and all other pairs is to implement the code to pull the column value in the getString(int) method and to force the getString(String) method to call the int parameter version. Unfortunately, it isn't that simple. Each call to the String parameter version makes an additional call to a method called findColumn(String). This method determines which column number the passed String represents. Thus, a single call to getString() could make an additional two calls. This is expensive, and you should use the getString(int) version as much as possible. Will you achieve a 20 percent performance increase? No, but 1 to 2 percent is always important.

Another performance increase can be realized when you use the proper get<type>() method to retrieve values from the ResultSet object. If you use a getString() to retrieve an integer values from an int column, Connector/J will need to do a cast from the Int to the String. The same is true for any of the columns and for using the "wrong" get method to pull the value. It is always better to retrieve the value from the object as its native value if possible.

Conclusion

In this chapter, we looked at different ways to achieve the best performance from MySQL, Connector/J, and your application.

APPENDIX A

MySQL Development and Test Environments

We developed and tested all of the code in this book on several different test architectures in order to provide some representative reference. This appendix briefly describes those environments and lists the installed software. In addition, we offer some notes for reproducing the configuration.

Test Architecture #1

For many of the examples in the book, we used a single test machine to handle both the database and applications. Figure A.1 shows an example of the architecture we used. This architecture is based on the following software:

- Windows XP Professional
- IIS Web Server
- MySQL 3.23.52-NT
- Java SDK 1.4.0
- Connector/J 3.0.1 beta
- Connector/J 2.1.4

No out-of-the-ordinary configuration was needed for any of the software. The MySQL database is executing a configuration file based on the my-large example from the installation.

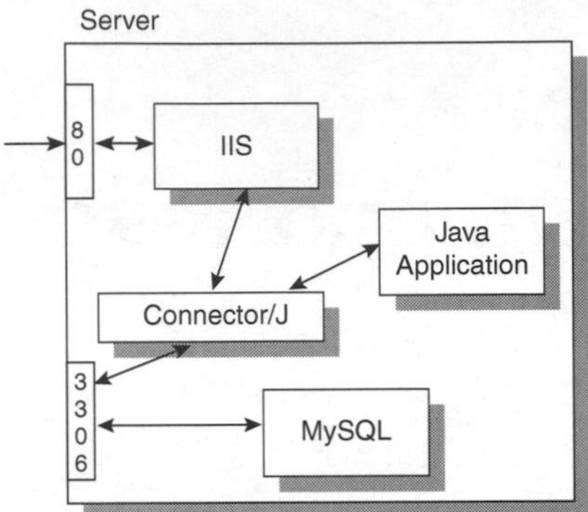

Figure A.1 A diagram of our test architecture #1.

Test Architecture #2

To show the cross-platform capabilities of the software and database, we created a two-tier architecture, as shown in Figure A.2. The application machine ran the following software:

- Windows 2000
- Java SDK 1.4.0
- Connector/J 3.0.1 beta
- Connector/J 2.1.4

The database machine ran the following software:

- Mandrake 8.2 Linux
- Java SDK 1.4.0 from Sun
- MySQL 4.0.4 beta

The machines were connected to each other over a 100MB LAN.

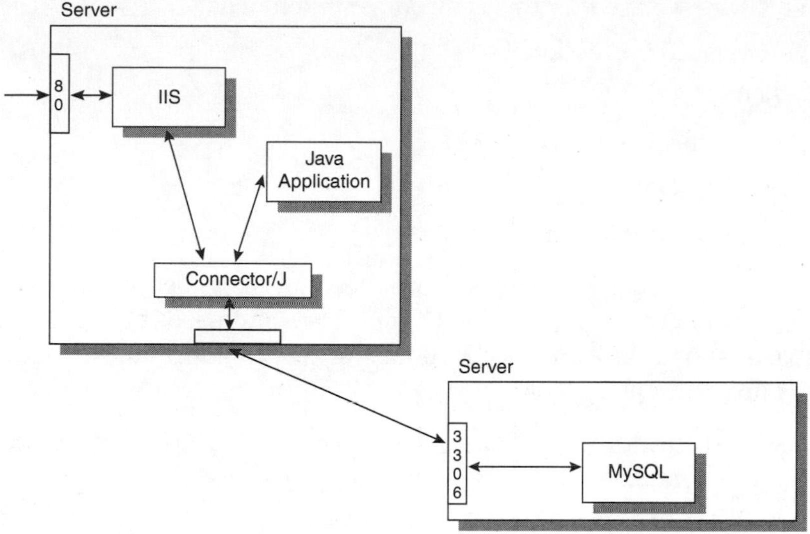

Figure A.2 A diagram of our test architecture #2.

Servlet Architecture

The environment we used to execute the servlet examples had a single machine that acted as both the application and database tier, as shown in Figure A.3.

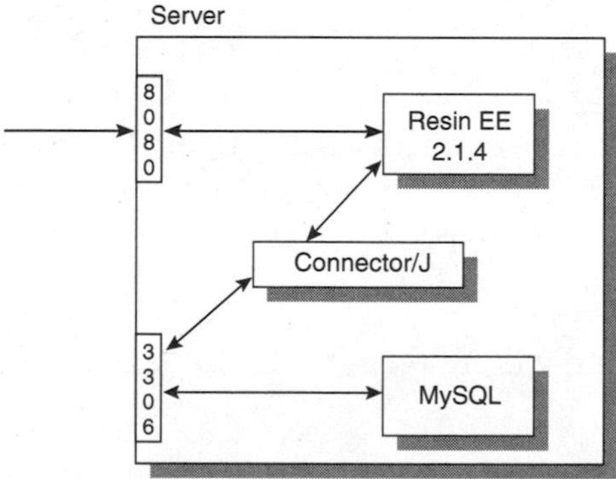

Figure A.3 Our servlet architecture.

The software we used for this environment included

- Windows XP Professional
- MySQL 3.23.52-NT
- Resin Enterprise Edition 2.1.4
- Java SDK 1.4.0
- Connector/J 3.0.1 beta

We installed MySQL (www.mysql.com) in c:\mysql, and copied the my-medium example configuration file to the C: root drive and used it as is. The accounts database, shown in Appendix B, holds all of the information needed by the servlet applications.

We installed Resin EE 2.1.4 (www.caucho.com) in a directory called servers. We made several configuration changes to execute servlets:

1. We downloaded Connector/J (www.mysql.com) and placed the JAR file from the zip file into the resin-ee-2.1.4/lib directory.
2. We added a <resource-ref> element to the resin.conf file located in the resin-ee-2.1.4/conf directory. The element we used is

```
<resource-ref>
  <res-ref-name>jdbc/ca</res-ref-name>
  <res-type>javax.sql.DataSource</res-type>
  <init-param driver-name="org.gjt.mm.mysql.Driver"/>
  <init-param url="jdbc:mysql://localhost:3306/accountsDB"/>
  <init-param user=""/>
  <init-param password=""/>
  <init-param max-connections="20"/>
  <init-param max-idle-time="30"/>
</resource-ref>
```

3. We added a <web-app> entry to the configuration file for Resin. The entry, which appears here, allows servlets to be executed from the accounts directory path:

```
<web-app id='/accounts'/>
```

4. We created a directory structure within /resin-ee-2.1.4/doc to handle requests:

```
/resin-ee-2.1.4/doc/accounts/WEB-INF
/resin-ee-2.1.4/doc/accounts/WEB-INF/classes
```

5. We added a web.xml file to the /resin-ee-2.1.4/doc/accounts/WEB-INF directory with the following entry:

```
<web-app>
  <servlet-mapping>
```

```
    <url-pattern id="/*"/>
    <servlet-name id="invoker"/>
  </servlet-mapping>
</web-app>
```

We placed the servlets described in this book in the WEB-INF/classes directory. We placed the HTML files that use the servlets in the /resin-ee-2.1.4/doc directory.

Since Resin uses port 8080 in a development setting and by default, we used the following URL to execute the HTML and servlets:

```
http://localhost:8080/accounts.html
```

The EJB Architecture

We based all of the code for handling Enterprise JavaBeans on the same architecture described for the servlets. We expanded the web.xml file to include the following declaration to relate the beans to the proper JNDI source:

```
<resource-ref>
    <res-ref-name>java:comp/env/cmp</res-ref-name>
    <class-name>com.caucho.ejb.EJBServer</class-name>
    <init-param data-source="java:comp/env/jdbc/ca"/>
 </resource-ref>
```

We placed all of the bean source files in the /doc/WEB-INF/classes directory.

Databases and Tables

This appendix provides a comprehensive listing of all databases and tables used in all of the examples throughout this book. You can find the SQL we used to create these databases and tables at the book's Web site: www.wiley.com/compbooks/matthews.

The accounts Database and Tables

The accounts database consists of the following tables:

- **acc_acc**—Holds primary accounts information and defines acc_id as the key to other tables.
- **acc_add**—Holds multiple addresses for accounts; acc_id is the foreign key.

The acc_acc table is described as

```
mysql> describe acc_acc;
+----------+---------------+------+-----+---------+-------+
| Field    | Type          | Null | Key | Default | Extra |
+----------+---------------+------+-----+---------+-------+
| acc_id   | int(11)       |      | PRI | 0       |       |
| username | varchar(64)   | YES  |     | NULL    |       |
| password | varchar(64)   | YES  |     | NULL    |       |
| ts       | timestamp(14) | YES  |     | NULL    |       |
| access   | varchar(15)   | YES  |     | NULL    |       |
+----------+---------------+------+-----+---------+-------+
```

The SQL to build the table is

```
create table acc_acc(
  acc_id int not null primary key,
  username varchar(64),
  password varchar(64),
  ts timestamp,
  access varchar(15));
```

The acc_add table is described as

```
mysql> describe acc_add;
+----------+--------------+------+-----+---------+-------+
| Field    | Type         | Null | Key | Default | Extra |
+----------+--------------+------+-----+---------+-------+
| add_id   | int(11)      |      | PRI | 0       |       |
| acc_id   | int(11)      |      | PRI | 0       |       |
| address1 | varchar(64)  | YES  |     | NULL    |       |
| address2 | varchar(64)  | YES  |     | NULL    |       |
| address3 | varchar(64)  | YES  |     | NULL    |       |
| address4 | varchar(64)  | YES  |     | NULL    |       |
| city     | varchar(32)  | YES  |     | NULL    |       |
| state    | char(2)      | YES  |     | NULL    |       |
| zip      | varchar(10)  | YES  |     | NULL    |       |
| ts       | timestamp(14)| YES  | PRI | NULL    |       |
| act_ts   | timestamp(14)| YES  |     | NULL    |       |
+----------+--------------+------+-----+---------+-------+
```

The identification Database and Tables

The identification database consists of a single table, named thumbnail, which holds fingerprint information for accounts. The table's foreign key is acc_acc.acc_id.

The SQL to build the identification table is

```
create table thumbnail(thumb_id int not null,
                       acc_id int not null,
                       pic blob,
                       ts timestamp,
                       act_ts timestamp,
                       primary key(thumb_id, acc_id, ts));
```

The thumbnail table is described as

```
mysql> describe thumbnail;
+----------+--------------+------+-----+---------+-------+
| Field    | Type         | Null | Key | Default | Extra |
+----------+--------------+------+-----+---------+-------+
| thumb_id | int(11)      |      | PRI | 0       |       |
| acc_id   | int(11)      |      | PRI | 0       |       |
| pic      | blob         | YES  |     | NULL    |       |
| ts       | timestamp(14)| YES  | PRI | NULL    |       |
| act_ts   | timestamp(14)| YES  |     | NULL    |       |
+----------+--------------+------+-----+---------+-------+
```

Test Databases

We used two database tables for testing purposes in this book.

Database Products

We executed the performance tests against a product table found in the products database.

The SQL used to create the table is

```
create table product(id int auto_increment primary key,
                     string varchar(32),
                     test double,
                     supplier varchar(128),
                     ts timestamp,
                     value int);
```

The product table is described as

```
mysql> describe product;
+----------+--------------+------+-----+---------+----------------+
| Field    | Type         | Null | Key | Default | Extra          |
+----------+--------------+------+-----+---------+----------------+
| id       | int(11)      |      | PRI | NULL    | auto_increment |
| string   | varchar(128) | YES  |     | NULL    |                |
| test     | decimal(6,2) | YES  |     | NULL    |                |
| supplier | varchar(128) | YES  |     | NULL    |                |
| ts       | timestamp    | YES  |     | NULL    |                |
| value    | int(11)      | YES  |     | NULL    |                |
+----------+--------------+------+-----+---------+----------------+
6 rows in set (0.00 sec)
```

The Database Test

In the code that demonstrates how ENUMs are used, we used a table called enumtest within a database test in Chapter 6.

The SQL to create the table is

```
Create table enumtest(
             ID int,
             Status enum('contact', 'contacted', 'finished');
```

The enumtest table is described as:

```
mysql> describe enumtest;
+--------+---------------------------+------+-----+---------+-------+
| Field  | Type                      | Null | Key | Default | Extra |
+--------+---------------------------+------+-----+---------+-------+
| ID     | int(11)                   | YES  |     | NULL    |       |
| status | enum('contact',           |      |     |         |       |
|        | 'contacted','finished')   | YES  |     | NULL    |       |
+--------+---------------------------+------+-----+---------+-------+
2 rows in set (0.00 sec)
```

APPENDIX C

The JDBC API and Connector/J

At the core of Java's support for data sources such as the MySQL relational database server is the JDBC API. This API provides a wide range of support for establishing database sessions, obtaining meta-information associated with a database, executing SQL statements, and processing data returned from a database. The API is split between two java packages, java.sql and javax.sql. The former provides the core JDBC API, while the latter adds a number of server-side extensions. As of version 1.4 of the Java 2 Platform, Standard Edition, both packages are included in the standard release and adhere to the JDBC 3.0 specification. It is version 3.0 of the specification that this appendix addresses.

While the JDBC API provides a number of predefined classes, the bulk of the API consists of interfaces that the JDBC driver is responsible for implementing. The official JDBC driver for MySQL is known as Connector/J. As of this writing, there are two versions of the driver available. The first is version 2.0.14, which is considered the stable release. The second is version 3.0.2 Beta, which is considered a development release. Since Connector/J 3 appears to be well on its way to becoming a stable release, that is the version this appendix focuses on. Tables C.2 and C.4 summarize the extent to which Connector/J 3 implements the JDBC interfaces. Where an interface is partially implemented, the section dedicated to that interface groups the method signatures according to whether or not they are implemented. Note that much of the currently unimplemented functionality is due to a lack of corresponding support from MySQL.

The java.sql Package

The java.sql package represents the core of the JDBC API. It provides 11 classes and 18 interfaces focused on connecting to and communicating with a data source. The classes, listed in Table C.1, are all implemented and delivered as part of the package. On the other hand, classes implementing the package interfaces are the responsibility of the JDBC driver developer. Implementation of all 18 interfaces is not a requirement for a useful driver. In fact, depending on the nature of the underlying data source, attempting to implement all of the interfaces may not even be practical. Table C.2 summarizes the java.sql package interfaces, including the level of implementation provided by the Connector/J driver.

Table C.1 java.sql Classes

NAME	DESCRIPTION
BatchUpdateException	Exception indicating a failed batch update
DataTruncation	Exception indicating unexpected data truncation
Date	Representation of a SQL DATE
DriverManager	Management service for JDBC drivers
DriverPropertyInfo	Representation of a JDBC driver connection property
SQLException	Base JDBC exception type
SQLPermission	Permission used by applet SecurityManager
SQLWarning	Representation of a database warning
Time	Representation of a SQL TIME
Timestamp	Representation of a SQL TIMESTAMP
Types	JDBC types

Table C.2 java.sql Interfaces (continues)

NAME	DESCRIPTION	IMPLEMENTED
Array	Representation of SQL ARRAY type	No
Blob	Representation of SQL BLOB type	Partially
CallableStatement	SQL stored procedure support	No
Clob	Representation of SQL CLOB type	Partially

Table C.2 java.sql Interfaces (continued)

NAME	DESCRIPTION	IMPLEMENTED
Connection	Representation of database session	Partially
DatabaseMetaData	Information about database and driver	Yes
Driver	Interface implemented by all JDBC drivers	Yes
ParameterMetaData	PreparedStatement parameter metadata accessor	No
PreparedStatement	Precompiled SQL statement	Partially
Ref	Representation of SQL REF type	No
ResultSet	Data table abstraction for query results	Partially
ResultSetMetaData	ResultSet metadata accessor	Yes
Savepoint	Transaction savepoint	No
SQLData	Mapping from SQL UDT to Java class	No
SQLInput	UDT input stream	No
SQLOutput	UDT output stream	No
Statement	Static SQL Statement	Yes
Struct	Representation of a SQL structured type	No

Array

The Array interface represents the Java language mapping of the SQL ARRAY type defined by the SQL99 standard. Classes implementing this interface provide methods for accessing values from the underlying SQL ARRAY in the form of either Java arrays or JDBC ResultSet objects. Methods are also provided for accessing type information associated with the SQL ARRAY elements. MySQL does not currently support the SQL ARRAY type, and as such, Connector/J does not implement this interface.

Methods

```
Object getArray()
Object getArray( long index, int count )
Object getArray( long index, int count, Map map )
Object getArray( Map map )
int getBaseType()
String getBaseTypeName()
ResultSet getResultSet()
```

```
ResultSet getResultSet( long index, int count )
ResultSet getResultSet( long index, int count, Map map )
ResultSet getResultSet( Map map )
```

BatchUpdateException

The BatchUpdateException class is a Java exception class derived from SQLException. Instances of BatchUpdateException are thrown by the executeBatch() method specified in the Statement interface when one or more commands in a batch update fail. Exceptions of this type provide update counts for each successful update command. If an update command fails, the driver is allowed to either throw an exception immediately or continue processing the remaining commands, setting the respective update count to Statement.EXECUTE_FAILED for each failed command. The Connector/J implementation, as of this writing, takes the latter approach.

Constructors

```
BatchUpdateException()
BatchUpdateException( int[] updateCounts )
BatchUpdateException( String reason, int[] updateCounts )
BatchUpdateException( String reason,
                      String SQLState, int[] updateCounts )
BatchUpdateException( String reason, String SQLState,
                      int vendorCode, int[] updateCounts )
```

Method

```
int[] getUpdateCounts()
```

Blob

The Blob interface represents the Java language mapping of the SQL BLOB (Binary Large Object) type. Classes implementing this interface provide methods for accessing and updating BLOB values. In the context of Connector/J, an object implementing the Blob interface is capable of holding any column type that maps to a Java byte array. The Blob interface is only partially implemented by Connector/J.

Methods (Implemented)

```
InputStream getBinaryStream()
byte[] getBytes( long pos, int length )
long length()
long position( Blob pattern, long start )
long position( byte[] pattern, long start )
```

Methods (Not Currently Implemented)

```
OutputStream setBinaryStream( long pos )
int setBytes( long pos, byte[] bytes )
int setBytes( long pos, byte[] bytes, int offset, int len )
void truncate( long len )
```

CallableStatement

The CallableStatement interface extends the PreparedStatement interface, adding support for execution of SQL stored procedures. Classes implementing this interface provide methods for preparing, executing, and processing the results of SQL stored procedures. As of this writing, MySQL does not support SQL stored procedures, and as such, Connector/J does not provide such support. Currently, Connector/J does provide a class that implements the CallableStatement interface; however, it is intended only as an UltraDev-related workaround and is in truth simply a PreparedStatement implementation masquerading as a CallableStatement.

Methods

```
Array getArray( int i )
Array getArray( String parameterName )
BigDecimal getBigDecimal( int parameterIndex )
BigDecimal getBigDecimal( String parameterName )
Blob getBlob( int i )
Blob getBlob( String parameterName )
boolean getBoolean( int parameterIndex )
boolean getBoolean( String parameterName )
byte getByte( int parameterIndex )
byte getByte( String parameterName )
byte[] getBytes( int parameterIndex )
byte[] getBytes( String parameterName )
Clob getClob( int i )
Clob getClob( String parameterName )
Date getDate( int parameterIndex )
Date getDate( int parameterIndex, Calendar cal )
Date getDate( String parameterName )
Date getDate( String parameterName, Calendar cal )
double getDouble( int parameterIndex )
double getDouble( String parameterName )
float getFloat( int parameterIndex )
float getFloat( String parameterName )
int getInt( int parameterIndex )
int getInt( String parameterName )
long getLong( int parameterIndex )
long getLong( String parameterName )
Object getObject( int parameterIndex )
```

```
Object getObject( int i, Map map )
Object getObject( String parameterName )
Object getObject( String parameterName, Map map )
Ref getRef( int i )
Ref getRef( String parameterName )
short getShort( int parameterIndex )
short getShort( String parameterName )
String getString( int parameterIndex )
String getString( String parameterName )
Time getTime( int parameterIndex )
Time getTime( int parameterIndex, Calendar cal )
Time getTime( String parameterName )
Time getTime( String parameterName, Calendar cal )
Timestamp getTimestamp( int parameterIndex )
Timestamp getTimestamp( int parameterIndex, Calendar cal )
Timestamp getTimestamp( String parameterName )
Timestamp getTimestamp( String parameterName, Calendar cal )
URL getURL( int parameterIndex )
URL getURL( String parameterName )
void registerOutParameter( int parameterIndex, int sqlType )
void registerOutParameter( int parameterIndex,
                           int sqlType, int scale )
void registerOutParameter( int paramIndex,
                           int sqlType, String typeName )
void registerOutParameter( String parameterName, int sqlType )
void registerOutParameter( String parameterName,
                           int sqlType, int scale )
void registerOutParameter( String parameterName,
                           int sqlType, String typeName )
void setAsciiStream( String parameterName,
                     InputStream x, int length )
void setBigDecimal( String parameterName, BigDecimal x )
void setBinaryStream( String parameterName,
                      InputStream x, int length )
void setBoolean( String parameterName, boolean x )
void setByte( String parameterName, byte x )
void setBytes( String parameterName, byte[] x )
void setCharacterStream( String parameterName,
                         Reader reader, int length )
void setDate( String parameterName, Date x )
void setDate( String parameterName, Date x, Calendar cal )
void setDouble( String parameterName, double x )
void setFloat( String parameterName, float x )
void setInt( String parameterName, int x )
void setLong( String parameterName, long x )
void setNull( String parameterName, int sqlType )
void setNull( String parameterName,
              int sqlType, String typeName )
void setObject( String parameterName, Object x )
void setObject( String parameterName,
                Object x, int targetSqlType )
```

```
void setObject( String parameterName,
                Object x, int targetSqlType, int scale )
void setShort( String parameterName, short x )
void setString( String parameterName, String x )
void setTime( String parameterName, Time x )
void setTime( String parameterName, Time x, Calendar cal )
void setTimestamp( String parameterName, Timestamp x )
void setTimestamp( String parameterName,
                   Timestamp x, Calendar cal )
void setURL( String parameterName, URL val )
boolean wasNull()
```

Clob

The Clob interface represents the Java language mapping of the SQL CLOB (Character Large Object) type. Classes implementing this interface provide methods for accessing and updating CLOB values. In the context of Connector/J, an object implementing the Clob interface is capable of holding any column type that maps to a Java String. The Clob interface is only partially implemented by Connector/J.

Methods (Implemented)

```
InputStream getAsciiStream()
Reader getCharacterStream()
String getSubString( long pos, int length )
long length()
long position( Clob searchstr, long start )
long position( String searchstr, long start )
```

Methods (Not Currently Implemented)

```
OutputStream setAsciiStream( long pos )
Writer setCharacterStream( long pos )
int setString( long pos, String str )
int setString( long pos, String str, int offset, int len )
void truncate( long len )
```

Connection

The Connection interface represents a session with a particular database. Classes implementing this interface provide a variety of methods for managing the session and interacting with the database. Common uses of this interface include management of transaction and commit properties, creation and preparation of statements, definition of type maps, and access to comprehensive database metadata. Connector/J currently implements most of the Connection interface; several methods involving savepoints, type maps, and stored procedures remain unimplemented due to a lack of corresponding support at the MySQL level.

Methods (Implemented)

```
void clearWarnings()
void close()
void commit()
Statement createStatement()
Statement createStatement( int resultSetType,
                           int resultSetConcurrency )
Statement createStatement( int resultSetType,
                           int resultSetConcurrency,
                           int resultSetHoldability )
boolean getAutoCommit()
String getCatalog()
int getHoldability()
DatabaseMetaData getMetaData()
int getTransactionIsolation()
SQLWarning getWarnings()
boolean isClosed()
boolean isReadOnly()
String nativeSQL( String sql )
PreparedStatement prepareStatement( String sql )
PreparedStatement prepareStatement( String sql,
                                    int autoGeneratedKeys )
PreparedStatement prepareStatement( String sql,
                                    int[] columnIndexes )
PreparedStatement prepareStatement( String sql,
                                    int resultSetType,
                                    int resultSetConcurrency )
PreparedStatement prepareStatement( String sql,
                                    int resultSetType,
                                    int resultSetConcurrency,
                                    int resultSetHoldability )
PreparedStatement prepareStatement( String sql,
                                    String[] columnNames )
void rollback()
void setAutoCommit( boolean autoCommit )
void setCatalog( String catalog )
void setHoldability( int holdability )
void setReadOnly( boolean readOnly )
void setTransactionIsolation( int level )
```

Methods (Not Currently Implemented)

```
Map getTypeMap()
CallableStatement prepareCall( String sql )
```

```
CallableStatement prepareCall( String sql, int resultSetType,
                               int resultSetConcurrency )
CallableStatement prepareCall( String sql, int resultSetType,
                               int resultSetConcurrency,
                               int resultSetHoldability )
void releaseSavepoint( Savepoint savepoint )
void rollback( Savepoint savepoint )
Savepoint setSavepoint()
Savepoint setSavepoint( String name )
void setTypeMap( Map map )
```

Fields

```
static int TRANSACTION_NONE
static int TRANSACTION_READ_COMMITTED
static int TRANSACTION_READ_UNCOMMITTED
static int TRANSACTION_REPEATABLE_READ
static int TRANSACTION_SERIALIZABLE
```

DataTruncation

The DataTruncation class is a Java exception class derived from SQLWarning. Instances of DataTruncation are thrown when a JDBC operation unexpectedly truncates data on a read or write. Methods of this class provide access to additional information regarding the nature of the data truncation.

Constructors

```
DataTruncation( int index, boolean parameter,
                boolean read, int dataSize, int transferSize )
```

Methods

```
int getDataSize()
int getIndex()
boolean getParameter()
boolean getRead()
int getTransferSize()
```

DatabaseMetaData

The DatabaseMetaData interface represents a collection of information that provides a comprehensive characterization of a particular database and associated JDBC driver implementation. The interface consists of over 200 methods and fields spanning the full range of useful database metadata. A number of methods defined by this interface include parameters that accept pattern strings. In such cases, a '_' matches any one character, and a '%' matches any substring of 0 or more characters. This interface is fully implemented by Connector/J, though not all of the methods necessarily make sense in the context of MySQL. Where a method requests information that is not applicable to MySQL, Connector/J tries to respond in a reasonable and nondisruptive manner (e.g., by returning an empty ResultSet).

Methods

```
boolean allProceduresAreCallable()
boolean allTablesAreSelectable()
boolean dataDefinitionCausesTransactionCommit()
boolean dataDefinitionIgnoredInTransactions()
boolean deletesAreDetected( int type )
boolean doesMaxRowSizeIncludeBlobs()
ResultSet getAttributes( String catalog, String schemaPattern,
                         String typeNamePattern,
                         String attributeNamePattern )
ResultSet getBestRowIdentifier( String catalog, String schema,
                                String table,
                                int scope, boolean nullable )
ResultSet getCatalogs()
String getCatalogSeparator()
String getCatalogTerm()
ResultSet getColumnPrivileges( String catalog, String schema,
                               String table,
                               String columnNamePattern )
ResultSet getColumns( String catalog, String schemaPattern,
                      String tableNamePattern,
                      String columnNamePattern )
Connection getConnection()
ResultSet getCrossReference( String primaryCatalog,
                             String primarySchema,
                             String primaryTable,
                             String foreignCatalog,
                             String foreignSchema,
                             String foreignTable )
int getDatabaseMajorVersion()
int getDatabaseMinorVersion()
String getDatabaseProductName()
String getDatabaseProductVersion()
int getDefaultTransactionIsolation()
int getDriverMajorVersion()
int getDriverMinorVersion()
String getDriverName()
String getDriverVersion()
ResultSet getExportedKeys( String catalog,
                           String schema, String table )
```

```
String getExtraNameCharacters()
String getIdentifierQuoteString()
ResultSet getImportedKeys( String catalog,
                           String schema, String table )
ResultSet getIndexInfo( String catalog, String schema,
                        String table, boolean unique,
                        boolean approximate )
int getJDBCMajorVersion()
int getJDBCMinorVersion()
int getMaxBinaryLiteralLength()
int getMaxCatalogNameLength()
int getMaxCharLiteralLength()
int getMaxColumnNameLength()
int getMaxColumnsInGroupBy()
int getMaxColumnsInIndex()
int getMaxColumnsInOrderBy()
int getMaxColumnsInSelect()
int getMaxColumnsInTable()
int getMaxConnections()
int getMaxCursorNameLength()
int getMaxIndexLength()
int getMaxProcedureNameLength()
int getMaxRowSize()
int getMaxSchemaNameLength()
int getMaxStatementLength()
int getMaxStatements()
int getMaxTableNameLength()
int getMaxTablesInSelect()
int getMaxUserNameLength()
String getNumericFunctions()
ResultSet getPrimaryKeys( String catalog,
                          String schema, String table )
ResultSet getProcedureColumns( String catalog,
                               String schemaPattern,
                               String procedureNamePattern,
                               String columnNamePattern )
ResultSet getProcedures( String catalog, String schemaPattern,
                         String procedureNamePattern )
String getProcedureTerm()
int getResultSetHoldability()
ResultSet getSchemas()
String getSchemaTerm()
String getSearchStringEscape()
String getSQLKeywords()
int getSQLStateType()
String getStringFunctions()
ResultSet getSuperTables( String catalog, String schemaPattern,
                          String tableNamePattern )
ResultSet getSuperTypes( String catalog, String schemaPattern,
                         String typeNamePattern )
```

```
String getSystemFunctions()
ResultSet getTablePrivileges( String catalog,
                              String schemaPattern,
                              String tableNamePattern )
ResultSet getTables( String catalog, String schemaPattern,
                     String tableNamePattern, String[] types )
ResultSet getTableTypes()
String getTimeDateFunctions()
ResultSet getTypeInfo()
ResultSet getUDTs( String catalog, String schemaPattern,
                   String typeNamePattern, int[] types )
String getURL()
String getUserName()
ResultSet getVersionColumns( String catalog, String schema,
                             String table )
boolean insertsAreDetected( int type )
boolean isCatalogAtStart()
boolean isReadOnly()
boolean locatorsUpdateCopy()
boolean nullPlusNonNullIsNull()
boolean nullsAreSortedAtEnd()
boolean nullsAreSortedAtStart()
boolean nullsAreSortedHigh()
boolean nullsAreSortedLow()
boolean othersDeletesAreVisible( int type )
boolean othersInsertsAreVisible( int type )
boolean othersUpdatesAreVisible( int type )
boolean ownDeletesAreVisible( int type )
boolean ownInsertsAreVisible( int type )
boolean ownUpdatesAreVisible( int type )
boolean storesLowerCaseIdentifiers()
boolean storesLowerCaseQuotedIdentifiers()
boolean storesMixedCaseIdentifiers()
boolean storesMixedCaseQuotedIdentifiers()
boolean storesUpperCaseIdentifiers()
boolean storesUpperCaseQuotedIdentifiers()
boolean supportsAlterTableWithAddColumn()
boolean supportsAlterTableWithDropColumn()
boolean supportsANSI92EntryLevelSQL()
boolean supportsANSI92FullSQL()
boolean supportsANSI92IntermediateSQL()
boolean supportsBatchUpdates()
boolean supportsCatalogsInDataManipulation()
boolean supportsCatalogsInIndexDefinitions()
boolean supportsCatalogsInPrivilegeDefinitions()
boolean supportsCatalogsInProcedureCalls()
boolean supportsCatalogsInTableDefinitions()
boolean supportsColumnAliasing()
boolean supportsConvert()
boolean supportsConvert( int fromType, int toType )
boolean supportsCoreSQLGrammar()
```

```
boolean supportsCorrelatedSubqueries()
boolean supportsDataDefinitionAndDataManipulationTransactions()
boolean supportsDataManipulationTransactionsOnly()
boolean supportsDifferentTableCorrelationNames()
boolean supportsExpressionsInOrderBy()
boolean supportsExtendedSQLGrammar()
boolean supportsFullOuterJoins()
boolean supportsGetGeneratedKeys()
boolean supportsGroupBy()
boolean supportsGroupByBeyondSelect()
boolean supportsGroupByUnrelated()
boolean supportsIntegrityEnhancementFacility()
boolean supportsLikeEscapeClause()
boolean supportsLimitedOuterJoins()
boolean supportsMinimumSQLGrammar()
boolean supportsMixedCaseIdentifiers()
boolean supportsMixedCaseQuotedIdentifiers()
boolean supportsMultipleOpenResults()
boolean supportsMultipleResultSets()
boolean supportsMultipleTransactions()
boolean supportsNamedParameters()
boolean supportsNonNullableColumns()
boolean supportsOpenCursorsAcrossCommit()
boolean supportsOpenCursorsAcrossRollback()
boolean supportsOpenStatementsAcrossCommit()
boolean supportsOpenStatementsAcrossRollback()
boolean supportsOrderByUnrelated()
boolean supportsOuterJoins()
boolean supportsPositionedDelete()
boolean supportsPositionedUpdate()
boolean supportsResultSetConcurrency( int type,
                                      int concurrency )
boolean supportsResultSetHoldability( int holdability )
boolean supportsResultSetType( int type )
boolean supportsSavepoints()
boolean supportsSchemasInDataManipulation()
boolean supportsSchemasInIndexDefinitions()
boolean supportsSchemasInPrivilegeDefinitions()
boolean supportsSchemasInProcedureCalls()
boolean supportsSchemasInTableDefinitions()
boolean supportsSelectForUpdate()
boolean supportsStatementPooling()
boolean supportsStoredProcedures()
boolean supportsSubqueriesInComparisons()
boolean supportsSubqueriesInExists()
boolean supportsSubqueriesInIns()
boolean supportsSubqueriesInQuantifieds()
boolean supportsTableCorrelationNames()
boolean supportsTransactionIsolationLevel( int level )
boolean supportsTransactions()
boolean supportsUnion()
```

```
boolean supportsUnionAll()
boolean updatesAreDetected( int type )
boolean usesLocalFilePerTable()
boolean usesLocalFiles()
```

Fields

```
static short attributeNoNulls
static short attributeNullable
static short attributeNullableUnknown
static int bestRowNotPseudo
static int bestRowPseudo
static int bestRowSession
static int bestRowTemporary
static int bestRowTransaction
static int bestRowUnknown
static int columnNoNulls
static int columnNullable
static int columnNullableUnknown
static int importedKeyCascade
static int importedKeyInitiallyDeferred
static int importedKeyInitiallyImmediate
static int importedKeyNoAction
static int importedKeyNotDeferrable
static int importedKeyRestrict
static int importedKeySetDefault
static int importedKeySetNull
static int procedureColumnIn
static int procedureColumnInOut
static int procedureColumnOut
static int procedureColumnResult
static int procedureColumnReturn
static int procedureColumnUnknown
static int procedureNoNulls
static int procedureNoResult
static int procedureNullable
static int procedureNullableUnknown
static int procedureResultUnknown
static int procedureReturnsResult
static int sqlStateSQL99
static int sqlStateXOpen
static short tableIndexClustered
static short tableIndexHashed
static short tableIndexOther
static short tableIndexStatistic
static int typeNoNulls
static int typeNullable
static int typeNullableUnknown
static int typePredBasic
static int typePredChar
```

```
static int typePredNone
static int typeSearchable
static int versionColumnNotPseudo
static int versionColumnPseudo
static int versionColumnUnknown
```

Date

The Date class extends the java.util.Date class in a manner providing a representation of the SQL DATE type. Essentially, Date serves as an adaptor that allows a java.util.Date object to be treated as only consisting of the date part (i.e., year, month, and day).

Constructor

```
Date( long date )
```

Methods

```
void setTime( long date )
String toString()
static Date valueOf( String s )
```

Driver

The Driver interface represents the interface to which all JDBC database drivers must adhere. Classes implementing this interface provide methods for accessing information about the driver and building session connections. This interface is fully implemented by Connector/J.

Methods

```
boolean acceptsURL( String url )
Connection connect( String url, Properties info )
int getMajorVersion()
int getMinorVersion()
DriverPropertyInfo[] getPropertyInfo( String url,
                                      Properties info )
boolean jdbcCompliant()
```

DriverManager

The DriverManager class provides a management service for JDBC drivers. In addition to loading and registering drivers specified by the jdbc.drivers system property, the class provides methods for manually registering and deregistering

JDBC drivers. When a connection is requested, the DriverManager assumes responsibility for locating the proper driver and using it to establish a new session. The class also provides methods for handling logging and timeouts associated with session setup.

Methods

```
static void deregisterDriver( Driver driver )
static Connection getConnection( String url )
static Connection getConnection( String url, Properties info )
static Connection getConnection( String url,
                                 String user, String password )
static Driver getDriver( String url )
static Enumeration getDrivers()
static int getLoginTimeout()
static PrintWriter getLogWriter()
static void println( String message )
static void registerDriver( Driver driver )
static void setLoginTimeout( int seconds )
static void setLogWriter( PrintWriter out )
```

DriverPropertyInfo

The DriverPropertyInfo class encapsulates a single driver-related property. Each property consists of a name-value pair, and optionally, supplemental information describing the name-value pair and providing associated constraints. Objects of this type are returned by the getPropertyInfo() method specified by the Driver interface. They are useful primarily for dynamic discovery of a particular JDBC driver's supported connection properties.

Constructor

```
DriverPropertyInfo( String name, String value )
```

Fields

```
String[] choices
String description
String name
boolean required
String value
```

ParameterMetaData

The ParameterMetaData interface represents a parameter metadata accessor. Classes implementing this interface provide methods for accessing the properties and type information associated with a parameter contained by a PreparedStatement object. Connector/J does not currently implement the ParameterMetaData interface.

Methods

```
String getParameterClassName( int param )
int getParameterCount()
int getParameterMode( int param )
int getParameterType( int param )
String getParameterTypeName( int param )
int getPrecision( int param )
int getScale( int param )
int isNullable( int param )
boolean isSigned( int param )
```

Fields

```
static int parameterModeIn
static int parameterModeInOut
static int parameterModeOut
static int parameterModeUnknown
static int parameterNoNulls
static int parameterNullable
static int parameterNullableUnknown
```

PreparedStatement

The PreparedStatement interface extends the Statement interface, adding support for precompiled SQL statements. Classes implementing this interface provide methods for setting parameters, executing statements, and accessing parameter and result set metadata. PreparedStatement objects are created by objects implementing the Connection interface. Connector/J currently implements most of the PreparedStatement interface; only the metadata accessors and setters for Array and Ref types remain unimplemented.

Methods (Implemented)

```
void addBatch()
void clearParameters()
boolean execute()
ResultSet executeQuery()
int executeUpdate()
void setAsciiStream( int parameterIndex,
                     InputStream x, int length )
void setBigDecimal( int parameterIndex, BigDecimal x )
void setBinaryStream( int parameterIndex,
```

```
                        InputStream x, int length )
void setBlob( int i, Blob x )
void setBoolean( int parameterIndex, boolean x )
void setByte( int parameterIndex, byte x )
void setBytes( int parameterIndex, byte[] x )
void setCharacterStream( int parameterIndex,
                         Reader reader, int length )
void setClob( int i, Clob x )
void setDate( int parameterIndex, Date x )
void setDate( int parameterIndex, Date x, Calendar cal )
void setDouble( int parameterIndex, double x )
void setFloat( int parameterIndex, float x )
void setInt( int parameterIndex, int x )
void setLong( int parameterIndex, long x )
void setNull( int parameterIndex, int sqlType )
void setNull( int paramIndex, int sqlType, String typeName )
void setObject( int parameterIndex, Object x )
void setObject( int parameterIndex, Object x, int targetSqlType
)
void setObject( int parameterIndex,
                Object x, int targetSqlType, int scale )
void setShort( int parameterIndex, short x )
void setString( int parameterIndex, String x )
void setTime( int parameterIndex, Time x )
void setTime( int parameterIndex, Time x, Calendar cal )
void setTimestamp( int parameterIndex, Timestamp x )
void setTimestamp( int parameterIndex,
                   Timestamp x, Calendar cal )
void setURL( int parameterIndex, URL x )
```

Methods (Not Currently Implemented)

```
ResultSetMetaData getMetaData()
ParameterMetaData getParameterMetaData()
void setArray( int i, Array x )
void setRef( int i, Ref x )
```

Ref

The Ref interface represents the Java language mapping of the SQL REF type defined by the SQL99 standard. Classes implementing this interface provide methods for setting and retrieving the instance objects referenced by the corresponding SQL REF. MySQL does not currently support the SQL REF type, and as such, Connector/J does not implement this interface.

Methods

```
String getBaseTypeName()
Object getObject()
```

```
Object getObject( Map map )
void setObject( Object value )
```

ResultSet

The ResultSet interface represents a query result that is best expressed as a table of data. Although intended primarily for capturing the results of SQL query execution, the ResultSet interface is used to good advantage throughout the JDBC API. Viewed as a table, a ResultSet consists of columns that may be referenced either by column name or column number; column numbering begins with 1 and increases left to right. Unlike columns, rows are referenced via a cursor that must be moved to the row of interest. Initially, a ResultSet cursor is placed immediately before the first row.

While the most common scenario probably involves using next() to step through the rows of a result set, it is also possible to move the cursor by a number of rows relative to the current position and jump to an absolute position, assuming the ResultSet is scrollable. For the purpose of specifying an absolute position, the first row is row number 1, the second row is row number 2, etc; row number 0 corresponds to the position immediately preceding the first row. For the most part, the methods provided by classes implementing this interface fall into four categories: result set metadata access, cursor manipulation, column value access, and column value update. Connector/J currently implements most of the ResultSet interface.

Methods (Implemented)

```
boolean absolute( int row )
void afterLast()
void beforeFirst()
void cancelRowUpdates()
void clearWarnings()
void close()
void deleteRow()
int findColumn( String columnName )
boolean first()
InputStream getAsciiStream( int columnIndex )
InputStream getAsciiStream( String columnName )
BigDecimal getBigDecimal( int columnIndex )
BigDecimal getBigDecimal( String columnName )
InputStream getBinaryStream( int columnIndex )
InputStream getBinaryStream( String columnName )
Blob getBlob( int i )
Blob getBlob( String colName )
boolean getBoolean( int columnIndex )
boolean getBoolean( String columnName )
byte getByte( int columnIndex )
```

```
byte getByte( String columnName )
byte[] getBytes( int columnIndex )
byte[] getBytes( String columnName )
Clob getClob( int i )
Clob getClob( String colName )
int getConcurrency()
String getCursorName()
Date getDate( int columnIndex )
Date getDate( int columnIndex, Calendar cal )
Date getDate( String columnName )
Date getDate( String columnName, Calendar cal )
double getDouble( int columnIndex )
double getDouble( String columnName )
int getFetchDirection()
int getFetchSize()
float getFloat( int columnIndex )
float getFloat( String columnName )
int getInt( int columnIndex )
int getInt( String columnName )
long getLong( int columnIndex )
long getLong( String columnName )
ResultSetMetaData getMetaData()
Object getObject( int columnIndex )
Object getObject( String columnName )
int getRow()
short getShort( int columnIndex )
short getShort( String columnName )
Statement getStatement()
String getString( int columnIndex )
String getString( String columnName )
Time getTime( int columnIndex )
Time getTime( int columnIndex, Calendar cal )
Time getTime( String columnName )
Time getTime( String columnName, Calendar cal )
Timestamp getTimestamp( int columnIndex )
Timestamp getTimestamp( int columnIndex, Calendar cal )
Timestamp getTimestamp( String columnName )
Timestamp getTimestamp( String columnName, Calendar cal )
int getType()
URL getURL( int columnIndex )
URL getURL( String columnName )
SQLWarning getWarnings()
void insertRow()
boolean isAfterLast()
boolean isBeforeFirst()
boolean isFirst()
boolean isLast()
boolean last()
void moveToCurrentRow()
void moveToInsertRow()
boolean next()
```

```
boolean previous()
void refreshRow()
boolean relative( int rows )
void setFetchDirection( int direction )
void setFetchSize( int rows )
void updateAsciiStream( int columnIndex,
                        InputStream x, int length )
void updateAsciiStream( String columnName,
                        InputStream x, int length )
void updateBigDecimal( int columnIndex, BigDecimal x )
void updateBigDecimal( String columnName, BigDecimal x )
void updateBinaryStream( int columnIndex,
                         InputStream x, int length )
void updateBinaryStream( String columnName,
                         InputStream x, int length )
void updateBoolean( int columnIndex, boolean x )
void updateBoolean( String columnName, boolean x )
void updateByte( int columnIndex, byte x )
void updateByte( String columnName, byte x )
void updateBytes( int columnIndex, byte[] x )
void updateBytes( String columnName, byte[] x )
void updateCharacterStream( int columnIndex,
                            Reader x, int length )
void updateCharacterStream( String columnName,
                            Reader reader, int length )
void updateDate( int columnIndex, Date x )
void updateDate( String columnName, Date x )
void updateDouble( int columnIndex, double x )
void updateDouble( String columnName, double x )
void updateFloat( int columnIndex, float x )
void updateFloat( String columnName, float x )
void updateInt( int columnIndex, int x )
void updateInt( String columnName, int x )
void updateLong( int columnIndex, long x )
void updateLong( String columnName, long x )
void updateNull( int columnIndex )
void updateNull( String columnName )
void updateObject( int columnIndex, Object x )
void updateObject( int columnIndex, Object x, int scale )
void updateObject( String columnName, Object x )
void updateObject( String columnName, Object x, int scale )
void updateRow()
void updateShort( int columnIndex, short x )
void updateShort( String columnName, short x )
void updateString( int columnIndex, String x )
void updateString( String columnName, String x )
void updateTime( int columnIndex, Time x )
void updateTime( String columnName, Time x )
void updateTimestamp( int columnIndex, Timestamp x )
void updateTimestamp( String columnName, Timestamp x )
boolean wasNull()
```

Methods (Not Currently Implemented)

```
Array getArray( int i )
Array getArray( String colName )
Reader getCharacterStream( int columnIndex )
Reader getCharacterStream( String columnName )
Object getObject( int i, Map map )
Object getObject( String colName, Map map )
Ref getRef( int i )
Ref getRef( String colName )
boolean rowDeleted()
boolean rowInserted()
boolean rowUpdated()
void updateArray( int columnIndex, Array x )
void updateArray( String columnName, Array x )
void updateBlob( int columnIndex, Blob x )
void updateBlob( String columnName, Blob x )
void updateClob( int columnIndex, Clob x )
void updateClob( String columnName, Clob x )
void updateRef( int columnIndex, Ref x )
void updateRef( String columnName, Ref x )
```

Fields

```
static int CLOSE_CURSORS_AT_COMMIT
static int CONCUR_READ_ONLY
static int CONCUR_UPDATABLE
static int FETCH_FORWARD
static int FETCH_REVERSE
static int FETCH_UNKNOWN
static int HOLD_CURSORS_OVER_COMMIT
static int TYPE_FORWARD_ONLY
static int TYPE_SCROLL_INSENSITIVE
static int TYPE_SCROLL_SENSITIVE
```

ResultSetMetaData

The ResultSetMetaData interface represents a result set metadata accessor. Classes implementing this interface provide methods for accessing the types and properties associated with a ResultSet object. This interface is fully implemented by Connector/J.

Methods

```
String getCatalogName( int column )
String getColumnClassName( int column )
int getColumnCount()
int getColumnDisplaySize( int column )
String getColumnLabel( int column )
String getColumnName( int column )
```

```
int getColumnType( int column )
String getColumnTypeName( int column )
int getPrecision( int column )
int getScale( int column )
String getSchemaName( int column )
String getTableName( int column )
boolean isAutoIncrement( int column )
boolean isCaseSensitive( int column )
boolean isCurrency( int column )
boolean isDefinitelyWritable( int column )
int isNullable( int column )
boolean isReadOnly( int column )
boolean isSearchable( int column )
boolean isSigned( int column )
boolean isWritable( int column )
```

Fields

```
static int columnNoNulls
static int columnNullable
static int columnNullableUnknown
```

Savepoint

The Savepoint interface represents a specific point in a transaction to which the overall transaction can be rolled back if necessary. Savepoints are established and used for rollback by objects implementing the Connection interface. Connector/J does not currently implement the Savepoint interface.

Methods

```
int getSavepointId()
String getSavepointName()
```

SQLData

The SQLData interface represents a custom mapping between a SQL user-defined type (UDT) and a Java language class. Instances of classes implementing this interface are placed in a Connection object's type map and used to read UDTs from and write UDTs to the database associated with the session. MySQL does not currently support UDTs, and as such, Connector/J does not implement this interface.

Methods

```
String getSQLTypeName()
void readSQL( SQLInput stream, String typeName )
void writeSQL( SQLOutput stream )
```

SQLException

The SQLException class extends java.lang.Exception and serves as the base JDBC exception type; all other JDBC exceptions are derived from SQLException. Information contained by objects of this type include a description of the exception, a SQL state that is to follow either X/Open or SQL99 conventions, a vendor-specific error code, and a hook from which additional SQLException objects can be chained.

Constructors

```
SQLException()
SQLException( String reason )
SQLException( String reason, String SQLState )
SQLException( String reason, String SQLState, int vendorCode )
```

Methods

```
int getErrorCode()
SQLException getNextException()
String getSQLState()
void setNextException( SQLException ex )
```

SQLInput

The SQLInput interface represents an input stream for reading SQL user-defined types (UDTs) from a database. Classes implementing this interface provide a variety of methods for extracting values from the underlying stream. MySQL does not currently support UDTs, and as such, Connector/J does not implement this interface.

Methods

```
Array readArray()
InputStream readAsciiStream()
BigDecimal readBigDecimal()
InputStream readBinaryStream()
Blob readBlob()
boolean readBoolean()
byte readByte()
byte[] readBytes()
Reader readCharacterStream()
Clob readClob()
Date readDate()
double readDouble()
float readFloat()
int readInt()
```

```
long readLong()
Object readObject()
Ref readRef()
short readShort()
String readString()
Time readTime()
Timestamp readTimestamp()
URL readURL()
boolean wasNull()
```

SQLOutput

The SQLOutput interface represents an output stream for writing SQL user-defined types (UDTs) to a database. Classes implementing this interface provide a variety of methods for inserting values into the underlying stream. MySQL does not currently support UDTs, and as such, Connector/J does not implement this interface.

Methods

```
void writeArray( Array x )
void writeAsciiStream( InputStream x )
void writeBigDecimal( BigDecimal x )
void writeBinaryStream( InputStream x )
void writeBlob( Blob x )
void writeBoolean( boolean x )
void writeByte( byte x )
void writeBytes( byte[] x )
void writeCharacterStream( Reader x )
void writeClob( Clob x )
void writeDate( Date x )
void writeDouble( double x )
void writeFloat( float x )
void writeInt( int x )
void writeLong( long x )
void writeObject( SQLData x )
void writeRef( Ref x )
void writeShort( short x )
void writeString( String x )
void writeStruct( Struct x )
void writeTime( Time x )
void writeTimestamp( Timestamp x )
void writeURL( URL x )
```

SQLPermission

The SQLPermission class is a Java permission class that extends java.security.BasicPermission. This permission is checked by the SecurityManager when an applet invokes DriverManager.setLogWriter(). Unless a permission value of setLog is defined, a SecurityException is thrown. At this time, setLog is the only permission supported by the SQLPermission class.

Constructors

```
SQLPermission( String name )
SQLPermission( String name, String actions )
```

SQLWarning

The SQLWarning class extends SQLException and provides for tracking database access warnings. As with SQLException, it is possible to chain multiple SQLWarning objects. Classes implementing the Connection, ResultSet, and Statement interfaces use such SQLWarning chains. Each database warning encountered is added to the chain, with the chain made accessible through the getWarnings() method. The SQLWarning class provides support for stepping through warning chains.

Constructors

```
SQLWarning()
SQLWarning( String reason )
SQLWarning( String reason, String SQLstate )
SQLWarning( String reason, String SQLstate, int vendorCode )
```

Methods

```
SQLWarning getNextWarning()
void setNextWarning( SQLWarning warning )
```

Statement

The Statement interface represents a static SQL statement. Classes implementing this interface provide methods for executing SQL statements, as well as managing properties associated with the results of execution. The statement execution methods automatically close any ResultSet object previously associated with the Statement object. Objects implementing the Connection interface are responsible for creating statements. The Statement interface is fully implemented by Connector/J.

Methods

```
void addBatch( String sql )
void cancel()
void clearBatch()
```

```
void clearWarnings()
void close()
boolean execute( String sql )
boolean execute( String sql, int autoGeneratedKeys )
boolean execute( String sql, int[] columnIndexes )
boolean execute( String sql, String[] columnNames )
int[] executeBatch()
ResultSet executeQuery( String sql )
int executeUpdate( String sql )
int executeUpdate( String sql, int autoGeneratedKeys )
int executeUpdate( String sql, int[] columnIndexes )
int executeUpdate( String sql, String[] columnNames )
Connection getConnection()
int getFetchDirection()
int getFetchSize()
ResultSet getGeneratedKeys()
int getMaxFieldSize()
int getMaxRows()
boolean getMoreResults()
boolean getMoreResults( int current )
int getQueryTimeout()
ResultSet getResultSet()
int getResultSetConcurrency()
int getResultSetHoldability()
int getResultSetType()
int getUpdateCount()
SQLWarning getWarnings()
void setCursorName( String name )
void setEscapeProcessing( boolean enable )
void setFetchDirection( int direction )
void setFetchSize( int rows )
void setMaxFieldSize( int max )
void setMaxRows( int max )
void setQueryTimeout( int seconds )
```

Fields

```
static int CLOSE_ALL_RESULTS
static int CLOSE_CURRENT_RESULT
static int EXECUTE_FAILED
static int KEEP_CURRENT_RESULT
static int NO_GENERATED_KEYS
static int RETURN_GENERATED_KEYS
static int SUCCESS_NO_INFO
```

Struct

The Struct interface represents the Java language mapping of a SQL structured type, which is a kind of user-defined type (UDT). Classes implementing this interface are responsible for storage of and access to attribute values associated with the represented SQL structured type. MySQL does not currently support UDTs, and as such, Connector/J does not implement this interface.

Methods

```
Object[] getAttributes()
Object[] getAttributes( Map map )
String getSQLTypeName()
```

Time

The Time class extends the java.util.Date class in a manner providing a representation of the SQL TIME type. Essentially, Time serves as an adaptor that allows a java.util.Date object to be treated as only consisting of the time part (i.e., hours, minutes, and seconds).

Constructor

```
Time( long time )
```

Methods

```
void setTime( long time )
String toString()
static Time valueOf( String s )
```

Timestamp

The Timestamp class extends the java.util.Date class in a manner providing a representation of the SQL TIMESTAMP type. In addition to extending Date, this class adds a nanosecond field. Given this addition and its effect on the behavior of the interface, it is recommended that Timestamp objects not be mixed with regular Date objects. The Timestamp class provides a number of methods specifically for accessing, setting, and comparing Timestamp values.

Constructor

```
Timestamp( long time )
```

Methods

```
boolean after( Timestamp ts )
boolean before( Timestamp ts )
int compareTo( Object o )
int compareTo( Timestamp ts )
```

```
boolean equals( Object ts )
boolean equals( Timestamp ts )
int getNanos()
long getTime()
void setNanos( int n )
void setTime( long time )
String toString()
static Timestamp valueOf( String s )
```

Types

The Types class defines a set of constants representing the SQL types. These constants are referred to as the JDBC types and are used throughout the API to assist with type mapping issues. The numeric values of the constants follow the X/Open conventions. This class has no methods, other than those inherited from java.lang.Object.

Fields

```
static int ARRAY
static int BIGINT
static int BINARY
static int BIT
static int BLOB
static int BOOLEAN
static int CHAR
static int CLOB
static int DATALINK
static int DATE
static int DECIMAL
static int DISTINCT
static int DOUBLE
static int FLOAT
static int INTEGER
static int JAVA_OBJECT
static int LONGVARBINARY
static int LONGVARCHAR
static int NULL
static int NUMERIC
static int OTHER
static int REAL
static int REF
static int SMALLINT
static int STRUCT
static int TIME
static int TIMESTAMP
static int TINYINT
static int VARBINARY
static int VARCHAR
```

The javax.sql Package

The javax.sql package extends the core JDBC API. It provides 2 classes and 12 interfaces focused primarily on providing database services. As with the core API, the classes, listed in Table C.3, are provided by the package, but responsibility for classes implementing the interfaces lies outside the package. Unlike the core API, delegation of interface responsibility is not so clear-cut. The interfaces include event listeners that might be implemented by any party interested in events of corresponding types. There are also interfaces for custom readers and writers that need be implemented only under special circumstances. Current Connector/J support is limited to implementation of the interfaces associated with basic and pooled data source connections. Table C.4 summarizes the interfaces and level of support.

Table C.3 javax.sql Classes

NAME	DESCRIPTION
ConnectionEvent	Connection pool event
RowSetEvent	RowSet change event

Table C.4 javax.sql Interfaces

NAME	DESCRIPTION	IMPLEMENTED
ConnectionEventListener	Connection pool event listener	No
ConnectionPoolDataSource	PooledConnection factory	Yes
DataSource	Basic connection factor	Yes
PooledConnection	Connection managed by a connection pool	Yes
RowSet	JavaBeans-compatible data source interface	No
RowSetInternal	Internal view of a RowSet object	No
RowSetListener	RowSet change event listener	No
RowSetMetaData	Column type metadata for a RowSet	No
RowSetReader	Custom reader used by a RowSet object	No
RowSetWriter	Custom writer used by a RowSet object	No
XAConnection	Connection for distributed transactions	No
XADataSource	XAConnection factory	No

ConnectionEvent

The ConnectionEvent class represents a Java event used for signaling events associated with connection pools. Instances of this class are generated both when an error occurs and when a connection is closed. The methods defined for this class provide access to the associated ConnectionPool object and, in the case of an error, the corresponding SQLException object.

Constructors

```
ConnectionEvent( PooledConnection con )
ConnectionEvent( PooledConnection con, SQLException ex )
```

Method

```
SQLException getSQLException()
```

ConnectionEventListener

The ConnectionEventListener interface represents a Java event listener that receives notification of connection pool events. Classes implementing this interface provide methods for responding to connection closures and connection pool errors. Parties interested in connection pool events are responsible for implementing this interface.

Methods

```
void connectionClosed( ConnectionEvent event )
void connectionErrorOccurred( ConnectionEvent event )
```

ConnectionPoolDataSource

The ConnectionPoolDataSource interface represents a ConnectionPool object factory. Classes implementing this interface provide methods for building and distributing connections associated with a particular data source; these connections are suitable for inclusion in a connection pool. Methods are also available for managing timeouts and logging. Connector/J fully implements this interface.

Methods

```
int getLoginTimeout()
PrintWriter getLogWriter()
PooledConnection getPooledConnection()
PooledConnection getPooledConnection( String user,
```

```
                                        String password )
    void setLoginTimeout( int seconds )
    void setLogWriter( PrintWriter out )
```

DataSource

The DataSource interface represents a Connection object factory. Classes implementing this interface provide methods for building and distributing connections associated with a particular data source. Methods are also available for managing timeouts and logging. The Connection objects provided by a DataSource are equivalent to those provided through the java.sql.DriverManager service. Connector/J fully implements this interface.

Methods

```
Connection getConnection()
Connection getConnection( String username, String password )
int getLoginTimeout()
PrintWriter getLogWriter()
void setLoginTimeout( int seconds )
void setLogWriter( PrintWriter out )
```

PooledConnection

The PooledConnection interface represents a data source connection associated with a connection pool. Classes implementing this interface provide methods for accessing and managing an associated pooled connection. Connector/J fully implements this interface.

Methods

```
void addConnectionEventListener(
                      ConnectionEventListener listener )
void close()
Connection getConnection()
void removeConnectionEventListener(
                      ConnectionEventListener listener )
```

RowSet

The RowSet interface extends the ResultSet interface, adding support for the JavaBeans component model. In addition to ResultSet handling, classes implementing this interface provide methods for session management, SQL statement execution, and event listener registration. In a sense, a RowSet class can be viewed as something that wraps the rest of the JDBC API, providing an alternative, but familiar, way to interact with a data source. Connector/J does not currently implement the RowSet interface.

Methods

```
void addRowSetListener( RowSetListener listener )
void clearParameters()
void execute()
String getCommand()
String getDataSourceName()
boolean getEscapeProcessing()
int getMaxFieldSize()
int getMaxRows()
String getPassword()
int getQueryTimeout()
int getTransactionIsolation()
Map getTypeMap()
String getUrl()
String getUsername()
boolean isReadOnly()
void removeRowSetListener( RowSetListener listener )
void setArray( int i, Array x )
void setAsciiStream( int parameterIndex,
                     InputStream x, int length )
void setBigDecimal( int parameterIndex, BigDecimal x )
void setBinaryStream( int parameterIndex,
                      InputStream x, int length )
void setBlob( int i, Blob x )
void setBoolean( int parameterIndex, boolean x )
void setByte( int parameterIndex, byte x )
void setBytes( int parameterIndex, byte[] x )
void setCharacterStream( int parameterIndex,
                         Reader reader, int length )
void setClob( int i, Clob x )
void setCommand( String cmd )
void setConcurrency( int concurrency )
void setDataSourceName( String name )
void setDate( int parameterIndex, Date x )
void setDate( int parameterIndex, Date x, Calendar cal )
void setDouble( int parameterIndex, double x )
void setEscapeProcessing( boolean enable )
void setFloat( int parameterIndex, float x )
void setInt( int parameterIndex, int x )
void setLong( int parameterIndex, long x )
void setMaxFieldSize( int max )
void setMaxRows( int max )
void setNull( int parameterIndex, int sqlType )
void setNull( int paramIndex, int sqlType, String typeName )
void setObject( int parameterIndex, Object x )
void setObject( int parameterIndex,
```

```
                Object x, int targetSqlType )
void setObject( int parameterIndex, Object x,
                int targetSqlType, int scale )
void setPassword( String password )
void setQueryTimeout( int seconds )
void setReadOnly( boolean value )
void setRef( int i, Ref x )
void setShort( int parameterIndex, short x )
void setString( int parameterIndex, String x )
void setTime( int parameterIndex, Time x )
void setTime( int parameterIndex, Time x, Calendar cal )
void setTimestamp( int parameterIndex, Timestamp x )
void setTimestamp( int parameterIndex,
                   Timestamp x, Calendar cal )
void setTransactionIsolation( int level )
void setType( int type )
void setTypeMap( Map map )
void setUrl( String url )
void setUsername( String name )
```

RowSetEvent

The RowSetEvent class represents a Java event used for signaling events associated with RowSet objects. Instances of this class are generated both by cursor movement and changes in the contents of a RowSet object. Instances of this class provide access to the associated RowSet object.

Constructor

```
RowSetEvent( RowSet source )
```

RowSetInternal

The RowSetInternal interface represents an internal view of a RowSet. Classes implementing the RowSetReader and RowSetWriter interfaces rely on this view for interaction with RowSetInternal objects. Connector/J does not currently implement the RowSetInternal interface.

Methods

```
Connection getConnection()
ResultSet getOriginal()
ResultSet getOriginalRow()
Object[] getParams()
void setMetaData( RowSetMetaData md )
```

RowSetListener

The RowSetListener interface represents a Java event listener that receives notification of RowSet change events. Classes implementing this interface provide methods for responding to cursor movement, row modifications, and complete RowSet modifications. Parties interested in RowSet change events are responsible for implementing this interface.

Methods

```
void cursorMoved( RowSetEvent event )
void rowChanged( RowSetEvent event )
void rowSetChanged( RowSetEvent event )
```

RowSetMetaData

The RowSetMetaData interface extends the ResultSetMetaData interface, adding methods for setting values associated with the RowSet column types. Classes implementing this interface are intended primarily for use with RowSetReader objects, which are responsible for reading data into RowSet objects. Connector/J does not currently implement the RowSetMetaData interface.

Methods

```
void setAutoIncrement( int columnIndex, boolean property )
void setCaseSensitive( int columnIndex, boolean property )
void setCatalogName( int columnIndex, String catalogName )
void setColumnCount( int columnCount )
void setColumnDisplaySize( int columnIndex, int size )
void setColumnLabel( int columnIndex, String label )
void setColumnName( int columnIndex, String columnName )
void setColumnType( int columnIndex, int SQLType )
void setColumnTypeName( int columnIndex, String typeName )
void setCurrency( int columnIndex, boolean property )
void setNullable( int columnIndex, int property )
void setPrecision( int columnIndex, int precision )
void setScale( int columnIndex, int scale )
void setSchemaName( int columnIndex, String schemaName )
void setSearchable( int columnIndex, boolean property )
void setSigned( int columnIndex, boolean property )
void setTableName( int columnIndex, String tableName )
```

RowSetReader

The RowSetReader interface represents a custom data source reader for RowSet objects that support the reader/writer paradigm and do not maintain a continuous data source connection. A RowSetReader object replies on the RowSetInternal interface for access to the RowSet object. Connector/J does not implement the RowSetReader interface; it is intended primarily for application programmers who must customize the behavior of a RowSet implementation.

Method

```
void readData( RowSetInternal caller )
```

RowSetWriter

The RowSetWriter interface represents a custom data source writer for RowSet objects that support the reader/writer paradigm and do not maintain a continuous data source connection. A RowSetWriter object relies on the RowSetInternal interface for access to the RowSet object. Connector/J does not implement the RowSetWriter interface; it is intended primarily for application programmers who must customize the behavior of a RowSet implementation.

Method

```
boolean writeData( RowSetInternal caller )
```

XAConnection

The XAConnection interface extends the PooledConnection interface, providing a data source connection interface suitable for working with distributed transactions. Classes implementing this interface are capable of providing an appropriate javax.transaction.xa.XAResource object to the transaction manager. Connector/J does not currently implement the XAConnection interface.

Method

```
XAResource getXAResource()
```

XADataSource

The XADataSource interface represents an XAConnection object factory. Classes implementing this interface provide methods for building and distributing connections associated with a particular data source; these connections are suitable for distributed transactions. Methods are also available for managing timeouts and logging. Connector/J does not currently implement this interface.

Methods

```
int getLoginTimeout()
PrintWriter getLogWriter()
XAConnection getXAConnection()
XAConnection getXAConnection( String user, String password )
void setLoginTimeout( int seconds )
void setLogWriter( PrintWriter out )
```

APPENDIX D

MySQL Functions and Operators

One of your responsibilities as a developer is to determine when the database should handle computations versus the application. To aid in this analysis, this appendix provides all of the functions and operators defined within MySQL. Each of them has been described with a short query to show their operation. Before you perform an operation in Java with the data, check to see if the operation could be handled at the database server.

Following is a list of all the functions and operators discussed in this appendix:

+, -, *, /, unary

ABS

CEILING

DEGREES

EXP

FLOOR

GREATEST

LEAST

LOG

MOD

PI

POW, POWER

RADIANS

RAND

ROUND

SIGN

SQRT

Trig functions

COS, SIN, TAN, ACOS, ASIN, ATAN, ATAN2, COT

TRUNCATE

=

!=, <>

<, <=, >, >=

<=>

BETWEEN x AND Y

COALESCE

IN, NOT IN

INTERVAL

IS NULL

IS NOT NULL

ISNULL

!, NOT

||, OR

&&, AND

CASE f WHEN c1 THEN t1 WHEN c2... ELSE f1 END

IF(x1,x2,x3)

IFNULL(x1,x2)

NULLIF(x1,x2)

ASCII

BIN

CHAR

CONCAT, CONCAT_WS

CONV

ELT

FIELD

FIND_IN_SET

HEX

INSERT

LCASE, LOWER

LEFT

LENGTH, OCT_LENGTH, CHAR_LENGTH, CHARACTER_LENGTH

LIKE pattern [ESCAPE 'char'], NOT LIKE pattern [ESCAPE 'char']

LOCATE, POSITION, INSTR

LOCATE

LPAD

LTRIM

MATCH (c1, c2) AGAINST

MID

OCT

ORD

REGEXP pattern, RLIKE pattern, NOT REGEXP pattern, NOT RLIKE pattern

REPLACE

REPEAT

REVERSE

RIGHT

RTRIM

STRCMP

SUBSTRING

SOUNDEX

TRIM([both | leading | trailing] remove FROM string)

UCASE, UPPER

AVG

COUNT

MIN

MAX

SUM

STD

STDDEV

CURDATE, CURRENT_DATE

CURTIME, CURRENT_TIME

DATE_FORMAT, TIME_FORMAT

DAYNAME

DAYOFMONTH

DAYOFWEEK

DAYOFYEAR

FROM_DAYS

FROM_UNIXTIME

HOUR

MINUTE

MONTH

MONTHNAME

NOW, SYSDATE, CURRENT_TIMESTAMP

PERIOD_DIFF

QUARTER

SECOND

SEC_TO_TIME

TIME_TO_SEC

TO_DAYS

UNIX_TIMESTAMP

WEEK

WEEKDAY

YEAR

YEARWEEK

BINARY

CONNECTION_ID

DATABASE

DECODE

ENCRYPT

ENCODE

FORMAT

LAST_INSERT_ID

MD5

PASSWORD

USER, SYSTEM_USER, SESSION_USER

VERSION

Arithmetic Functions/Operators

MySQL offers a wide variety of operations/functions to handle both comparisons and limit the results of an expression. Most of the operators are self-explanatory, so no examples are provided.

+

Performs mathematical addition.

-

Performs mathematical subtraction.

*****

Performs mathematical multiplication.

/

Performs mathematical division.

unary –

Returns complement of argument.

ABS(number)

Returns the absolute value of the provided number parameter.

CEILING(*number*)

CEILING returns an integer value representing the integer round-up of *number*. Defined as min(z: z integer, z >= *number*).

DEGREES(*number*)

DEGREES() returns a float value representing degrees after converting from *number* in radians.

EXP(*number*)

EXP will return a float value based on the equation e^{number}.

FLOOR(*number*)

FLOOR returns an integer value representing the integer round-down of *number*. Defined as max(z: z integer, z <= *number*).

GREATEST(*x, y, ...*)

The GREATEST() function offers the same functionality as LEAST(), but returns the greatest value.

LEAST(*x, y, ...*)

The LEAST() function can be used to return all values or a value that is the least of the set. For example, LEAST(1, 5, 6) will return 1. Can be used in a query with column field names. When used in a query, all values over *y* will be displayed as *y*. Example:

```
mysql> SELECT login, LEAST(salary, 100000)
FROM login;
+---------+-----------------------+
| login   | LEAST(salary, 100000) |
+---------+-----------------------+
| johnd   |                100000 |
| janed   |                 91000 |
| timd    |                100000 |
| jamesr  |                100000 |
| jaysong |                 42000 |
| Mattm   |                 46000 |
| bobs    |                 24000 |
+---------+-----------------------+
7 rows in set (0.06 sec)
```

LOG(*number*)

LOG returns a float value based on the natural log of *number*.

LOG10(*number*)

LOG10 returns a float value based on the equation $\log_{10}$(*number*). If the result cannot be calculated, NULL is returned.

MOD(*n*,*m*)

The MOD function returns an integer representing the remainder for the equation *n* / *m*.

PI()

The function PI returns a value of 3.141593.

POW(*x*,*y*),POWER(*x*,*y*)

Both the POW and POWER functions return a float value based on the equation x^y.

RADIANS(*number*)

RADIANS() returns a float value representing radians after converting from *number* in degrees.

RAND(),RAND(*seed*)

The RAND function returns a float value between the range of 0 to 1. If the RAND(*seed*) function is used, the *seed* will be used as a seed value.

ROUND(*number*)

The ROUND function returns an integer rounded up the next larger whole number.

ROUND(*number*,*d*)

The 2 parameter ROUND function returns a float value where *number* is rounded to *d* decimal places. A whole number will be returned.

SIGN(*number*)

Returns:

-1 if *number* < 0

0 if *number* = 0

1 if *number* > 0

SQRT(*number*)

The SQRT function returns a float value based on the square root of *number*. If the value cannot be calculated, a NULL is returned.

Trigonometric Functions

COS(*number*),

SIN(*number*),

TAN(*number*),

ACOS(*number*),

ASIN(*number*),

ATAN(*nubmer*),

ATAN2(*x*,*y*),

COT(*number*)

The trigonometric functions return a float value.

TRUNCATE(*number, d*)

The TRUNCATE function returns a float value representing *number* truncated to the *d*th decimal place.

Comparison Functions/Operators

When SELECT queries are created, comparison functions and operators are used to limit or narrow the results as needed by the application. In this section, we examine all of the comparison functions and operators available in MySQL. For those that are obvious, examples won't be given. It should be noted that comparison functions and operators work left to right and ignore case. However, if a binary column type is used in the definition of the database table or the BINARY operator is used, the comparison will consider case.

=

The equality operator is used to compare two values and return true or false based on the result. The operator does not work on NULL values, and <=> should be used.

<>, !=

MySQL allows the use of either syntax for testing inequality. A value of true is returned if the operands are not equal.

<=, <, >=, >

The less than and greater than operators work on both numeric and alphanumeric operands; they return true or false based on their obvious function.

<=>

When using the equality operator on column fields, a NULL value will play havoc with queries. If column values might be NULL, use this operator. For example:

```
mysql> select login from login where closedate = null;
Empty set (0.00 sec)

mysql> SELECT login
FROM login
WHERE closedate <=> null;
+-------+
| login |
+-------+
| johnd |
| bobs  |
+-------+
2 rows in set (0.00 sec)
```

BETWEEN *min* AND *max*

Many queries will require an expression to bring back results in a range of values. For example, WHERE salary > 10000 and salary < 100000. The operator BETWEEN *min* AND *max* is a convenience operator for this range type query.

Example:

```
mysql> SELECT login, salary
FROM login
WHERE salary BETWEEN 10000 AND 100000;
+---------+--------+
| login   | salary |
+---------+--------+
| janed   |  91000 |
| jaysong |  42000 |
| Mattm   |  46000 |
| bobs    |  24000 |
+---------+--------+
4 rows in set (0.00 sec)
```

COALESCE(*list, text*)

If you want to retrieve a list of the row in a database where a NULL exists in a column, but you would like to have a more pleasing message appear than the string *null*, then COALESCE can be used. The string *text* will be displayed for all NULL values in *list*; otherwise, the current column value is displayed.

The COALESCE function returns either NULL or *<value>* when a NULL is found in list. Example:

```
mysql> SELECT login, opendate, COALESCE(closedate, 'Closedate
is NULL') as 'WARNING'
FROM login;
+---------+---------------------+---------------------+
| login   | opendate            | WARNING             |
+---------+---------------------+---------------------+
| johnd   | 2002-10-10 00:00:00 | Closedate is NULL   |
| janed   | 0000-00-00 00:00:00 | 0000-00-00 00:00:00 |
| timd    | 0000-00-00 00:00:00 | 0000-00-00 00:00:00 |
| jamesr  | 0000-00-00 00:00:00 | 0000-00-00 00:00:00 |
| jaysong | 0000-00-00 00:00:00 | 0000-00-00 00:00:00 |
| Mattm   | 0000-00-00 00:00:00 | 0000-00-00 00:00:00 |
| bobs    | 2003-01-10 09:51:27 | Closedate is NULL   |
+---------+---------------------+---------------------+
7 rows in set (0.00 sec)
```

Expr IN (*value*, ...)
Expr NOT IN (*value*, ...)

In the previous BETWEEN operator, a range of values will be selected. If the expression needs only to match a set of values, the IN operator can be used. If the expression needs to not match a set of values, the NOT IN expression can be used. Example:

```
mysql> SELECT login, opendate
FROM login
WHERE role IN ('SE', 'CS');
+---------+---------------------+
| login   | opendate            |
+---------+---------------------+
| jaysong | 0000-00-00 00:00:00 |
| Mattm   | 0000-00-00 00:00:00 |
| bobs    | 2003-01-10 09:51:27 |
+---------+---------------------+
3 rows in set (0.00 sec)
```

INTERVAL(*n*, *n1*, *n2*, *n3*)

If the values supplied to the INTERVAL function can pass the test defined as n $< n1 < n2 < n3$.

IS NULL

The IS NULL operator is functionality equivalent to <=>.

IS NOT NULL

The IS NOT NULL allows a column value to be tested against NULL and return true if the value is not equal to NULL.

ISNULL(*expression*)

MySQL includes the ISNULL() function for limiting rows based on the value of an expression begin NULL.

Example:

```
mysql> SELECT login, opendate
FROM login
WHERE ISNULL(closedate);
+-------+---------------------+
| login | opendate            |
+-------+---------------------+
| johnd | 2002-10-10 00:00:00 |
| bobs  | 2003-01-10 09:51:27 |
+-------+---------------------+
2 rows in set (0.02 sec)
```

Logical Operators

In many of the comparison and other functions defined in this appendix, using the logical operators provides the ability to further limit and narrow results returned from the database. Again, many of these are self-explanatory and thus do not contain examples.

NOT, !

The NOT and ! operators are used to invoke logical negation.

OR, ||

The OR and || operators handle logical OR. One or more operands are required to be TRUE for a TRUE result.

In the following examples, we see two separate queries, and then one with them combined, to illustrate how the correct result is returned.

```
mysql> SELECT login, role
FROM login
WHERE salary < 100000;
```

```
+---------+------+
| login   | role |
+---------+------+
| janed   | CFO  |
| jaysong | SE   |
| Mattm   | SE   |
| bobs    | CS   |
+---------+------+
4 rows in set (0.00 sec)

mysql> SELECT login, role
FROM login
WHERE ISNULL(closedate);
+-------+-------+
| login | role  |
+-------+-------+
| johnd | owner |
| bobs  | CS    |
+-------+-------+
2 rows in set (0.00 sec)

mysql> SELECT login, role
FROM login
WHERE salary < 100000 OR ISNULL(closedate);
+---------+-------+
| login   | role  |
+---------+-------+
| johnd   | owner |
| janed   | CFO   |
| jaysong | SE    |
| Mattm   | SE    |
| bobs    | CS    |
+---------+-------+
5 rows in set (0.00 sec)
```

AND
&&

For the AND and && operators, both of the operands must be TRUE to return a true result. Building off the previous, we can return the rows where both criteria are satisfied.

```
mysql> SELECT login, role
FROM login
WHERE salary < 100000 AND ISNULL(closedate);
+-------+------+
| login | role |
+-------+------+
| bobs  | CS   |
+-------+------+
1 row in set (0.00 sec)
```

Control Functions

The output from a query can be displayed based on a condition supplied in the query.

CASE *f*
WHEN *c1* THEN *t1*
WHEN *c2*...
ELSE *f1*
END

Convenience syntax for using multiple conditions. Commonly used to return values from the database yet hiding the true values. Example:

```
mysql>
SELECT login,
CASE
  WHEN salary > 249000 THEN 'No Bonus'
  WHEN salary < 95000 THEN 'Full Bonus'
  ELSE '1/2 Bonus'
END AS 'Bonus'
FROM login;
+---------+------------+
| login   | Bonus      |
+---------+------------+
| johnd   | No Bonus   |
| janed   | Full Bonus |
| timd    | 1/2 Bonus  |
| jamesr  | No Bonus   |
| jaysong | Full Bonus |
| Mattm   | Full Bonus |
+---------+------------+
6 rows in set (0.00 sec)
```

IF(*x1*,*x2*,*x3*)

The IF expression works like the statement IF THEN ELSE. If $x1$ is true, then return the value of $x2$; otherwise $x3$. Example:

```
mysql>
SELECT login, opendate,
IF (description like "Chief%", "Executive Team",
"Development Staff") AS "Group"
FROM login;
+---------+---------------------+-------------------+
| login   | opendate            | Group             |
+---------+---------------------+-------------------+
```

```
| johnd   | 2002-10-10 00:00:00 | Development Staff |
| janed   | 0000-00-00 00:00:00 | Executive Team    |
| timd    | 0000-00-00 00:00:00 | Executive Team    |
| jamesr  | 0000-00-00 00:00:00 | Executive Team    |
| jaysong | 0000-00-00 00:00:00 | Development Staff |
| Mattm   | 0000-00-00 00:00:00 | Development Staff |
+---------+---------------------+-------------------+
6 rows in set (0.00 sec)
```

IFNULL(*x1,x2*)

If you are performing database cleanup or maintenance, you can have the database inform you of row fields that are currently NULL and need a value. IFNULL, will display the value in the column if it is not NULL; if it is NULL, the value in *x2* will be displayed. Example:

```
mysql> SELECT login, IFNULL(role, 'Must Have Role')
FROM login;
+---------+--------------------------------+
| login   | IFNULL(role, 'Must Have Role') |
+---------+--------------------------------+
| johnd   | owner                          |
| janed   | CFO                            |
| timd    | CTO                            |
| jamesr  | CEO                            |
| jaysong | SE                             |
| Mattm   | SE                             |
| bobs    | Must Have Role                 |
+---------+--------------------------------+
7 rows in set (0.03 sec)
```

NULLIF(*x1,x2*)

NULLIF is another function to handle NULL values in the database. If *x1* is equal to *x2*, a NULL is returned in the result. Example:

```
mysql> SELECT login, NULLIF(role,"CEO") as "Role" FROM login;
+---------+-------+
| login   | Role  |
+---------+-------+
| johnd   | owner |
| janed   | CFO   |
| timd    | CTO   |
| jamesr  | NULL  |
| jaysong | SE    |
| Mattm   | SE    |
| bobs    | CS    |
+---------+-------+
7 rows in set (0.01 sec)
```

String Functions/Operators

The MySQL database includes a large number of functions and operators for dealing with text strings found in the column data.

ASCII(*string*)

The ASCII function returns the ASCII value of the first character in *string*.

BIN(*number*)

The BIN function converts *number* to its binary equivalent.

CHAR(*N, N1, N2, ...*)

The CHAR function converts all numbers provided as parameters to ASCII characters, concatenate them, and return as a string.

CONCAT(*s1, s2, ...*)

The CONCAT function appends all string parameters and returns the resulting string. Example:

```
mysql> SELECT CONCAT("current login = ", login) AS 'login'
FROM login;
+------------------------+
| login                  |
+------------------------+
| current login = bobs   |
| current login = jamesr |
| current login = janed  |
| current login = jaysong |
| current login = johnd  |
| current login = Mattm  |
| current login = timd   |
+------------------------+
7 rows in set (0.00 sec)
```

CONCAT_WS(*delimiter, s1, s2, ...*)

The CONCAT_WS function concatenates all supplied string parameters separating all of the string by the *delimiter* character.

CONV(*number, frombase, tobase*)

The CONV() converts *number* from base *frombase* to base *tobase*. The acceptable values range from 2 to 36 for the *frombase* and *tobase* parameters.

ELT(*number, s1, s2, ...*)

The ELT function returns string *S1* if number = 1, string *s2* if number = 2, and so on.

FIELD(*string, s1, s2, ...*)

The FIELD function returns a value starting at 1 if *string* equals *s1*, 2 if *string* equals *s2*, and so on.

FIND_IN_SET(*string, strlist*)

The FIND_IN_SET function attempts to find *string* within the set *strlist* where *strlist* is a comma-delimited list of values. The function returns 1 if *string* is the first element in *strlist* set.

HEX(*number*)

The HEX function converts *number* to its hexadecimal equivalent.

INSERT(*string, position, length, newstring*)

The INSERT function inserts *newstring* into *string* starting at *position* and returns the result.

LCASE(*string*)
LOWER(*string*)

These functions return *string* after converting to lowercase.

LEFT(*string, length*)

The LEFT function returns *length* characters from the left part of *string*.

LENGTH(*string*)
OCT_LENGTH(*string*)
CHAR_LENGTH(*string*)
CHARACTER_LENGTH(*string*)

All of these functions return the length of the supplied *string* parameter.

LIKE pattern [ESCAPE '*char*']
NOT LIKE pattern [ESCAPE '*char*']

When attempting to match against columns containing character strings, missing a single character will kept the row from being matched. The LIKE operator can be used to search through character string columns to find a match. The LIKE operator uses two wildcards: _ character matches a single characters, and % matches any number of characters. Example:

```
mysql> SELECT login, description
FROM login
WHERE description LIKE "CHIEF%";
+--------+-------------------------+
| login  | description             |
+--------+-------------------------+
| janed  | Chief Financial Officer |
| timd   | Chief Technical Officer |
| jamesr | Chief Executive Officer |
+--------+-------------------------+
3 rows in set (0.00 sec)
```

LOCATE(*substring, string*)
POSITION(*substring* IN *string*)
INSTR(*s, sub*)

If you need to find the location of a string with another string, the LOCATE and POSITION functions can be used. Both functions will return the numerical position of *substring* within *string*. If the substring is not found, a value of 0 is returned.

LOCATE(*substring, string, position*)

Additional substrings can be found by supplying a position value in this LOCATE method. The database will start looking for the match at the specified *position*.

LPAD(*string, len, pads*)

The LPAD and RPAD methods will return *string* with *len* number of *pads* characters to the left (LPAD) or right (RPAD) of the *string*.

LTRIM(*string*)

The LTRIM function removes all spaces from the front of *string* and returns the result.

MATCH (*c1*, c2) AGAINST (*expression*)

If you've defined a table column type using MySQL's full text-searching capabilities, the MATCH function can be used to locate appropriate text. Example:

```
mysql> SELECT *
FROM documents
MATCH(bibliography) AGAINST ('distributed');
```

MID(*string, position, length*)

Specific parts of a string can be returned using these functions. The functions will return a string *length* characters in size from *string* starting at character *position*.

OCT(*number*)

The OCT function converts *number* to its octal equivalent.

ORD(*string*)

The ORD function will return the ASCII value of the first character in *string* using Unicode.

REGEXP *pattern*
RLIKE *pattern*
NOT REGEXP *pattern*
NOT RLIKE *pattern*

If you are familiar with regular expressions, you will like to use the RLIKE or REGEXP operators. These operators will allow you to search in character columns for patterns. Example:

```
mysql> SELECT login, description
FROM login
WHERE login RLIKE "^ja[a-z]*";
+---------+------------------------+
| login   | description            |
+---------+------------------------+
| janed   | Chief Financial Officer |
| jamesr  | Chief Executive Officer |
| jaysong | Software Engineer      |
+---------+------------------------+
3 rows in set (0.02 sec)
```

REPLACE(string, *from*, *to*)

The characters in a string can be converted before being returned to the application with the REPLACE function. The function will return a string where all *from* occurrences are converted to *to* characters before being returned. Example:

```
mysql> SELECT login, REPLACE(description, 'Engineer', 'Coder')
AS description
FROM login;
+---------+------------------------+
| login   | description            |
+---------+------------------------+
| johnd   | owner john doe         |
| janed   | Chief Financial Officer |
| timd    | Chief Technical Officer |
| jamesr  | Chief Executive Officer |
| jaysong | Software Coder         |
| Mattm   | Software Coder         |
| bobs    | Client Services        |
+---------+------------------------+
7 rows in set (0.00 sec)
```

REPEAT(*string, count*)

The REPEAT function returns a string where *string* is repeated *count* times.

REVERSE(*string*)

The REVERSE function returns *string* with all characters presented in reverse order.

RIGHT(*string, length*)

The RIGHT function returns *length* characters from the right part of *string*.

RTRIM(*string*)

The RTRIM function removes all spaces from the end of *string* and returns the results.

STRCMP(*e1, e2*)

The STRCMP function is designed to match string *e1* to string *e2*. The results of the match are

0 if identical

-1 is *e1* < *e2*

1 if *e1* > *e2*

The function does not consider case.

SUBSTRING(*string, position, length*)
SUBSTRING(*string* FROM *position* FOR *length*)
SUBSTRING(*string, position*)
SUBSTRING(*string* FROM *position*)

The SUBSTRING function will return a part of *string* starting at character *position* until the end of *string* is found.

SUBSTRING_INDEX(*string, delimiter, count*)

The SUBSTRING_INDEX function is designed to read *count*-1 delimiter characters from *string* and return all characters left until the end of the string.

SOUNDEX(*string*)

If you are interested in using the SoundEx encoding in your application, the MySQL data can create the value for you using the SOUNDEX function.

TRIM([both | leading | trailing] remove FROM *string*)

The TRIM method can be used to remove characters *remove* from *string* in a variety of situations including both the front and back, front, or back of *string*, and return the results.

UCASE(*string*)
UPPER(*string*)

These functions return *string* after converting to uppercase.

Grouping Functions

In addition to the GROUP BY clause found in the SELECT command, MySQL provides several other functions defined to help pull together the right rows.

AVG(*expression*)

The AVG function is used to provide an average based on the expression and the rows pulled using the query. The query must have a GROUP BY clause. Example:

```
mysql> SELECT login, AVG(salary) as 'Average Salary'
FROM login
GROUP BY current group;
+-------+----------------+
| login | Average Salary |
+-------+----------------+
| johnd |         137000 |
| janed |         182400 |
+-------+----------------+
2 rows in set (0.01 sec)
```

COUNT(*expression*)

The COUNT function will return the total number of rows based on the current query of the database. Example:

```
mysql> SELECT COUNT(*)
FROM login;
+----------+
| COUNT(*) |
+----------+
|        7 |
+----------+
1 row in set (0.05 sec)
```

COUNT(DISTINCT *expression, ...*)

This version of the COUNT function will count only distinct rows based on one or more expressions. Example:

```
mysql> SELECT COUNT(DISTINCT role)
FROM login;
+----------------------+
| COUNT(DISTINCT role) |
+----------------------+
```

```
|                    6 |
+----------------------+
1 row in set (0.02 sec)
```

MAX(*expression*)

The MAX function returns the maximum value for the supplied *expression*. The GROUP BY clause must be in the query.

MIN(*expression*)

The MIN function returns the minimum value for the supplied *expression*. The GROUP BY clause must be in the query. Example:

```
mysql> SELECT login, MIN(salary) as 'Minimum Salary'
FROM login
GROUP BY currentgroup;
+-------+----------------+
| login | Minimum Salary |
+-------+----------------+
| johnd |          24000 |
| janed |          42000 |
+-------+----------------+
2 rows in set (0.00 sec)
```

STD(*expression*)
STDDEV(*expression*)

The STD and STDEV functions return the standard deviation for the supplied *expression*. The GROUP BY clause must be part of the query.

SUM(*expression*)

The SUM function will calculate the sum of all selected rows. The GROUP BY clause must be part of the query. Example:

```
mysql> SELECT login, SUM(salary) as 'Sum of Salaries'
FROM login
GROUP BY currentgroup;
+-------+-----------------+
| login | Sum of Salaries |
+-------+-----------------+
| johnd |          274000 |
| janed |          912000 |
+-------+-----------------+
2 rows in set (0.01 sec)
```

Date and Time Functions

MySQL allows for extensive date and time manipulation.

CURDATE()
CURRENT_DATE

These functions will return the current date in YYYY-MM-DD format. Example:

```
mysql> SELECT CURDATE(), CURRENT_DATE;
+------------+--------------+
| CURDATE()  | CURRENT_DATE |
+------------+--------------+
| 2003-01-10 | 2003-01-10   |
+------------+--------------+
1 row in set (0.00 sec)
```

CURTIME()
CURRENT_TIME

These functions return the current time. Example:

```
mysql> SELECT CURTIME(), CURRENT_TIME;
+-----------+--------------+
| CURTIME() | CURRENT_TIME |
+-----------+--------------+
| 15:55:08  | 15:55:08     |
+-----------+--------------+
1 row in set (0.00 sec)
```

DATE_FORMAT(*date, format*)
TIME_FORMAT(*time, format*)

The DATE_FORMAT function is a very powerful formatter of a *date* parameter. The *format* parameter can be built to display a specific date/time string using the following placeholders:

TAG	DESCRIPTION
%M	Month name (*January*)
%W	Weekday name (*Sunday*)
%D	Day with English suffix (*1st*, *2nd*,)
%Y	4-digit year
%y	2-digit year

TAG	DESCRIPTION
%X	4-digit year for the week, where Sunday is the first day of the week combined with '%V'
%x	4-digit year for the week, where Monday is the first day of the week combined with '%v'
%a	Abbreviated weekday name (*Sun*)
%d	Day of the month
%e	Day of the month
%m	Month (*01*)
%c	Month (*1*)
%b	Abbreviated month name (*Jan*)
%j	Day of the year (*001*)
%H	Hour (*00..23*)
%k	Hour (*0..23*)
%h	Hour (*01..12*)
%I	Hour (*01..12*)
%l	Hour (*1..12*)
%i	Minutes, numeric (*00..59*)
%r	Time, 12-hour (*hh:mm:ss [AP]M*)
%T	Time, 24-hour (*hh:mm:ss*)
%S	Seconds (*00..59*)
%s	Seconds (*00..59*)
%p	*AM* or *PM*
%w	Day of the week (0=*Sunday*)
%U	Week (*0..53*), where Sunday is the first day of the week
%u	Week (*0..53*), where Monday is the first day of the week
%V	Week (*1..53*), where Sunday is the first day of the week combined with '%X'
%v	Week (*1..53*), where Monday is the first day of the week combined with '%x'

Example:

```
mysql>
SELECT login, opendate, DATE_FORMAT(opendate, "%W %M %D")
FROM login
WHERE opendate <> 0;
+-------+---------------------+-----------------------------------+
| login | opendate            | DATE_FORMAT(opendate, "%W %M %D") |
+-------+---------------------+-----------------------------------+
| johnd | 2002-10-10 00:00:00 | Thursday October 10th             |
| bobs  | 2003-01-10 09:51:27 | Friday January 10th               |
+-------+---------------------+-----------------------------------+
2 rows in set (0.00 sec)
```

DAYNAME(*date*)

The DAYNAME function returns the name of the day on which the supplied *date* occurred. Example:

```
mysql> SELECT login, opendate, DAYNAME(opendate)
FROM login
WHERE opendate <> 0;
+-------+---------------------+-------------------+
| login | opendate            | DAYNAME(opendate) |
+-------+---------------------+-------------------+
| johnd | 2002-10-10 00:00:00 | Thursday          |
| bobs  | 2003-01-10 09:51:27 | Friday            |
+-------+---------------------+-------------------+
2 rows in set (0.00 sec)
```

DAYOFMONTH(*date*)

The DAYOFMONTH function returns the day of the month the supplied *date* occurred. Example:

```
mysql> SELECT login, opendate, DAYOFMONTH(opendate)
FROM login
WHERE opendate <> 0;
+-------+---------------------+----------------------+
| login | opendate            | DAYOFMONTH(opendate) |
+-------+---------------------+----------------------+
| johnd | 2002-10-10 00:00:00 |                   10 |
| bobs  | 2003-01-10 09:51:27 |                   10 |
+-------+---------------------+----------------------+
2 rows in set (0.00 sec)
```

DAYOFWEEK(*date*)

The DAYOFWEEK function will return an integer based on a value of 1 for Sunday for *date*. Example:

```
mysql> SELECT login, opendate, DAYOFWEEK(opendate) AS 'Day of week'
FROM login
WHERE opendate <> 0;
+-------+---------------------+-------------+
| login | opendate            | Day of week |
+-------+---------------------+-------------+
| johnd | 2002-10-10 00:00:00 |           5 |
| bobs  | 2003-01-10 09:51:27 |           6 |
+-------+---------------------+-------------+
2 rows in set (0.00 sec)
```

DAYOFYEAR(*date*)

The DAYOFYEAR function returns the day of the year the supplied *date* occurred. Example:

```
mysql> SELECT login, opendate, DAYOFYEAR(opendate)
FROM login WHERE opendate <> 0;
+-------+---------------------+---------------------+
| login | opendate            | DAYOFYEAR(opendate) |
+-------+---------------------+---------------------+
| johnd | 2002-10-10 00:00:00 |                 283 |
| bobs  | 2003-01-10 09:51:27 |                  10 |
+-------+---------------------+---------------------+
2 rows in set (0.00 sec)
```

FROM_DAYS(*days*)

The FROM_DAYS function calculates the date represented by *days*.

FROM_UNIXTIME(unix_timestamp)
FROM_UNIXTIME(unix_timestamp, format)

These functions take a Unix timestamp and return a date/time value.

HOUR(*time*)

The HOUR function returns the hour the supplied time occurred. Example:

```
mysql> SELECT login, opendate, HOUR(opendate)
FROM login
WHERE opendate <> 0;
+-------+---------------------+----------------+
| login | opendate            | HOUR(opendate) |
+-------+---------------------+----------------+
| johnd | 2002-10-10 00:00:00 |              0 |
| bobs  | 2003-01-10 09:51:27 |              9 |
+-------+---------------------+----------------+
2 rows in set (0.00 sec)
```

MINUTE(*time*)

The MINUTE function returns the minute the supplied time occurred. Example:

```
mysql> SELECT login, opendate, MINUTE(opendate)
FROM login
WHERE opendate <> 0;
+-------+---------------------+------------------+
| login | opendate            | MINUTE(opendate) |
+-------+---------------------+------------------+
| johnd | 2002-10-10 00:00:00 |                0 |
| bobs  | 2003-01-10 09:51:27 |               51 |
+-------+---------------------+------------------+
2 rows in set (0.00 sec)
```

MONTH(*date*)

The MONTH function returns the month the supplied date occurred. Example:

```
mysql> SELECT login, opendate, MONTH(opendate)
FROM login
WHERE opendate <> 0;
+-------+---------------------+-----------------+
| login | opendate            | MONTH(opendate) |
+-------+---------------------+-----------------+
| johnd | 2002-10-10 00:00:00 |              10 |
| bobs  | 2003-01-10 09:51:27 |               1 |
+-------+---------------------+-----------------+
2 rows in set (0.00 sec)
```

MONTHNAME(*date*)

The MONTHNAME function returns the name of the month the supplied date occurred. Example:

```
mysql> SELECT login, opendate, MONTHNAME(opendate)
FROM login
WHERE opendate <> 0;
+-------+---------------------+---------------------+
| login | opendate            | MONTHNAME(opendate) |
+-------+---------------------+---------------------+
| johnd | 2002-10-10 00:00:00 | October             |
| bobs  | 2003-01-10 09:51:27 | January             |
+-------+---------------------+---------------------+
2 rows in set (0.00 sec)
```

NOW()
SYSDATE()
CURRENT_TIMESTAMP

These functions will return the current date and time in the format YYYY-MM-DD HH:MM:SS. Example:

```
mysql> SELECT NOW(), SYSDATE(), CURRENT_TIMESTAMP;
+---------------------+---------------------+---------------------+
| NOW()               | SYSDATE()           | CURRENT_TIMESTAMP   |
+---------------------+---------------------+---------------------+
| 2003-01-10 15:56:18 | 2003-01-10 15:56:18 | 2003-01-10 15:56:18 |
+---------------------+---------------------+---------------------+
1 row in set (0.00 sec)
```

PERIOD_DIFF(*date1, date2*)

The PERIOD_DIFF function returns the difference in number of months between date1 and date2. Example:

```
mysql> SELECT login, opendate, PERIOD_DIFF(ts, opendate)
FROM login
WHERE opendate <> 0;
+-------+---------------------+---------------------------+
| login | opendate            | PERIOD_DIFF(ts, opendate) |
+-------+---------------------+---------------------------+
| bobs  | 2003-01-10 09:51:27 |                        67 |
+-------+---------------------+---------------------------+
1 rows in set (0.00 sec)
```

QUARTER(*date*)

The QUARTER function returns an integer representing the quarter the supplied date occurred. The values will be in the range 1 to 4. Example:

```
mysql> SELECT login, opendate, QUARTER(opendate)
FROM login
WHERE opendate <> 0;
+-------+---------------------+-------------------+
| login | opendate            | QUARTER(opendate) |
+-------+---------------------+-------------------+
| johnd | 2002-10-10 00:00:00 |                 4 |
| bobs  | 2003-01-10 09:51:27 |                 1 |
+-------+---------------------+-------------------+
2 rows in set (0.02 sec)
```

SECOND(*time*)

The SECOND function returns the second the supplied time occurred. Example:

```
mysql> SELECT login, opendate, SECOND(opendate)
FROM login
WHERE opendate <> 0;
+-------+---------------------+------------------+
| login | opendate            | SECOND(opendate) |
+-------+---------------------+------------------+
| johnd | 2002-10-10 00:00:00 |                0 |
| bobs  | 2003-01-10 09:51:27 |               27 |
+-------+---------------------+------------------+
2 rows in set (0.00 sec)
```

SEC_TO_TIME(*seconds*)

The SEC_TO_TIME function converts *seconds* into a time value with the format HH:MM:SS.

TIME_TO_SEC(*time*)

The TIME_TO_SEC function converts the supplied *time* to its equivalent in seconds.

TO_DAYS(*date*)

The TO_DAYS function returns the total days starting at 0 to *date*.

UNIX_TIMESTAMP()
UNIX_TIMESTAMP(*date*)

These functions return a Unix timestamp based on the total number of seconds since 1970-01-01 00:00:00 GMT. The optionally supplied *date* parameter will cause the total number of seconds from *1970* to *date* instead of the current time.

Example:

```
mysql> SELECT UNIX_TIMESTAMP();
+------------------+
| UNIX_TIMESTAMP() |
+------------------+
|       1042239404 |
+------------------+
1 row in set (0.00 sec)

mysql> SELECT UNIX_TIMESTAMP('2001-12-10');
+------------------------------+
| UNIX_TIMESTAMP('2001-12-10') |
+------------------------------+
|                   1007967600 |
+------------------------------+
1 row in set (0.00 sec)
```

WEEK(*date*)

The WEEK function returns an integer representing the week the supplied date occurred. The value returned will be in the range 0 to 53. All weeks are started on Sunday. Example:

```
mysql> SELECT login, opendate, WEEK(opendate)
FROM login
WHERE opendate <> 0;
```

```
+-------+---------------------+----------------+
| login | opendate            | WEEK(opendate) |
+-------+---------------------+----------------+
| johnd | 2002-10-10 00:00:00 |             41 |
| bobs  | 2003-01-10 09:51:27 |              2 |
+-------+---------------------+----------------+
2 rows in set (0.02 sec)
```

WEEK(*date, start*)

This WEEK function returns an integer representing the week the supplied date occurred. The value returned will be in the range 0 to 53. A *start* value of 0 indicates the week should begin on Sunday, and a value of 1 indicates the week should begin on Monday.

WEEKDAY(*date*)

The WEEKDAY function returns an integer using 0 for Monday for the supplied *date*. Example:

```
mysql> SELECT login, opendate, WEEKDAY(opendate) AS 'Day of week'
FROM login
WHERE opendate <> 0;
+-------+---------------------+-------------+
| login | opendate            | Day of week |
+-------+---------------------+-------------+
| johnd | 2002-10-10 00:00:00 |           3 |
| bobs  | 2003-01-10 09:51:27 |           4 |
+-------+---------------------+-------------+
2 rows in set (0.00 sec)
```

YEAR(*date*)

The MONTHNAME function returns the year the supplied date occurred. Example:

```
mysql> SELECT login, opendate, YEAR(opendate)
FROM login
WHERE opendate <> 0;
+-------+---------------------+----------------+
| login | opendate            | YEAR(opendate) |
+-------+---------------------+----------------+
| johnd | 2002-10-10 00:00:00 |           2002 |
| bobs  | 2003-01-10 09:51:27 |           2003 |
+-------+---------------------+----------------+
2 rows in set (0.00 sec)
```

YEARWEEK(*date*)

The YEARWEEK function returns the year and month the supplied date occurred in the format YYYYMM. Example:

```
mysql> SELECT login, opendate, YEARWEEK(opendate)
FROM login
```

```
WHERE opendate <> 0;
+-------+---------------------+--------------------+
| login | opendate            | YEARWEEK(opendate) |
+-------+---------------------+--------------------+
| johnd | 2002-10-10 00:00:00 |             200241 |
| bobs  | 2003-01-10 09:51:27 |             200302 |
+-------+---------------------+--------------------+
2 rows in set (0.00 sec)
```

YEARWEEK(*date, start*)

The YEARWEEK function returns the year and month the supplied date occurred in the format YYYYMM. A *start* value of 0 indicates the week should begin on Sunday, and a value of 1 indicates the week should begin on Monday.

Other Functions

The server includes a number of miscellaneous functions.

BINARY

If you have an ASCII or character column in a table, and you want the various comparison functions and operators to handle case sensitivity, use the BINARY operator to convert the column value to binary.

CONNECTION_ID()

The CONNECTION_ID function returns an integer representing the thread_id for the database server connection. Example:

```
mysql> SELECT connection_ID();
+-----------------+
| CONNECTION_ID() |
+-----------------+
|              23 |
+-----------------+
1 row in set (0.15 sec)
```

DATABASE()

The DATABASE function returns the name of the current database being used. Example:

```
mysql> SELECT DATABASE();
+--------------+
| DATABASE()   |
+--------------+
| entitlements |
+--------------+
1 row in set (0.00 sec)
```

DECODE(*string, string2*)

The DECODE function decrypts *string1* based on *string2*. It is assumed that ENCODE was used to encrypt *string1* using *string2*. Example:

```
mysql> SELECT DECODE('?Å≈L_', 'password');
+-----------------------------+
| DECODE('?Å≈L_', 'password') |
+-----------------------------+
| johnd                       |
+-----------------------------+
1 row in set (0.00 sec)
```

ENCRYPT(*string[,seed]*)

The ENCRYPT function is a wrapper with MySQL to the Unix crypt() system call. The function will encrypt the supplied *string* based on the optional *seed* value. If MySQL cannot find the crypt() system call, the function will return NULL.

ENCODE(*string, string2*)

The ENCODE function will encrypt *string* based on the supplied *string2*.

Example:

```
mysql> SELECT ENCODE('johnd', 'password');
+-----------------------------+
| ENCODE('johnd', 'password') |
+-----------------------------+
| ?Å≈L_                       |
+-----------------------------+
1 row in set (0.00 sec)
```

FORMAT(*value, d*)

The FORMAT function will add commas for number formatting to the *value* parameter as well round the value to *d* decimal places. Example:

```
mysql> SELECT FORMAT(0824098394.334, 2);
+---------------------------+
| FORMAT(0824098394.334, 2) |
+---------------------------+
| 824,098,394.33            |
+---------------------------+
1 row in set (0.01 sec)
```

LAST_INSERT_ID()

When a database table has a column defined to automatically increment using the auto_increment clause, the LAST_INSERT_ID function can be used to obtain the incremented value. Example:

```
mysql> SELECT LAST_INSERT_ID();
```

MD5(*string*)

The MD5 function will calculate and return a checksum value for the supplied *string*. The MD5 returns a checksum for string *s*. Example:

```
mysql> SELECT MD5('This is a string');
+----------------------------------+
| MD5('This is a string')          |
+----------------------------------+
| 41fb5b5ae4d57c5ee528adb00e5e8e74 |
+----------------------------------+
1 row in set (0.00 sec)
```

PASSWORD(*string*)

The PASSWORD function will convert the supplied *string* into a proprietary-based encrypted string. Example:

```
mysql> SELECT PASSWORD('johnd');
+-------------------+
| PASSWORD('johnd') |
+-------------------+
| 0c4e736925ab7792  |
+-------------------+
1 row in set (0.00 sec)
```

USER()
SYSTEM_USER()
SESSION_USER()

All of these functions will return the current user logged in the MySQL database server. Example:

```
mysql> SELECT USER();
+----------------+
| USER()         |
+----------------+
| ODBC@localhost |
+----------------+
1 row in set (0.00 sec)
```

VERSION()

The VERSION function will return a string representing the current MySQL server version. Example:

```
mysql> SELECT version();
+-----------+
| version() |
+-----------+
| 3.23.52-nt |
+-----------+
1 row in set (0.00 sec)
```

APPENDIX E

Connector/J Late-Breaking Additions

Updating the Connector/J driver is difficult enough; simultaneously writing a book and timing it to release with the driver is that much more difficult! After the final copyedit of the pages of this book, a gamma version of Connector/J 3.0 was released. This appendix provides information on the most important additions. Any future changes not listed in this appendix can be found on the change page at http://www.mysql.com/downloads/api-jdbc-dev.html. The vast majority are minor bug fixes, but some enhancements were important enough to mention here.

Failover Support

One of the most important considerations when developing a database-oriented system is availability. MySQL handles availability by supporting replication. A master database server writes updates to the database both to a table and a log file. Slave servers access the log file and duplicate the updates. Updates to the system are allowed on the master server and read on both the master and slave servers. There can be any number of slaves to the primary master.

If you are writing an application that accesses the master database server, you normally have to write code to handle a failure on the master and switch to a slave machine for all reads. Updates are postponed until the master server is put back online.

The Connector/J 3.0.4 Gamma supports automatic fail-over support at the JDBC level. By setting various options in the database URL, the driver will support automatic read-only queries across any number of slave hosts. The format for the new URL is

```
jdbc:mysql://[hostname][,failoverhost1,
failoverhost2...][:port]/[dbname]....
```

For example:

```
jdbc:mysql://192.168.120, 192.168.1.24/test
```

One requirement for the use of JDBC fail-over is that the autocommit variable must be set to true for the current connection because fail-over support isn't appropriate across a transaction. Two other URL connection variables affect the fail-over. The first is queriesBeforeRetryMaster, which has a default value of 50. When a fail-over occurs, this variable will be used to determine how many queries to perform on a fail-over server before trying the master server.

The second parameter is autoReconnect. If this variable is false, the driver will fail-over to a slave database only during a connection attempt on the master server. If the master server isn't available, the driver will fail to a slave. If this variable is true, the system will check the connection upon every query and fail-over to a slave if the master is no longer available.

Windows Named Pipes

If you are executing MySQL and an application on Windows NT/2000/XP, you can use Named Pipes to connect to the database. Support for Named Pipes is through a new socket factory plugin added to Connector/J. To use a named pipe between the JDBC driver and a local MySQL database, add the following parameter to the URL connection string:

```
SocketFactory=com.mysql.jdbc.NamedPipeSocketFactory
```

A specific pipe path can be used by specifying the namedPipePath and a pipe string, or the default pipe of \\.\pipe\MySQL will be used. Note that if the NamedPipeSocketFactory is used in a URL, the hostname, failover hosts, and port number will naturally be ignored. An application using named pipes instead of TCP/IP will execute faster due to the reduction in overhead.

Batch Processing Error Continuation

Connector/J 3.0 supports batch processing in which multiple queries are sent to the database in a batch to reduce overhead involved in creating statement and connections to the database. You can set up a URL parameter called continueBatchOnError, which tells the system whether an error in one query should cause the batch to fail or not. The default value of the variable is true. To change the value, use a string like this one:

```
continueBatchOnError=true
```

Strict Updates

When using updatable ResultSet objects, changes to the object are automatically sent to the database without writing an insert query. The parameter strictUpdates can be used to tell the server whether or not an update should be allowed when all of the primary keys for the table have not been included in the result set.

In other words, if we have a table with two primary keys, prim_id and prim_id_two, a ResultSet object would need to have both of the columns in it in order to allow the rows of the ResultSet object to be updated. The default for this parameter is true. To change the value, use a string like this one:

```
strictUpdates=true
```

Profile SQL

If you are interested in profiling queries to the database including the queries generated from Container Managed Persistent Enterprise Java Beans, use the profilesSql parameter. This parameter, which defaults to false, will dump all queries as well as execution times to STDERR. To change the value, use a string like this one:

```
profilesSql=true
```

SSL

The MySQL database server supports client connections using Secure Socket Layer (SSL). Connector/J 3.0.4 Gamma supports creating a SSL connection as well. In order for the driver to build such a connection, several criteria must be met:

- MySQL version 4.0.4 or later
- JDK 1.4 (which includes Java Secure Sockets Extension) or JDK 1.2/1.3 with the extensions added

- A MySQL certificate included with the current 4.0.4 or greater server
- A client certificate

It should be noted that using SSL will affect the performance of the system due to the added overhead of encrypting and decrypting all communication between the JDBC and the database. Since this feature is still in the gamma phase, we refer you to the instructions provided in the Readme file of the latest Connector/J 3.0 download.

Index

Symbols

A

B

C

D

E

T